THEATER HISTORIOGRAPHY ∾

Theater Historiography

Critical Interventions

Henry Bial and *Scott Magelssen*, editors ∾

The University of Michigan Press / Ann Arbor

For our teachers, especially
RICHARD SCHECHNER *and*
MICHAL KOBIALKA ℘

Copyright © by the University of Michigan 2010
All rights reserved
Published in the United States of America by
The University of Michigan Press
Manufactured in the United States of America
♾ Printed on acid-free paper

2013   2012   2011   2010   4   3   2   1

A CIP catalog record for this book is available from the British Library.

Library of Congress Cataloging-in-Publication Data

Theater historiography : critical interventions / Henry Bial and Scott
   Magelssen, editors.
       p.   cm.
   Includes bibliographical references and index.
     ISBN 978-0-472-07133-3 (cloth : alk. paper) — ISBN 978-0-472-
05133-5 (pbk. : alk. paper)
     1. Theater—Historiography.   I. Bial, Henry, 1970–   II. Magelssen,
Scott, 1974–
PN2115.T44   2010
792.09—dc22   2010030243

Acknowledgments

The critical questions addressed by the authors in the following essays are only possible because of the time, generosity, inspiration, and passion of our teachers and mentors. There is not enough room to thank all the individuals whose work and energy have informed the scholarship in this collection, but the contributors would like to acknowledge some of those who have been particularly influential. They are, in alphabetical order: Karen Ahlquist, Sally Banes, Rosemarie K. Bank, Jack Beasley, Sarah Blackstone, John L. Brooke, Marvin Carlson, Una Chaudhuri, Dwight Conquergood, Tim Cribb, Robert Croghan, Mary Karen Dahl, Tracy C. Davis, Greg Dening, Jill Dolan, Harry J. Elam Jr., J. Ellen Gainor, Susan C. Haedicke, Peter Holland, John Houchin, Jean Howard, Ric Knowles, Michal Kobialka, Sonja Arsham Kuftinec, Carol Martin, Theresa May, Bruce A. McConachie, Brooks McNamara, Martin Meisel, Julie Stone Peters, Peggy Phelan, Della Pollock, Thomas Postlewait, Martin Puchner, Joseph Roach, David Román, Richard Schechner, Laurence Senelick, Vladimir Stamenkovic, Diana Taylor, Tamara Underiner, and Leigh Woods. More than a few of us owe a debt to Oscar Brockett, who often said that "facts are inert, history is in the narrative."

The editors would like to thank each of our departments and institutions, as well as those of our contributors, for the sustained institutional and collegial support necessary for endeavors like this one. A special note of thanks is due the officers and voting members of the Mid-America Theatre Conference (MATC), who selected us to cochair MATC's 2007 Theatre History Symposium, sowing the seeds for what would become a fruitful and nourishing professional collaboration. We thank also the University of Michigan Press for its faith in the project, Scott Ham and Marcia LaBrenz for all their tremendous assistance, and especially senior executive editor LeAnn Fields, whose sound advice and constant encouragement have been invaluable in shepherding this project from "the back of a napkin" to the volume you now hold in your hands.

Many thanks are due to each of our families—Christine, Anna, and

Emily Bial; Theresa, Trygg, and Ari Magelssen—for their deep reservoirs of support and patience.

A different version of Odai Johnson's "Unspeakable Histories: Terror, Spectacle, and Genocidal Memory" appeared in *Modern Language Quarterly*, and we thank that journal for allowing portions to reappear here. Portions of Erin B. Mee's "But Is It Theater? The Impact of Colonial Culture on Theatrical History in India" appeared in different form in Mee's book *Theatre of Roots: Redirecting the Modern Indian Stage* (Seagull, 2008), and we thank her for allowing them to be reprinted here. Finally, we thank our contributors, whose cutting-edge research and intellectual rigor both prompted this volume and brought it into being. The success of *Theater Historiography: Critical Interventions* belongs to them. Any errors of commission or omission herein belong to the editors.

HENRY BIAL, *University of Kansas*
SCOTT MAGELSSEN, *Bowling Green State University*

Contents

Introduction

HENRY BIAL AND SCOTT MAGELSSEN ∾

Theater historiography means the study of the foundational assumptions, principles, and methodologies that determine how theater history is written. To practice theater historiography means to look beyond the record of "what happened" to analyze *how* and *why* such records are constructed. Thus we might say that theater historiography is to theater history as physics is to engineering or economics is to business: the fundamental theories and hypotheses from which all subsequent decisions flow. Compared to those other disciplines, however, theater historiography has come late to the party. It is only in the last thirty years or so that theater scholars have paid critical attention to how theater history is written, and many if not most theater history textbooks give the subject scant attention . . . or no attention at all.

This is not because earlier generations of theater historians lacked a clear methodology. Neither were they lacking in conscientiousness or self-awareness. On the contrary, theater historiography did not—and, in a sense, could not—emerge as long as theater history was defined strictly as the accumulation of factual knowledge about the dramatic literature and staging practices associated with the canon of Western civilization. This starting assumption pointed clearly to a methodology that valorized the archival document and the archaeological record over all other ways of understanding the theatrical past. Theater historians might (and did) dispute each other's interpretation of the archival record, but virtually all of them presumed the existence of an empirical truth that existed a priori—a truth it was their job to reveal.

Late in the twentieth century, however, theater history, like most of the humanities and social sciences, was jolted by the postmodern recognition that even on the rare occasions that facts and events themselves are verifiable, the narratives through which we order those facts and events are necessarily subjective. Interpretations of the past are thus always already shaped by the values, judgments, and desires of the present. Or, as historian and theorist Michel de Certeau argued in *The Writing of History* (1975), facts and events only exist as such because they have at some point been deemed worth remembering—and have no inherent meanings outside those that have been generated and imposed upon them through the "discursive formations" and "acquired rationalizations" of historians.

Meanwhile, members of previously "unhistoried" populations—women, ethnic and racial minorities, non-Western nations—began to enter the academy in large numbers. In theater studies, this shift—combined with postmodern philosophy's critique of hierarchical structures of knowledge—had two lasting consequences: first, many theater scholars gained a greater cognizance of and appreciation for the contributions of oppressed or marginalized persons to the history of world drama; second, because the embodied traditions of such populations did not seem to fit the category of "theater" as conventionally defined in the Euro-American tradition, a significant number of scholars chose instead to pursue their research under the broader heading of "performance." Over time, the first approach led theater historians to develop new historiographic approaches, methods more suitable to a nonhierarchical and multicultural understanding of theater, while the second approach led many in the emerging discipline of performance studies to break from theater history, which they dismissed as overly concerned with unimaginative recounting of historical fact. Performance studies drew its methods not only from theater but also from a wide range of other scholarly disciplines, including but not limited to anthropology, psychology, and gender studies. Over time, performance studies diverged from theater history to the point where the two disciplines often seem to be rivals, wielding competing assumptions, terms, and methods.

Today, those who would write theater history stand on the threshold of another epistemological shift. A new generation of would-be scholars, raised on the shifting sands of the Internet and global media culture, reads history from a fundamentally different perspective than prior generations. The hard-won understanding that history is not and cannot be an impartial record of facts and events is, for such students, a commonplace. They understand that history is a complex and contested act of cultural memory. What they don't know is what to do about it. This is especially true in regard to the theater history classroom, where strategies for critical engagement with the archive must often be learned in parallel with a wealth of names, dates, and entire plays that students are expected to commit to memory. At the institutional level, theater and performance history is under siege in many university theater departments, even as its methods and paradigms gain traction elsewhere in the academy. Are we merely preserving the best of a medium whose glory days lie in the past? Or are we marshaling the resources of theater's resurgence? Interdisciplinarity and multiculturalism have become our watchwords, but as theater students and historians continue to broaden the scope of our research, considering texts and performances hitherto ignored, our term papers, syllabi, and curricula are in a losing race, trying to square a twentieth-century ideal of encyclopedic knowledge with the twenty-first-century explosion of ideas and information. Even as we embrace more complex and embodied forms of knowledge, we continue to rely on the archival document. As we forge bridges with other disciplines, we face the potential of losing those things that make theater history unique. There has never been a more critical time to intervene in the practice of theater historiography.

This book is designed to help students and theater historians chart their own trajectory through this complex intellectual atmosphere. The twenty-one essays in the pages that follow have been written by scholars conducting fresh, dynamic, and interesting new work in theater history across a wide range of subject areas, from classical antiquity to the contemporary American musical. The methodologies these authors employ are equally diverse, spanning from the literary to the anthropological, from the archival to the phenomenological. This is not an accident. From the beginning we knew that for this book to truly make a critical intervention into theater historiography, we would need to assemble a group of theater historians who represent as many schools (literally and figuratively) as possible.

Some of the authors' approaches are practical. Some are speculative. Some deploy old established principles and methodologies in new ways for new purposes. Several look to what we might call the history of theater historiography, grounding their contemporary interventions in close readings of historical accounts that have themselves passed into history. Several more draw their ideas and terms in equal measure from both theater history and performance studies, demonstrating that these once-rival schools of thought are moving toward reconciliation. Regardless of method, each chapter seeks in its own way to demonstrate how theater history can be more ethically practiced, more incisively written, and more cogently read.

The book's organization is intended to demonstrate that historiographic approaches need not be lumped together by geographic or chronological perspectives. Part I, "Unearthing the Past," presents a series of methodological dilemmas, questions of the sort that each historian must learn to confront on his or her own terms. Though they vary widely in the cultures and periods they address, these authors all recognize the necessity of assembling evidence in support of historical inquiry. The question of what constitutes sufficient evidence runs throughout the section, as does the responsibility of the historian to respect that evidence. Odai Johnson brings *defixiones*, the buried archaeological remnants of Roman slaves' anger, to bear on a reading of classical Roman comedy and tragedy, inviting us to "unsilence" the narratives that have heretofore been buried beneath the historiographic record. In a similar manner, Ellen MacKay plumbs the depths of classical theater history to interrogate the traditional regard for "plausible" evidence, taking up Richard Beacham's invitation to consider nontraditional or even "unlikely" evidence as a crucial method of rethinking a history reined in by what past scholars have deemed plausible. Where MacKay considers the implausible, Robert B. Shimko shows us what happens when historical facts reveal a truth stranger than fiction. Considering the offstage career of seventeenth-century English theater impresario William Davenant, Shimko suggests that the pleasurable moments of the "unexpected" in the archive can, by embracing what de Certeau terms "bouts of surprise," enliven the sometimes limited discourse of conventional histories. Heather S. Nathans concludes this section with an investigation of the role of Jewish actors and audiences in the early American theater. Offering a "fugue history" that synthesizes multiple methodologies, Nathans investigates how historians' dismissive claims about that which ought to be obvious often hide histories much less obvious than those dismissals would lead us to believe.

Part II, "The Stakes of Historiography," illustrates that methodological concerns are not innocent of political agendas. Ranging again through several times and places, these chapters focus on the ways that theater history, in remembering a cultural past, stakes a claim on that culture's present and future. Branislav Jakovljevic opens Part II by positing that political and historiographic moves in the twentieth century fundamentally shifted historical discourse from a conventional approach to the object of inquiry to a "contemporary attitude" that completely transforms our understandings and stagings of the theatrical past, citing Martin Esslin's concept of the "Theater of the Absurd" as a prime example. By exposing the culturally Darwinist and racist foundations of nineteenth-century ethnography, E. J. Westlake draws our attention to the fact that the archives on which we rely for our most valuable material about so-called primitive societies are laced with an incredibly problematic "legacy" that must be considered if we are to work responsibly in these areas. Where Westlake advocates for the need to extract and salvage what we can from a problematic liaison of racial politics and ethnography, Alan Sikes's essay calls for joining approaches that too often stand apart. In his examination of the Licensing Act of 1737,

Sikes suggests that approaching particular historical moments as sites of convergence of class-based and sex-based anxieties reveals much more about their complexities than past approaches that have privileged a single axis of identity over all others. Erin B. Mee's essay analyzes the way that the historiography of pre-independence India, specifically the determination of which cultural practices have been deemed fit to remember as performance, has been motivated by colonial understandings and aesthetics, demonstrating how Indian theatrical history is being rewritten by necessary acts of decolonialization. At the level of contemporary politics, John Fletcher charges us to consider the difficult question of whether the traditionally celebrated and affirmed activist theater on our syllabi and in our research ought to be expanded to include far-right performances, often excluded because they have run counter to our own sympathies. More pointedly, however, Fletcher asks how we ought to deal with these performances in our research and teaching and how they might expose our own intellectual and ethical blind spots.

Politics, of course, is not the only challenge faced by contemporary theater historians. As theater history expands its perspective to consider other media and other ways of understanding human experience, historians often struggle to integrate our traditional methods with broader intellectual and societal paradigm shifts. The four essays in Part III, "Historiography for a New Millennium," present four very different ways of coming to terms with a new "order of things." Sarah Bay-Cheng asks how the relatively recent emergence of digital technology in theater will explode the manner in which we approach the archive. Is it possible that, in the case of digital performance, the historian's experience of digital documentation will "eventually supersede the experience of the performance itself"? Harvey Young, noting the tendency of text-based histories to exclude marginalized peoples, offers a model of history based on visual, rather than textual, analysis. Considering the work of nineteenth-century landscape painter Robert Duncanson, Young shows us the potential of such visual analysis to illuminate previously obscure parts of the field. Both Wendy Arons and Jonathan Chambers explore the implications of even larger paradigm shifts and how the enterprise of theater and performance research has been structured by the contours of "being" as they have been conceptually cemented. Surveying recent work in ecocriticism and evolutionary biology, Arons directs us to move beyond the simplistic modernist divide between nature and culture. Her essay considers theater and performance not as a product of culture, but as a result of biologically conferred "natural advantage"—and considers what that means for our future on the planet. Chambers argues that the modern approach to acting as fundamentally (but invisibly) driven by the ontological binary between life and death (and the privileging of the former at all costs) is a problematic template for understanding works outside the modern moment. What if, pace Freud, death were not unthinkable? How would that change our approach to performing premodern dramas?

Part IV, "Performance as Historiography," invokes the parallel between performance and history. It is not, perhaps, groundbreaking to suggest that theater is "history by other means." But these essays push that understanding to a deeper level, demonstrating that performance can be read not only as history but as historiography. Indeed, as demonstrated in these case studies, the complex and contested nature of performance makes it an ideal venue for critical reflexivity with regard to the remembrance and retelling of past experience. As theater people know, "dying on stage" has a particular meaning for actors, one that Mechele Leon explores in the context of Molière. The French actor and playwright's final hour, itself a theatrical historical event, offers an occasion to trace the complex ways that the relationship between performance and history is marked with the "unforeseen fiascos of death." Nicholas Ridout's study of Alvis Hermanis's 2005 performance that invited the audience to collectively read Vladimir Sorokin's novel *Ice* illuminates the ways that theater and performance can self-reflexively allow a community to work through—and perform—its own history and memory while at the same time working through and performing its contemporary political and social tensions. The last two essays in Part IV, by Suk-Young Kim and Scott Magelssen, explore the opportunities and problems that occur when the methodology of performance is invoked to historiographically supplement the archive in cases where the record may be incomplete. Kim addresses the epistemological and ethnographic dilemmas theater scholars face when asking interview subjects who have been through trauma to reperform their pasts in order to fill in the gaps of theater history. Kim uses her own recent work on twentieth-century North Korean theater, and her interviews with North Korean expatriate choreographer Kim Young-sun, to illustrate these dilemmas. Magelssen suggests ways in which learner-driven historiographic performance might be used in the theater history classroom, as a way of bearing witness to the pasts that may be underserved by traditional pedagogy.

Finally, Part V, "Theater History's Discipline," considers the disciplinary and institutional imperatives shaping the work of theater historians today. Questions of discipline and methodology cannot, after all, be separated from the realpolitik of academe. Nevertheless, in calling for various interventions in the institutionalization of theater history, these authors offer strategies by which theater historians can reconcile the demands of the academy with the press of historiographical urgency. While Margaret Werry approves of the "rapproachment" between theater and performance studies, and the subsequent opportunities afforded by interdisciplinarity across other fields, she is duly alarmed by how some of the most promising trajectories of new thinking have been stalled as we continue to default to culturally specific modes of defining performance. Werry levels challenges at scholars of theater and performance studies to consider paradigms of performance not tied to Western notions of representation, but rather to think "oceanically" about it. We can start, suggests Werry, by looking not only to traditions outside our remit but to disciplines that have gotten short shrift in our own culture within the last centuries. Werry's call to look outward is counterbalanced by James Peck's challenge for theater historians to look inward: while theater historiography has benefited from interdisciplinarity, Peck argues, it often overlooks the resources for approaching the past within its own companion disciplines in theater studies. He uses a Brechtian example to show how we must value *intra*disciplinarity as well. Patricia Ybarra's essay engages in a close analysis of what every student and scholar of theater history experiences in the trenches, but is not being addressed in terms of its impact on our work. By uncovering the trends toward entrepreneurism and neoliberalism in our administrations and our society, Ybarra demonstrates the ways in which our modes of historiography are increasingly made to answer to more "fungible" markers of success than those for which we have previously been held accountable. This shift in criteria takes its toll not only on theater research but on the relationships between junior and senior scholars in our field. Judith Sebesta's collaboration with musicologist Jessica Sternfeld on the history of *Rent* bridges historically entrenched discursive gaps that divide colleagues within and outside of our programs and models a new interdisciplinarity and cooperation between theater historians and music scholars. Their subject, musical theater, is one of the most popular theater forms of all—and thus stands to suffer the most from a perpetuation of traditional discursive divides.

Finally, Henry Bial concludes the collection with a reconsideration of the supposed antagonism between theater history and performance studies. Tracing a genealogy of the dispute between the two fields (as well as the disciplinary exigencies that led to their alleged differences), Bial highlights the ways in which the essays in this book, in so aptly mobilizing intersections between performance studies and theater historiography, demonstrate that the question of whether performance studies and theater history are reconcilable has already been decisively answered.

From the outset, this collection has been shaped with an eye toward use in the classroom. The editors invited each author to compose a short piece (in the neighborhood of four thousand words) addressing what they perceived as the most "critical" issues they currently face as theater historians. By keeping their essays short, each author has been able to distill his or her "intervention" down to its most urgent and exciting historiographic ideas. The brevity of the chapters also makes them ideal for reading assignments: two or even three may be selected and assigned together for a particular class session. Our own experience has shown that a combination of short pieces written from contrasting viewpoints provides a dynamic and interesting foundation for discussion.

The chapters are ordered so that each contribution might speak meaningfully to the work that appears immediately before and after it. Yet such juxtapositions are necessarily limited by the linear technology of the codex. Because historiography is rarely so linear, particular lines of thought cut across the book in many directions, and readers may reasonably choose to group essays together for discussion in combinations other than those suggested by the running order. For example, James Peck's essay in Part V invites us to be more willing to apply contemporary practical theory to past subjects, while Branislav Jakovljevic holds in Part II that we've been applying contemporary practical theory to past subjects for decades without sufficiently thinking of how that theory is historicized. Robert B. Shimko writes in Part I that we might turn back to the archive with an openness to "bouts of surprise" that have heretofore been neglected in theater history's dry reworking of old ground, even as Mechele Leon finds in Part IV that theater historiography, like audiences, thrives on "stories of mishaps, disrupted performances, and other events in which actors and audiences are treated to the thrill of breakdown in the representational apparatus, to those moments when the curtain is drawn back, so to speak, on the past." And we hope and trust that each and every chapter will invite connections with emerging conversations as our discipline continues to shift. Taken in any order, however, we believe that the essays in *Theater Historiography: Critical Interventions* point toward a future in which theater historians are more informed, innovative, and intellectually engaged than ever before. Theater history demands nothing less.

PART I

Unearthing the Past

Unspeakable Histories

Terror, Spectacle, and Genocidal Memory

ODAI JOHNSON ✧

Alexander Solzhenitsyn, in his preface to *The Gulag Archipelago*, described the discovery, in Siberia, of a small school of prehistoric fish frozen in a glaciated subterranean stream. The fish were thought to be tens of thousands of years old, perfectly preserved from the last ice age. The importance of the find was recognized immediately, but while a team of Soviet scientists were quarreling over the direction of the discovery, the prison laborers from the gulag who had found the site broke open the ice, thawed the ancient fish, roasted them, and ate them on the spot. Solzhenitsyn, of all people, understood and sympathized with the need to devour history.[1]

This study lives in exactly such moments: of survivors who endure by swallowing their history, by eating their own memory. It is, in this regard, an excavation of the already consumed.

The kinds of atrocities that Solzhenitsyn documented became the bloody signature of the twentieth century, but today I turn to an earlier, equally brutal period, indeed, one of the earliest recorded genocidal periods of Western history—Rome in the second century (BCE), between the fall of Greece and the fall of Carthage, ironically the golden age of Roman comedy—to begin an excavation of genocidal memory buried in a bleak landscape and scarred body sites of the unhistoried, who left few memorials.

i: Genocide: Carthage, North Africa

146 BCE: The Roman orders were concise: kill everyone, spare no one; and so they slaughtered, indiscriminately, pausing only to loot along the way. Fatalities were never accurately counted. Carthage was once a city of seven hundred thousand. When the soldiers left, it was emptied and razed to the ground. Atrocities were committed as privileges of the victors: rapes,

mutilations, cultural desecrations. Temples were plundered for their precious metals. Priests were murdered for their ornaments.[2] The city was leveled and systematically burned block by block for seventeen days. It is the kind of destruction implied in the Greek word *holocaust*, a total burning. When the ashes cooled, Roman soldiers plowed up the ruins and sowed salt into the earth, with the curse that neither crops nor houses might ever rise again. So complete was the destruction of Carthage, it was erased from the map of Africa. The survivors—the prisoners of war, on the brink of starvation—who filed out of the wreckage were shackled and marched off as slaves. Many of these were then redisplayed, first in a triumph to the Roman general Scipio Aemilianus Africanus, who executed the destruction, and later in the theater of state as they, the *noxii* (condemned), ritualistically completed their own eradication as gladiators in the Roman arena. The victory games that marked the third and final Punic War lasted for three festive days, during which, for a good laugh, Plautus's *The Carthaginian* was remounted, its central characters all displaced Carthaginians, including two young girls stolen and sold into a brothel.[3]

Just across the strait of Gibraltar, in Iberia (Spain), an identical fate befell the northern colony of Carthage, Nova Carthago, at the hands of the same Roman family. Polybius recounted the extermination that had become a standard Roman practice:

> When Scipio [Africanus] thought the number of those who had entered the city adequate, he dispatched the majority of the troops against those in the city, according to the Roman custom, instructing them to kill anyone they met and to spare no-one, and not to start plundering before the signal was given. The purpose of this Roman custom [is] to instill terror; for one can often see in cities taken by the Romans not only the bodies of humans, but dogs cut in half and the severed limbs of other animals. On this occasion indeed there was much of this kind to be seen because of the [great] number of people in the city.[4]

Roman historians never deployed terms like *genocide* (though they considered the Carthaginians an alien race, as they did the Greeks or the Gauls); the slaughtering of noncombatants was a routine tactical approach to domination.[5] But even to the modern reader, accustomed to the excesses of twentieth-century atrocities, the numbers of casualties accumulated by Roman campaigns during this period remain staggering. Classical writers tend to cite numbers symbolically rather than statistically, so documentation was loose and exaggeration widespread.[6] Still, during one lifetime of Roman expansion (roughly from the first Macedonian war in 215 to the destruction of Carthage and Corinth in 146), we have claims of over two and half million casualties, and those but a rough estimate of the actual figures.

In the Second Punic War, there were three hundred thousand casualties. When Carthage fell at the close of the third war, fewer than fifty thousand were marched into a life of captivity, the only survivors of a city of seven hundred thousand. When Corinth fell the same year, all the males were slaughtered, all the women and children were sold into slavery, and the entire city was burned to the ground. Village by village, tribal armies who resisted Rome were starved or slaughtered into submission,[7] from the eastern borders of Spain, to the Rhone Valley, transalpine Gaulia, the Aegean, the Greek east (Pergamum), and down to Numidia. One could circumscribe the Mediterranean mapping Roman carnage in a grim census of the dead, the defeated, and the displaced.

Roman historians (Polybius, Suetonius, Livy, Strabo), who knew where their bread was buttered, have characterized the wars of the second century as retaliations, or as delivery from tribal tyrannies.[8] Nonetheless, it is a chilling fact that within seven decades Rome became the military master of the Mediterranean—statistically speaking, it had subjugated as much as a fifth of the world's population—and even the Roman historians recognized this had not been accomplished through diplomacy.[9] What causes the shudder in the recitation of the death toll is not the scope of the brutality, so much as the grim regularity of it all. For nearly a century, as William Harris observed, almost every year, legions went out and did massive violence to someone, and this regularity gives the phenomenon a pathological character.[10]

If terrorism was the harsh voice of empire, equally disturbing was the silence of the vanquished, the survivors whose unhistoried voices were left mute in the wake of conquest; and given the scope of this conquest, Rome's unhistoried subjects represent a sizeable silence. The displaced, the defeated, the enslaved—in Carlin Barton's apt and ugly phrase, the refuse of Rome's wars—carried that war-memory back to Rome.[11] They were the genocide survivors, the amputated, the castrated, the expurgated, and the plentiful. Period historians like Strabo described the practice in fish-market terms: "Slaves were easily caught, and there was a large and wealthy market not at all far away, Delos, which could receive and dispatch tens of thousands of slaves on the same day."[12]

Among the unhistoried was one occupation that might have left something behind. Occasionally, the displaced found their way into the theater.

For four hundred years, the acting profession was occupied almost exclusively by slaves and, during the expansive centuries, prisoners of war. The same is true for many of those who wrote for the stage. Livius Andronicus was one, a Greek slave from Tarentum, a casualty to Roman expansion into Magna Graeca. Plautus was another victim of the same campaign to control the Italian peninsula. Caecilius Statius (ca. 219–168), the comic playwright who first encouraged Terence, was another captured slave, from Insubrian Gaulia, near Milan. Most germane to this project is Publius Terentius Afer (Terence), who came to Rome as a slave from Carthage. And this is where the problem begins. The victims of Roman atrocities, who when they wrote, when they spoke, speak nothing of their past, may share a transhistorical problem of traumatized people anywhere, but I am most interested in the ontological applications of the problem of trauma theory for the theater, as both spectacle of genocide and the burial ground of such horrific memories. Though the texts themselves are compositionally incapable of speaking to such things (these are comedies, after all), there are moments of profoundly legible silence, cavities that betray the trauma behind the text and the horrific histories beneath it. Slice into any Roman comedy of the second century and you find them, behind the running slaves and the senex, behind the inherited masks of Menander, the *mutae personae*, staring back at us from the shadows of the stage with their unspeakable histories, terrified, traumatized. Violent and violated victims, young girls, young men, slaves, kidnapped, castrated, sold to brothels, raped, beaten, stolen again from their slavers, silently staring out from the peripheries of the plots of Roman comedy, staged on the occasions of Roman victories. But rage, as Seneca reminds us, cannot be hidden.[13] One slave, in Plautus's *Carthaginian (Poenulus)*, bites back a curse he cannot deliver:

> SYNECRASTUS: They (the gods) won't blast me, but I can make 'em curse him, if I liked, yes, blast that master of mine, if I . . . If I . . . If I . . . [14]

It's the biting of the tongue I'm after here, that swallowed curse of suppressed rage, and the whole history of the speechless whose only mark was their aphasia.

ii: *Mutae Personae*

Under conditions that tend to annihilate the imagination, a few witnesses survived the atrocities of the century to bear the burden of the memory of the defeated and the dispossessed back as trophies of the victor.[15] Their stories and voices were ventriloquized to the imperial market of the comic stage. Though the form of Roman comedy was itself circumscribed (by Greek originals, by regulations of content, by the ludic nature of performance), it was nonetheless composed by victims of the wars of Roman territorial expansion, occasionally very direct victims. In this regard, I think one can fairly ask to what extent Roman comedies can be read as documents of repressed terror. "How can I express the great anger that burns in my fevered liver?" asked Juvenal, who suffered no worse than poverty and exile to Egypt. How indeed does one express great anger for a race that is no more? How does one expunge from the head what the survivors have lived through? Starvation and cannibalism, the slaughter of the city, dismemberment, rape, suicide, or slavery, year after year, nation after nation, race by race . . . What does Rome do with it all? Where is the burial ground of genocidal memory?

As I am speaking of unspeakable things, of buried *ira* (rage), I want to evoke a Roman model that metaphorically and materially articulates both burial and rage: curse tablets.

Greco-Roman curse tablets have been found by the hundreds, written secretly, venomously, many by slaves or servants on lead tablets, or written for them, nailed shut (hence their names, *defixiones*) and buried because they speak of what cannot be spoken. Like voodoo pins of hatred, the tablets call down the wrath of the gods to curse and bind the slave's or servant's master, enemies, sometimes rival lovers, and because they were buried, many have survived.[16] The *defixio* in the image here was found beneath the floor of the circus of refounded Carthage. Here is another one, from a body who was owned (slave or servant), who inventoried the body site, piece by piece, to curse and bind his master's health and wealth:

Malcius, belonging to Nicona: [his] eyes, hands, fingers, arms, nails, hair, head, feet, thigh, belly, buttocks, navel, chest, nipples, neck, mouth, cheeks, teeth, lips, chin, eyes, forehead, eyebrows, shoulder blades, shoulders, sinews, bones, merilas [?], belly, penis, shin: in these tablets I bind his income, profit, and health.[17]

The burial of the slave's curse seems a uniquely Roman mode of expression for the rage of *mutae personae*. I'm fascinated by the image of a thin but enduring subterranean stratum of anger running below the triumphal arches and coliseums, an articulate subsoil littered with the silent and irrepressible rage of its victims.

Figure 1.1. *Defixio* found beneath the floor of the circus of refounded Carthage. University of Colorado, University of Georgia, and University of Michigan excavations in the Circus of Carthage. Photograph by S. Carl, used by kind permission of Naomi Norman.

Consider the *mutae personae* of Terentian comedy, like the character of the young Pamphila, in *The Eunuch*, a free Athenian girl, sixteen, kidnapped by slavers, sold to a brothel, and briefly displayed before buyers and audience alike en route to her new life: "What's your impression of this little item, fresh from the market?" asks the auctioneer salaciously (476). One act later she will be raped by a young patrician, her clothes torn off, her hair ripped out, and then married off to the same rapist, and she never speaks a line.[18] But she is not offstage; she is not invisible. Pamphila cries. And it is a deeply poignant, scarred, and ghosting moment. It is also a moment that Terence replicated in the same tragic sequence in three of his six comedies, in which *mutae personae*, all young women, all stolen into slavery, all raped, all scream in childbirth just offstage and become for one moment unmuted, storied, by a pain that rips through the text and lives always just beyond, promising a history it cannot deliver but refuses entirely to deny.

If there is a repressed terror to Roman comedy, it lies in its aphasia, in its inability to speak the horrors. As Herb Blau has written of the Donner Party diaries, it is what the text doesn't say that reveals the deepest scars.[19] It is the terror of absence, the trauma that leaves no words. The image of the palimpsest here is an apt one: the slaves of Roman comedy are characters without a past, and the playwrights are slaves without a memory; both strive to elide the atrocity that brought them to that ludic moment in Rome.[20] Both rewrite themselves; both swallow their own history.

Still, occasionally one finds moments even in palimpsests when the original voice leaks through, when the tongue of the text seems to struggle against the mouth of it and betrays a reflexive rasp of old pain, a brief, nearly inaudible eruption of casual cruelty and buried *ira* that lived just outside the world of the play, just beyond; occasionally one can find cavities of trauma that seem to hemorrhage and startle the reader with a sound of something brutal, just out of reach.

One such moment is preserved in Terence's play *The Eunuch*, when Parmeno, a slave, to secure his master's love interest, plays an auctioneer selling other slaves, including his own master, Chaerea, who dresses as a eunuch. A small but complicated moment of display follows when two "slaves" are trotted out for the "buyer," a military man, Thraso, and his parasite. It is, in essence, both a representation and a parody of a slave market in which prisoners and victims of some foreign war stand on the block for the perusal of the soldier:

PARMENO: Send that pair. Out on the double. You first, right this way.—Direct from darkest Ethiopia!
THRASO: Three minae.
GNATHO: At most. Pure schlock.
PARMENO: Hey Dorus! Where are you? [Chaerea appears dressed as a Eunuch.]
Over here. Now there, I submit, is a eunuch! Kindly note the thoroughbred features, the flawless freshness. . . .
THRASO: Damnation, Handsome beast.
PARMENO: Well, Gnatho, any observations? No faults to pick at? Thraso? How about you? —The ultimate accolade: Silence. Inspect him, please. Examine his literature. Music. Athletics. Guaranteed performance in all the pursuits deemed fit and proper for a well-brought up young gentleman.
THRASO: —Know a pursuit I wouldn't mind trying with him. If forced, of course. Or even sober. . . . (iii.2.471–81)[21]

But Chaerea is neither slave nor eunuch, as he violently demonstrates. His body bears no scarred memory of the vanquished. Yet it is he, not those on the auction block, from whom, in an imagined voice, the buried *ira* erupts in a vendetta of the victimized: "Place me inside [the brothel]," he tells his slave, "to pay them back, to victimize them as they do us."[22] Us? Chaerea is a young and privileged, free-born Athenian playboy, playing at slavery to get laid, who rages as if he were the castrated slave who cannot, or the mute Ethiopian girl in the scene who does not. Us? One finds this kind of displacement in Terence, where the venom is authentic, but the voicing is not. When Chaerea does succeed in entering the brothel, his first act is to victimize, to violently rape Pamphila. He later shares his "conquest" with his friend:

CHAEREA: Meantime, the girl fell asleep. I sneaked a sideways peek, through the fan, like this. I took a careful look around. The coast was clear. I locked the door.

ANTIPHO: Then what? . . .

CHAEREA: A chance like this, no matter how short—do you think I'd miss it? Temptation, aspiration, surprise, and passion all mixed in one? Just what do you think I am, a eunuch? (599–606)[23]

It is the maid at the brothel (another slave) who discloses the real damage of the assault on the girl:

PYTHIAS: When he'd had his fun with the girl, did he stop? Oh, no—atrocity wasn't enough for him. He shredded her dress and ripped out her hair in handfuls! . . .

PHAEDRIA: What do you mean?

PYTHIAS: What do I mean? . . . Your eunuch raped our virgin!
(645–53)

Where does this anger of Chaerea's come from? From the character of the free-born and privileged playboy? Or the manumitted Carthaginian slave Terence? It is as if a text behind the text suddenly, briefly betrays the repressed rage of captivity, the memory of atrocity (his own abuse?), and the rage erupts to victimize another victim.

The most frightening part of Roman comedy is that I really don't think these moments are compositional (borrowed from Menander or invented originally), but rather that they represent a rage that lived beyond a text too barren for vengeance, a kind of curse tablet, buried and leaching into the text, hemorrhaging out in unaccountable moments from the other side. To recognize the unsettling moments that erupt terrified voices from *mutae personae* is to evaporate the humor from the canon of Roman comedy. But to ignore it is to consign away the violent history that preceded those ludic occasions. And this is the heart of the problem: how to exhume and honor a history that is largely unacknowledged by the survivors on a stage constitutionally incapable of remembering it.

iii: History's Disappearances

When Clifford Geertz noted that in Balinese society, the owner of the victorious fighting cock eats the remains of the loser, it was the old historiographic problem of history's disappearances.[24] The Romans were no different in this regard; they consumed their victims, one way or another. Driven by an impossible desire to reconcile the atrocities of the past, victors and vanquished, we try to make all these disappearances—what de Certeau called "all these zones of silence"—more audible, more legible, by looking below, beyond, beneath, running fingers over the rough edges, prying open the ellipses, listening for the offstage voices that betray an opening into the unstoried histories.

Herodotus reminds us of the importance of the sub rosa in his account of the exiled Spartan Demaratus, who caught wind of the plan for a Persian invasion of Sparta and tried to alert his city:

> As the danger of discovery was great, there was only one way in which he could contrive to get the message through: this was by scraping the wax off a pair of wooden folding tablets, writing on the wood underneath what Xerxes intended to do [invade], and then covering the messages over with wax again. In this way the tablets, being apparently blank, would cause no trouble with the guards along the road. (vii.239).

We, too, must look for the tablets that are apparently blank, beneath, behind, just beyond which is written the imperative missive. Of the two, it is the words beneath the wax that are the more indelible and infinitely more urgent. "I continue to be troubled," wrote Paul Ricoeur, "by the unsettling spectacle offered by an excess of memory here, and an excess of forgetting elsewhere."[25] I consider the idea of a more just allotment of memory a historiographical mandate of the highest order.

NOTES

1. From Aleksander Solzhenitsyn, *The Gulag Archipelago, 1918–1956*, trans. Thomas Whitney (New York: Harper and Row, 1973), xv.

2. The two classical descriptions of the final destruction of Carthage are Polybius, *Rise of the Roman Empire*, and Appian, *Wars of the Romans in Iberia*, from which the description here is culled. I am relying on J. S. Richardson's translation of *Appian, Wars of the Romans in Iberia* (Warminster: Aris and Phillips, Ltd., 2000) and Ian Scott-Kilvert's *Polybius* (London: Penguin, 1979). Polybius describes the rampage as standard Roman practice (X.18, 19.3–5).

3. The play concerns a Carthaginian father looking for his daughters, who have been kidnapped and sold to a brothel somewhere, many of which the father is obliged to visit. The Roman joke—such as it was—is that the father, on his brothel tour, may very well end up sleeping with his own daughters.

4. Polybius X.15.4–6.

5. For a more thorough discussion of the Roman conception of race, see Benjamin Isaac, *The Invention of Racism in Classical Antiquity* (Princeton: Princeton University Press, 2004). Pliny succinctly puts it thus: "the Greeks are a most wicked and intractable race" ("Anequissimum et indocile genus") (*Natural History* xxix.14).

6. Donald Kyle, *Spectacles of Death in Ancient Rome* (London: Routledge, 1998), 76. Consider, e.g., the imprecise but categoric tone of Plutarch's description of Sulla's conquest of Athens: "There was no numbering the slain; the amount is to this day conjectured only from the space of ground overflowed with blood. For without mentioning the execution done in other quarters of the city, the blood that was shed about the market place spread over the whole Ceramicus within the Double-gate, and according to most writers, passed through the gate and overflowed the suburb" (trans. Dryden). A more comprehensive catalog of the dead can be gleaned from William V. Harris, *War and Imperialism in Republican Rome* (Oxford: Clarendon Press, 1979), additional notes, ix, 263–64. Valerius Maximus (II.8.1) also notes that triumphs could not be granted to any who killed fewer than five thousand in any single engagement.

7. Appian, *Wars of the Romans in Iberia*, trans. and ed. J. S. Richardson (Warminster: Aris and Phillips, 2000), 5.

8. See, e.g., Polybius xxxi.23. For Polybius's complex relationship to the Aemilius Paullus family, see Polybius xviii.46, x.40.2.

9. Keith Hopkins's phrase: "By the close of the 2nd century Rome had conquered perhaps one fifth or one sixth of the world's then population" (*Death and Renewal* [Cambridge, Cambridge University Press, 1983], 1). Polybius I: "Rome succeeded in less than fifty-three years in bringing under their rule almost the whole of the inhabited world, an achievement which is without parallel in human history."

10. William V. Harris, *War and Imperialism in Republican Rome* (Oxford: Clarendon Press, 1979), 52.

11. Carlin Barton, *The Sorrows of the Ancient Romans* (Princeton: Princeton University Press, 1993), 13.

12. Strabo xiv.5.2.

13. *De ira* I.i.5

14. Loeb edition (London: William Heinemann Ltd., 1932); Janet Burroway, trans. *Plautus: the Comedies*, ed. David R. Slavitt and Palmer Bovie (Baltimore: Johns Hopkins University Press, 1995), 3: 1062–65.

15. Beyond the campaigns themselves, a second and no less profound expression of Roman genocide played out in the gladiatorial arena. Inside that forum of war memory and myth-making, the survivors of Carthage, Corinth, Nova Carthago, re-created their own destruction in the ultimate display of the subjected: by slaughtering each other. This was not yet on the scale of the early Empire, two centuries later, when the games could offer as many ten thousand pairs of gladiators over a five-day period, a feat sponsored by Augustus and Trajan both (*The Achievements of the Divine Augustus*, ed. P. A. Brunt and J. M. Moore [Oxford: Oxford University Press, 1967], 29; Dio. 68.15). But we recall it was the excess of the civic celebrations of the Punic Wars of the second century (BCE) that established the senatorial limits on the numbers slaughtered (Dio. 54.2). Much has been written about the games and their value to Rome. See, e.g., Barton, *Sorrows of the Ancient*

Romans; Keith Hopkins, "Murderous Games," in Hopkins, *Death and Renewal*, 2: 1–30.

16. The image of the voodoo pin is literal here, as images pierced with pins were often employed. Cf. Ovid: "Has some Thessalian poison bewitched my body, is it some spell or drug that has brought this misery upon me. Has some sorceress written my name on crimson wax, and stuck a pin in my liver" (*Amores* 3.7.27–30). Quoted in John Gager, ed., *Curse Tablets and Binding Spells from the Ancient World* (New York: Oxford University Press, 1992), 250–51.

17. Undated, from Nomentum, near Rome. Quoted in William Harris, *Restraining Rage: The Ideology of Anger Control in Classical Antiquity* (Cambridge: Harvard University Press, 2001), 13. For a fuller discussion of curse tablets, their authors, and their subjects, see Gager, *Curse Tablets*. There is a subtly subversive moment in Plautus's *Carthaginian* in which the slave Milphio recites a similar inventory of his own body as a courtship address to his master's mistress: "My life, my lips, my eyes, my ears, nose, throat, my bosom" (458–60). One wonders if the slave is not rehearsing the familiar trope of a binding curse as well, speaking exclusively ("signifying") to the knowing. His master seems to acknowledge as much and beats him for it (490–92). And again, in *Mostellaria* (The Haunted House), Tranio, trapped on the altar and threatened by his master:

THEOPROPIDES—I'm going to make an example of you.
TRANIO—Like me that well, do you?
THEOPROPIDES: Just tell me something: what sort of man was my son when I left him in your care?
TRANIO—Oh, he was a man with feet, hands, fingers, ears, eyes, mouth.
THEOPROPIDES—That's not what I asked you.
TRANIO—That's not what I answered you, either. (1117–24)

18. The tragic sequence is replicated in Terence's *Adelphoe*, with the additional consequence of a child from the rape. The victim's name is also Pamphila, and the only line attributed to her is a cry of the pain of childbirth, offstage. Similarly, in his *Hecyra* (The Mother-in-Law), the unseen Philumena is only heard offstage, crying in the delivery of another child of a rape (iii.315).

19. Herbert Blau, *Take Up the Bodies* (Urbana: University of Illinois Press, 1982), 184–85.

20. Matthew Leigh, *Comedy and the Rise of Rome* (Oxford: Oxford University Press, 2004), 57; Moses I. Finley, *Ancient Slavery and Modern Ideology* (London: Chatto and Windus, 1980), 75–77, traces the Roman strategy of breaking the family bonds of prisoners and slaves.

21. Douglass Parker, trans., *Complete Comedies of Terence* (New Brunswick: Rutgers University Press, 1974).

22. Literally "to pay back these torturers" ("deducar et illis crucibus") (383).

23. Literally, "to be what I was pretending to be" ("ego is essem vero qui simulabar") (606).

24. Clifford Geertz, "Deep Play: Notes on the Balinese Cockfight," in *The Interpretation of Cultures* (New York: Basic Books, 1973), 421.

25. Paul Ricoeur, *Memory, History, Forgetting* (Chicago: University of Chicago Press, 2004), xv.

Against Plausibility

ELLEN MACKAY ❧

This essay means to put under scrutiny the generalization that theater historians have tended to begin with: that the theatrical past stands in dire need of some discipline. Here is E. K. Chambers, making this point at the start of his epic study *The Medieval Stage* (1935):

> The history of the mediaeval theatre had never, from an English point of view, been written. The initial chapter of Collier's *Annals of the Stage* is even less adequate than is usual with this slovenly and dishonest antiquary.[1]

A somewhat milder version of the same vexation shows up in A. M. Nagler's introduction to *A Source Book in Theatrical History:*

> It is true that the nineteenth century contributed to our knowledge of earlier stage history, but it is rather obvious that the bulk of the biographies of players and monographs on the theatrical traditions of certain cities were more inspired by personal enthusiasm and local patriotism than guided by scholarship.[2]

Assessing the state of things at the midpoint of the twentieth century, Nagler concludes that the field of theater history is "still waiting for a methodology" that would "allow for a scientific approach to theatrical facts."[3] Until then, we remain constrained by "the dilettantism and anecdotalism" of the "pseudo-historians" on whose shoulders we stand.[4]

Theater history, I submit, is still bound by Nagler's mandate. Written at "Easter, 1952," his introduction describes our messianic awaiting for the method that we have yet to encounter face to face.[5] In the meanwhile, we continue the labor of disenthralling ourselves from the enthusiasms of our forebears, seeking the truth that by ignorance, jingoism, and rank dishonesty has been hidden. "Only a strictly scholarly path" can bring us "to the goal," writes Nagler, insinuating the religious spirit of this travail.[6] For the *Source book* at its outset gathers its readership to an ecumenical council: like exegetes sifting the apocrypha from the canon, we "por[e] over" "scholia, letters, archival statistics, eyewitness accounts, prefaces, reviews, drawings, prints, etc. . . . of very unequal value" to purify our tainted archive.[7] Hence, the purge of past "scholarship" with which theater history perpetually re-begins itself: in pursuit of a cleaner slate, much of what has been said before must be discarded.

The Matter of Fact

What kinds of things does history find out? I answer *res gestae:* actions of human beings that have been done in the past.

Patrick Collinson, *The Idea of History*

No one can dispute that Nagler's concerns are well-founded. Thanks to the "anecdotalism" of "pseudo-historians," the annals of the theatrical past announce the necessity of their correction. Take, for instance, the oft-told chestnut regarding the theater's first tragedian: "When, at the performance of *The Eumenides*, Aeschylus introduced the chorus in wild disorder into the orchestra, he so terrified the crowd that children died and women suffered miscarriage."[8] Modern scholarship calls this "sheer fancy"; "in thirty years of lecturing on the *Oresteia*," William Calder writes, "I have always dismissed the anecdote as rubbish."[9] At the very root of theater history, we are thus confronted by the problem Nagler tackles: much of what we have as evidence of the theater's "*res gestae*" is to history what fish stories are to marine science.

But though I do not dispute Nagler's call to sobriety, my aim is to make a case for the preservation of enchantment. Or rather, my aim is to show the case Nagler seems to be making for it, even as he agitates for methodological improvement. His book's most striking characteristic, after all, is its anecdotalism; the dubiety and contingency that define this form are exuberantly manifest in entries titled "Showman Pompey" and "Sir Charles Steals the Show." Only slightly less whimsical is "Aeschylus—Man of the Theater," the second of the book's selected contents. Under this heading, Nagler unfolds the same scene of women and children fatally convulsed by the *Eumenides* that Calder calls "rubbish" and that, by Easter of 1952, has already been thoroughly debunked. (In his 1907 study *The Attic Theatre*, A. E. Haigh calls it "a foolish invention.")[10] To be sure, Nagler doesn't hold this story up as scientific truth; "we must be aware," he writes, "that the anonymous biographer compiled his accounts from rather spurious sources."[11] But the disclaimer only raises the question of what our disposition toward this evidence ought to be. What sort of "aware[ness]" can explain the canonization of such "spurious sources" in *A Source Book In Theatrical History*?

There are, of course, good evidentiary uses to which this sort of implausible anecdote can be put. Calder lists two of them: "the fables about the *eklepsis* because of the *Eumenides* only inform us of the effect the play had on later readers" (this is Ulrich von Wilamowitz-Moellendorff's assessment, in 1914);[12] or "the tradition [is] an irresponsible biographer's elaboration of hints in the play itself" (Calder's paraphrase of Mary Lefkowitz's reading, from 1981).[13] But what claims my interest is the precarious move Calder finally makes to champion its plausibility. After thirty years of taking the *Eumenides'* abortifacience as a myth, he discovers "a remarkable and well attested parallel" in the German premiere of *Othello*. According to the testimony of an "eyewitness" (the secretary of the Danish Constitutional Assembly, in fact), "the daemonic passion of the African, the satanic malice of his ensign, [and] the cruel slaughter of the innocent Desdemona" proved more than "the women of 1776 Hamburg could bear":

> The closer the performance approached the catastrophe, the more uneasy the audience grew. "Swoons followed upon swoons," reports an eyewitness. "The doors of the boxes opened and closed. People left or when necessary were carried out; and (according to trustworthy reports) the premature miscarriages of various prominent Habsburg women were the result of seeing and hearing the overly tragic play.[14]

It is easy enough to point out the weak science of this corroboration: its "trustworthy reports" are merely hearsay; the racial "shock" of this play for eighteenth-century audiences is deeply conventional;[15] the *Oresteia's* legendary production history may have shaped the secretary's account.[16] As Calder himself admits, the "parallel does not assure the historicity of the Aeschylean anecdote."[17] More difficult to explain is Calder's decision to sweep past the obvious reasons that one report cannot verify the other. At the cost of good practice—at history's sacrifice, we might even say—Calder makes the claim that the Aeschylean "anecdote cannot be dismissed on the grounds of intrinsic absurdity."[18] Oddly enough, years of following "a strictly scholarly path" lead him right back to the enthusiasms of Nagler's "pseudo-historians."

To look to the "sources" of theater historiography is thus to recognize that alongside skepticism—indeed, in the midst of skepticism's strongest promulgation—there remain strong expressions of wonder and belief. This double-mindedness owes, I think, to the divide of theory from practice, though not in the sense typically bemoaned by theater departments. Because it leaves behind no matter to anchor its fact, performance has been conceptualized as a kind of ghost-work; over the past couple of decades, the summons and summoning of its "traceless"[19] iterations have been richly "hauntologized"[20] in key works by Peggy Phelan, Herbert Blau, Marvin Carlson, Alice Rayner, Joe Roach, Richard Schechner, and Diana Taylor, among others.[21] Yet consensus on the subject of performance's spectrality creates an impasse for the sort of "ever-questioning scholar" to whom Nagler addresses his *Source Book*—the scholar who practices "a scientific approach to theatrical facts."[22] As Derrida writes, riffing on Marcellus's great line—"Thou art a scholar—speak to it Horatio"—"There has never been a scholar who really, and as a scholar, deals with ghosts. A traditional scholar does not believe in ghosts."[23] Inasmuch as it is epistemologically necessary to "believe in the sharp distinction of the real and the unreal, the actual and the inactual," in order to keep from straying into "theatrical fiction, literature and speculation," the "traditional" scholar, bound by the Jamesonian imperative to "always historicize," is bound also to recognize the hauntology of the stage as "the end of history" as we know we should practice it.[24]

This dilemma is the subject of the *Source Book*'s most acute intervention. At the very outset of his preface, Nagler describes the problem: "The theater historian is expected to reconstruct, both vividly and accurately, the conditions under which the plays of Sophocles, Corneille, Calderón, Lyly, Goldoni, Hebbel, or Gorky were first performed. And yet, the very essence of the theater is absolute transitoriness."[25] Because the archive "cannot faithfully convey the ephemeral impression made on contemporary audiences," Nagler takes it as his book's mission to simulate the experience.[26] "Under the guidance of an academician," he tells us, the reader is turned spectator: made to "watch the metamorphoses of Thespis with fascination" and "witness" a "masque performance" or "the first Park Theater."[27] For in Nagler's final assessment, we are "bound to concede that the theater historian is not a person who has ceased to feel as a playgoer, but one who is amply rewarded when he can share the transient emotional experiences of former generations of spectators."[28]

To Collinson's question, "What kinds of things does history find out?" Nagler's answer is thus a conjuring trick. By his own account, theater his-

tory does not so much find things out as purvey an imagined approximation of the "emotional experience" of vanished audiences. This confession
produces a stark shift in metaphors: what begins as an excavational effort—
for "the theatre historian's task approximates most closely that of the
archeologist"—becomes a spectatorial diversion when Nagler tells us that
each item in his compilation "is preceded by an introduction" that "set[s]
the scene for the entrance of the source itself."[29] Acting as the impresario
of his evidences, Nagler unfolds his work of "science" within the stage's apparatus of beguilement and illusion, destabilizing the very grounds where
he would, as an archeologist, dig.

My return to Nagler is thus to show how implacably the work of con-
ceptualizing the theater means abandoning anything like a scientific approach to theatrical facts. Long before Derrida tells us, Nagler shows us
that a strictly scholarly path cannot avail the historian whose object of
study lies somewhere between the real and the unreal, the actual and the
inactual. The fact that the *Source Book* begins as *Henry V* does—"Let us
. . . / On your imaginary forces work"—is therefore its best methodological insight, inasmuch as it reminds us that to deal in performance is always
and inescapably to deal in conjuration.[30] What Derrida adds to this precept
is its cutting edge; if to "*con-jure*," or make a pact, with the lost experience
of former generations is, as he says, the only means of doing justice to the
past, then theater scholars are at the vanguard of histogiography's best
practice.[31]

The Persistence of Enchantment

But how, without indulging in fatuous suppositions or egregious
anachronism, are we to do justice to these, too often silent, though
sensed, presences, that lie beneath the surface of scholarly
accounts?
Richard Beacham, "Architectural, Pictorial and
Virtual Spaces: Theatrical Phantasia in Antiquity and Today"

By turning briefly to the naumachia, a Roman naval spectacle that continues to perplex scholarly posterity, I mean now to prove that the theater has
always evinced the messianism that Derrida preaches: the dredging of its
past leads us to the "emancipatory" recognition that "what remains irre-
ducible" is the necessity of trying to do right by the dead.[32] Whereas
Nagler's treatment of Aeschylus (among others) shows us that the disposi-
tive yearnings of "archeo-historicism" are confuted by the theater's dubi-

ous remains, the naumachia, and the urge to "solve" it by scientific means, is a cautionary lesson in the inanity that comes of failing to acknowledge as much.[33]

An entertainment that sometimes doubled as mortal combat, the Roman naumachia is proof, as I. M. Barton writes, of the "vast depths of inhumanity which [its] organizers—and the spectators—could plumb."[34] At least, it would be proof if we could be more sure of how, or even if, it ever happened. Replete with sea monsters, Tritonic automata, and (according to Tacitus) floating "fancy boys," accounts of the water spectacles of ancient Rome are bound to fail the smell test of a more disciplined historicism, not least for their lack of material evidence.[35] Because man-made lakes and river basins are such poor repositories of history's traces, they are the archeo-historical equivalent of gaps in the record; the naumachia, we might say, is a largely foundationless form. The productions attributed to the Coliseum only confuse the matter further; in her assiduous study of this subject, K. M. Coleman begins by voicing an understandable incredulity: "Are we really to believe," she asks, "that aquatic spectacles were staged in the Flavian Amphitheatre?"[36] What surprises is how neatly her question recapitulates the record of the naumachia's event. Consider Martial's first epigram on the subject:

> If you happen to have only just arrived from remote shores to watch, and this has been your first day at the sacred games, don't be deceived by this naval war-goddess with her ships and sea-like waves; here not long ago there was land. Don't you believe it? Watch while the water tires the War-god out. They'll be a short delay, and then you'll say: "here just a moment ago there was sea."[37]

It is no exaggeration to say that Martial's question—"Don't you believe it?"—has polarized classical archaeology. At least since the Napoleonic age of excavation and expropriation, strenuous efforts have been made to prove that the amphitheater's "systems of drains" either could or could not have supported the aquadramatics that Emperor Titus is reported to have called for.[38] Which is to say that studies of the naumachia, and the "vast depths of inhumanity which [its] organizers—and the spectators—could plumb," have degenerated for centuries into heated arguments about the Coliseum's plumbing.

To be fair, we can recognize the rush to measure conduits and pipes as a properly scientific approach to the question of how to substantiate the-

Figure 2.1. The hard science of archeo-historicism: a detail from one of Antoine Desgodets's plates of the Coliseum, from his magnum opus, *The ancient edifices of Rome, precisely drawn and measured* (1682). Courtesy of the Lilly Library of Indiana University.

atrical facts—especially "facts" of so suspect an order. As one nineteenth-century encyclopedia entry demonstrates, it is no easy task to reconcile the naumachia's record with the project of knowledge gathering:

> These sea-fights are said to have been exhibited on such a scale of magnificence and splendour as almost to surpass our belief. In the naumachia exhibited by Nero there were sea-monsters swimming about in the artificial lake (Suetonius, *Nero*, 12), and Claudius caused a Triton, made of silver, to be placed in the middle of the lake Fucinus, who was made, by machinery, to give the signal for attack with a trumpet (Suetonius, *Claud.*, 21).[39]

And yet the technicism of our historiographic recourse—the jerk back to a reality so mundane as the Coliseum's pipework—is no cure for the doubt that ails us. Since it is by now clear that no conclusion can be drawn on this basis—the consensus of scholars is that "the structural evidence for the hydraulic system of the Coliseum and other amphitheaters is open to interpretation"—the perpetual effort to plumb a practice that is self-professedly unfathomable has only served to prove that it is not merely the "personal enthusiasm[s]" of "pseudo-historians" that vex theater history's enterprise.[40] We are equally hamstrung by our own hermeneutic of suspicion.

I do not mean to insinuate that the naumachia hasn't earned the skepticism with which scholars have repeatedly greeted it; assuredly, Martial, Seutonius, and Tacitus have bequeathed to us some of the fishiest stories in the theatrical archive. My aim, instead, is to point out that the form itself defies the resolution that a positivist practice of historiography would like to give it. Because its textual remains preserve nothing so much as the "emotional experience" of its own implausibility ("Don't you believe it?"), any attempt to definitively answer the question of whether or not there were aquatic spectacles in the Flavian Amphitheater by inching out the building's architectural specifications is bound to send scholarship down the drain. Instead, by all surviving accounts, the naumachia is a type of experience designed to force "the suspension of mastery, certainty, knowingness itself," to quote Mary Blaine Campbell's deft characterization of "wonder."[41] The story that its "history" tells is thus an injunction to remember that performance refuses the straightening-out that would deliver us from centuries of methodological flailing. It is, rather, an agent of looseness, always toggling between the "flat unraised spirits" of scholastic inquiry and the "imaginary forces" of spectatorial enchantment.[42] Any attempt to lay down some discipline must therefore take into account the fact that "the sharp distinction of the real and the unreal," or of the "pseudo" and the bona fide, will necessarily fail to take into account the theater's history, which is to say, the "transient emotional experiences of former generations of spectators." To heed Beacham's appeal and do justice to performance is thus to get past the illusion of empirical factuality and make peace with the dream of being there.

NOTES

1. E. K. Chambers, *The Medieval Stage: Two Volumes Bound as One* (New York: Dover, 1903; rept., 1996), v.

2. A. M . Nagler, *A Source Book in Theatrical History (Sources of Theatrical History)* (New York: Dover, 1952), xx.

3. Nagler, *Source Book*, xxi.

4. Nagler, *Source Book*, xx.

5. Nagler, *Source Book*, x.

6. Nagler, *Source Book*, xxiii.

7. Nagler, *Source Book*, ix.

8. "Bios Aischylou," trans. John J. Walsh, S. J., from *Aeschyli Tragoediae*, ed. Ulrich von Wilamowitz-Moellendorff (Berlin, 1914), secs. 2–16, quoted in Nagler, *Source Book*, 5.

9. William Calder, "Miscarriages in the Theatre of Dionysos," in *Theatrokratia: Collected Papers on the Politics and Staging of Greco-Roman Tragedy*, ed. Scott Smith (Hildesheim: Georg Olms Verlag, 2006), 63.

10. A. E. Haigh, *The Attic Theatre*, ed. A. W. Pickard-Cambridge (Oxford: Oxford University Press, 1907), 327, quoted in Calder, "Miscarriages," 63.

11. Nagler, *Source Book*, 4.

12. *Aischylos Interpretationen* (Berlin: Weidmann, 1914), 249, trans. and quoted in Calder, "Miscarriages," 63.

13. Mary Lefkowitz, *The Lives of the Greek Poets* (Baltimore: Johns Hopkins University Press, 1981) 71–72, quoted in Calder, "Miscarriages," 63.

14. Johann Friedrich Schutze, Kgl. dänische Kanzleisekretär, *Hamburgische Theater-Geschichte* (Hamburg, 1794), 208–9, cited in Jocza Savitz, *Shakespeare und die Bühne des Dramas: Erfahrungen and Betrachtungen* (Bonn, 1917), 31, trans. and quoted in Calder, "Miscarriages," 64.

15. For a thorough account of *Othello*'s "disturbed response," see Michael Neill, "Unproper Beds: Race, Adultery and the Hideous in Othello," first published in *Shakespeare Quarterly*, collected in *Putting History to the Question: Power, Politics and Society in English Renaissance Drama* (New York: Columbia University Press, 2000), 237–68, 268.

16. In a footnote, Calder admits this is a "remote[ ]" possibility ("Miscarriages," 65).

17. Calder, "Miscarriages," 65.

18. Calder, "Miscarriages," 65.

19. Peggy Phelan, *Unmarked: The Politics of Performance* (New York: Routledge, 1993), 149.

20. Derrida coins the term *hauntology* in *Specters of Marx: The State of Debt, the Work of Mourning, and the New International*, trans. Peggy Kamuf (New York: Routledge, 1994), 10.

21. Herbert Blau, *The Audience* (Baltimore: Johns Hopkins University Press, 1990); Marvin Carlson, *The Haunted Stage: The Theatre as Memory Machine* (Ann Arbor: University of Michigan Press, 2003); Phelan, *Unmarked*; Alice Rayner, *Ghosts: Death's Double and the Phenomena of Theatre* (Minneapolis: University of Minnesota Press, 2006); Joseph Roach, *Cities of the Dead: Circum-Atlantic Performances* (New York: Columbia University Press, 1996); Richard Schechner, *Between Theater and Anthropology* (Philadelphia: University of Pennsylvania Press, 1985); Diana Taylor, *The Archive and the Repertoire* (Durham: Duke University Press, 2003).

22. Nagler, *Source Book*, ix, xxi.

23. William Shakespeare, *Hamlet*, ed. Ann Thompson and Neil Taylor, in *The Arden Shakespeare* (London: Thomson Learning, 2006), 1.1.41; Derrida, *Specters of Marx*, 11.

24. Derrida, *Specters of Marx*, 11; Fredric Jameson, *The Political Unconscious* (London: Methuen, 1981), 9; Derrida, *Specters of Marx*, 11, 10. The end of history is one-half the title of Francis Fukuyama's *The End of History and the Last Man* (New York: Avon Books, 1992), with which Derrida does battle in *Specters of Marx*.

25. Nagler, *Source Book*, ix.

26. Nagler, *Source Book*, ix.

27. Nagler, *Source Book*, x.

28. Nagler, *Source Book*, x.

29. Nagler, *Source Book*, ix, x.

30. William Shakespeare, *Henry V*, ed. T. W. Craik, in *The Arden Shakespeare* (London: Thomson Learning, 1995), prologue, 17–18.

31. Derrida, *Specters of Marx*, 31.

32. Derrida, *Specters of Marx*, 59.

33. The term comes from Robert D. Hume, *Reconstructing Contexts: The Aims and Principles of Archeo-Historicism* (Oxford: Clarendon Press, 1999). See Jacky Bratton, *New Readings in Theatre History* (Cambridge: Cambridge University Press, 2003), 3–16, for a compelling critique of Hume's positivism.

34. I. M. Barton, "Buildings for Entertainment," in *Roman Public Buildings*, ed. I. M. Barton (Exeter Studies in History 20, 1989), 120.

35. Tacitus *Annals* XV.37.2–7. The translation is in K. M. Coleman, "Launching into History: Aquatic Displays in the Early Empire," *Journal of Roman Studies* 83 (1993): 48–74, 51.

36. Coleman, "Launching into History," 49.

37. Martial *De Spectaculis* 24, trans. and quoted in Coleman, "Launching into History," 60.

38. D. S. Potter and D. J. Mattingly, *Life, Death, and Entertainment in the Roman Empire* (Ann Arbor: University of Michigan Press, 1999), 233.

39. Charles Knight, *Arts and Sciences; or, The Fourth Division of "The English Encyclopedia"* (London: Bradbury, Evans & Co., 1867), 5: 893.

40. Potter and Mattingly, *Life, Death, and Entertainment*, 233.

41. Mary Blaine Campbell, *Wonder and Science: Imagining Worlds in Early Modern Europe* (Ithaca: Cornell University Press, 1999), 3.

42. Shakespeare, *Henry V*, prologue, 9.

The Spark of Strangeness

William Davenant, Piracy, and Surprises in Theater History

ROBERT B. SHIMKO ❧

This essay revolves around a web of extraordinary events with the seventeenth-century theater impresario William Davenant at their center. I proffer it as an object lesson in what might be termed "historiographical detouring," a deliberate act of scholarly deviation from the well-worn narratives surrounding some accustomed aspect of theater history for the purpose of placing the familiar facts in tension with truths stranger than fiction. Investigating certain curiosities surrounding Davenant shows how some of the dustier figures encountered in the archives of the theatrical past can be destabilized and opened up to intriguing and more deeply contextualized interpretations—if we revisit them via what Michel de Certeau has characterized as "bouts of surprise . . . the sudden jubilatory, semi-ecstatic forms of 'astonishment' or 'wonder' which have been, from Aristotle to Wittgenstein, the inaugurators of philosophical activity."[1] In a eulogy for his friend Michel Foucault, de Certeau compares Foucault the reader to Foucault the bicyclist in the city, each navigating his particular terrain "with exact and vigilant attention, poised to catch, at the turn of a page or a street, the spark of some strangeness lurking there unnoticed."[2] This is an intensely personal utterance given the context, but it also serves as an apt description of a too infrequently discussed moment in historiographic work: the unanticipated appearance of some nearly forgotten yet fascinating element of the past that opens up new avenues of inquiry into a given subject.

Bouts of surprise remind us that the writers of history are also its wondering readers. And for teachers of history, they suggest the power of defamiliarizing habitual historical narratives in the classroom. De Certeau's description speaks to those instances when scholars find ourselves beguiled by the affective powers of the archive as we uncover occurrences and connections that are "quite readable, but unread because they take the ex-

pected and the codified by surprise."[3] It is just such an experience of astonishment and captivation in the face of history that I wish to relate, regarding piracy (of the high seas, rather than the literary sort) as a previously unrecognized leitmotif in the writings and life of William Davenant.

While Davenant continues to occupy a position as one of the de rigueur
figures in the history of seventeenth-century English theater, Davenant
scholarship has become decidedly stagnant. Even the most recent work on
him merely calls for further embellishment of traditional avenues of study:
his lengthy and varied literary and theatrical careers, his introduction of
opera to England, and his associations with other notables like Dryden and
Hobbes.[4] Such work, though potentially valuable, would embellish but not
otherwise transfigure an already existing portrait. Lamenting a falling off
of scholarly attention paid to a particular historical personage seems in itself less than enough cause to reignite major critical interest, especially if
that figure, like Davenant, has gradually become wrapped in an aura of
vaguely contemptible familiarity (I suspect few readers felt umbrage when
I implied that Davenant was "dusty").

In the realm of theater history, a longstanding tradition of cursory coverage has effectively consolidated and condensed ideas about Davenant's
noteworthiness into a standard list of accomplishments that can be found
repeated in nearly all contemporary surveys.[5] Put briefly, it runs as follows.
As a young playwright, he worked on some of the splendid pre–Civil War
court masques, including the last of them: *Salmacida Spolia*, which he conceived in collaboration with Inigo Jones.[6] In 1656 he staged the *Siege of
Rhodes*, which was the first major stage production since the theater ban of
1642 and which introduced opera, the (noncourtly) female performer, and
Italianate scenography to England.[7] At the outset of the Restoration, he
and Thomas Killigrew ultimately secured, after some finagling, the two
sole royal patents to operate playhouses in London.[8] As manager of the
Duke's Company from 1660 until his death in 1668, he continued to advance the use of Italianate stage spectacle while producing revivals of
Shakespeare as well as debuting Dryden's early plays.[9]

Of the nine general histories I consulted, three also note that William
Shakespeare may have been Davenant's godfather.[10] Two of those accounts
refer to the contention that Shakespeare may have actually sired him.[11]
And only one of them references (and obliquely, at that) the story, which
goes back to John Aubrey's seventeenth-century collection of biographical
sketches, *Brief Lives*, about how it was Davenant himself who propagated
the rumor.[12] However, this last book politely avoids Aubrey's pert but correct observation that such a claim amounted to calling his mother a cuck-

olding whore.[13] The frontispiece from the 1673 folio edition of his collected works (fig. 3.1) adds a visual signifier to one book's discussion of Davenant,[14] though it goes unmentioned that the portrait juxtaposes the highs and lows of his life: the bays he wore as poet laureate and his syphilis-ravaged nose.

As far as thumbnail sketches in theater history textbooks go, Davenant's is not entirely uninteresting, even when such juicy details are glossed over. But it is precisely the neatness and stability of this accrued identity that present a problem because the implication of its consistency is that it encompasses the broad strokes of everything worth knowing about the man, his work, and his enmeshment in history. The experience of surprise is important here. It differs from other modes of taking in of new information in that, in some way or other, the surprise does not agree with what is pre-supposed—a drastic realignment of expectations occurs in an instant. My own bout of surprise with Davenant occurred while I was conducting dissertation research on the writing of theater history during the Interregnum and early Restoration. I came across a biography of Davenant from 1938 that included a chapter titled "General, Knight, and Pirate."[15] Pirate? This was not the Davenant I thought I knew; my curiosity was piqued.

Prompted to return to Davenant qua pirate a few years later,[16] I wondered how he might fit into the guiding question of Hans Turley's excellent book *Rum, Sodomy, and the Lash:* "How did the Pirate—a serious menace to mercantilism and trade in early-modern Britain—become the outrageously masculine antihero familiar to us through novels, movies, plays, and other outlets of popular culture?"[17] As it turns out, Davenant's writings on the subject show a shift from the former attitude in his early adulthood toward something both like and unlike the latter description after his own real-life piratical experiences.

Pirates figured prominently in the young Davenant's imagination, particularly those from Dunkirk, then a pseudo-independent Flemish state that served as a base for channel pirates, many of them financially tied to the Spanish crown.[18] In an early poem, Davenant celebrated the public sale of wares from a Spanish ship, recently captured by the English Navy, which had allegedly been trafficking in stolen goods with the Dunkirkers. The poem is narrated by a barker who seems to derive particular delight in offering for sale

> Souldiers Cassocks, both old and new,
> Which *Valdes* unto *Dunkirke* sent,
> But now the rogues must lie perdue
> Starke-naked, and keep perpetuall Lent;[19]

Figure 3.1. Engraved portrait of Sir William Davenant from the frontispiece of the 1673 folio edition of Davenant's *Works*, reproduced by permission of the Bodleian Library, Oxford.

As a patriotic young Englishman, Davenant saw pirates, especially the Span-ish-aligned Dunkirkers, as detestable villains deserving of such humiliation. In fact, the Dunkirk pirates so inflamed his thoughts that in 1628 Davenant wrote to the secretary of state, Dudley Carleton, with a plan to blow up the port of Dunkirk using a huge quantity of gunpowder. He concludes the let-ter with the claim that "I shall performe the service, though with the losse of my life."[20] The letter was cataloged by the secretary of state's office, but no official offer was extended to Davenant to execute his plan.

Two years later, the twenty-four-year-old Davenant again returned to the subject of piracy with a narrative poem, equal in imaginativeness to his letter to Carleton though less deadly earnest in its conception. The occasion was the safe return of Jeffrey Hudson to the English court after he and his traveling companions had been held hostage and robbed by Dunkirk pirates. Hudson, who held the position of "Queen's Dwarf," was returning from France as part of a delegation sent to collect ten Capuchin friars for the household of Queen Henrietta Maria and, more importantly, a midwife named Madame Peronne, who a few months later would deliver the infant prince who would become Charles II. Hudson was included in the traveling party in order to delight the French court with his eighteen-inch frame, and he had been lavished with gifts.[21] Not far from the French coast, the ship was boarded, and Hudson, Madame Peronne, and three others were taken prisoner and held for ransom. When it became clear that stealing a pregnant queen's midwife had earned them more attention than they had bargained for, the pirates released all of their captives, who were safely returned to England after just two days.[22]

The diminutive Hudson had been a favorite of Henrietta Maria since their initial meeting (the first Duke of Buckingham had arranged for Hudson to emerge from a pie crust at the end of a banquet, surprising the young queen, who was poised, knife in hand, to slice into the pie).[23] Davenant no doubt saw an opportunity to curry favor with her through some verses on the happy occasion of their reunion. Titled "Jeffereidos, on the Captivitie of Jeffrey," Davenant's mock romance portrays a comical version of Hudson's ordeal with the Dunkirk pirates, who are presented as caricatured miscreants:

> A sayle! A sayle! Cry'd they, who did consent
> Once more to break the eighth commandment
> For a few Coles, of which by theft so well
> Th'are stor'd; they have enow to furnish hell[24]

In short order the devilish crew overtakes the vulnerable English vessel. "After having rifled all her precious Freight," the pirates, whom Davenant depicts as infernal beings composed of "Tar and Pitch," discover the hyperbolically tiny Hudson hiding beneath a candlestick. Taken for a spy and bound in chains, Hudson resists, calling the captain a "Pirat-Dogge."[25] He is then put on the rack and interrogated in an attempt to glean any English or French state secrets that the pirates might then sell to the Spanish crown. Unable to coerce Hudson, the pirates strip him of his jewels and send him off to Brussels on the back of a poodle, signaling the poem's final abandonment of any connection to reality.[26] The second canto concerns Hudson's adventures as a small man in a fantastic landscape. The centerpiece is a battle between Hudson and a turkey, from which he is ultimately rescued by the midwife Madame Peronne. This fanciful, swashbuckling tale offers a high degree of retrospective irony, given the harrowing events that awaited both Davenant and Hudson during the English Civil War.[27]

In 1642, shortly before the outbreak of open hostilities between the forces of Charles I and Parliament, Queen Henrietta Maria fled for the continent to begin raising funds for the war effort. She enlisted Davenant to sail to The Hague in order to pawn some of her jewels. Soon, Davenant was also acting as the personal go-between for the queen and the royalist general William Cavendish, Earl of Newcastle.[28] Davenant, it should be noted, had long been one of the queen's most trusted cat's-paws. For example, a letter written by Sir John Suckling during the 1639 Scottish uprising against Charles I, known as the First Bishops' War, indicates that Davenant maintained a personal flock of carrier pigeons (which Suckling refers to as "Mr. Davenant's Barbary pigeons") that he used to convey messages on the queen's behalf, allowing her to communicate with her husband in the field.[29] Finding himself again in Henrietta Maria's employ, Davenant began regularly conveying money, supplies, and information from Holland to Newcastle's outpost in Yorkshire. These dealings were often less secret than the parties involved would have wished, however, and record of them was preserved primarily through the reports of a parliamentary agent named Walter Strickland, who was working in Holland as a diplomat and spy and who would, a few years later, become Davenant-as-pirate-captain's chief nemesis.[30]

During the first year of the war, Davenant proved to be a bold servant of the crown, ultimately earning knighthood from Charles I. As the fighting intensified throughout 1643, he began to incorporate the raiding of enemy vessels into his gun-and-secret-running expeditions. A report in the parliamentarian news sheet the *True Informer* decried the fact that "whole Ships full of plundered goods, and some very rich," were being sold off to profiteering merchants in Rotterdam. And among the royalist Englishmen blamed for conducting this business, the "chief was Davenant the Poet (now Knighted)."[31] The parliamentarians, however, had their own cunning agent in Rotterdam: Walter Strickland. When Davenant purchased a Dutch frigate for twenty-five hundred pounds and crewed it with one hundred men at his own expense, Strickland saw to it that the ship was detained in port whenever the winds were favorable for sailing and that it was given clearance to depart only when they were still or blowing inland. This game kept up for four months until the infuriated Davenant finally resold the ship at a loss of roughly one thousand pounds.[32]

Davenant then took the step of obtaining a legal commission from

Charles I to operate in the channel. This was important because it would have given him the status of a privateer, defined in Hans Turley's useful taxonomy as "a working member of society" with permission from a monarch to "prey on enemy ships during wartime."[33] With his letter of marque in hand, Davenant took command of a second small frigate, which he named the *Newcastle* in honor of his former superior officer. The *Newcastle* soon captured two English ships loaded with supplies, bound for the parliamentary army. But when Davenant tried to sell the contents to his usual contacts in Rotterdam, Dutch officials stepped in, ignored his royal commission, and confiscated the haul, which was estimated at roughly six thousand pounds.[34] A privateer serves at the pleasure of a sitting monarch, after all, and in the context of a civil war that made the English king's authority nebulous at best, the Dutch evidently felt at liberty to treat Davenant as a pirate (i.e., a stateless criminal) when it served their interest.

Beyond his mutable status with the Dutch, Davenant was viewed unambiguously as a pirate by the parliamentarian faction in England. On 8 March 1644, the House of Commons heard reports by an agent named Peters about the largely unchecked flow of arms from Holland to the royal army, as well as the taking of various parliamentary ships in the channel. The Commons responded to Peters's presentation by issuing a set of four resolutions declaring that Davenant and three royalist merchants based in Holland "shall be forthwith accused of high treason for levying war against the King and Parliament."[35] The inclusion of "the King" in this last phrase is a curious piece of rhetoric, for it denies Davenant's obvious allegiance to King Charles. The intent seems to be to mark Davenant as an enemy to all of England, rather than an antagonist to one faction in a civil war. Indeed, this is reminiscent of the definition of the pirate as "*hostis humani generis*, the common enemy against all mankind," used by Turley.[36] Davenant promptly disproved this characterization, however, by returning to England for a short time to serve in the king's army, and it was reported in the *Parliament Scout* that he was killed in the battle of Marston Moor.[37] Reports of his death were, of course, greatly exaggerated, and he reappears in the historical record going about the business of securing a new ship, although he remained commander in absentia of the still-operating raider *Newcastle* as well.[38] Using letters of request from the highly placed royalist commanders Lord George Digby and Sir Hugh Pollard, Davenant was able to obtain from the commander of the port of Dartmouth a packet boat—a relatively small and speedy vessel usually used for the rapid transport of packages and other mail.[39] Once again Davenant was set for action as a conveyor of information and supplies.

Back at sea, Davenant focused his energies primarily on smuggling arms past an increasingly dangerous parliamentary blockade. By one account he delivered fully thirteen thousand pounds' worth of guns and ammunition to the royal army.[40] The *Newcastle* continued to prowl the channel without Davenant directly in command, though as owner of the vessel he still received credit and blame for its exploits. One anonymous parliamentarian angrily recommended that "Sir William Davenant, the poet—now the great pirott—and he that was the agent in projecting and bring[ing] up the northerne army three years since, would be put into the exceptions for life. No man hath done you more hurt, and hath been a greater enemy to the parliament."[41] Despite such votes of confidence from his enemies, Davenant was only one facet of a royalist war effort grown increasingly hopeless. By the time King Charles surrendered himself to the Scots on 5 May 1646, Davenant had abandoned the channel and joined the exiled court in Paris, eventually taking up residence in an apartment at the Louvre.

Davenant next took to sea four years later, after being named first treasurer of Virginia and then lieutenant governor of Maryland by the self-proclaimed but uncoronated Charles II. Ironically, his ship was promptly captured by a parliamentary frigate called *Fortune* a day after beginning the journey to America. This led to four years of imprisonment, first at Cowes Castle on the Isle of Wight and then in the Tower of London.[42] After he was finally released in August of 1654, Davenant reentered a city dominated by forces hostile to royalists. Deeply in debt and truly qualified to work in only two arenas—war and the theater—he began making tentative steps toward the project for which he is today best remembered: staging hybrids of music, declamatory poetry, dance, and scenography designed to skirt the ongoing Puritan ban on stage plays. *The Siege of Rhodes* is usually accorded pride of place among these works. But if Davenant's piratical exploits have been neglected by theater historians because they have not been recognized as intersecting meaningfully with his theatrical accomplishments, then the last of Davenant's quartet of pre-Restoration operatic productions, in which he thoroughly exploited the subject of piracy/privateering, makes a strong case to the contrary.

The History of Sir Francis Drake premiered at the Cockpit in Drury Lane in early 1659 and was published later the same year.[43] Drawing on an account of Drake's adventures in the West Indies, written to win favor from Elizabeth I,[44] Davenant constructs Drake, and by extension the English privateer more generally, as a steely but just nationalist who puts honor before personal gain. His fictionalized Drake is unceasingly virtu-

ous, at least when understood from a seventeenth-century English chau-
vinist perspective. He allies himself with a group of "Symerons" (Cimar-
rons), African slaves escaped from their Spanish masters, and receives
from their king lavish praise in the heroic poetic mode for his courage and
power.[45] When the Symerons capture a Spanish wedding party, Drake intervenes but first hears out the Symeron spokesman, who explains that
they were seeking tit for tat against the Spanish, who "midst the triumphs
of our nuptial feasts / Have forced our brides and slaughtered all our
guests." Drake concludes the dispute with the verdict: "No length of studied torments shall suffice / To punish all unmanly cruelties," and the scene
concludes with a dance by the Spanish father of the bride and bridegroom
celebrating Drake's righteousness.[46]

In contrast with Drake's near-constant moralizing and absorption of
compliments, Davenant shows Drake's crew as much more concerned with
the capture of wealth for its own sake. The second entry opens with a sea
shanty that includes grumbling about the "bacon and peas" enjoyed by
"our master and his mate," a plot to hide captured loot from the ship's
sticky-fingered purser, and plans for sneaking up on the enemy. Later in
the play, a pair of seamen and a pair of land soldiers sing about why the two
groups they represent never get along. The crux is that each feels left out
of the spoils of the other's marauding, and they make peace based on the
thought of teaming up against the Spanish:

> Come let us join hands then, and ne'er part asunder,
> But, like the true sons of trusty old mothers,
> Make equally haste to a snap of the plunder,
> Then justly divide and spend it like brothers.[47]

The tone is less one of nationalist enthusiasm à la Drake, and more of bad
boys in good spirits, calling to mind works of twentieth-century musical
theater like *The Threepenny Opera* and *Guys and Dolls*, which celebrate crim-
inals as charming scoundrels. While Davenant assiduously avoids the status of willful outlaw for Drake, who is always adamant that he robs the
Spanish only to weaken them as a rival to England, Drake's crew project
the likable antihero aura commonly ascribed to pirates in popular culture
in later centuries. Davenant thus interweaves two affective tropes: the
roguish attractiveness of English pirates and the self-sacrificing nobility of
the patriotic privateer.

It was the latter that Davenant sought to attach to himself when in the
spring of 1664, approximately six months after he had revived *The History*

of Sir Francis Drake as the third act of his theatrical chimera *A Playhouse to Be Let*, he laid out the details of his purchase and employment of the *Newcastle*, as well as his related financial losses when Walter Strickand—described in the post-Restoration climate as "Agent to the Rebels"—conspired with the Dutch against him. Davenant's complaint for losses totaling one thousand pounds was filed among the Foreign State Papers in the Public Record Office, though no evidence shows him receiving any reimbursement from the English government.[48] In his argument, Davenant did his best to portray himself as a put-upon servant of Charles I, the implication being that he deserved some recompense from Charles II. However, the fact that he had incurred his expenses in pursuit of capturing and selling English ships, "rebel" or not, would always bind Davenant in a liminal space between privateer and pirate.

This paper ends with the reimagining of a picture. The William Faithorne engraving of Davenant that accompanies this essay is one of the most frequently reproduced images associated with the Restoration theater. If you like, the website allposters.com will even sell you an 18 x 24 print of it for $49.99. If not ubiquitous, it is at least readily available, and for many theater historians it is familiar. Davenant's portrait is thus not the first place one might look in order to be surprised. But I've seen, as part of end-of-the-term performative research projects, a hybrid of William Davenant and Johnny Depp's Jack Sparrow enacted by a young African American man from Texas. I've also seen a puppet Davenant, with a female student's voice, raiding cardboard ships before receiving his theater patent from a puppet Charles II. The point of these examples is not that they were amusing, though they were, but that they began with a moment of fascination ("That boring old guy from the textbook was a pirate?!") and ultimately became jumping-off points for serious discussions of the archive: how it functions; how it is based in the principles of selection and arrangement; and how the scholar's own selection and arrangement is itself always an interpretation, making legible some constituent of the historical record. One cannot force a surprise discovery in the archive, but we can, through practice, ready ourselves and our students to ask questions of the unexpected: what it indicates about what is already commonly known and how that common knowledge can be transformed by a new arrangement. That William Davenant was a pirate matters in the way that Aphra Behn and Christopher Marlowe were spies matters. These are more than fun pieces of trivia. They may seduce our imaginations in ways similar to fictional adventures, but they also function as part of what Foucault calls "the dramaturgy of the real," connecting personal histories to the exigencies of their times, showing what it was possible and necessary for individuals to become in those times.[49]

NOTES

1. Michel de Certeau, *Heterologies: Discourse on the Other*, trans. Brian Massumi (Minneapolis: University of Minnesota Press, 1986), 194.

2. de Certeau, *Heterologies*, 194.

3. de Certeau, *Heterologies*, 194.

4. See Andrew Shifflett and Ronald E. Miller, "Recent Studies in Sir William Davenant," *English Literary Renaissance* 36, no. 3 (2006): 466–81.

5. I am thinking here of the sort of overview-style theater history textbooks that might be used in university theater history courses: Oscar Brockett and Franklin Hildy, *History of the Theatre*, 10th ed. (New York: Pearson, 2008); Edwin Wilson and Alvin Goldfarb, *Living Theatre: History of Theatre*, 5th ed. (New York: McGraw Hill, 2008); Phillip Zarrilli, Bruce McConachie, Gary Jay Williams, and Carol Fisher Sorgenfrei, *Theatre Histories: An Introduction* (New York: Routledge, 2006); John Russell Brown, ed., *The Oxford Illustrated History of Theatre* (New York: Oxford University Press, 1995); Jack Watson and Grant McKernie, *A Cultural History of Theatre* (New York: Longman 1993); Glynne Wickham, *A History of the Theatre* (New York: Cambridge University Press, 1992); Phyllis Hartnoll, *The Theatre: A Concise History* (New York: Thames and Hudson, 1985); Ronald Harwood, *All the World's a Stage* (Boston: Little, Brown, 1984); Patti Gillespie and Kenneth Cameron, *Western Theater: Revolution and Revival* (New York: Macmillan, 1984). I have limited my sample to books published since the mid-1980s, roughly the period identified by Shifflett and Miller as marking a lull in studies of Davenant.

6. Brockett and Hildy, *History of the Theatre*, 134; Brown, *Oxford Illustrated History of Theatre*, 200; Hartnoll, *Theatre*, 113; Wickham, *History of the Theatre*, 132; Harwood, *All the World's a Stage*, 146–48.

7. Brockett and Hildy, *History of the Theatre*, 202; Wilson and Goldfarb, *Living Theatre*, 262; Watson and McKernie, *Cultural History of Theatre*, 218; Harwood, *All the World's a Stage*, 179; Wickham, *History of the Theatre*, 163–64. Hartnoll, *Theatre*, 113; Brown, *Oxford Illustrated History of Theatre*, 203–4; Gillespie and Cameron, *Western Theater*, 313.

8. Brockett and Hildy, *History of the Theatre*, 202–4; Wilson and Goldfarb, *Living Theatre*, 262; Zarrilli et al., *Theatre Histories*, 189; Wickham, *History of the Theatre*, 162; Hartnoll, *Theatre*, 113; Harwood, *All the World's a Stage*, 179; Watson and McKernie, *Cultural History of Theatre*, 218; Gillespie and Cameron, *Western Theater*, 312; Brown, *Oxford Illustrated History of Theatre*, 205.

9. Brockett and Hildy, *History of the Theatre*, 205–6; Zarrilli et al., *Theatre Histories*, 189; Wickham, *History of the Theatre*, 163; Harwood, *All the World's a Stage*, 179; Watson and McKernie, *Cultural History of Theatre*, 219–20; Brown, *Oxford Illustrated History of Theatre*, 205–6, 210.

10. Wilson and Goldfarb, *Living Theatre*, 262; Hartnoll, *Theatre*, 113; Harwood, *All the World's a Stage*, 178.

11. Hartnoll, *Theatre*, 113; Harwood, *All the World's a Stage*, 178. Knowledge of this part of the story evidently used to be more widespread. Seventy-five years ago, Davenant biographer Alfred Harbage claimed that "the one thing which everyone knows about Davenant is that he might have been Shakespeare's son" (*Sir William Davenant: Poet Venturer* [Philadelphia: University of Pennsylvania Press, 1935], 8).

12. Harwood, *All the World's a Stage*, 178.

13. John Aubrey, *Brief Lives*, ed. Oliver Lawson Dick (Ann Arbor: University of Michigan Press, 1957), 85.

14. Wilson and Goldfarb, *Living Theatre*, 262.

15. Arthur H. Nethercot, *Sir William D'avenant: Poet Laureate and Playwright-Manager* (Chicago: University of Chicago Press, 1938), 200–221.

16. The image of Davenant raiding parliamentarian ships in the English Channel would likely have remained a bit of theater trivia in my mind if not for a 2007 Mid-America Theatre Conference call for papers (written by the coeditors of this book) that centered on the theme "True North" and included pirates as a suggested topic. Professor Magelssen has since confirmed for me that in adding pirates to their list of map-related themes, he and Professor Bial were hoping to tap into the ongoing popular interest in pirates, which crystallized around the three *Pirates of the Caribbean* films. As it turned out, my paper was the only one at the conference to take the somewhat tongue-in-cheek pirate suggestion seriously.

17. Hans Turley, *Rum, Sodomy, and the Lash* (New York: New York University Press, 1999), 2.

18. Some historians of sixteenth- and seventeenth-century naval affairs refer to the Dunkirkers generally as "privateers" because the original Dunkirk fleet was employed by the Spanish crown expressly to raid Dutch ships. However, by the end of the sixteenth century, many of the vessels operating out of the port of Dunkirk represented privately controlled criminal enterprises. The Dutch government officially designated the whole Dunkirk fleet as pirates as early as 1587. English ships were technically neutral (i.e., noncombatants, though they were involved in trade with the Dutch) in this conflict, so from the English perspective, Dunkirkers who raided English ships deserved the label "pirate."

19. William Davenant, "The Wares put to sale which were lately taken in a Spanish Ship," in *The Works of Sir William Davenant* (London: Henry Herringman, 1673), 338.

20. Full text reprinted in Harbage, *Sir William Davenant*, 38.

21. Nethercot, *Sir William D'avenant*, 86–87.

22. Nick Page, *Lord Minimus* (New York: St. Martin's, 2001), 69–73.

23. Page, *Lord Minimus*, 1–2.

24. Sir William Davenant, "Jeffereidos, on the Captivity of Jeffery," in *Works*, 224.

25. Davenant, "Jeffereidos," 225.

26. Davenant, "Jeffereidos," 226.

27. Jeffry Hudson was among Henrietta Maria's inner circle who took refuge in France for much of the war. Hudson, who had long since tired of jokes and patronizing verses about his stature, let it be known to his fellow exiles that the next person to insult him would have to face him in a duel. A young man named Charles Crofts, brother to the Queen's Master of Horse, took the bait, though the actual in-

sult he used is unknown. Crofts evidently did not take the prospect of a duel with
Hudson seriously, for when asked to select a weapon he chose a "squirt"–an early
pump-action fire extinguisher. Hudson, however, insisted on pistols on horseback,
and when the two charged one another, Hudson promptly shot Crofts through the
forehead. Davenant was present at the shooting, the incident standing as a grim reminder that both he and Hudson now occupied a world far more dangerous,
though perhaps no less bizarre, than the one imagined in "Jeffereidos." For a fuller
account, see Page, *Lord Minimus*, 171–78.

28. Harbage, *Sir William Davenant*, 88.

29. John Suckling, *The Works of Sir John Suckling in Prose and Verse*, ed. A.
Hamilton Thompson (New York: Russell and Russell, 1964), 333–34, 415–16. For
more information on (and illustrations of) the specific breed once commonly called
Barbary pigeons, or "Barbs," see W. B. Tegetmeier, *Pigeons: Their Structure, Vari-
eties, Habits, and Management* (London: George Routledge and Sons, 1868),
133–38.

30. Mary Edmond, *Rare Sir William Davenant* (Manchester: Manchester University Press, 1987), 92.

31. *True Informer*, 13 Jan. 1644.

32. Nethercot, *Sir William D'avenant*, 211–12.

33. Turley, *Rum, Sodomy*, 29, 37.

34. Turley, *Rum, Sodomy*, 212.

35. House of Commons, *Journal*, volume 3, 8 Mar. 1644, 421.

36. Turley, *Rum, Sodomy*, 1–2, 28–43.

37. *Parliament Scout*, 18 July 1644.

38. Nethercot, *Sir William D'avenant*, 217.

39. Harbage, *Sir William Davenant*, 94.

40. Harbage, *Sir William Davenant*, 94–95.

41. Quoted in Harbage, *Sir William Davenant*, 95; Nethercot, *Sir William
D'avenant*, 221; Edmond, *Rare Sir William Davenant*, 96.

42. See Philip Bordinat and Sophia Blaydes, *Sir William Davenant* (Boston:
Twayne, 1981), 22–23.

43. Janet Clare, *Drama of the English Republic, 1649–60* (New York: Manchester
University Press, 2002), 263.

44. Philip Nichols, *Sir Francis Drake Revived* (London, 1626). See Clare,
Drama of the English Republic, 265–66.

45. Clare, *Drama of the English Republic*, 277–78.

46. Clare, *Drama of the English Republic*, 290. In an essay about reawakening interest in Davenant, I feel compelled to note that Davenant's representation of
Drake's relationship with the "Symerons," and the way both relate to the Spanish,
are ripe for in-depth postcolonial critique, which, unfortunately, would not fit
within the space allotted for this chapter.

47. Clare, *Drama of the English Republic*, 285.

48. Reprinted in E. S. De Beer, "A Statement by Sir William D'avenant," *Notes
and Queries* 153, 5 Nov. 1927, 327–28.

49. Michel Foucault, "Lives of Infamous Men," in *The Essential Foucault*, ed.
Paul Rabinow and Nikolas Rose (New York: New Press, 2003), 281.

Is There Too Much "History" in My Theater History?

Exploring the Roles of Jewish Actors and Audiences in the Early National Playhouse

HEATHER S. NATHANS ﾟ

In his 1891 history of the Rhode Island stage, author George O. Willard referred to the state's Jewish population as "conspicuous in their support" of the earliest theatrical ventures in the young country.[1] While Willard may have meant simply that Jewish Americans were easily noticeable, "conspicuous" is an adjective that makes the historian's mouth water, since it can also imply that history, motive, and meaning may be readily discerned.[2]

As I investigated the group so "conspicuous" to Willard, the question of what rendered them extraordinary grew increasingly complex and raised questions about the roles Jews envisioned for themselves in the formation of American culture. While theater historians have noted that eighteenth- and nineteenth-century British Jews often witnessed negative stereotypes on stage and violence in the playhouse, American Jews carved out a different role from the beginning of the first professional theatrical entertainments in America. They took an active part as performers, playwrights, critics, audience members, and theater shareholders.[3]

Willard's description also invites broader questions about the process and parameters for historical research in theater. As Peter Holland notes, while pursuing theater history "on the surface . . . doesn't look like much of a problem," the question of "what kind of history theatre history is" in fact continues to challenge scholars.[4] For example, in establishing a credible context for Jewish involvement in early American theater, do I unbalance the argument by interweaving other strains of history? I could begin with an exploration of actor biographies, repertoire, and audience composition, but those records have inherent limitations and frustrating gaps.

W. B. Worthen describes the "disciplinary frictions" that continually "remap the borders between and beyond humanities fields."[5] The word "friction," however innocently chosen, hints at inherent tensions and at a potential opacity between disciplines only resolved through a process of agitation. I offer an alternate image, framing my argument as a fugue, in which different voices—or in this case, different "kinds" of history—blend in counterpoint to create synthesis. This is not merely a rationale for interdisciplinarity, since, as recent and forthcoming studies demonstrate, most contemporary theater historians incorporate a range of historical methods and materials. My query engages with issues of *scope* and *transparency*. How does the theater historian recognize when the harmony created by many voices becomes cacophony? How can the theater scholar identify discordant elements in a chorus of otherwise complementary methods? In the particular case I examine here, how many types of history would be "too many" in establishing context for Jewish conspicuousness in early American theater?

In *Liberation Historiography*, John Ernest argues that traditionally oppressed groups develop "crooked" histories shaped in response and resistance to dominant narratives, but which are more than compensatory histories. Rather, they are "artful *untellings* that function always in the context of oppression, containment, and misrepresentations." He describes these "untellings" as "both calls to action and attempts to locate the ideological site for that action."[6] Ernest focuses on African American historiography, yet his approach can raise productive questions about Jewish involvement in the early American theater. As members of a traditionally marginalized group, American Jews felt the burden of performing their past *and* scripting their future histories. Did part of their interest in the theater spring from a wish to memorialize their identities in a form already inscribed with multiple cultural and ideological associations?

My questions thus fall equally between the historical and the historiographical. Willard's word "conspicuous" prompted a quest for connections between the colonies' comparatively small Jewish population and the country's early theatrical ventures. That research seems relatively straightforward: a matter of mapping social, familial, and entrepreneurial connections. However, my project grew more complicated when I tried to reconcile those patterns with an observation made by Errol Hill in his renowned work *The Jamaican Stage*. Hill comments: "Kingston Jews were most active in promoting professional and amateur productions. . . . Plays about Jews were therefore of particular interest to this sector of the theatre-going public. Shakespeare's *Merchant of Venice* was a favored piece with the American Company." How can a theater historian account for *positive* Jewish involvement in the playhouse, while simultaneously observing that Jews regularly saw themselves represented on stage as characters like Shylock? Hill wisely notes, "We have no report on how these plays were received by the Jewish community," adding that by the beginning of the nineteenth century, the stage enjoyed a much more philo-Semitic image of the Jew. Still, how did Jewish performers or advocates of the theater balance support for the drama with its often anti-Semitic rhetoric?[7]

While Willard's comment raises questions about theatrical history, Hill's observation prompts questions about textual analysis, documentary evidence, and historical speculation. The paradoxes in these sources challenge the theater historian to rethink historiographical frameworks for any exploration of racial and ethnic stereotypes. As Ernest might ask, what history needs to be *untold* here?

The upheaval of the Revolution meant that many states stripped Jewish citizens of their rights (for their refusal to swear loyalty oaths on a Christian Bible), and mobs routinely decried those who refused to comply with nonimportation agreements as "Shylocks" (regardless of their religious affiliation). These issues implicitly or explicitly infiltrated the post-Revolutionary playhouse. Each circumstance rendered the nation's Jewish population "conspicuous," but what mysterious historical alchemy will produce a persuasive explanation for Jews' passionate interest in publicly supporting the playhouse?

Untelling Histories: Jewish Actors and the Importance of Geography

Because they appear on stage, actors are often the most "conspicuous" part of theater history. However, little concrete information remains about these early performers, and so I turn to perhaps the most *inconspicuous* Jewish figures in my history as a way to "untell" the stories that have been created about Jews in the national playhouse. According to cast lists from 1785, a family of Jewish performers named Solomon (often spelled Solomons) appeared for one night in Baltimore with the Maryland Company of Comedians. Mr. Solomon sang the popular "The Top Sail Shivers in the Wind."[8] Between 1785 and 1793, the Solomons traveled as independent performers and singers, appearing with different companies on occasion, but not settling with one particular group for any length of time. For example, a 1791 notice in the *New York Advertiser* describes the visit of two vocalists (a Mr. and Mrs. Solomon) "from the south" who had previously appeared in South Carolina, Georgia, Virginia, and Boston.[9] Throughout their wanderings they ventured not only to major urban centers but to many smaller towns. In 1794 they returned to Philadelphia, where, by 1796, the family included a juvenile performer, "Miss Solomon," who, at the age of six, was regarded as something of an infant prodigy for her wonderful singing.[10] Two years after the family's move to Philadelphia, a poem about Miss Solomon appeared in the *Philadelphia Minerva*. Describing her as a "lisping tuner of Apollo's lyre," the author wished that her "skill might improve as thou increase in age / And prove the wonder of Columbia's page."[11] Whatever their previous history of wandering, by the mid-1790s the Solomons had established at least one family member as a star on the early national circuit.

While the Solomon family may not have been the only Jewish performers on the early national stage, they are—thus far—the only ones I can locate who have also been identified and claimed as Jewish actors in the *Jewish* historical record. This kind of claiming marks an effort to "untell" a traditional history about the lack of Jewish involvement in early American culture. In *The Jews of Philadelphia*, Henry Samuel Morais offers a list of Jewish performers and playwrights who graced the antebellum stage. The Solomons are the only pre-nineteenth-century names who appear on his list—suggesting that for some reason, they were the only "conspicuous" Jews performing in that early period.[12] Given the almost complete dearth of information about their backgrounds, what made them conspicuous is less clear. Mr. and Mrs. Solomon played supporting roles, rather than leads, and I have not determined they played any Jewish characters. Their comparative obscurity—juxtaposed with the notion of Jewish conspicuousness—made me fixate on them as a way to understand more about the lives of Jewish performers in the early American theater. Additionally, the fact that they were *not* famous actors suggested that their experience might have been more "typical" of the average Jewish American citizen during this period.

Much information about the Solomons' professional activities may be gleaned from daybooks, playbills, and early American newspapers. Harder to determine is where this family of performers actually came from. The players of the post-Revolutionary theater endured a peripatetic existence after the American Revolution as the nation struggled to reestablish the entertainments that had been largely (although not entirely) suspended by the war. America could offer little in the way of "homegrown" actors during the 1780s. Many professional performers were either former members of prewar touring companies or new recruits culled from England. Did the Solomons fall into either of those categories—or is there a third possibility that might point to their origins and help to illuminate the question of Jewish "conspicuousness" in this period?

For example, many members of the Old American Company spent the Revolution in Jamaica, and the fact that the Solomons joined the company after the Revolution may be suggestive. While it is possible that the Solomon family came from the British provincial touring population, they may also have gained entry into the company through the West Indian network that had evolved over the previous thirty years.[13] Odai Johnson's outstanding *Absence and Memory in Colonial American Theatre* notes that even when performers were not members of the same troupe, they often corresponded with or assisted each other (when it was not against their business interests to do so), and actors frequently moved among troupes during that tenuous period of reestablishing the nation's theater. He also observes that many spent time touring as solo performers to supplement their income. Thus it does not seem surprising that within such a relatively short period of time the Solomons appeared with the Maryland Company of Comedians, then as solo performers touring the colonies, then at the short-lived Board Alley Theatre in Boston, with the Old American Company in New York and Philadelphia, and eventually with Wignell's company at the Chestnut Street Theatre.

Settlement, Sanctuary, and Rights

In 1779, a group of almost thirty Jewish Americans joined the "Free Citizen" militia in Charleston, South Carolina, which soon became known as the "Jew Company" (though it contained a number of Gentiles). More than forty years later, on June 7, 1821, M. Jacob Cohen compiled a list of the members with whatever biographical information he remembered about the company. Number six on the list is a man with the last name Solomon (no first name is listed—there is a blank line instead). While there are other Solomons who appear on the list, the biographical information provided tentatively excludes them as possibilities for "my" Mr. Solomon. More importantly, written next to Solomon's name is the phrase "the Chozan." *Chosan* or *hazan* are Hebrew words that can identify either a religious figure *or* one who leads songs for the congregation (particularly solos) *or* a bridegroom. Another document dated February 7, 1779, describing the "Jew Company" notes that this Mr. Solomon was going to be married on the following Wednesday.[14]

This evidence is obviously far too sketchy to claim that Mr. Solomon the actor was part of the famous "Jew Company" of South Carolina, but the lack of a first name on the list (only one of two first names omitted) could suggest that the man who made the list had not been particularly well acquainted with Solomon, which would be likely if they were of different socioeconomic backgrounds (Cohen was a member of a wealthy merchant family).[15] Moreover, Mr. Solomon the actor was often praised for his excellent singing and most often appeared solely in singing parts or to perform songs during the entr'actes. Additionally, Solomon's name does *not* appear as the *hazan* of the postwar Charleston synagogue, suggesting that he may have moved out of the community. Do these facts on a list of Revolutionary War soldiers—a Southern origin, a missing name, a talent for singing, a notation of an impending marriage at a date that would be consistent with a family traveling with young children a decade later—lead me closer to "untelling" the story of ethnic identities in the early American playhouse?

Perhaps more importantly, is Solomon's potential identity as a "colonial" Jew actually significant to understanding the history of early American Jewish involvement in the playhouse? How could a possible military record be connected either to an acting career or to Solomon's Jewish and American citizenship? To understand the importance of the potential military history connection, I shift to a brief examination of the legal history of Jewish settlement in the colonies.

The real and vivid dangers European Jews faced in the eighteenth century may have made America's reputation for comparative religious tolerance more attractive.[16] As historian William Pencak has suggested, colonial anti-Semitism was almost "casual" in its content and often seemed more a force of cultural habit than the product of any active animus.[17] What rights of self-expression, cultural access, and agency might Jews have enjoyed in the colonies that they could not have in Europe, and how might that have affected their choice to become conspicuous performers in or supporters of the playhouse? In 1740, the British government had passed an act allowing the naturalization of Jews who were "settled or shall settle in any of his Majesty's Colonies in America."[18] Moreover, the act includes a special provision for rewording the general naturalization oath to allow Jews to take it without renouncing their faith: "Whenever any Person professing the Jewish Religion shall present himself to take the said Oath . . . the said Words (upon the true Faith of a Christian) shall be omitted out of the said Oath."[19] Aaron Lopez's oath of naturalization (taken in Massachusetts in 1762) shows the phrase "upon the true faith of a Christian" crossed out on the printed form. Underneath the formal oath, Lopez has added and witnessed in his own handwriting that he did, "from my heart, abhor, detest, and abjure as Impious and Heretical, that damnable doctrine that Princes Excommunicated or deprived by the Pope, or any authority of the See of Rome, may be deposed or murthered [*sic*] by their subjects, or any other whatsoever."[20]

The naturalization act of 1740 implicitly assumes that Jews will play a significant role in the colonial economy (the introduction to the act observes that "the Increase of a People is a Means of Advancing the Wealth and Strength of any Nation or Country").[21] At the same time, by creating a distinction in the oath of allegiance administered to Jewish citizens, it potentially rendered them more conspicuous among the other naturalized populations of the colonies—especially since it made their Jewish identity "visible" in the alteration of the official naturalization documents.[22] What kind of history were Jews performing by altering these documents? In one sense, they literally overwrote their faith on top of the history of the colonial empire. By "untelling" the narrative that imagined all colonial citizens as gentiles, they reconfigured the nascent American archive of citizenship around new racial and ethnic identities.[23] *If* Mr. Solomon the actor joined the "Free Citizen/Jew Company" militia of Charleston, he was making the ultimate statement about his allegiances and his sense of belonging both within the city's Jewish community and among his gentile American fellow soldiers. Many Jewish soldiers used their participation in the war to claim the privileges of citizenship in a postwar society that questioned their loyalties and their rights.[24]

"The Liberty to Invite his Friends": Jewish Social Networks

The laws of the colonies and the exigencies of revolution may have made Jews particularly visible among their gentile counterparts, but were there other practices, social networks, for instance, or markers beyond the law that rendered them both visible *and* strategically positioned to claim authority?[25] By the 1760s, colonial American Jews began to extend their familial and religious networks into social and cultural ventures.[26] For example, in 1761, a small group of Jewish men in Newport established a social club, at which "no talk relating to Synagogue affairs" was permitted (upon penalty of forfeiting "the value of four bottles of good wine" to the club's coffers).[27] While the club's agenda did not include either play-reading or play-going (the specific activities mentioned are card playing, dining, and conversation), there is a potential connection that might be fruitful for exploring Jewish involvement in the playhouse.

The founders of the Newport Social Club included Moses Lopez, Isaac

Polock, Jacob Isaacs, Abraham Sarzedas, Naphtali Hart, Moses Levy, Is-sachar Polock, Napthali Hart Jr., and Jacob Rivera.[28] In 1762 Rhode Island issued an antitheater ban that targeted social clubs as potentially allied to the playhouse. The ban is *not* unusual in decrying theater-going as calcu-lated to "increase immorality, impiety, and contempt for religion." It *is* in-triguing in declaring that "no persons by or under any pretense whatsoever [may] let or suffer to be used or improved any house, room, or place what-soever in this colony [for] acting, or carrying on any stage plays, or other theatrical entertainments."[29] What raised the colony's anxieties about sub rosa performances in unlicensed theater spaces? While clandestine theatri-cal entertainments often made their way into taverns or assembly rooms during the colonial period, there was another and perhaps more important avenue of access that could have caused concern among local Rhode Island authorities—the Masons.

Masonic alliances facilitated theatrical networks during the colonial and early national periods. Colonial theater manager and Mason David Douglass exploited those connections to establish his bona fides in each new community he entered.[30] He also maintained the practices of both calling on his wealthiest patrons in their homes *and* of circumventing an-titheatrical bias by using "nontheater" spaces, from tavern rooms to as-sembly halls, to stage his performances.[31] American Jews played a strong role in the Masons.[32] In terms of the Masons' connections to David Doug-lass, the Newport Social Club, and the antitheater law of 1762, it seems possible that Douglass would have known the most prominent members of the city's Jewish population and might have solicited their aid in locating a performance space—including the club's premises.

The Masons formed a significant part of Jewish social life through the Revolution and well into the early national period. Their potential con-nections to the theater remained active as well. Through the Masons my "*in*conspicuous" Mr. Solomon becomes visible again. A November 7, 1794, listing for Mrs. Solomon's benefit at Philadelphia's Southwark The-atre makes specific mention of a "Masonic Song" to be sung by "Brother Solomons." The references to the Masonic song and to "Brother" Solomon suggest that the family expected at least *part* of their benefit-night audience to be drawn from the city's Masonic population and that they used that affiliation to bring attention to their performances. It also suggests how an itinerant family of Jewish performers gained entry into the various communities they visited. "Brother" Solomon would have a ready-made network in both the larger and smaller communities in which the family played. The Masonic affiliation allowed its brethren to cross class lines, as well as those of ethnic or religious difference. While it could not eliminate awareness of class or ethnicity entirely, it allowed the negotiation of those identities through common rituals of brotherhood. Thus a humble Jewish actor such as Mr. Solomon might imagine himself as a "brother" to prominent gentile Mason George Washington.

"Touches of Sweet Harmony": Synthesizing Stories

The year 1794 marked a turning point for the Solomon family and for the role many Jewish Americans played in local and national politics for the next several years. It was in 1794, the same year that the Solomon family made their debut in Philadelphia, that the city witnessed the debut of its first and most scathing "homegrown" anti-Semitic character: the craven and treacherous Jew Ben Hassan in Susanna Rowson's 1794 *Slaves in Algiers*. What would be the next logical step for my exploration of Jewish identity in the early playhouse to take?[33] While Jews openly protested against negative characterizations of their faith and culture in the public press and in the political sphere, the theatrical representation of Jewish stereotypes presented a more slippery problem.

Kent Cartwright has argued, "We watch acting with a double intention: first to 'get' the character, that is to construe the signals of histrionic technique into a portrait, and second, to test the 'fit' of the acting itself to what it impersonates."[34] If the Solomon family declined to play Jewish characters in the early national repertoire (even the more benevolent ones), does that suggest a tacit refusal to perpetuate a Jewish stereotype or to provide a comparison between a staged Jew and a "real" one? Moreover, during the mid-1790s, members of the family toured in some of the most adamantly Federalist (and thus potentially anti-Semitic) states in the Union. How did they negotiate their identity as Jews among these communities? The Solomons, while they retained their family name (which made them highly visible as Jews or as citizens of Jewish extraction), seem to have downplayed any other markers of "Jewishness" in the public imagination. Similarly, their coreligionists in the audience invested in the *institution* of the theater, not necessarily in its artistic product. Perhaps they were wise to do so. Controlling the *content* of the early national theater proved a virtually impossible task, as managers and shareholders soon found, but affiliation with an institution conveyed status and cultural authority. It was not until the first decades of the nineteenth century, as Federalist power began to wane and as Thomas Jefferson's government ushered in an era of at least nominal religious tolerance, that a greater number of Jews allowed themselves to be more "conspicuous" in their support of the theater, as performers, playwrights, and critics.[35]

Conclusions

I have not yet "found" Mr. Solomon. Aside from the fact that he appears to have been the first known Jewish actor on the national stage and the father of a successful performer, he appears almost entirely irrelevant to the history of American theater. And yet, is his long-standing obscurity a product of the way in which theater historians may have approached the discipline in the past? Would following the paths I have suggested here—military history, Masonic history, legal history, political history—have remapped Mr. Solomon into the narrative of the early playhouse? How many of these various paths need to be followed in order to "untell" familiar narratives and create new "crooked" ones, and should the historian disclose the apparent blind alleys he or she pursues in order to produce a more transparent historiographical process?

Ultimately, the history and historiography of a marginalized group is not only a performative one, as Ernest notes, but an *improvisational* one as well. A successful improvisation, however, relies on *audience* participation to shape its direction. The very format of traditional scholarship unavoidably militates against this kind of organic exchange. Perhaps the key is to provide the reader the opportunity to improvise within the history. In his seminal work on theatrical improvisation, Keith Johnstone demands that actors accept every "offer" from their fellow performers and their audiences. For Johnstone, no offer is too large or too small. If I can imagine every branch of history as an "offer," can I liberate my own historiographical process and allow readers to do so as well? Can I transform a seemingly random list of militia members from 1779 into a way to understand the performance of Jewish patriotism? Can I see, in the fleeting mention of a benefit night from 1794, the extension of a social network that allowed Jews to transcend racial and ethnic prejudice? Can I persuade the reader that every path, no matter how unexpected or seemingly unconnected, may illuminate an untold history or untell a familiar one?

NOTES

    1. George O. Willard, *History of the Providence Stage, 1762–1891* (Providence: Rhode Island News Company, 1891), 5.
    2. See also Henry Samuel Morais, *The Jews of Philadelphia: Their History from the Earliest Settlements to the Present Time; a Record of Events and Institutions, and of*

Leading Members of the Jewish Community in Every Sphere of Activity (Philadelphia: Levytype Co., 1894), 382.

3. Their names appear alongside those of prominent gentile theater supporters in cities including Charleston, New York, and Philadelphia.

4. W. B. Worthen and Peter Holland, eds., *Theorizing Practice: Redefining Theatre History* (New York: Palgrave Macmillan, 2003), xv.

5. Worthen and Holland, *Theorizing Practice*, 1.

6. John Ernest, *Liberation Historiography: African American Writers and the Challenge of History, 1794–1861* (Chapel Hill: University of North Carolina Press, 2004), 37.

7. Errol Hill, *The Jamaican Stage, 1655–1900: Profile of a Colonial Theatre* (Amherst: University of Massachusetts Press, 1992), 81. See also Jacob Marcus, *The Colonial American Jew, 1492–1776*, vol. 3 (Detroit: Wayne State University Press, 1970); Frederic Cople Jaher, *A Scapegoat in the New Wilderness: The Origins and Rise of Anti-Semitism in America* (Cambridge: Harvard University Press, 1994); Edward Colman, "Plays of Jewish Interest on the American Stage, 1752–1821," *Publications of the American Jewish Historical Society* 33 (1934): 171–98.

8. David Ritchey, *A Guide to the Baltimore Stage in the Eighteenth Century: A History and Day Book Calendar* (Westport, CT: Greenwood Press, 1982), 101, 123.

9. Advertisement cited in Odell's *Annals of the New York Stage*. See George C. D. Odell, *Annals of the New York Stage*, vol. 1, *To 1798* (New York: Columbia University Press, 1927). Available online at http://asp6new.alexanderstreet.com.proxy-um.researchport.umd.edu/atho/atho.result.resourcetext.aspx?word=solomons&sortorder=type (accessed Feb. 10, 2009).

10. The *Aurora*, describing Miss Solomon's debut as the Girl in *Children of the Wood*, noted that she "personated the little girl with singular propriety and grace. Her manner is easy and natural, her voice strong and articulate, and in her singing remarkably clear" (Mar. 20, 1795).

11. "The Garland—No. III, To Miss Solomons," *Philadelphia Minerva*, Apr. 2, 1796. Miss Solomon(s) performed into the 1800s, often appearing with John Durang.

12. There may, of course, have been other Jewish performers on the early American circuit who were not "visible" as Jews, to either the Jewish or the gentile audience. I am in the process of pursuing this question.

13. The Solomons appear sporadically throughout the dramatic record, suggesting that they had *not* been recruited from England as potential new stars or even serviceable stock players (Jamaica is another possibility). Advertisements often described the Solomons as from "the South" or from "the Southward" (James M. Barriskill, "The Newburyport Theatre in the Eighteenth Century," *Essex Institute Historical Collection* 91 [July 1955]: 223). For more on Jewish actors in Britain, see Kalman A. Burnim, "The Jewish Presence in the London Theatre, 1660–1800," *Transactions of the Jewish Historical Society of England* 33 (1995): 65–96.

14. See Cohen Family Papers, Box 1, American Jewish Historical Society. Charles Reznikoff argues that the word is *chosan* (bridegroom), while scholars at the American Jewish Historical Society identify the word as *hazan*. See Charles Reznikoff, *The Jews of Charleston: A History of an American Jewish Community* (Philadelphia: Jewish Publication Society of America, 1950), 271.

15. Pursuing this research might lead me to explore histories of artisan and middle-class Jewish settlement.

16. As Kal Burnim suggests, the persecution of Jews in Spain and Portugal sent many Jewish performers to London in the late seventeenth and early eighteenth centuries—at least initially ("Jewish Presence," 66). However, the controversy over the 1753 Jew Bill sparked a wave of public violence against Britain's Jews, including outbursts in the playhouse (Michael Ragussis, "Jews and Other 'Outlandish Englishmen': Ethnic Performance and the Invention of British Identity Under the Georges," *Critical Inquiry* 26 [Summer 2000]: 773).

17. William Pencak, *Jews and Gentiles in Early America* (Ann Arbor: University of Michigan Press, 2005), 4.

18. Morris U. Schappes, ed., *A Documentary History of the Jews in the United States, 1654–1875* (New York: Citadel Press, 1952), 22.

19. Schappes, *Documentary History*, 29.

20. Document facsimile appears in Lee M. Friedman, *Early American Jews* (Cambridge: Harvard University Press, 1934), 13.

21. Schappes, *Documentary History*, 26.

22. See also Jacob Rader Marcus, *The Colonial American Jew, 1492–1776* (Detroit: Wayne State University Press, 1970); Pencak, *Jews and Gentiles in Early America*.

23. For an exploration of parallel issues in a more recent colonial context, see Durba Ghosh, "National Narratives and the Politics of Miscegenation: Britain and India," in Antoinette Burton, ed., *Archive Stories: Facts, Fictions, and the Writings of History* (Durham: Duke University Press, 2005), 27–44.

24. Obviously, the speculation on Mr. Solomon *is* largely speculation. However, Jewish playwright and theater critic Mordecai Manuel Noah proudly used his military title of *Major* Noah.

25. See the letters of Moses Franks, correspondence and documents, 1760–1802, Franks Family Papers, American Jewish Historical Society. For the quotation in the subheading title, see Rules for the Newport Social Club, Nov. 25, 1761; reprinted in Schappes, *Documentary History*, 35.

26. Some Jews participated in gentile social networks as well, including the City Dancing Assembly of Philadelphia. See Heather S. Nathans, *Early American Theatre from the Revolution to Thomas Jefferson: Into the Hands of the People* (Cambridge: Cambridge University Press, 2003).

27. William Pencak (*Jews and Gentiles in Early America*) argues that the club emerged partly in *reaction* to the colony's refusal to allow Aaron Lopez and Isaac Elizer to become naturalized, implying a rejection of some of the city's Jewish citizens on behalf of the gentile elite.

28. These same men were involved in financing and building the city's first synagogue, which opened in 1763. See Pencak, *Jews and Gentiles in Early America*, 94–95; Schappes, *Documentary History*, 35–37.

29. John Russell Bartlett, ed., *The Records of the Colony of Rhode Island*, vol. 6, 1757–1769 (Rhode Island: Knowles, Anthony, and Co., 1861), 325–26.

30. See Odai Johnson, *Absence and Memory in Colonial American Theatre* (New York: Palgrave, 2006).

31. Willard, *History of the Providence Stage*, 17. It was Douglass's "trick" of using nontheater spaces that angered the Rhode Island government.

32. The lodge structure facilitated relocation to new communities for Jews as

well. For more on Jewish involvement with the Masons, see Sandra Cummings Malamed, *The Jews in Early America: A Chronicle of Good Taste and Good Deeds* (McKinleyville, CA: Fithian Press, 2003).

33. I have written elsewhere about the philo-Semitic character on the early national stage (Heather S. Nathans, "A Much Maligned People: Jews On and Off the Stage in the Early American Republic," *Early American Studies, An Interdisciplinary Journal* 2 [Fall 2004]: 310–42). However, that study does not address Jewish audiences' response to Jewish stereotypes. For the quotation in the subheading title, see William Shakespeare, *The Merchant of Venice*, V, I; full text available online at http://shakespeare.mit.edu/merchant/full.html (accessed Feb. 2, 2008).

34. Kent Cartwright, *Shakespearean Tragedy and Its Double: The Rhythms of Audience Response* (University Park: Pennsylvania State University Press, 1991), 6.

35. That conspicuousness incited a new wave of American anti-Semitism in the 1820s, as Jews poured into America from Europe, as established elites sought to prevent Jews from settling in urban centers, and as the Second Great Awakening swept the nation.

PART II

The Stakes of Historiography

The Theater of the Absurd and the Historization of the Present

BRANISLAV JAKOVLJEVIC ∾

I

On 27 October 1957 Belgrade weekly newsmagazine NIN published the article "The Satellite and the Absurd" by philosopher Karlo Ostojic.[1] The occasion for Ostojic's article was the awarding of the Nobel Prize for Literature to Albert Camus, author of the novel *The Stranger* and the collections of essays *The Myth of Sisyphus* and *The Rebel*, which coincided, as Ostojic noted, with the two hundredth revolution around the Earth of the Soviet spacecraft *Sputnik*, the first man-made satellite successfully installed into the planet Earth's orbit. The author of the article saw the breakthrough in rocket science as a direct challenge to the "writer who immured human thought with the Chinese wall of the absurd."[2] While acknowledging that Camus's pessimistic vision of the human condition came as a response to the abuses of scientific progress in the first half of the twentieth century, Ostojic finds it only appropriate that the challenge to that philosophical attitude comes from science. In the "nearly apocalyptic atmosphere" of the Cold War, he writes, emerges "a strange messiah. It weighs 84 kilos, is spherical in shape, covered with metal, and from the altitude of 900 kilometers it sends messages to all of humanity." In *Sputnik*'s beep-peeps he recognizes a pompous summons: "I am at the threshold of the cosmos. Stars are no longer flickering mysteries. They are so close. Man, you tired soldier of the battlefield of the absurd, follow me!"[3]

There are at least three layers of reference to Ostojic's article. First, it signifies a certain warming up of the relations between Yugoslavia and the Soviet Union, which were strained following Tito's break with Stalin in 1948 and his strategic turn toward the West. This move was accompanied by ruthless political prosecutions of suspected sympathizers of the Soviet Union, which resulted in the establishment of the camps on the island Goli otok in the Adriatic Sea. Right before he launches into a prosopopoeia of

Sputnik's speech, Ostojic makes sure to note that "socialist realism is not the path that points the way out of the dead end of the absurd." In the late fifties, Yugoslavia saw itself as the USSR's partner, not its vassal.

Second, "The Satellite and the Absurd" can be read as the standard leftist critique of Camus. Whereas his international reputation culminated with the Nobel Prize for Literature, in France his undisputed position as the leading public intellectual in the first years following World War II was seriously damaged by the 1951 publication of *L'homme révolté* (translated into English in 1956 as *The Rebel*), which received severe criticism from his former friends on the literary left. In his responses to Camus's critique of revolutionary violence, Sartre claimed that the real problem is not Marxism, but nihilism.[4] We find these same accusations of nihilism in the reception of Camus in Eastern Europe, and especially in the USSR. Moreover, the allegations of hopelessness and despair carried over from Camus to other writers associated with postwar French literature, especially Beckett and Ionesco.[5]

Finally, Ostojic's readers could hardly miss the reference to the first public performance in Yugoslavia of Beckett's *Waiting for Godot*, which took place on 17 December 1956, some ten months before publication of "The Satellite and the Absurd." By the time of its official opening, this production had already achieved the status of cause célèbre in the struggle for artistic freedoms in post-1948 Yugoslavia. After being banned in the Belgrade Drama Theater in the spring of 1954, in June of the same year it was performed clandestinely in an artist's studio at Staro sajmiste (the Old Fair Grounds).

Staro sajmiste was a complex of exhibition pavilions built in the 1930s on the left side of the Sava River, directly facing downtown Belgrade. During World War II, these pavilions were turned into the concentration camp Judenlager Semlin, in which some seven thousand Jews and six hundred Roma perished during the war.[6] After the war, because of the shortage of housing in bombed-out Belgrade, the large pavilions were divided into smaller studios and apartments and given free of charge to young artists and intellectuals. For a short period of time in the 1950s, the former extermination camp housed a community of avant-garde artists and intellectuals. According to Vasilije Popovic, the director of *Waiting for Godot*, who at that time lived in Staro sajmiste, the idea of performing the play in the studio of the painter Mica Popovic came spontaneously.[7] It was the first theatrical performance in postwar Belgrade that took place outside of institutional theaters, without state approval and funding. The play was performed on an improvised stage, without curtain, elevated stage, or proper lighting, in front of an audience of some forty spectators. Midway through the performance a severe summer storm descended on Sajmiste. The electric lights went out, and the rest of the show was performed by candlelight. The séance-like performance of *Waiting for Godot* in a dark and dilapidated pavilion that had been used as a concentration camp only a decade earlier seems perfectly in concert with the absurdist reading of the play.

II

Martin Esslin famously opens his 1961 book *Theatre of the Absurd* with the description of a performance of *Waiting for Godot* in San Quentin prison, a setting as charged as the pavilion of the former concentration camp somewhere in Eastern Europe. In his approach to Camus, Esslin pursued a track that sharply diverged from that of Karlo Ostojic. Paying no heed to the utopian potential of Soviet technological performance, he took Camus's notion of the absurd as the conceptual cornerstone of his book on post–World War II experimental drama in Europe and America. Writing, like Ostojic, in the aftermath of Camus's Nobel Prize, Esslin ignored polemics on the French left concerning Camus's distancing from Marxism or his silence on the Algerian crisis. Instead, he took Camus's pronouncements about post–World War II Europe as the starting point for his analysis of the avant-garde theater, which seems to have started to reemerge, alongside with new literature and painting, after the (often physical) demise of the prewar European avant-garde. The new avant-garde was not the continuation of the old one, but a direct response to the new political and spiritual reality.

The Theater of the Absurd, Esslin claims, is a "reflection" of the "attitude most genuinely representative of our own time," whose "hallmark" is secularization, which until World War II was successfully obscured by scientific progress, the emergence of nation states, and "various totalitarian fallacies."[8] He relies on Camus to depict the world at the end of the long process of desacralization: it is an unfamiliar world that cannot be explained by reasoning, in which man is an exile and a stranger. Out of Camus's numerous statements about the absurd, Esslin selects the one that most strongly resonates with theater: "This divorce between man and his life, the actor and his setting, truly constitutes the feeling of Absurdity."[9] Esslin goes on to assert that the "sense of metaphysical anguish at the absurdity of the human condition" represents "the theme of the plays of Beckett, Adamov, Ionesco, Genet, and the other writers discussed in this book."[10] As Tony Judt demonstrates, the Camus of *The Myth of Sisyphus* and *The Rebel* is not a philosopher but a *moraliste*, and if that is correct, then to take his ethical judgments for philosophical propositions would mean to seriously misinterpret them.[11]

On the one hand, weaknesses and inconsistencies of the absurd as the critical paradigm used to interpret the works of authors as vastly different as Beckett, Adamov, Ionesco, and Genet were observed soon after the publication of Esslin's book. For example, Robert Brustein wrote that "though on one occasion (Beckett) the book performs a genuine critical act, its critical judgments are often faulty, inflated, or misleading: [Esslin] praises Ionesco's worst work, overvalues Adamov, elaborates on an unending host of insignificant imitators, and tries to make Genet an important part of a tradition to which he does not belong."[12] Lionel Abel was more concise and to the point: "the world can no more become absurd than it can sin, starve or fall down."[13] On the other hand, such as it was, the Theater of the Absurd was quickly accepted as an interpretative tool in American theater scholarship. It entered anthologies of modern drama with astonishing quickness: only a year after the publication of Esslin's book, Otto Reinert used it as a tool for categorization in his *Modern Drama: Nine Plays* (1962), and the next year Charles Aughtry followed suit in his *Landmarks in Modern Drama: From Ibsen to Ionesco*. The absurd seems to have entered critical discourse even more swiftly: it figured prominently in Herbert Blau's report from continental European theater, "The Popular, the Absurd, and the Entente Cordiale," published in the March 1961 issue of the *Tulane Drama Review*. In February of the following year Edward Albee's article "Which Theater Is the Absurd One?" was published, prominently, in the *New York Times Magazine*. In her valuable investigation of the Theater of the Absurd as a critical paradigm, Yael Zarhy-Levo concludes that even though Esslin's "definition of the corpus" of absurdist drama "remained controversial," his "claim concerning the new theatrical trend has generally been accepted by criticism."[14] What Esslin himself asserted about the "corpus" also applies to his critical paradigm: "the convention of the Absurd *works*."[15] In fact, it has worked so well that it surpassed its initial scope. Having passed through five editions between its first publication in 1961 and the latest reprint in 2004, *The Theatre of the Absurd* has become one of the most successful works of theater theory and criticism in English in the second half of the twentieth century.[16] What distinguished the Theater of the Absurd from other relatively contemporaneous theorizations of theater, such as Lionel Abel's Metatheatre, or Bonnie Marranca's Theater of Images, was its transformation from a speculative theoretical concept into a powerful interpretative model that not only explains current theatrical practices but is also projected into the past. In that way, the Theater of the Absurd comes not only to explain and enact what Esslin calls the "contemporary attitude" but also to create its own genealogy and transform our understanding (and staging) of the theatrical past. This operation of the projection of a contemporary theoretical reading into the past is based, I argue, on the historization of the present. This historization, for its part, is preconditioned by the aesthetization of new artistic idioms and their emptying of potentially disturbing political potential by dragging them to safe and familiar conceptual terrain. When it comes to Beckett's *Waiting for Godot*, this same operation is at work both in its acceptance by theater institutions in the former Yugoslavia and in its appropriation as the cornerstone of Esslin's "critical term."[17]

Brustein's praise for Esslin's reading of Beckett notwithstanding, the reason *The Theatre of the Absurd* worked was not because of the textual interpretation of the plays discussed in the book. Neither did it come from the faithful application of Camus's and Sartre's ideas on the theater of Genet or Beckett. Instead, it came from Esslin's studied infidelity to both the dramatists he analyzed and the theorists he used in that analysis. *The Theatre of the Absurd* did not offer an existentialist, that is to say Sartrean, or Camusean reading of Beckett, Ionesco and others. Likewise, it stayed outside of structuralist approaches to theater, which were gaining prominence on the continent, especially through the writings of Roland Barthes and Bernard Dort. What it offered instead was a certain theatrical interpretation of some of the most daring experiments in drama at that moment. In some of his central insights Esslin comes close to both existentialist and structuralist readings, but he manages to steer clear of them.

The absurdist paradigm shares with structuralism the concern with communication. However, whereas the latter breaks down language in order to isolate the linguistic sign as the model for analysis of other cultural phenomena, the former diagnoses the breakdown of language, which theater, unlike literature, proves able to survive. This language rendered useless by bureaucratic and mass-media clichés becomes dispensable, which brings a certain liberation to theater. In his discussion of Beckett, Esslin argues that the disappearance of "dialectical exchange" from his dialogues shifts the emphasis from language, that is to say speech, to the totality of the theatrical situation: "his continued use of language must," argues Esslin, "be regarded as an attempt to communicate on his own part, to communicate the incommunicable."[18] If this discovery of the absurdist sublime emerges from the discussion of Beckett, then its full affirmation comes in Esslin's comments on Ionesco. In *The Theatre of the Absurd*, Ionesco's plays serve as the prime demonstration of the new relationship between script and stage. Plays such as *The New Tenant* and *Chairs*, Esslin observes, are devoid of "the concepts of character, conflict, plot-construction," and yet they remain dramas with "mounting suspense, excitement, and poetic form," which no longer come from language but from the stage images and actions themselves.[19] This unique theatricality of the Theater of the Absurd Esslin recognizes in Ionesco's interest in *"theatrical form"* and his ambition to "rediscover the basic and purest principles of theater."[20] He argues that through the theatricality of "pure theater," the absurdist playwrights confront the audience with a "picture of a disintegrating world that has lost its unifying principle, its meaning, and its purpose—an absurd universe."[21] And it is precisely from this encounter between the illogical, outwardly funny, yet "somber, violent, and bitter" stage images and an astonished audience that the efficacy of the Theater of the Absurd emerges. The absurd sublime is but an instrument of the absurd alienation effect, through which, Esslin argues, Beckett, Ionesco, and others accomplish what Brecht "postulated in theory but failed to achieve in practice—the inhibition of the audience's identification with the characters on the stage . . . and its replacement by a detached, critical attitude."[22] Even though Esslin takes his central concepts from Camus and Sartre, his reading of the "absurdist playwrights" is not existentialist but squarely Brechtian. In fact, *The Theatre of the Absurd* can be read as a continuation of Esslin's first book, *Brecht: A Choice of Evils*, published only two years earlier.[23] Unlike Brechtian theater, which appeals to the audience's intelligence, the absurd drama

> speaks to a deeper level of the audience's mind. It activates psychological forces, releases and liberates hidden fears and repressed aggressions, and, above all, by confronting the audience with a picture of disintegration, it sets in motion an active process of integrative forces in the mind of each individual spectator.[24]

In short, Esslin discovers a deeper efficacy in the theater of the authors who asked their readers not to look for symbols where none were intended and who argued for the gratuitousness of all art. If the purposefulness does not come from the playwright, it will come from the spectator:

> The stage supplies *him* with a number of disjointed clues that *he* has to fit into a meaningful pattern. In this manner, *he* is forced to make a creative effort of *his* own, an effort at interpretation and integra-

tion. The time has been made to appear out of joint; the audience of the Theatre of the Absurd is being compelled to set it right, or, rather, by being made to see that the world has become absurd, in acknowledging that fact takes the first step in coming to terms with reality.[25]

Once set in motion, the hidden dialectics of the Theater of the Absurd works by its own fiat: "The greater the anxieties and the temptation to indulge in illusions, the more beneficial is this therapeutic effect—hence the success of *Waiting for Godot* at San Quentin."[26]

If this critical paradigm managed to group together a certain number of works, thus outlining what Zarhy-Levo describes as a "movement," it proved incapable of instigating one.[27] Interestingly, it was much more successful in interpreting the theatrical past. What Esslin merely indicated in the chapter "The Tradition of the Absurd" was soon transformed into a fully blown historiography of the absurd: from Walter Sokel's *Anthology of German Expressionist Drama: A Prelude to the Absurd* (1963), to George Gibian's *Russia's Lost Literature of the Absurd: A Literary Discovery* (1971), to Maurice Marc LaBelle's *Alfred Jarry: Nihilism and the Theater of the Absurd* (1980), the Theater of the Absurd was transformed from a critical to a historiographic paradigm. It was no longer just the instrument for interpretation of contemporary drama but also the means to organize and understand theater's past.

One effect of *The Theatre of the Absurd* was the adoption of existentialist rhetoric by theater criticism. The pathos of Camus's phrases such as "metaphysical rebellion" or "hostile heavens" seeps into Esslin's "metaphysical anguish" or "gaping hole of nothingness," and from there on to titles such as *World in Collapse: The Vision of Absurd Drama* (John Killinger, 1971) and *Fiction of the Absurd: Pratfalls in the Void* (Dick Penner, 1980). Likewise, the proliferation of the absurd in theater historiography pointed to possible critical readings and contemporary stagings of dramatic texts from the theatrical past. The most effective such projection of the absurd into the past was that of Polish theater critic Jan Kott in his books *Shakespeare, Our Contemporary* (1965) and *The Eating of the Gods: An Interpretation of Greek Tragedy* (1973). Yet to stop at these historical projections of the Theater of the Absurd would mean to stop at the level of its effects. The reason why this concept gives itself to historiographic discourse is because this paradigm is, to begin with, not only critical but deeply historical and historicizing. The engine of this historicization is the same as the one used for the production of meaning: the absurdist V-effect. By projecting meaning into performance, Esslin's imagined audience member engages in an eminently historicist operation. By filling the gaps in meaning, *he* effectively does with the present what a historian does with the past. As Jacques Rancière repeatedly warns, historiography demands that "everything speaks, everything has a meaning, to the degree that every speech production is assignable to the legitimate expression of a place."[28] And indeed, the absurd, that which is deprived of sense, begins to make sense once it is *placed* on stage. Furthermore, the stage not only makes meaning possible but is also able to project it back onto the world.

> A feeling of helplessness when confronted with the vast intricacy of the modern world, and the individual's impotence in making his own influence felt on that intricate and mysterious machinery, pervades the consciousness of Western man today. A world that functions mysteriously outside our conscious control, must appear absurd. It no longer has a religious or historical purpose; it has ceased to make sense.[29]

And this is precisely where the absurd V-effect intervenes. The Theater of the Absurd not only infuses intelligibility into the place from which it was exhausted, and thus strives to mend the gap of meaninglessness that yawns on stage, but also extends this operation into the world outside of theater. In doing so, it narrativizes and historicizes the present. *The Theatre of the Absurd* is not only a critical interpretation of a certain corpus of dramatic literature but a judgment about the conditions in which the audience of these plays live. It asks the audience to step back and observe their own reality as an aesthetic object. And it does that by resorting to the historicist strategy of storytelling. The critical analyses in *The Theatre of the Absurd* are tied together into a clear temporal trajectory: from "The Tradition of the Absurd," to major representatives, to "Parallels and Proselytes," to "Beyond the Absurd." It is a narrative about the breakdown of narratives, in theater and elsewhere.[30] To indicate the major consequence of this narrativization of the present, I return to the story with which I opened this chapter.

III

There are four existing accounts of the history of the first staging of *Waiting for Godot* in Belgrade, all done in different media. The first attempt to make a historical record of this event was the series of interviews with participants and witnesses that Radmila Gligic made for Radio Belgrade III in 1976, which were subsequently published in the journal *Teatron* (1978). In 1985, theater critic Feliks Pasic made a TV documentary about the "Godot affair." He used the material gathered on that occasion for the publication of a book on theater censorship in Yugoslavia: "How We Waited for Godot while Pumpkins Blossomed" (*Kako smo cekali Godoa dok su cvetale tikve*, 1992). In 1990, the director of *Godot*, Vasilije Popovic, published his reminiscences of the event in the form of a novel entitled "Warm Fifties" (*Tople pedeste*), which he signed with his pen name Pavle Ugrinov.

The official Yugoslav premiere of *Waiting for Godot* took place in a large conference room on the ground floor of the building of the daily newspaper *Borba*, located in the central part of Belgrade. This was a landmark event in the history of post–World War II theater in Belgrade and Yugoslavia, not only because it was one of the first performances of Beckett's play in Eastern Europe[31] but also because it inaugurated the new theater Atelje 212, which instantly became the leading experimental theater in the country.[32] The script reached Belgrade soon after its publication in the journal *Avant-scène* in 1953. The poet Dusan Matic, who was a member of the Serbian Surrealist Group before World War II, saw Roger Blin's production, which was performed at a gathering of European intellectuals in Genève, Switzerland. Matic, who after the war became the dean of the School of Drama at Belgrade University, gave the play to Vasilije Popovic, the member of the first class that graduated from the program in theater directing. He took the play to Belgrade Drama Theater, the first theater in Belgrade, which, after Yugoslavia's break with the USSR, started staging new dramas from Western Europe and United States. Even though the head of the theater, Predrag Dinulovic, was not enthusiastic about the play, he authorized the rehearsals, which started in the early spring of 1954. The commencement of rehearsals coincided with the biggest political crisis in post-1948 Yugoslavia. This time, the crisis was internal, concerning the ousting from power of the high-ranking party official Milovan Djilas, which came as a result of his critique of the bureaucratization of Yugoslav socialist society. *Waiting for Godot* was never officially given a spot in the repertory of the Belgrade Drama Theater. According to Popovic, his arrangement with the head of the theater was to bring the play up on its feet, at which point the theater's artistic directors would see it and decide what to do with it. During the months of rehearsals, the word spread among Belgrade theatrical and artistic circles about the new and unusual play rehearsed by a young director and actors at the Belgrade Drama Theater. As the rehearsals progressed, the political crisis worsened. Finally, the leadership of the theater asked Popovic and his group of actors to hold a closed dress rehearsal. The theater's doors were barred, and theater guards were asked not to allow anyone to enter the building during the rehearsal. Still, a few people slipped in and managed to see the production. These illegal audience members, among whom were some prominent theater critics and young intellectuals, spread the word about the terminated production. The interest in the censored play led to the production at Staro sajmiste.

Neither Popovic nor the chroniclers of this performance report the therapeutic effects that Esslin recognized in San Quentin. Popovic and his friends saw this performance as proof of the necessity for an experimental theater that would work outside of state institutions. In the wake of this performance, they started searching for a space where they could stage other productions, and they eventually stumbled onto the unused conference room in the building of the *Borba* newspaper. There was still powerful resistance to the "free stage," which was now epitomized in Beckett's *Godot*. In his novel, Ugrinov notes the hypocrisy of the authorities, who, while mercilessly persecuting the opponents of the regime, objected to Beckett's images of despair and abandonment in the name of "humanism": "It was now clear that Beckett decisively took under protection all of those were abject and despondent."[33]

From the mid-1950s until the country's demise in the early 1990s, the Yugoslav paradox consisted in the fact that the same authorities who ruthlessly curtailed political freedoms were seeking to embrace and promote economic liberalism. This liberalization of the economy first affected culture. In 1956, the status of the "free artist" was made legal for the first time in the history of socialist Yugoslavia. That meant that cultural workers did not have to be affiliated with an institution in order to legally practice their trade. In this strange realignment, avant-garde artists found themselves on the same side as entertainers. According to Ugrinov, the producer of the unofficial theater group that emerged from the production of *Godot* at Staro sajmiste was clearly aware of the commercial side of newly accessible "independence." Soon after the discovery of the space at *Borba*, the group was joined by young theater director Mira Trailovic, who secured from Belgrade municipal authorities substantial financial backing for the new theater.[34] Ugrinov writes that the opening performance of *Waiting for Godot* was sold out and that even those who had censored it three years earlier now showed up to congratulate actors on their persistence. Champagne was opened already during the intermission to celebrate the "victory over the Administration," as if, comments Ugrinov, "it was not the Administration itself that made this theater possible."[35] He writes that even though the theater was small and improvised, without proscenium, lobby, or green room, the ceremony of the opening resembled those routinely performed in the national theater on the main city square: "they forced me to accept that which disgusted me: the old threadbare theater against which I rebelled."[36] Already in the next production he started rehearsing, he observed the change in the atmosphere within the group: "The sacrifice and the sacrificial act, the necessity of which was so clear to us in the beginning, and which we took as a sine qua non of our work, was now disturbed; as if we were no longer capable of self-renunciation, that most supreme form of freedom; as if the time of certain selfishness ensued, of certain need for personal promotion and accomplishment."[37] The "theater of spiritual need" was drowned by its own success.[38] A year after *Godot* Popovic stopped making theater and turned to writing. Between 1954 and 1957, the mechanism of censorship in Yugoslavia evolved from suppression to appropriation. The legitimization of the avant-garde limited its reach to the aesthetic sphere, which ultimately resulted in its depoliticization. There is a strict parallel between the institutionalization of *Waiting for Godot* in Yugoslav theater and its canonization in *Theatre of the Absurd*. The operations such as the absurd sublime and the absurd alienation effect transform an event into aesthetic object, and this aestheticization is the necessary precondition for the historization of the present.

NOTES

1. NIN is the acronym of *Nedeljne informativne novine*. This weekly newsmagazine was published in Belgrade before World War II and was revived in 1951, during the period of liberalization of Yugoslav society following the breakup with Stalin's USSR. It soon gained a reputation as the leading liberal magazine in Serbia and in Yugoslavia.

2. Karlo Ostojic, "Satelit i apsurd," *Nedeljne informativne novine*, Oct. 27, 1957, n.p.

3. Ostojic, "Satelit i apsurd."

4. Tony Judt, *The Burden of Responsibility: Blum, Camus, Aron, and the French Twentieth Century* (Chicago: University of Chicago Press, 1998), 103.

5. For example, in one of the rare publications on Beckett in the Soviet Union during the 1950s, the leading theater journal *Teatr* (Theater) published an article by French leftist theater critic Guy Leclerc, in which he criticizes the "snobbery and hopelessness" of Beckett's plays and summarily dismisses his and Ionesco's "absurdist language." Guy Leclerc, "Sudby avangardistskgo teatra vo Francii," *Teatr* (Sept. 1959): 184–88. *Waiting for Godot* was translated into Russian in 1966 and was

staged some twenty years later, during the heady days of Perestroika. Its Soviet premiere took place in 1987, in Theater Yermolova.

6. Milan Koljanin. *Nemacki logor na Beogradskom Sajmistu, 1941–1944.* (Belgrade: Institut Za savremenu istoriju, 1992), 61.

7. No relation to the director Vasilije Popovic.

8. Martin Esslin, *The Theatre of the Absurd,* 2nd ed. (New York: Anchor Books, 1969), 5.

9. Camus, as quoted in Esslin, *Theatre of the Absurd,* 5.

10. Esslin, *Theatre of the Absurd,* 5.

11. Judt, *Burden of Responsibility,* 121.

12. Robert Brustein, *Seasons of Discontent: Dramatic Opinions, 1959–1965* (New York: Simon and Schuster, 1965), 61.

13. Lionel Abel, *Metatheatre: A New View of Dramatic Form* (New York: Hill and Wang, 1964), 140.

14. Yael Zarhy-Levo, *The Theatrical Critic as Cultural Agent: Constructing Pinter, Orton and Stoppard as Absurdist Playwrights* (New York: Peter Lang, 2001), 15.

15. Esslin, *Theatre of the Absurd,* 362 (emphasis in original).

16. The first and second edition (1961 and 1969) were published by Anchor. (The official policy of this publisher is not to reveal the print run of its books. The frequent reprints suggest without any doubt that the popular demand for the book was significant.) The third edition (1980) and its reprint (1991) were published by Penguin, while the 2004 edition, with the new foreword by the author (Esslin passed away two years earlier), was published by Vintage Books.

17. I borrow the phrase "critical term" from Marvin Carlson's *Theories of the Theatre: A Historical and Critical Survey, from the Greeks to the Present* (Ithaca: Cornell University Press 1984), 411.

18. Esslin, *Theatre of the Absurd,* 64. In *Notes and Counter Notes,* Ionesco routinely invokes the "communication of the incommunicable." Unlike Esslin, however, he insists on the absence of efficacy in theater that uses this device. See Eugene Ionesco, *Notes and Counter Notes: Writings on the Theatre,* trans. Donald Watson (New York: Grove Press, 1964), 93, 105, 129.

19. Esslin, *Theatre of the Absurd,* 135.

20. Ionesco, *Notes and Counter Notes,* 122, 157 (emphasis in the original).

21. Esslin, *Theatre of the Absurd,* 361.

22. Esslin, *Theatre of the Absurd,* 360.

23. Esslin's focus on the audience carries over from his book on Brecht to his book on the "absurdists." In the former he argues that "Brecht's most original contribution to the theory of the theatre—but also most disputable—concerns the reaction of the audience." See Martin Esslin, *Brecht: A Choice of Evils* (London: Eyre and Spottiswoode, 1959), 148.

24. Esslin, *Theatre of the Absurd,* 362.

25. Esslin, *Theatre of the Absurd,* 363 (emphasis added). It is hardly surprising that Esslin genders this active, creative, and critical spectator the way he does.

26. Esslin, *Theatre of the Absurd,* 364.

27. See Zarhy-Levo, *Theatrical Critic as Cultural Agent,* 15 and passim.

28. Jacques Rancière, *The Names of History: On the Poetics of Knowledge,* trans. Hassan Melehy (Minneapolis: University of Minnesota Press, 1994), 65.

29. Esslin, *Theatre of the Absurd*, 185.

30. In that sense, it is not surprising that the new paradigm that replaced the Theater of the Absurd was that of postmodern performance.

31. In his essay "The Seriousness of Theater" Jan Kott writes that "*Waiting for Godot* made its debut in Warsaw just a little less than a year after its premiere in Paris" and provides the date as Jan. 2, 1957. *Waiting for Godot* opened in Théâtre de Babylone on Jan. 5, 1953, almost four years before the date Kott mentions in his essay. See Jan Kott, *The Theater of Essence and Other Essays* (Evanston: Northwestern University Press, 1984), 209.

32. In 1965, Atelje 212 moved from the improvised black-box theater into a newly erected modern theater building not far from its original location. Already two years later, Atelje 212 became the home of Belgrade International Theater Festival (BITEF), a festival that showcased premier experimental theater from both East and West: from Grotowski to the Living Theater, and from Peter Brook and Robert Wilson to Andrei Lyubimov to Anatoli Vasiliev. *Waiting for Godot* remained in the repertory of Atelje 212 for full seventeen years. It closed at the end of the 1973–74 season and was remounted in 1981 for another four-year run.

33. Pavle Ugrinov, *Tople pedesete* (Belgrade: Nolit, 1990), 205.

34. Feliks Pasic reports that she asked for two million dinars, which was an incredible sum of money. To the surprise of the group, this amount was granted, and that made possible the conversion of the conference room into a black-box theater. See Feliks Pasic, *Kako smo cekali Godoa kad su cvetale tikve* (Belgrade: Bepar Press, 1992), 47.

35. Ugrinov, *Tople pedesete*, 232.

36. Ugrinov, *Tople pedesete*, 235.

37. Ugrinov, *Tople pedesete*, 244.

38. Ugrinov, *Tople pedesete*, 245.

No Hint as to the Author Is Anywhere Found

Problems of Using Nineteenth-Century
Ethnography in Latin American
Theater History

E. J. WESTLAKE ⟡

Writing about the dance-drama *El Güegüence* in 1967, Pablo Antonio Cuadra called the title character the "first character of Nicaraguan litera-ture and certainly also one of the first of the Hispanic popular literature."[1] Scholars in the United States point to the dance-drama's unique mestizo heritage, owing to the fact that it was the first drama to emerge in the blending of indigenous and European culture.[2] Dating from the seven-teenth or eighteenth century, it appears to be the oldest comedy and the first mestizo play in the Americas. The Nicaraguan Ministry of Culture named *El Güegüence* the national dance-drama, and UNESCO recently granted it the status of Intangible Heritage. While dancers continue to perform the dance every year in Diriamba, said to be the birthplace of the dance-drama, the text of the drama is what enabled its "rediscovery" and caught the attention of Nicaraguan artists and intellectuals primed to em-ploy folk culture into the service of nationalism.

The text has its own history. In the late eighteenth century, Juan Eligio de la Rocha, a Nicaraguan lawyer and philologist, obtained two written versions. After his death, a German ethnographer, Karl Hermann Berendt, visited de la Rocha's brother and copied an interpolated version of the two texts. He then sold his text with many of his papers and artifacts to Daniel Brinton at the University of Pennsylvania. Brinton, an expert in languages of the Americas, published Berendt's text along with his own translation in his *Library of Aboriginal Literature* in 1883.

The preservation of text over context warrants a closer and more thor-ough examination of the play, its history, and the artifacts that make up the historical record. Indeed, even the existence of *El Güegüence* as a historical document raises important questions about the way we read Latin American history. While the privileging of text and nationalist reimaging of history have obscured and distorted the view, nineteenth-century racism and detached Victorian ethnographic practice have warped the historical record even further. In general, the rise of ethnography as a discipline, following the paradigm-shifting publication of *The Origin of the Species* by Darwin, provides theater historians with a wealth of texts, removed from the context of the "primitive" societies ethnographers sought to categorize. As Brinton reveals in his landmark book *Races and Peoples*, the primary responsibility of the anthropologist was to discern the various paths of evolution, first through measurements of physical bodies and only later through tracing linguistic variation, both of which would tell the men of science, working from the comfort of their libraries, the origins of various ethnic groups and their place within a hierarchy of racial superiority. *El Güegüence* becomes important to Brinton's cause as he attempts to discern the origins of indigenous Americans.

While the fruits of the labor of the early ethnographers have left us with valuable resources for the study of theater history of the Americas, it has also left us with a legacy rooted in the search for scientific evidence in support of racism. Understanding this legacy is a valuable key to determining how cultural artifacts were preserved and what cultural facts may have been ignored or erased.

Diriamba

I traveled to Diriamba for the Día de San Sebastian in 2008 and in 2009, where I observed performances of *El Güegüence* that preceded the devotional procession. In 2008, two groups attempted some of the dialogue. In 2009, the group presenting *El Güegüence* performed only the dance. The dance comprises only part of the day's celebration, the highlight of which is the procession, where the saints are carried down the street from the cathedral. The saints are greeted by *promesantes*, people (usually women) who walk toward Saint Sebastian on their knees in fulfillment of a promise. Some people physically support the *promesantes* while others lay blankets down in front of them. The devotional act is a communal one.

The dance of *El Güegüence* in this context consists of men in mule masks (the *machos*) doing a sweeping step forward and back as they travel around the other dancers. The dancers in the center are the human characters, the men wearing masks of colonial figures and the women unmasked. Without exception, the masks I saw of the men had light hair and blue eyes, although I have read accounts of masks of mestizo characters with brown eyes.[3]

El Güegüence has also entered the repertoire of folk dance groups throughout the country. It can occasionally be seen at the Jueves de Verbena in Masaya and the Ballet Folklorico Nicaragüense in Managua.[4] These presentations are more elaborate than the repetitive dance presented on the Día de San Sebastian and involve more complex dance steps for both the human and the mule characters. But there continues to be wide debate about how much of the original dance has survived through the centuries and what constitutes an "authentic" performance of *El Güegüence*. As folklorist Irene López notes of Diriamba: "The dance *El Güegüence*, that is this moment performed in the procession of Diriamba . . . , involves little of the dance, involves only a few of the people dressed in some of the masks of the *machos* and the others of the Spaniards, practically walking and beating the drum a lot. . . . It is dead folklore."[5] The anthropologists who retrieved the document preserved the text of the dance-drama, but the dance was never formally recorded. How much of the dance was successfully transmitted, and how much the dance may have changed over time, remain a subject for debate.

History of the Text

Many philologists believe *El Güegüence* has decisively indigenous roots. Before the Conquest, anthropologists believe two distinct groups, the Chorotegan (or Mangue) and the Nahua people, migrated from Mexico to southwestern Nicaragua and settled in the mountainous region between the Pacific and Lake Nicaragua. The Chorotegan people arrived first and were displaced by the Nahuas. Indeed, as the Mangue language died out, a hybrid Nahuatl-Spanish replaced it as the common language of the region. The people of Diriamba are ethnically Chorotegan. However, they perform *El Güegüence* as it was recorded by Berendt, in the hybrid Nahuatl-Spanish.

Brinton notes that dance played an important role in the indigenous cultures of Central America. Explorers and ethnologists, such as Berendt, noted some of the elements of indigenous dances and ritual dramas that were often performed as part of a religious festival or rite.[6] *El Güegüence* shares some elements with ritual dance-drama (such as *Rabinal Achí*), including music, dancing, masks, and the repetition of dialogue. As Brinton observed, the Church and colonial authorities attempted to destroy the native culture and to replace indigenous performance with Spanish *autos*.

However, indigenous performance persisted, interwoven with the new customs.[7] Scholars suppose that native and mestizo people created hybrid forms of performance, often subversive to colonial authority.[8] Brinton also believes that indigenous people preserved their history within the stories of ritual drama and dance-drama. He quotes nineteenth-century priest and historian José Antonio Urrutia: "In most of the Indian towns, the custom is still general of preserving a knowledge of great events in their history by means of representation called *bailes* [dances], which are, in fact, dances in the public squares on the days or evenings of great solemnities."[9] In many ways, *El Güegüence* fits this syncretic tradition, blending indigenous dance with local history to accompany a holy procession for the patron saint of Diriamba.

The story, however, reflects the colonial time in which the text emerged, a more modern history than the pre-Columbian stories Urrutia may have observed in other dance-dramas: it presents a mestizo trader fighting to survive at the hands of a corrupt colonial government. In the play, Güegüence and his two sons appear before Governor Tastuanes.[10] Initially, Tastuanes means to get the old man's money by taxing him, but Güegüence tricks the governor with double talk. He eventually succeeds in tricking the governor into marrying his daughter to Güegüence's favorite son.

The hybrid language of early colonial times, the blend of Nahuatl and Spanish, sets *El Güegüence* apart from the indigenous dance-dramas, in a combination that often creates clever double meanings. The entire play hinges on misunderstanding. These moments allow Güegüence to gain the upper hand by avoiding payment and to make jokes, often sexual, at the expense of his adversaries. For instance, when Güegüence counts out his payment to Alguacil,[11] he counts: "the half of this half of a *real* makes two *cuartillos*, a *cuartillo* is two *octavos*, an *octavo* is two *quartos*," and so on, until Alguacil, still reeling from the confusion of the scene, winds up receiving much less than he thinks.[12]

Many of the double meanings arise out of the blended language. A presentation of their goods ends with Güegüence introducing his favorite son, Don Forcico. Güegüence says Forcico has his "hand in many trades," in a way that suggests Forcico demonstrated talent in stealing the goods that they carry. He lists Forcico's virtues and his professions: sculptor, metalworker, grinder, and pilot. But these words, in the indigenous language, sound like words for "scoundrel," "thief," "sloth," and "garbage collector."[13]

Other misunderstandings allow Güegüence to insult authority. When Alguacil introduces himself as "a servant of the Lord Governor Tastuanes," Güegüence pretends to mis-hear the masculine form of servant, *criado*, as *criada*, the feminine. He proceeds to ask Alguacil what kind of servant-girl or wash-woman he is and will not accept Alguacil's attempts to correct him.[14] In Diriamba in 2008, the actor playing Güegüence in the older group underscored the sexual nature of Güegüence's advances, making Alguacil's desire to clear up the misunderstanding all the more desperate.[15]

Güegüence wins by dazzling the governor with stories of his wealth. Güegüence performs the colonial subject he knows the governor imagines him to be: an industrious, wealthy merchant ripe for exploitation. He boasts of his inventory and induces his sons to corroborate his story, each account further whetting the appetite of the governor as Güegüence pushes for the marriage, a one-sided deal that only benefits Güegüence. With Güegüence's trickery and playful sexual humor, the text seems to be full of examples of subversion, both of colonial authority and of oppressive social norms. It is not surprising, then, that Nicaraguan nationalists would seize upon this figure as an example of resistance, which adds yet another layer to the reading of the performance and the text.

El Güegüence and Nicaraguan Nationalism

According to Les Field, Brinton's English copy of *El Güegüence* came to the attention of the Nicaraguan literary intelligentsia at the beginning of the twentieth century through the writing of Rubén Darío and also through comments made by José Martí.[16] Both conservative Pablo Antonio Cuadra and Leftist Alan Bolt make references to using the street-theater format of *El Güegüence* in prefaces to their own plays.[17]

Cuadra felt that subversive potential lay in the play of language. The uniquely Nicaraguan form of hybrid language is *inherently* subversive to Cuadra. Güegüence can stand in front of the governor and tell him to his face that Don Forcico is a thief because the Nahuatl words he uses have double meanings. As Cuadra notes, Güegüence's power lies in "subtle games with not only the possible double meaning of a word but with the quid pro quo of translation from one language to another; what is revealed to us is a spirit of mischievous, playful, and satirical weaving of a new language with great creative freedom."[18] Cuadra's nationalist Vanguardia movement saw recapturing this language as an important part of their nationalist project, as something inherently resistant in the Nicaraguan national character. The mestizo wins in *El Güegüence* because he upsets the terms of the balance of power and sets new terms with the new hybrid language, impenetrable to the colonial authority. Taking this a step further, Cuadra holds Güegüence up as a kind of Nicaraguan Everyman.

Güegüence represents the Nicaraguan, who in resistance to oppression *is* a trickster by birthright: "The old rogue—illuminating our unstable Nicaraguan family, [is the] fruit of our mestizaje."[19]

The idea that Nicaraguans are natural tricksters, always in search of clever ways to thwart imperialist authority, gives nationalists an appealing symbol during a century of struggle against intervention from imperialist forces, namely the United States. This became an important component of nationalist doctrine during the Sandinista government of the 1980s, which sought to revive folk culture for nationalist purposes. It is tempting to read *El Güegüence* as a text of resistance, but reading it only as resistance means ignoring part of its long history.

"Discovery"

The text of the dance-drama made a remarkable journey on its way back into Pablo Antonio Cuadra's hands, and many Nicaraguans can recite the passage: Cuadra got it from Brinton, who got it from Berendt, who got it from de la Rocha. The circumstances of the recording of the performance into a text, and the progression of one text to the next, leave several questions, the answers to which we can only guess. The biographical and social frames—the lives of the people involved, their ideas about the text, and the nature of nineteenth-century anthropology in general—can offer some clues.

Karl Hermann Berendt left Germany after the 1848 Revolution. Finding himself on the wrong side of the conflict, Berendt lost his university post at Breslau, where he taught medicine, and headed for the Americas. He traveled throughout Mexico and Central America, examining the physical evidence he could find of indigenous peoples and cataloging what he could identify of indigenous languages. The Mangue and Nahuatl dialects of southeastern Nicaragua were of particular interest to Berendt. It is possible that Berendt sought texts like *El Güegüence* because he thought they would help him solve a particularly vexing ethnological puzzle. He had read several conflicting accounts of the origins of the Mangue-speaking people in Nicaragua and had decided to make a study of his own. When he came to Nicaragua in 1874, however, he was disappointed:

> I found that the Indian population near the Nicoya and the Fonseca bays had entirely disappeared. . . . I had, however, the good luck to ferret out some old people who still remembered words and phrases they had heard in their childhood; and I was enabled to collect ma-

terial sufficient to convince myself and others of the identity of this Mangue or Chorotegan idiom with the Chapaneco language of Mexico. . . . It may be possible to trace their history and descent backwards to one of the nations that were living in Anahuac [the seat of the Aztec Empire] in the earliest times of which our records speak.[20]

Berendt's main project in the region was to find proof of the migration of Mangue people from Mexico to Nicaragua, rather than the reverse, as some believed. Obtaining his copy of *El Güegüence* may have been part of that plan. In his written version, he even calls it a "comedia de los Indios Mangues." Although, as Pablo Antonio Cuadra notes, even as the drama has been performed in the Mangue communities, "most of the Indian language used in the play El Güegüence is Nahuatl."[21] If Berendt was hoping the text would help him solve this problem, it probably did not.

Brinton, on the other hand, was interested in native people throughout the Americas. Beyond his medical career, he spent much of his life classifying native languages and collecting documents. He and Berendt met several times when Berendt visited the United States, during which time Brinton purchased Berendt's documents for his own collection.[22] Berendt did not see a live performance of *El Güegüence*, nor did he obtain any description. This and comments from Brinton's colleagues, such as Earl Flint, caused Brinton to speculate that it was no longer ever performed in Nicaragua.[23]

To Brinton, Berendt's copy of the text must have seemed mysterious. The blended language, the unique characters, the spoken dialogue mixed with music and dance, were difficult for him to categorize. In his introduction, he attempts to imagine a single author, one that could not possibly be European:[24]

No hint as to the author is anywhere found. There are, however, reasons . . . to believe that it is the production either of a native Indian or a half-caste. That there are no monologues nor soliloquies; that there is no separation into scenes, the action being continuous throughout; that there is neither prologue, epilogue nor chorus; and especially that the wearisome repetition of the same phrases, and by one speaker of what a previous one has said—a marked characteristic of the native scenic orations—are all traits which we can scarcely believe any Spaniard sufficiently cultivated to write at all, would exhibit. . . . The devices for exciting laughter are scarcely more than three in number; one the assumed deafness of the Güegüence, the second . . . , amusing quid-pro-quos, and third, the introduction of obscene references. . . . The absence of all reference to the emotions of love, and the naive coarseness indicated in the passages about women, point rather to a native than a European hand.[25]

Brinton finds the play to be obscene, coarse, and wearisome, evidence of a primitive mind at work.

To understand Brinton's chauvinistic attitude in his analysis, one needs to understand the development of anthropology as a discipline in the nineteenth century. Brinton was the last of a kind of amateur anthropologist, taking up the practice of cataloging and understanding indigenous languages as part of a hobby. While he himself argued for anthropology to become a serious field of study and was instrumental in establishing one of the first departments of anthropology in the United States, he did not formally study anthropology himself. He was a doctor who loved collecting Native American folklore. Brinton's interest grew to include all the native people of the Americas, and to understanding the migration of people throughout both continents.[26]

Within this context, it is not surprising that Brinton did not engage in the kind of fieldwork considered essential in later anthropological study. The functions of explorers and ethnologists were neatly divided, hence his need to purchase artifacts and documents from explorers, such as Berendt. In fact, it should be noted that Brinton never traveled to Nicaragua, never saw the dance-drama of *El Güegüence* performed nor met any people who had ever performed it. His overlap with the rise of the career of Franz Boas makes this lack of firsthand knowledge painfully clear, although he continued to defend his methodology even as he exchanged letters with the latter.

I have found myself strangely compelled to understand Brinton; as a Quaker myself, I want to believe Brinton was probably motivated to learn about indigenous people because of his Quaker upbringing, which would suggest he held relatively enlightened ideas about the intelligence and beliefs of other peoples. Indeed, he believed that the spiritual lives of all people were interconnected and that religions of the people of the Americas were primitive expressions of the same spiritual world he valued as a Quaker.[27] On the other hand, while he dedicated his life to examining the commonalities between peoples, he was equally concerned with discerning the differences.[28] And these differences were put into the service of establishing a racial hierarchy.[29] Brinton lays out his views on racial inferiority in *Races and Peoples* (1890) when he professes:

We are accustomed familiarly to speak of "higher" and "lower" races, and we are justified in this even from merely physical considerations. These indeed bear intimate relations to mental capacity. . . . The European or white race stands at the head of the list, the African or negro at its foot.[30]

As Baker notes, Brinton often had positive things to say about indigenous peoples of the Americas.[31] But Brinton came to the defense of his Indians only because he fiercely believed they were direct descendants of Europeans, as he notes in *The American Race*, coming to the Americas by a north Atlantic land bridge instead of being descendants of the people of Asia.[32] Therefore, they occupied a higher position in the racial hierarchy than many other nonwhite races, and he spends the following chapter categorizing the evidence of their superiority, going as far as to say that, in art, "the American stands next to the white race."[33]

It is no accident that Brinton and Berendt were both physicians before becoming anthropologists. It is safe to say that the earliest projects of anthropologists involved this kind of racial classification, initially based on the physical measurements of human beings. *Races and Peoples* contains hundreds of references to physical features, their shapes and their sizes: "medium height, oval faces, handsome regular features, symmetrical in body, the skull dolichocephalic."[34] Educated people began to debate the theory of evolution in the first half of the nineteenth century following the publication of the work of Lamarck and Darwin. This sparked a drive to study human beings in light of the new paradigm of a natural scale and to understand the different human "species" in progressive and hierarchical terms.[35] Both Brinton and Berendt became interested in cataloging the languages of the Americas as linguistics held another, similar key to mapping out who evolved from whom and when. *El Güegüence* becomes an artifact, a piece of evidence that would help gauge the origins and measure the success of Americans.

The racist lens through which *El Güegüence* is "discovered" and analyzed does not end with Berendt and Brinton. Cuadra's own writing about Nicaraguan literature, while celebrating the indigenous elements, seems to reflect the European-centric notion that all things from Europe are superior to any culture inherited from the Americas. He writes:

The Greco-Roman tradition is more accessible through our language. . . . The indigenous is more difficult because it has scarcely been expressed in language and what is there becomes a challenge.

But this challenge, I believe, inspires creativity and opens mysterious zones of human thought and feeling that the western world,
with its excess of rationalism, has forgotten.[36]

To Cuadra, Nicaraguans inherited the primitive—dreams, the subcon-
scious, vivid imagery—from indigenous people and the ability to reason
and to write from Europe. Europeans were rational; the indigenous people
were not. And although he is celebrating a mestizo culture that has the best
of both worlds, the devaluing and erasure of indigenous people are clear in
his statement.

Suspended Reading

I have tried to illuminate some of the issues that arise when examining the
performance evidence of colonized peoples. First, the historical record of
the dance itself is largely missing. Any recording that exists of the colonial
dance-drama rests on the dramatic text alone. Second, the text has been deployed as a tool of nationalism. Much of the twentieth-century description
and analysis of the play encourages the reader to understand the text in a
particular framework. Third, the text was "discovered," disseminated, and
examined, to the exclusion of other products of culture, as a project of a
discipline with a particular agenda.

I think the most productive way to read such a performance is to read it
in a state of suspension. Attempts to fasten the text (both performance and
written) ultimately fail because it escapes modernist frames of authentica-
tion. When I attended the festival in Diriamba in 2008, I was concerned
because I was forced to leave before I thought the performers were
finished. I was certain they were going to perform the rest of the dialogue,
and I returned in 2009 to see the rest. The fact that the dialogue was not
performed at all made me aware of the fact that 2008 had been an experi-
ment, that the organizers had abandoned the idea in order to accommodate the regular timeline of the procession, and that it was unclear as to
whether they would attempt it again. This caused me to see the problem
with what I thought was a series of contradictions among Field's report of
having talked to people who were part of a tradition of performing *El
Güegüence* that went back for generations, López's comment that it was
"dead folklore," and Flint's assertion to Brinton that it was no longer performed. To say that *El Güegüence* is performed is not to say that a particular *El Güegüence* is performed, but that any combination of dances, with or
without dialogue, may be performed. Yet fixed ideas about what it means to

perform the dance-drama have caused conflicts over what the "authentic" performance might be. López's version of El Güegüence, a new dance-drama called El Gran Pícaro, actually reconstructs El Güegüence from her own research of colonial times and the dances of that era.[37] But López hasn't escaped criticism for performing something that is not "authentic."

The nationalist interpretation also threatens to unravel in a twenty-first-century reading of the text as the very government that advocated the use of the protagonist as a symbol of resistance to imperialism wraps itself in the corruption of Tastuanes's office. The figure of Güegüence looks more like a symbol of greed than a symbol of liberation in the face of the consolidation of power by the Sandinistas and the pact Daniel Ortega made with the embezzling PLC president, Arnoldo Alemán.[38] There are also many people who question the idea of Güegüence as an Everyman as the universalizing discourse of nationalism gives way to a vision of Nicaragua as a land of diversity. Indeed, who does the figure of Güegüence represent? As Erick Blandón observes in Barroco descalzo, Güegüence is "part of an imaginary homogeneity . . . and nothing is said of any differentiation of classes, of the Caribbean Africans, homosexuals, or women."[39]

And while the conditions of the dance-drama's "discovery" and preservation have little bearing on its signification in the present day, a reader must wonder what was preserved through the screen of the nineteenth-century anthropological project and what was sifted out. No doubt a whole constellation of context pulls the dance-drama away from original meaning and sets it adrift in the sea of later signs. Ultimately, when examining the performance itself, its analysis, or its historical record, the reader can be aware of this suspension, allowing for the possibilities that are spun from the unraveling.

NOTES

1. Pablo Antonio Cuadra, El Nicaragüense (Managua: Editorial Unión, 1967), 65.

2. See Judith Weiss, et al., Latin American Popular Theatre: The First Five Centuries (Albuquerque: University of New Mexico Press, 1993); Diana Taylor and Sarah Townsend, eds., Stages of Conflict: A Critical Anthology of Latin American Theater and Performance (Ann Arbor: University of Michigan Press, 2008); and Don Rubin and Carlos Solórzano, The World Encyclopedia of Contemporary Theatre: The Americas (New York: Routledge, 2001).

3. See Taylor and Townsend, Stages of Conflict.

4. The current director of the Managua company, Ronald Abud Vivas, is a native of Diriamba.

5. Irene López, interview with the author, 7 June 2008.

6. For explorers, see Gonzalo Fernández de Oviedo y Valdés, *Historia general y natural de las Indias, islas y tierre-firme del mar océano, por el capitan Gonzalo Fernández de Oviedo y Valdés . . . publicala la Real Academia de la Historia, cotejada con el códice original, enriquecida con las enmiendas y adiciones del autor, é ilustrada con la vida y el juicio de las obras del mismo por d. José Amador de los Ríos . . . primera [-tercera] parte* (Madrid: Real Academia de la Historia, 1851–55); Ephraim G. Squier, *The States of Central America; Their Geography, Topography, Climate, Population, Resources, Productions, Commerce, Political Organization, Aborigines, etc., etc., Comprising Chapters on Honduras, San Salvador, Nicaragua, Costa Rica, Guatemala, Belize, the Bay Islands, the Mosquito Shore, and the Honduras Inter-Oceanic Railway; by E. G. Squier, Formerly Charge d'Affairs of the United States to the Republics of Central America, With Numerous Original Maps and Illustrations* (New York: Harper and Brothers, 1858); and Pablo Levy, *Notas geográficas y económicas sobre la república de Nicaragua y una exposición completa de la cuestion del canal interoceánico y de la de inmigración, con una lista bibliográfica, las mas completa hasta el dia, de todos los libros y mapas relativos á la América central y general y á Nicarrgua [sic] en particular* (E. Denné Paris: Schmitz, 1873).

7. Daniel G. Brinton, "Introduction," in *The Güegüence; a Comedy Ballet in The Nahuatl-Spanish Dialect of Nicaragua*, ed. and trans. Daniel Brinton (Philadelphia: D. G. Brinton, 1883, Library of Aboriginal American Literature 3; rept., New York: AMS Press, 1969), xxiii.

8. See Weiss et al., *Latin American Popular Theatre*; Adam Versenyi, *Theatre in Latin America: Religion, Politics, and Culture from Cortes to the 1980s* (Cambridge: Cambridge University Press, 1993); and Max Harris, *The Dialogical Theatre: Dramatizations of the Conquest of Mexico and Questions of the Other* (New York: St. Martin's Press, 1993).

All. e.g., note the apparently contradictory semiotics of *La Conquista de Jerusalén* (The Conquest of Jerusalem, 1539).

9. Quoted in Brinton, "Introduction," xxiii.

10. "Güegüence" is a name that some have supposed comes from the Nahuatl word *huehue*, or "old man." "Tastuanes" literally means "governor," and so his name is "Governor Governor."

11. "Alguacil" means "sheriff."

12. Carlos Mántica Abaunza, *El Cüecüence o El gran sinvergüeza: Obra maestra de la picaresca indoamerica* (Managua: Academia Nicaragüence de la Lengua, 2001), 54. I am relying mostly on the translation from the hybrid language into Spanish by Carlos Mántica. The translation from his Spanish text to English is my own.

13. *Güegüence*, ed. and trans. Brinton, 74 (subsequent quotations are from the Brinton translation).

14. *Güegüence*, 36.

15. The bulk of the sexual humor comes when the governor brings up the mules or "machos" for a dance-procession to celebrate the marriage agreement. Güegüence again feigns deafness when Forcico says that they have been corralled, or "cogidos." Güegüence misunderstands the word to be "encogidos," or "shriveled" and asks if it is from the cold (*Güegüence*, 106). Of one of the mules, Güegüence muses: "How can [this one] be well if it has such a stick in the front of it? Where did this mule get this stick run into himself, boy?" (110). Don Forcico

replies that it is from the colt yard, or the "potrero," but Güegüence replies that that's what he gets for running from *potrero* to *putrero*, suggesting a double meaning of colt yard for "putero," or whorehouse.

16. See Les W. Field, *The Grimace of Macho Ratón: Artisans, Identity, and Nation in Late-Twentieth-Century Western Nicaragua* (Durham: Duke University Press, 1999).

17. See, e.g., Alan Bolt, "Banana Republic," *Cuadernos universitarios* 28 (1982): 9–40.

18. Pablo Antonio Cuadra, "*El Güegüence y El Macho Ratón*," in *Baile de El Güegüence, o Macho Ratón*, ed. Carlos Mántica Abaunza (Managua: Editorial Hispamer, Costado Este de la UCA, 1998), 23.

19. Cuadra, "*El Güegüence y El Macho Ratón*," 19.

20. C. Hermann Berendt, "Remarks on the Centres of Ancient Civilization in Central American and Their Geographical Distribution: Address Read Before the American Geographical Society, July 10th 1876, by Dr. C. Hermann Berendt, Reprinted from the Bulletin of the American Geographic Society Session 1875–76. No. 2" (New York: Douglas Taylor, 1876), 13.

21. Cuadra, "*El Güegüence y El Macho Ratón*," 23.

22. This collection is now archived at the University of Pennsylvania, where Brinton worked to establish one of the United States' first programs in anthropology.

23. Brinton, "Introduction," xli.

24. It is interesting to note that Brinton, perhaps because he felt he was an apt critic of dramatic literature, collected quite a few dramatic texts from Central America, most from criollo (white) writers, and even wrote a drama himself. See Daniel G. Brinton, *Maria Candelaria: An Historic Drama from American Aboriginal Life* (Philadelphia: David McKay, 1897).

25. Brinton, "Introduction," xlii–xliv.

26. John M. Weeks, *The Library of Daniel Garrison Brinton* (Philadelphia: University of Pennsylvania Museum of Archaeology and Anthropology, 2002).

27. See Daniel G. Brinton, *Religions of Primitive Peoples* (New York: G. P. Putnam, 1897).

28. Lee D. Baker, "Daniel G. Brinton's Success on the Road to Obscurity, 1890–99," *Cultural Anthropology* 15, no. 3 (2000), 394–423, 397.

29. Baker, "Daniel G. Brinton's Success," 400.

30. Daniel G. Brinton, *Races and Peoples: Lectures on the Science of Ethnography* (New York: Hodges, 1890), 47–48.

31. Baker, "Daniel G. Brinton's Success," 400.

32. Daniel G. Brinton, *The American Race* (Philadelphia: David McKay, 1891), 32.

33. Brinton, *American Race*, 43.

34. Brinton, *Races and Peoples*, 169.

35. Alfred C. Haddon specifically names Brinton when mentioning evolution in his short *History of Anthropology* (1934): "In the United States . . . the earlier anthropologists such as . . . D. G. Brinton, and others, were under the spell of evolution" (*History of Anthropology* [London: Watts & Co., 1934 (1910)], 116).

36. Steven F. White, *Culture and Politics in Nicaragua: Testimonies of Poets and Writers* (New York: Lumen Books, 1986), 33.

37. *El Gran picaro: Una recreación basada en la historia de "El Güegüese,"* DVD, dir. Irene López (Mántica, Waid, and Company, 2005); Irene López, *El Gran picaro*, rehearsal, 7 June 2008.

38. For a more involved analysis of how the characters of *El Güegüence* are read in the current political environment, see E. J. Westlake, "The Güegüence Effect: The National Character and the Nicaraguan Political Process," in *Political Performances: Theory and Practice*, ed. Susan C. Haedicke, Deirdre Heddon, Avraham Oz, and E. J. Westlake (New York and Amsterdam: Rodopi Press, 2009).

39. Erick Blandón Guevara, *Barroco descalzo* (Managua: URACCAN, 2003), 130.

Sodomitical Politics

The 1737 Licensing Act and
The Vision of the Golden Rump

ALAN SIKES ❧

Most theater history students learn that in the year 1737 the English Parliament passed the first in a series of licensing acts that restricted performance events to licensed theaters and subjected performance scripts to government censorship. Most theater history instructors will recall that the Licensing Act of 1737 was precipitated by official outrage over satiric portrayals of King George II and his court. And most experts in the theater of the eighteenth century are probably familiar with the detailed study of the act and its passage published several years ago by Victor Liesenfeld.[1] There readers will discover that the act was ratified in response to the threatened theatricalization of an anonymous pamphlet entitled *The Vision of the Golden Rump*, a text that scandalously depicted the king as a sort of automated idol possessed of the protuberant posterior that lent the essay its name. This grotesque image of the royal rump garnered a great deal of public interest and dealt a significant blow to the dignity of the sovereign; Parliament prevented its presentation on the stage by passing the restrictive act—a decision that influenced the English theater for centuries to follow.

Yet given the fact that a theatrical version of *The Golden Rump* was never produced, it may seem odd at first glance that this ephemeral satiric pamphlet could weigh so heavily upon English theater history. In this essay, however, I will attempt to shed some light on the reasons for such weight. Specifically, I argue that the various ministrations performed upon the titular Rump qualified the pamphlet as a site of sodomitical attentions, one at which a number of potent political anxieties could converge; given the political instabilities of the moment in question, neither Court nor Parliament could afford for such anxieties to appear within so volatile a venue of public expression as the eighteenth-century English stage.

I also hope that this essay can raise broader questions for the field of theater history, questions that invite us to rethink our organization of the theatrical archive and the knowledges that it can either foster or foreclose. Given its sodomitical subject matter, I locate *The Golden Rump* at the intersection of two lines of inquiry frequently pursued within our field along more or less parallel tracks: the role of theater in class politics, on the one hand, and its role in sexual politics, on the other. Of course, the politics of both sex and class figure centrally in many landmark theatrical texts and productions. Too often, however, they are categorized within the archive as exemplars for one set of political practices over another. At times such archival categorizations are matters of convenience, at other times matters of necessity; consider the hard choices a theater instructor must make when selecting texts for a course on "Women in Theater" or a lecture series on "Theater and Revolution." Yet at times such archival alignments obscure the complex political potential we may derive from our objects of study. As a theater scholar invested in both class and sexual politics, I wonder about the insights that might issue from efforts to view our archival materials as loci for both sets of struggles simultaneously.[2]

The Golden Rump may be usefully viewed as one such locus. In fact, I consider the text emblematic of other missed opportunities to link sex-based and class-based politics, for the threatened play based on the original pamphlet is likewise missing from history; the script, if it was ever actually completed, has yet to surface within or without the theatrical archive. Yet a closer look at the pamphlet itself may shed light upon other archival omissions that we produce through our organization and arrangement of historical objects. Certainly our lack of access to a theatrical script should not deter us from attending to the impact of the original pamphlet upon theater history, for there we can learn much not only about the political perils that issued from the specter of royal sodomy but also about the perils that might have issued from its presentation in the theater. Cameron McFarlane argues that "just as sodomy is conceived as creating a wide variety of social disorders, so can a wide variety of social disorders be conceived of as being sodomitical," and indeed, *The Golden Rump* employs sodomy to figure a host of intertwined inversions that turned the politics of both sex and class upon their ears.[3] I look now to the pamphlet to show just why such inversions proved "too hot to handle" for the English stage.

The Vision of the Golden Rump was first published in two installments within the weekly journal *Common Sense*. The periodical began publication in February 1737, and the appearance of *The Golden Rump* in its March 19 and 26 issues gained it early notoriety. That an essay so critical of George II appeared in *Common Sense* was scarcely surprising; Liesenfeld notes that the journal was founded by Charles Molloy, an Irish attorney who apparently supported the claims of the Jacobite line to the English throne over those of the Hanoverian George II.[4] These rival claims first emerged in 1688, when James II abandoned his throne and sailed for France; a suspected Catholic, James governed a nation inimical to papist monarchs, and widespread antipathy to his reign eventually forced him to flee for his life. Parliament responded by inviting William of Orange and his wife, Mary, the Protestant daughter of James II, to ascend the throne as coregents. The precedents set by this so-called Glorious Revolution were reinforced upon the accession of Anne, younger sister of Mary, in 1702. Parliament granted Anne the throne by approving the Act of Settlement, which not only validated her reign but also stipulated that upon her death the crown would pass to George Lewis, a great-grandson of Charles I and the present Protestant Elector of Hanover. In 1714 the elector took the British throne as George I, and upon his death in 1727 his son was crowned George II. Yet the new dynasty did not sit well with the entire English population; a significant fraction believed that Parliament had no business meddling with royal succession and argued that the son of James II—also named James but called the Pretender by the Hanoverian court—was the rightful heir to the kingdom.

Liesenfeld also notes that the Pretender, eager to use *Common Sense* as his mouthpiece in London, would not permit the journal to appear overtly Jacobite in its leanings—one reason, perhaps, that *The Golden Rump* contains no open call for his return to power.[5] Significantly, however, the essay later appeared in another pamphlet entitled *A New Miscellany for the Year 1737*, a publication clearly sympathetic to the Jacobite cause; the pamphlet includes not only *The Golden Rump* but also *Thanksgiving for the Restoration of King Charles II*, which offers ample evidence of Jacobite loyalties. The anonymous author of the *Thanksgiving* invokes the execution of Charles I and the confusion of the Commonwealth era as the lowest ebb in English history; only the restoration of Charles II returned the nation to its former strength and security. How much more odious, then, the author asks, is the fact that the English have learned nothing from their earlier tribulation and have once again deprived the nation of its rightful sovereign: "If *King Charles the Second* was restored to HIS OWN JUST AND UNDOUBTED RIGHT, and if we return Publick Thanks to the *Almighty* for that *Happy Restoration*, how could we ever deprive his Heirs of THAT JUST AND UNDOUBTED RIGHT, that was THEIR OWN JUST AND UNDOUBTED RIGHT at his Death, They being his *Just and Undoubted*

THE FESTIVAL OF THE GOLDEN RUMP.
Rumpatur *quisquis* Rumpitur *invidia*.

Figure 7.1. *The Vision of the Golden Rump*, reprinted with permission from the British Museum.

Heirs?"[6] The author therefore argues for the restoration of the Jacobite line and ends the text by insisting that to deny the rightful king his crown is to "trifle with God, and make a Jest of Heaven: For, by the common Prayers of this Day, we assert the Hereditary Right to the Throne of *Great Britain*, and renounce that of Election, which we have *now and then usurped*."[7]

Yet if *The Golden Rump* is less open in its call for Jacobite restoration, its skewering of the current Hanoverian monarch leaves little doubt where the loyalties of its author actually lay. The text begins with a preface that muses upon the animated idols of the pagan past, noting how these idols often acted as oracles. The author wryly notes that such oracles—like that of Apollo at Delphi, for instance—wielded considerable power in the ancient world, remarking, "For the God of *Delphos* was frequently bribed to accommodate his Responses to the ambitious and political Views of his Votaries."[8] The preface thereby sets the stage for the appearance of the titular Rump, an animated idol invested with a similar degree of political power. The author encounters this idol—or Pagod, as he is called within the text—in a dream; after a canoe ride on a swiftly flowing river, the author comes ashore at a temple and is led inside by a Conductor who explains the visions that unfold within. The author first encounters the Rump himself, described as "an human Figure, excepting only that he had Goats Legs and Feet, like those which are given by Poets and Statuaries to the old *Satyrs*. His Head was made of Wood, his Body down to the waist of Silver; and his Posteriors, which were large and prominent, and from whence he deriv'd his Title, were of solid Gold."[9] That the Rump represents George II is made plain by the fact that the Pagod, like the monarch, attained his exalted position through election:

> By this Description the Reader will easily conceive that the Back of the IDOL was turned to the Congregation. . . . My friendly Conductor informed me, that he had placed himself in this Posture upon his first Entrance into the Temple, as well to shew his Politeness, as to testify his Respect and Gratitude to a Nation which had elected him into the Number of the *Dii Majores*, or *Greater Gods*.[10]

The author, moreover, makes the most of this comparison between Pagod and monarch, for the boorish posture of the Rump suggests that George II—himself often accused of arrogance and ill temper—likewise "shows his ass" to his subjects: "Here I could not help smiling to think how widely the Custom of this Country differed from mine, where the same Thing which passed here for Civility, and good Manners, would be reckoned a Mark of Insolence and Brutality."[11]

The author next describes two figures attendant on the Pagod. To the right of the Rump stood the High Priestess, also called the Tapanta; the author remarks that she was "dressed in the Habit of a *Roman* Matron," then notes that "she had a Silver Bell in one Hand, and a small Golden Pipe or Tube in the other, with a large Bag or Bladder at the End of it."[12] This curious device "exactly resembled a common Clyster pipe, and was used, as my Friend explained it to me, in the same manner. For the Bladder was full of *Aurum potabile*, compounded with Pearl Powders, and other choice Ingredients. This Medicine, at proper Seasons, was injected by TAPANTA into the f—d—t of the PAGOD to comfort his Bowels and preserve Complexion."[13]

With this description of the enema administration the author invokes a potent image of sexual inversion, one in which a powerful male is penetrated by his attendant female. Moreover, the fact that the Tapanta represents Queen Caroline extends the inversion beyond the person of the king himself. In his history of the Hanoverians, Jeremy Black remarks that the headstrong and outspoken queen wielded considerable power in her own right, serving as regent whenever her husband made his frequent trips to his native Hanover.[14] By taking the reins of office, then, Caroline assumed a masculine position much like the one assumed by the Tapanta when she penetrates the Rump with her clyster pipe.

To the left of the Rump stood the Chief Magician, also called the Gaster Argos; the author remarks that "he had a Rod or Wand in his Hand, which he waved continually to and fro," then notes that the rod "belonged heretofore to *Pharaoh's* chief Magician, and still retained its marvelous Virtue; that is, would change itself into Serpent or Dragon, whenever GASTER ARGOS cast it upon the Ground."[15] The Argos was responsible for managing the golden tribute offered the Rump by his worshippers and employed his magic wand to secure the booty. The Argos threw his rod to the floor before the massed offerings, and the dragon that appeared greedily devoured the golden tribute. The Argos then seized the monster by the tail, transformed it into a wand again, and with a final flourish transferred the accumulated wealth to the Rump himself. "The MAGICIAN gently stroked the GOLDEN RUMP with the small End of his Rod, when behold! that Part of the IDOL swelled to such an enormous Size, that (as I conjecture) the unnatural Protuberance, of additional Weight of Gold, was sufficient to make a Statue as large as the Statue in *Grosvenor Square*, Horse and all."[16]

Again the author proffers a powerful image of sexual inversion as the Argos strokes the Rump with his rod of office, an action that causes the Rump to swell as if impregnated by such attentions. Moreover, the inversion again besmirches individuals other than the king alone, for the Argos represents Robert Walpole, his first minister. In his own history of the Hanoverians, S. E. Ayling notes that Walpole had served George I in the same capacity and won renewal of his post from George II after proving handy at raising revenue for his sovereign.[17] The king therefore became increasingly dependent on Walpole, especially as his frequent visits to Hanover steadily increased in expense, and the monarch came to count upon him to swell the state coffers in much the same way that the Argos swells the posterior of the Pagod.

Near the end of the vision, the Argos announced to the congregation that "his *Pagodship* was engaged to sup with *Jupiter* that evening in *Aethiopia*; where they were to settle Affairs of the greatest Importance. . . .

Saying this, he laid down his Rod with great Reverence at the Feet of the
PAGOD. The Rod, as before, was immediately changed into a huge
Dragon . . . who took the IDOL on his Back, and flew with him out of the
Temple."[18] The ceremony completed, the author and Conductor prepared
to take their leave, but before parting the Conductor shared a bit of temple
gossip when he turned to the author and whispered, "You see the Power of
our PAGOD; but a Word in your Ear: Do not imagine he is really gone to
sup in *Aethiopia*. He never mounts the Dragon, but when he is in an
amorous Fit. He had beheld, among his Votaries, some mortal Female,
who had smitten him to the Heart."[19] Such a tryst with a mortal mistress
would first seem to neutralize the sexual inversions so far attributed to the
Pagod; rather than a passive and, by extension, feminized recipient of sex-
ually suggestive attentions to his rump, the Pagod now appears as an active
agent in pursuit of a dalliance with his female devotee. Yet a final parsing of
the parallels between Pagod and king will reveal further insinuations of inversion. If the Rump has been figuratively penetrated and rendered pregnant, then it stands to reason he should eventually give birth. And indeed,
his counterpart the king does produce illicit progeny—two sorts, in fact,
both linked to his frequent trips to Hanover.

Like the Rump, the king too had a mistress—the Hanoverian Countess
Amalia Sophie Marianne von Walmoden—and she provided the major im-
petus for his frequent and expensive travels to his homeland. The affair was
something of an open secret, but so was the fact that the long coach rides
between London and Hanover produced the first sort of progeny I have in
mind: the constant jolting of the carriage gave the king terrible hemor-
rhoids. Liesenfeld reports that after a stay of some eight months in
Hanover, the monarch at last returned to London in January 1737; he arrived ostensibly suffering from a cold, but "it was soon a matter of conversation that he was 'extremely out of order' from fever, shooting pains in the
head, and an excruciating case of the piles complicated by a fistula in the
same area."[20] This delicate condition of the king likely explains the decision to call his satiric namesake the Divine Rump, and given the other sexual inversions visited upon him, it does not seem a great stretch to consider
the royal piles an inverse form of royal progeny.

Yet this first progeny is a comic counterpart to the second sort I had in
mind: the king, as everyone knew, had sired a son by his mistress. Black
notes that "Madame Walmoden's second son, John, born in 1736, who was
reputed to be the King's child, rose to Field Marshall in the Hanoverian
army."[21] Certainly the existence of this bastard son inflamed the already
bitter feud that raged between the king and his heir, the Crown Prince

Frederick. George II had suffered a stormy relationship with his own father during his years as crown prince, and history repeated itself in the relationship between George II and Frederick. Ayling observes that the prince "tenanted Leicester House, as his father had done in his own days as Prince of Wales, and there held a sort of rival court to which wits, men of fashion, and ambitious politicians with an eye to the future found it natural to gravitate."[22] Generations of wrangling between fathers and sons had tarnished the Hanoverian dynasty, and the existence of a bastard son further compromised its image in the eyes of critics—for the Jacobites, after all, George II had no more claim to the throne than his illegitimate offspring.

Thus *The Golden Rump* offers a Jacobite vision of a miscreant king, one whose relations with his queen and first minister, as well as his foreign mistress and her progeny, are tainted by sodomitical spectacle. Such a spectacle of sexual inversion, moreover, invites conflation with a similar inversion of class, for according to the Jacobites George II had no legitimate right to the throne in the first place. In the eyes of the court, this conflation posed a significant political threat, for the image of a sodomitical sovereign could be marshaled to incite sedition against the state. And as that most public forum for political expression, the theater was the venue in which this linkage of class and sexual inversion held the greatest potential for fomenting insurrection—hence, perhaps, the reason that the Court moved so swiftly to prevent the appearance of *The Golden Rump* upon the stage.

A confluence of other social shifts doubtless rendered this prevention even more imperative. On the one hand, the libertine spirit of the Restoration had given way to the more conservative moral climate of the Hanoverian era. Rakish aristocrats no longer touted the joys of sodomy in their poems and panegyrics, and court records of the day show a steady increase in prosecutions for sodomitical acts among the middling and working classes. The growing public opprobrium attached to sodomy could only encourage dissenters to link it to their claims of political malfeasance.[23] On the other hand, both the size and the number of theater spaces had grown considerably since the Restoration. The two theaters still holding the original patents issued by Charles II had both moved into larger houses, and ambiguities concerning the patent monopolies had resulted in a proliferation of performance spaces offering short farces, ballad operas, pantomimes, puppet shows, and various other entertainments. As a result, the burgeoning theater scene had become an increasingly public forum for political expression.[24] Given the threatened appearance of a theatrical *Golden Rump*, therefore, conditions proved ripe for prompt and radical state intervention.

Walpole launched the court efforts to pass the Licensing Act by regaling Parliament with scenes from the now apocryphal stage version of *The Golden Rump*. To fuel the fire, he attributed the script to Henry Fielding, who had presented several successful political farces throughout the decade at the Little Theatre in the Haymarket. Fielding, for his part, publicly denied authorship, and others in the press insinuated that Walpole had commissioned the scenes himself with the purpose of pushing the act through Parliament. At any rate, the Licensing Act passed in the House of Commons on June 1, 1737 on a voice vote; no division of the House is recorded for any of the three readings of the bill. In the House of Lords, the bill faced more vocal, if not more widespread, opposition. Philip Dormer Stanhope, Fourth Earl of Chesterfield, decried the bill as an infringement on English liberties—censorship of the theaters today, he argued, would lead to censorship of the press in future days: "No Country ever lost its *Liberty* at *once*, 'tis by *Degrees* that Work is to be done; by *such* Degrees as creep insensibly upon you, till 'tis *too late* to stop the Mischief," he advised.[25] Despite this warning, the Licensing Act passed in the House of Lords on June 6, 1737, with a division of the House after the third reading: thirty-seven in favor of passage; five opposed. George II gave his approval to the act at the close of Parliament on June 21, alluding to its passage in his final address: "You cannot be insensible what just Scandal and Offence the Licentiousness of the present Times, under the Colour and Disguise of Liberty, gives to all honest and sober Men, and how absolutely necessary it is to restrain this excessive Abuse, by a due and vigorous Execution of the Laws."[26]

Passage of the act shaped the contours of the English stage for generations to come. The two patent companies at Drury Lane and Covent Garden held monopolies on full-length spoken drama until 1843; the censorship of play texts intended for public performance persisted until 1968. The impact of this and subsequent theatrical legislation doubtless offers theater historians much material for further investigation; I hope that such investigations will also interrogate our arrangement and organization of these archival materials. Given my own activist approach to theater scholarship, I advocate exploration into the insights that performance can offer us about the intersections of seemingly disparate political agendas. My own efforts foreground the links between the politics of sex and class, and the lessons learned from *The Golden Rump* may prove instructive in understanding the complexities of such links at given historical moments both past and present. In the England of 1737, implications of sodomy supported efforts to debunk claims to hereditary class privilege. Our present day bears witness to a greatly changed and much more flexible conception of class status—at least in certain economically advantaged sectors of the globe. Yet transgressive sexualities continue to inform and inflect class identities; consider how current debates over same-sex marriage in the United States and elsewhere are overdetermined by struggles over the accumulation and preservation of both cultural and economic capital.[27] Perhaps this short study of *The Golden Rump* will spark other theater scholars to consider the multiple political valences of their own objects of study, especially the ways in which one line of political discourse may either support or stymie the impact of another. The theatrical archive can offer a wealth of opportunities to pursue multiple axes of conjoined political struggles; this essay is an invitation to precisely such pursuits.

NOTES

1. Victor Liesenfeld, *The Licensing Act of 1737* (Madison: University of Wisconsin Press, 1984).

2. To be sure, several prominent theater scholars consistently link sex and class politics within their work. See, among others, Sue-Ellen Case, *The Domain-Matrix* (Bloomington: University of Indiana Press, 1996); Jill Dolan, *Geographies of Learning* (Middletown, CT: Wesleyan University Press, 2001); and David Savran, *A Queer Sort of Materialism* (Ann Arbor: University of Michigan Press, 2003). I am indebted to such scholars, whose work deeply informs my own.

3. Cameron McFarlane, *The Sodomite in Fiction and Literature: 1660–1750* (New York: Columbia University Press, 1997), 37.

4. Liesenfeld, *Licensing Act of 1737*, 92.

5. Liesenfeld, *Licensing Act of 1737*, 92–93.

6. Anonymous, "Thanksgiving for the Restoration of King Charles II," in *A New Miscellany for the Year 1737* (London, 1737), 17; italics in original.

7. "Thanksgiving," 17; italics in original.

8. Anonymous, "The Vision of the Golden Rump," in *New Miscellany for the Year 1737*, 2.

9. "Golden Rump," 3.

10. "Golden Rump," 3.

11. "Golden Rump," 3.

12. "Golden Rump," 3.

13. "Golden Rump," 3. *Aurum potabile*, or literally "drinkable gold," was a legendary panacea produced by alchemists through a series of complex operations involving the dissolution of solid gold into a suitable liquid medium. The term "f—d—t" refers to the "fundament" or posterior of the Pagod, here abbreviated as an ostensible gesture of propriety.

14. Jeremy Black, *The Hanoverians: History of a Dynasty* (London: Hambledon and London, 2004), 107.

15. "Golden Rump," 4.

16. "Golden Rump," 7. The Grosvenor Square statue in question represented George I, father of George II, and its invocation at this juncture recalls the frequent claims that both kings drained the public treasury with their lavish expenditures.

17. S. E. Ayling, *The Georgian Century: 1714–1837* (London: George G. Harrop, 1966), 103.

18. "Golden Rump," 10–11.

19. "Golden Rump," 11.

20. Liesenfeld, *Licensing Act of 1737*, 96.

21. Black, *Hanoverians*, 107.

22. Ayling, *Georgian Century*, 122.

23. On the self-posturing of Restoration sodomite rakes, see McFarlane, *Sodomite in Fiction and Literature*, 12–24, 42–49. On the increase in public prosecution of middle- and working-class sodomites, see Rictor Norton, *Mother Clap's Molly House* (London: GMP Publishers, 1992), 9–13. Yet note also how McFarlane cogently argues that shifts in the public visibility of sodomy vis-à-vis class status does not necessarily imply shifts in understandings of sexual identity or gender hierarchy; see the McFarlane pages noted earlier, as well as 174–81.

24. For detailed information on the expansion and proliferation of theater spaces in the years 1660–1737, see Emmett L. Avery and Arthur H. Scouten, *The London Stage: 1660–1700: A Critical Introduction* (Carbondale: Southern Illinois University Press, 1968), xxxi–xlviii; Emmett L. Avery, *The London Stage: 1700–1729: A Critical Introduction* (Carbondale: Southern Illinois University Press, 1968), xxii–li; Arthur H. Scouten, *The London Stage: 1729–1747: A Critical Introduction* (Carbondale: Southern Illinois University Press, 1968), xix–xlvii.

25. Philip Dormer Stanhope, Fourth Earl of Chesterfield, "The Lord C—d's Speech Against the Bill for Restraining the Stage," in *New Miscellany for the Year 1737*, 21.

26. Quoted in Liesenfeld, *Licensing Act of 1737*, 155.

27. For a detailed materialist analysis of class issues embedded in contemporary GLBT activism, see Rosemary Hennessy, *Profit and Pleasure: Sexual Identities in Late Capitalism* (New York: Routledge, 2000). For specific analysis of marriage, see chap. 2, 64–68.

But Is It Theater?

The Impact of Colonial Culture on Theatrical History in India

ERIN B. MEE ℺

In the nineteenth century, the British introduced European theater to the colonial cities of Bombay and Calcutta by touring productions to entertain their expatriate communities; by supporting productions of English plays staged by the expatriates themselves in newly erected British-style playhouses; and by teaching English drama in Indian universities, where Shakespeare was presented as the apex of British civilization.[1] The spread of English drama was part of the colonization of Indian culture. It was designed not only to shape artistic activity but to impose on Indians a way of understanding and operating in the world and to assert colonial cultural superiority. By the mid-nineteenth century, urban middle-class intellectuals had begun to build their own proscenium stages, to translate English plays into Indian languages, and to write their own plays in the style of the European drama to which they had been exposed.

Through these productions, the British introduced the proscenium stage to India, which changed the performer-spectator relationship and the ways in which spectators participated in productions. They commercialized theater-going, turning theater into a commodity rather than a community event related to annual harvests and religious occasions. Most significantly, however, they introduced a conceptualization of theater as dramatic literature, a construction that shaped the very definition of theater, the aesthetics of the emerging modern Indian theater, and the way Indian theatrical history was understood. The widespread teaching of Shakespeare in the newly established colleges, and the associated number of productions, translations, and adaptations of his plays, valorized playwright-initiated, text-based, plot-driven productions that followed a tightly constructed five- or three-act structure. This sensibility influenced the development of modern drama, which by the early twentieth century was expected to have human rather than divine characters, conversational dialogue, behavior that was psychologically motivated, events that were causally linked, and realistic settings that allowed spectators to believe in the present-tense reality of the action on stage while eliminating anything that would shatter the illusion of the fictional world of the play.

Most "indigenous" performance-driven genres of theater in India to that point often included improvisation, were often composed of short and unrelated pieces of entertainment or song-and-movement sequences, and oftentimes took place over an entire night or a series of days and nights.[2] The new definition of modern theater as dramatic literature marginalized these genres, which came to be thought of as "theatrical" but not as "theater" per se and were therefore left out of the histories of theater. In this manner, histories of Indian theater not only erased indigenous theater forms from the record but actively participated in the construction of theater as a form of literary activity. Similar developments affected theatrical practice, ways of defining theater, and theatrical history in Nigeria, Indonesia, and elsewhere—for the sake of clarity I focus on Indian theater as one example of a larger phenomenon.[3] We can agree that dramaturgical structures organize our experiences, affecting the way we process them; and that visual practices socialize us in ways of seeing the world. Thus ways and modes of understanding the world are embedded in theatrical practice. When histories of theater valorize certain kinds of theater, then, as was the case in colonial India, they elide or erase other ways of seeing the world, other modes of interpersonal interaction, and other ways of structuring experience.

In this essay, I examine the "colonization of Indian theatrical history" to show what the colonial definition of theater excluded and to examine the literary bias it introduced via Shakespeare and other European playwrights such as Ibsen and Shaw. In *Shakespeare and the Authority of Performance*, W. B. Worthen asks: "what are the consequences for an understanding of [theatre and theatrical history] of seeing the theatre as a kind of paper stage, its work and the audience's response already scripted by the hand of" the writer?[4] I offer a short answer to that question here as I chart the effect of a literary bias on Indian theater and theater history, and the ways in which post-Independence-era histories reversed the bias, valorizing performance-driven theaters that offer us a performance-oriented understanding of theater and the world. A performance-oriented understanding of theater emphasizes the ways in which we communicate through images, fragments of music or sound, and kinesthetic interactions between bodies, acknowledging that these modes of experience exist outside language and are cognitively different from language-based exchanges and experiences.

It also allows for the inclusion of a wide variety of dramaturgical structures, acknowledging that there are many ways to think about our experiences and that these structures both reflect and constitute culture.

The first modern history of Indian drama, according to historiographer Rakesh Solomon, was Horace Hayman Wilson's *Select Specimens of the Theatre of the Hindus*, published in Calcutta in 1827.[5] The significance of Wilson's book was its literary bias: "Wilson's avowed goal in his study was to champion Sanskrit plays as great literature."[6] His book included a "Treatise on the Dramatic System of the Hindus," translations of six Sanskrit plays, and commentaries on twenty-three Sanskrit plays. Wilson conflated "Indian theater" with "Sanskrit dramatic literature," which led him to ignore everything except Sanskrit plays and to ignore staging practices. His work was enormously influential: it was translated into French (1828) and German (1828), and two editions were printed in London (1835 and 1871). His conceptual framework for Indian theater (theater = play texts) has been used by a number of theater historians since, including Sylvain Lévi, whose book *Le théâtre Indien* (The Indian Theatre, 1890) took Wilson's literary bias even further: "We have, without hesitation," he wrote, "reserved the term 'Indian theatre' for the Sanskrit drama. . . . We think that the Sanskrit theatre is the Indian theatre *par excellence*." He dismissed popular non-Sanskrit theater as "'unsophisticated,' 'indifferent to literary qualities,' and offering 'very little originality.'" He went on to say that "the popular theatre has no history."[7] The next history of Indian theater, published as *The Indian Theatre: A Brief Survey of the Sanskrit Drama*, by Ernest Philip Horrwitz (1912), made its bias clear in its title.

Indian theater historians adopted the literary bias of Wilson, Lévi, and Horrwitz. For example, R. K. Yajnik, in his book *The Indian Theatre: Its Origins and Its Later Developments under European Influence*, was interested exclusively in dramatic literature, and he measured the quality of the theater in terms of its literary merit: "Gradually, the dignity of drama as literature and as a fine art is being generally recognized."[8] He credited the British with raising the standards of Indian dramatic literature in his review of one new play, saying that "only a student of British drama could have attained the polish and refinement of treatment that this playwright brings to bear on his material."[9] Equating theater with dramatic literature contributed to a construction of theater history that effectively erased several centuries of performance-based theater. According to this definition, there was no significant theater between the decline of Sanskrit drama around 1000 CE and the nineteenth century, when colonial theater took hold in India, because there were very few theatrical genres that produced dramatic literature as a stand-alone product outside the context of performance.[10] Consequently, it appeared that modern theater was a gift to India from the British, proving their cultural superiority.

In reality, numerous genres of theater developed between the first and nineteenth centuries. Although it is often difficult to pin down dates of origin for many of these genres, *svang* and *kathakali*, two examples from very different geographical locations, clearly originated in the period that is often ignored. Director Neelam Man Singh Chowdhry tells us that the term *svang*, which literally means "masquerade" but refers to the art of mimicry and to specific skits, appears in the religious writings of Guru Nanak (1469–1538),[11] and references to svang can be found in a play written in 1686–89, as well as in nineteenth-century texts.[12] *Nautanki*, which is the name of both a heroine and the genre of musical stage plays that tell her story, was known as svang until the 1920s and continues to be known as such in certain areas. Nautanki developed out of and has been influenced by svang, by the style of performed poetic composition known as *lavani*, by operatic drama (*sangeet*), by *khyal* (musical plays performed by troupes in Rajasthan in the late eighteenth and nineteenth centuries), and by court dramas.[13] Nautanki scholar Kathryn Hansen points out that "theatre was a principal pursuit of a number of kings across Northern India from 1600 to 1850, and they patronized theatrical performances held in their palaces as well as in public to amuse and edify the populace."[14] Clearly, there was a wealth of dramatic performance in Northern India before the nineteenth century. In the Southwestern state of Kerala, kathakali came into its own as an art form between 1750 and 1800 under the royal patronage of Maharaja Kartika Tirunal (1724–98) and Veera Kerala Varma (1766–1828), although it developed out of and shares a number of characteristics and practices with *kutiyattam* (a particular way of performing Sanskrit drama in Kerala), *Ramanattam* (dramatization of stories from the Ramayana), *Krishnattam* (dramatization of stories about Krishna), *kalarippayattu* (a martial art), and *mudiyettu* (ritual enactments of the fight between Goddess Kali and the demon Darika), which developed even earlier. Some of the most highly regarded *attakkathas* (source texts for kathakali performances) were written by the poets Unnayi Varrier (1665–1725) and Kottayam Tampuran (1675–1725), while the earliest date back to Kottarakkara Tampuran (1625–85), proving that kathakali, along with many other genres, flourished in the seventeenth and eighteenth centuries.

Prior to the imposition of text-dominated theater, the majority of the many and varied performance genres throughout India, while unique and particular in many ways (artistic goals and aesthetics, dramaturgical structures, social roles, political agendas, the specific cultures they reflect, and the regional languages of their performance), were and continue to be similar in that they are not text-driven stagings of dramatic literature. This does not mean they do not work with literary texts, but that the logic and experience of the event are not derived solely from the text, and the performance is not judged (by spectators, critics, or performers themselves) in terms of its "fidelity" to the text or its fidelity to the purported intentions of a playwright. *Tamasha, jatra,* and kutiyattam offer three very different examples of performance-driven theater. Tamasha, which developed in the 1600s as court entertainment for the Peshwa rulers and an entertainment and inspiration for Maratha soldiers, combines elements of *kathak* (a genre of classical North Indian dance that developed as court entertainment), *dasavatar* (mime, pageantry, music, and dance that together tell the story of any one of Vishnu's ten incarnations, proceeding episodically), *lalit* (devotional entertainment performed as part of several festivals, usually incorporating some kind of social critique), and *bharud* (dramatic songs distinguished by their humorous double entendres), along with other musical and performance genres.[15] It incorporates a section known as *batavani;* jokes that satirize a current event or person in power; and, later, in the nineteenth century, a *vag,* or plot-based scenario. A tamasha performance can contain as many as thirty lavanis (sung poetic narratives with a specific metric form).

An evening of jatra, outdoor theater popular in both urban and rural areas of Bengal, Bihar, and Orissa, does follow the plot of a play, although the plot is interrupted by a figure known as the Vivek, who functions as the conscience of a given character by singing about the character's inner moral conflicts, and (in the nineteenth century) by fifty to sixty songs throughout each performance, some sung by the actors themselves, some sung for them by musicians. Jatra actors improvise their dialogue, so the length and focus of a scene can vary in performance.

Kutiyattam is the most text-based of the examples I use here. But because the stories (from epic and mythological sources) are already familiar to the spectator, the focus of a given performance is on the way a particular performer interprets the text by elaborating on it. The elaboration is so complex that the performance of a single play can take anywhere from five to thirty-five nights to complete. Each scene has its own title and is meant to be performed as its own entity; within each scene, a performer may spend up to an hour illuminating a line of text by making political and social analogies, exploring emotional associations, and telling related or background stories. On the first night of a kutiyattam performance, a character enters, introduces himself by narrating his personal history and some important details from his own life, presents some of the important events leading up to the play, and expands on details found in the first few lines of text. On the second and third nights the same character (possibly played by a different actor) tells stories connected to, but not found in, the main story of the play. On the fourth night a second character introduces himself, presents personal background leading up to the moment the play begins, and tells the story from his point of view. On each successive night another character appears until all the characters have been introduced, each offering his or her own history and version of the story. On other nights the *vidushaka* appears. His job is to translate the Sanskrit text of the play into Malayalam (the language spoken in Kerala, where kutiyattam is performed) and to make political and social analogies between events in the play and events in the real world. In this way the story is told and retold from many points of view, the background to the story is fully explored, and the story is made relevant to the audience. On the final night "the play" is performed. Thus "the play"—the text sans elaborations—is only a tiny fraction of the total experience, and the *attaprakarams* (the acting manuals that contain guidelines for the improvised elaborations) are valued even more highly than the text itself.

Genres like kutiyattam, jatra, and tamasha were excluded from books on Indian theater in the pre-Independence period. In 1980 theater scholar Kapila Vatsyayan published an influential book called *Traditional Indian Theatre: Multiple Streams*, in which she wrote about genres of performance that flourished between the first and nineteenth centuries—the era erased by Wilson, Lévi, Horrwitz, Yajnik, and others—in order to legitimize previously denigrated genres of performance and reinstate them in the history books. She accomplished this by focusing on their literary aspects: "the prolific literary activity of medieval India convinced me that the origins of the so-called folk rural forms lay as much in regional literatures as in the oral traditions."[16] Vatsyayan argued against the notion that performance-driven genres were completely divorced from literature: while not text-based or plot-driven, many of them nonetheless employ highly poetic speeches, dialogue, and song lyrics. She created a linear history of Indian theater by linking these genres to their "origins" in the venerated Sanskrit drama: "What appeared on the surface as belonging only to the rural masses without history and ancient links indeed embodied elements which were the continuation of [the] tradition of the *Natyashastra* [the Sanskrit treatise on aesthetics]."[17] Vatsyayan's assertion, made with the memory of Partition still fresh in mind, was also designed to show that the regional performing arts of India (and therefore the regions themselves) were culturally connected through their relationship to a common Sanskritic dramatic tradition. However, while she succeeded in legitimizing these genres by pointing out their literary aspects, Vatsyayan did not challenge the literary bias itself. Other post-Independence theater historians did.

After Independence, a number of playwrights and directors turned to classical dance, religious ritual, martial arts, and popular entertainment—genres that had come to be identified as "Indian" in contradistinction to the "Europeanized" modern theater—to see what dramaturgical structures, acting styles, and staging techniques could be used to create an "indigenous" nonrealistic style of production that in turn could define an "Indian theater." This impulse became known as the theater of roots movement—a post-Independence effort to decolonize the aesthetics of modern Indian theater.[18] One of the characteristics of theaters such as kutiyattam and tamasha, and of the work of the theater of roots movement, which absorbed and re-created numerous aspects of these performance-driven theaters, is that actors, directors, and playwrights complicate the linear narrative, allowing for multiple voices and perspectives on a particular theme or story, which then have to be analyzed by the spectator. Director Kavalam Narayana Panikkar (who is inspired by the dramaturgical structure of kutiyattam) asks his actors to elaborate on the text so the audience can explore many interrelated thematic threads; playwright Girish Karnad (whose dramaturgical structures are inspired by the dance-drama *yakshagana*) surrounds the central plot of his most famous play with a chorus, two talking dolls, and a number of songs and dances, giving the audience multiple ways of experiencing and processing the "main story." In these situations, the performance is an opportunity for multivocality, for privileging voices other than just that of the playwright. Director Ratan Thiyam employs a physicality and vocality that emphasize experiences that are beyond language. In his case, as in Panikkar's, vocal expression and physicality are not subordinated to the text but serve as equal channels of communication, and the information they provide is not always based on or derived from the text. Because the commentary is conveyed through physical movement, vocal gestures, music, and percussion, these productions honor nonverbal modes of expression, communication, and experience. Panikkar is well known for re-creating text in the body, where language becomes visual, embodied, and experienced. To make sense of the physical vocabulary, the spectator has to engage as cocreator of the event rather than as passive observer. These theaters assert the value of other (non-text-based, nonlinear) ways of perceiving, structuring, and processing experience.

At the same time, and as part of the roots movement, theatrical history was being reconceived and rewritten. Theater historians (many of whom were also playwrights) challenged the narratives established in nineteenth- and early twentieth-century histories of Indian theater and the assumptions that gave rise to them. In 1971, playwright and historian Adya Rangacharya traced a new history of modern Indian theater. His book *The Indian Theatre* begins with the statement: "When the Western scholars first interested themselves in research into Vedic and Sanskrit literature, the Indian theatre meant usually dramatic works in Sanskrit."[19] He goes on to say that because the Sanskrit plays they studied did not conform to Aristotelian dramaturgy, these scholars treated the texts as dramatically inferior to classical Greek plays: they were considered bad drama but, because of their poetry, viewed as good literature. Rangacharya said that "Oriental" scholarship was "not only continued by us but unfortunately we were content to accept the conclusion of one or another scholar as the final word."[20] His book was an attempt to set the record straight. By focusing on the performance aspects of the *Natyashastra*, and linking contemporary performance to Sanskrit drama by pointing out that numerous theatrical conventions mentioned in the *Natyashastra*, such as the use of the hand-held entrance curtain, are still in evidence "in the present day in many forms of village plays,"[21] he created a link between Sanskrit drama and theater of the fifteenth century. Rangacharya was one of the first historians to point out that "when we say that there was no Indian drama from the tenth century to the fifteenth or sixteenth century, we only mean that there were no written dramas."[22] Rangacharya contended that dramatic talent continued developing after 1000 CE through *Harikatha* (stories about Hari or Vishnu), "in which through songs, narration, intonation and acting, devotional stories were enacted by only one artist to a mixed audience," necessitating the creation of character,[23] and he traced the development of Indian theater through the dramatic songs of the fifteenth-century poet-saint Purandaradasa, claiming they required two or more actors to perform and concluding, "here, one could say confidently, is the beginning of modern Indian drama."[24] Rangacharya's history of modern Indian theater legitimized the many traditional performance genres (as theaters that developed before the rise of modern theater are known) and reinstated them in the history books.

Similarly, Nemichandra Jain set out to "decolonize" the history of Indian theater by tracing its development before, during, and after the influence of British aesthetics through traditional performance. In *Indian Theatre: Tradition, Continuity and Change* Jain asserted that "our theatre has now reached a point where it cannot make much headway without coming to terms with its own unique and unparalleled tradition."[25] In his third chapter, Jain asserted that the British arrived in India precisely at the moment theater reached a point of stagnation: in Jain's history, the British did not bring theater to India; they destroyed what was there. Discussing the rise of cities, he said, "A new type of theatre began to take shape there which had a very tenuous or no relation at all with our own long performance tradition."[26] As a result, "a fatal alienation between our rural and urban theatre developed."[27] Jain believed that the "natural" development or continuity of Indian theater had been destroyed by the British, and his project was to reestablish that continuity. Consequently, he advocated renewing the contact between rural and urban theaters: his history is both descriptive and prescriptive; it is an effort to rewrite and reroute the history of Indian theater.[28]

In 1951 (twenty years before Jain's book appeared), Mulk Raj Anand made a similar argument in a book titled *The Indian Theatre*, which was a significant departure from earlier books of the same title. Anand called for a new modern theater that would be uniquely Indian.[29] His move was to define "the Indian theater" in terms of "folk theater" and to assert its value and vitality. His agenda was to promote a "synthesis" of urban theater and rural performance, which "will bring us to the basis of a new kind of theatrical expression."[30] Anand's prescription for modern Indian theater was to "adapt our knowledge of the survivals [*sic*] of the old folk theatre to the needs of today," which would make possible "a new indigenous tradition of the Indian theatre . . . unique to our country."[31] Anand's book, like Jain's, is a manifesto as well as a history—it is as prescriptive as it is descriptive, and it helped explain and justify the theater of roots movement.

In 1964, J. C. Mathur published *Drama in Rural India*, in which he focused on theatrical practices and aesthetics ignored by the urban theater.[32] Mathur's book marked the beginning of a stream of books focused on performance-driven theaters, which together served to legitimize these genres as worthwhile fields of study. A partial list of titles in English (there are many others in English and other languages) includes Balwant Gargi's *Folk Theatre of India* (1966); Sudha Desai's *Bhavai: A Medieval Form of Ancient Indian Dramatic Art as Prevalent in Gujarat* (1972); K. Shivarama Karanth's *Yakshagana* (1975); *Lesser Known Forms of Performing Arts in India*, edited by Durgadas Mukhopadhyay (1978); Samar Devilal's *Folk Entertainments in Rajasthan* (1979); and *Folk Entertainment in India* (1981), edited by P. N. Chopra.[33] Although they have their own problems, these books represent a radically new approach to theater in terms of what they value.

Post-Independence theater historians in India, in their attempt to "decolonize" their theatrical history by valorizing "indigenous" genres of theater and a performative understanding of theater, were instrumental in shifting the conceptual frameworks governing the understanding of Indian theatrical history and in rewriting that history. The work of these post-Independence historians serves as a model for other theater historians and theorists, because it focuses on the politics of aesthetic choices, and it acknowledges and promotes a multiplicity of dramaturgical structures, visual practices, modes of interaction, and cognitive processes that contribute to a wider range of experience.

NOTES

1. Bombay and Calcutta were renamed Mumbai and Kolkata in the 1990s. To avoid being anachronistic, I use their old names when discussing events that occurred before the 1990s and their new names when I am speaking about events during or after the 1990s.

2. It is difficult in India to distinguish what is "indigenous" from what is "imported." The term *indigenous* as it is used in discussions of modern Indian theater usually refers to performance genres that were fully developed and established in the precolonial era, although they were clearly influenced by colonial theater. Whenever I use the term, I follow this usage.

3. For a brief discussion of the politics of the terms *literature* and *drama* in Africa, see the introduction to *Pre-colonial and Post-colonial Drama and Theatre in Africa*, ed. Lokangaka Losambe and Devi Sarinjeive (Asmara, Eritrea: Africa World Press, 2001). For a discussion of *tradisi baru*, an Indonesian theatrical movement similar to India's theater of roots, see Cobina Gillitt's dissertation, "Challenging Conventions and Crossing Boundaries: A New Tradition of Indonesian Theatre from 1968–1978" (New York University, 2001).

4. W. B. Worthen, *Shakespeare and the Authority of Performance* (Cambridge: Cambridge University Press, 1997), location 71–75 (all Worthen quotations are from the Kindle edition).

5. See Rakesh Solomon, "From Orientalist to Postcolonial Representations: A Critique of Indian Theatre Historiography from 1827 to the Present," *Theatre Research International* 29, no. 2 (2004): 113. Cf. H. H. Wilson, *Select Specimens of the Theatre of the Hindus*, 3 vols. (Calcutta: V. Holcroft, 1827).

6. Solomon, "From Orientalist to Postcolonial Representations," 114.

7. Sylvain Lévi, *Le théâtre Indien* (Paris: E. Buillon, 1890); translated by Narayan Mukerji as *The Theatre of India* (Calcutta: Writer's Workshop, 1978); quoted in Solomon, "From Orientalist to Postcolonial Representations," 115.

8. R. K, Yajnik, *The Indian Theatre: Its Origins and Its Later Developments under European Influence* (New York: Haskell House Publishers, [1934] 1970), 238.

9. Yajnik, *Indian Theatre*, 239.

10. This generalized perception persisted despite the fact that in the case of certain genres such as Nautanki, texts were published and widely circulated.

11. In Ananda Lal, ed., *The Oxford Companion to Indian Theatre* (Delhi: Oxford University Press, 2004), 459.

12. Kathryn Hansen, *Grounds for Play: The Nautanki Theatre of North India* (Berkeley: University of California Press, 1992), 56–62.

13. Hansen, *Grounds for Play*, 56–73.

14. Hansen, *Grounds for Play*, 74.

15. See Tevia Abrams, "Tamasha: People's Theatre of Maharashtra State, India," Ph.D. diss. (Michigan State University, 1974).

16. Kapila Vatsyayan, *Traditional Indian Theatre: Multiple Streams* (Delhi: National Book Trust, 1980), viii.

17. Vatsyayan, *Traditional Indian Theatre*, viii.

18. See Erin B. Mee, *Theatre of Roots: Redirecting the Modern Indian Stage* (Calcutta: Seagull Books, 2009).

19. Adya Rangacharya, *The Indian Theatre* (Delhi: National Book Trust, 1971), 1.

20. Rangacharya, *Indian Theatre*, 1.

21. Rangacharya, *Indian Theatre*, 46.

22. Rangacharya, *Indian Theatre*, 55.

23. Rangacharya, *Indian Theatre*, 54.

24. Rangacharya, *Indian Theatre*, 64.

25. Nemichandra Jain, *Indian Theatre: Tradition, Continuity and Change* (Delhi: Vikas Publishing House, [1971] 1992), 10.

26. Jain, *Indian Theatre*, 61.

27. Jain, *Indian Theatre*, 61.

28. One response to the attempt to reunite the two purportedly divergent streams of urban and rural theater shows how entrenched the conceptual divide had become and still remains. Amitava Roy has written, "The term 'folk theatre' is itself a misnomer. What we do on the proscenium stage is 'theatre'; what our 'folks' have been doing throughout the centuries is best termed 'performance'" ("Folk Is What Sells Well," in *Rasa, The Indian Performing Arts in the Last Twenty-Five Years*, vol. 2, *Theatre and Cinema*, ed. Bimal Mukherjee and Sunil Kothari [Calcutta: Anamika Kala Sangam Trust, 1995], 10). Roy's anxiety about the mixing of "theater" and "performance" perpetuates the application of colonial theoretical frameworks to current theatrical activity. This is precisely the mindset that Jain's history attempted to change.

29. Mulk Raj Anand, *The Indian Theatre* (New York: Roy Publishers, 1951), 60.

30. Anand, *Indian Theatre*, 59.

31. Anand, *Indian Theatre*, 60.

32. J. C. Mathur, *Drama in Rural India* (Bombay: Asia Publishing House, 1964).

33. Balwant Gargi, *Folk Theatre of India* (Calcutta: Rupa and Co., [1966] 1991); Sudha R. Desai, *Bhavai: A Medieval Form of Ancient Indian Dramatic Art as Prevalent in Gujarat* (Ahmedabad: Gujarat University, 1972); K. S. Karanth, *Yakshagana* (Delhi: Abhinav Publications, 1997); Durgadas Mukhopadhyay, ed., *Lesser Known Forms of Performing Arts in India* (Delhi: Sterling Publishers, 1978); Samar Devilal, *Folk Entertainments in Rajasthan* (Udaipur: Bhartiya Lok Kala Mandal, 1979); P. N. Chopra, ed., *Folk Entertainment in India* (Delhi: Ministry of Education and Culture, Government of India, 1981).

Sympathy for the Devil

Nonprogressive Activism and the Limits of Critical Generosity

JOHN FLETCHER ∿

In *Acts of Intervention*, his study of gay men's performance practices during the initial years of the U.S. AIDS epidemic, David Román introduces the term *critical generosity*. Surveying the range of shows, protests, demonstrations, and cabarets responding to the emerging AIDS crisis, Román considers and rejects the use of standard aesthetic or canonical criteria to evaluate the shows' quality. More important, he argues, is "to attend to the context and ambition of the performances under discussion . . . as an attempt to honor the potential inherent in all AIDS performances to help us more effectively understand AIDS."[1] Román refutes the assumption that critics write from objective vantage points set apart from or above the subjects they investigate, particularly when the subjects' political aims overlap with or otherwise affect the life situation of the scholar. Critical generosity reimagines the relationship between performances for social change and the scholar who studies them as "a cooperative endeavor and collaborative engagement with a larger social mission."[2]

How does critical generosity—or lack thereof—toward the political goals of the performers we study affect the historiography of activist performance? This question suggests two others. First, what level of critical generosity—avowed sympathy with the causes of one's subjects—is proper for historians? Second, and more subtly, what level of generosity does current scholarly discourse about social-change performance oblige historians to adopt? To address these questions, I explore some of my own historiographic research into pro- and anti-gay activist performances. I find, in general, that many of the critical and analytic tools available to me presuppose a degree of alignment with and endorsement of progressive causes, causes I regard as laudable in that they aim at realizing liberatory and egalitarian aims. Simpatico scholarship of this sort works as long as I remain a progressive critic investigating progressive performances. I face some difficulty, however, when historicizing nonprogressive activisms, which by virtue of being conservative get cast as antiliberatory or antiegalitarian. How and why, then, might I practice critical generosity toward my enemy?

Román's arguments about an ethical historiography of AIDS performances inform my own investigations into activist performances, by which I mean performances whose intent involves altering the attitudes, structures, or practices of the society in which they operate. I study a range of plays, rallies, community-based productions, parades, sidewalk happenings, demonstrations, protests, performance art, museums, flash mobs, and online videos—events united not by form or style but by their having been produced to serve a political cause. Like many other scholars of activist performance, I do my best to couple historiographic tasks of description and contextualization with a critically generous attempt to gain a deep sense of the "larger social mission" to which the performers see their acts as contributing. Where such missions encompass what Chantal Mouffe and Ernesto Laclau call a "radical democratic" project of expanding and deepening the scope of liberty and equality (a stance that overlaps with the adjective *progressive*) I align myself with the performances' larger intent.[3]

But not all social missions aim at radical democratic ends, and the net I cast with my definition of activist theater captures more than just performances whose politics I endorse. Consider, for example, an anti-gay demonstration such as the Mayday for Marriage Rally, held in Washington, D.C., shortly before the 2004 elections. There, a number of conservative groups staged a massive demonstration on the National Mall, delivering a message to Congress that they wish to see a particular civil right—the right to state-recognized marriage—restricted to heterosexual couples. Is a nonprogressive activist performance like the rally due a degree of critical generosity? If not, then what *instead* of generosity?

Complicating any answer to these questions is the fact that the critical vocabulary of activist performance scholarship often assumes a generally progressive stance. Although exceptions exist, "activist performance" generally connotes a performance with progressive aims, and studies of nonprogressive activism must often explicitly mark themselves as such (as I do in my title).[4] Similar patterns obtain in other disciplines where social-change initiatives are studied. Writing from sociological and ethnographic perspectives, for example, Kathleen M. Blee notes a tendency for researchers to focus on movements "attempting to broaden opportunities and advance social equality," movements whose social or political beliefs researchers tend to share. "Indeed," she continues, "some social movement concepts are nearly synonymous with progressive movements."[5] This identity between the language of scholarship and the political orientations of scholars, I argue, impacts the historiographic representation and analysis of social-change performances, forging a degree of assumed or obligatory consonance between progressive scholars and progressive artists.

My own work illustrates this concord. In my first published article, I wrote about a solo show by Tim Miller, 2002's *Glory Box*. Miller's semiautobiographical piece focuses on the plight of binational gay couples like Miller and his partner.[6] I linked aspects of Miller's performance—his text, his staging, and his activism regarding the gay marriage issue—to several larger relevant discourses circulating at the time of the event, analyzing in detail his particular dramaturgical interaction with these discourses. In doing so, I mobilized a number of terms from the arsenal of social change performance scholarship: *radical democracy, community-based theater, utopian performative, queer activism, liberation,* and *human rights.*

Complex as they are, each of these phrases operates on two levels, one overt and one tacit. First, these terms grant a degree of critical context required of any historiographic study, fleshing out what would otherwise be a thin piece of reportage ("Here's what happened") or a personal-reaction blog entry ("It sure was neat!"). Some of these terms, like *radical democracy, human rights,* or *queer activism,* connect Miller's performance to contemporary (relative to Miller) cultural conversations regarding the proper content of civil rights, the morality of tolerance, or the ethics of immigration law. Others, like *utopian performative* or *community-based theater,* link Miller's dramaturgy to particular styles or movements in performance, suggesting or clarifying a frame through which others may view Miller's work. But these terms do more than describe. In the way I used them, in the critical conversation to which my article contributes, descriptors like *community-based* or *utopian* carry a normative charge. They register a value judgment, endorsing Miller's work as well as describing it. By reading Miller's performance in 2002 through the lens of Jill Dolan's writings about the utopian performative, for example, I not only cited Dolan's model for describing an audience-performer gestalt of shared hope;[7] I tapped into the undeniably positive associations that a word like *utopian* conjures, incorporating Miller's performance into the glow of those positive associations. A similar aura of approval attends phrases like *community-based, democratic,* or *liberatory,* power words ensconced within analytic and theoretical models.[8] In this way, then, my critical generosity operated in part via an analytic/descriptive vocabulary that endorses the aims of its object.

But what effects does such vocabulary have when either the historian or the subject lacks the progressive politics assumed by the language of scholarship? Consider how the very term *progressive* implies that only movements based on left-leaning philosophies (i.e., in favor of broadened rights and equality for increasingly pluralized groups) actually possess qualities of *movement* or *action* in a positive direction; progressive movements are by definition those that strive toward a social or political Good. By necessary contrast, nonprogressive movements become enemies of the Good: inactive, retrogressive, or even altogether evil. The vocabularies born of critical generosity toward progressive activist historiographies, then, render the "larger social missions" of nonprogressive activist performances either unintelligible or repugnant. Indeed, the question presents itself: does being for democracy or human rights mandate that the critic take an actively oppositional stance against conservative or otherwise nonprogressive work?

Or, to reverse this question, what if the critic of progressive work isn't herself progressive? Imagine, for instance, if I had written about Miller's *Glory Box* from a stance not aligned with, or even opposed to, the normalization or political equality of GLBT people.[9] In such a scenario, Miller's show, his body of work, his activism, and even the audience's reactions—all of these would remain the same, and I would as a historian be tasked with reporting these accurately. But the analysis I as "pro-family" critic would write would presumably differ. Assuming for the sake of argument I avoid writing an article consisting of outright lies or pure anti-gay propaganda, either of which would indicate not a lack of critical generosity but plain shoddy scholarship,[10] to what extent would my nonprogressive political stance affect my scholarly treatment of Miller? Were I "pro-family" in the conservative sense, I would likely pass over or problematize descriptors like *utopian performative;* if I believe homosexuality to be harmful, I am not likely to join or endorse a utopian meditation on the joys of same-sex partnership. I might even import phrases like *same-sex addiction* or *gay agenda* from other pro-family discourses to contextualize Miller's performance, suggesting that he acts as part of a subculture (like crack addicts, sex workers, or neo-Nazis) unified by marginal or quasi-criminal lifestyles. Most likely I would adopt a cooler, more reserved tone in describing Miller and his work. I might even mark my discomfort at being a part of his mostly GLBT and GLBT-friendly audience (much as I mark my own discomfort in pieces I have written about attending conservative evangelical performances).

But, although indicating a distance from Miller's political stance, would such critical antipathy necessarily register as anti-democratic or anti–human rights, opposed to progressive power words like *community, liberty,* and *democracy*? I submit that it would not. The obvious point bears repeating: nonprogressive, pro-family groups in the United States typically do not imagine themselves as acting apart from or against liberal democratic values. Beneath culture-war catchphrases like *gay agenda* or *protecting marriage* lie not negative values of "exclusion" or "privilege" but ideals such as "a healthy community" or "the will of the people." My research into (non-hypothetical) pro-family discourse reveals a striking degree of similarity in the motivating vocabularies of left and right activisms.

Shifting from my hypothetical pro-family critic to a historical pro-family performance, consider the aforementioned Mayday for Marriage rally in Washington, D.C.[11] A series of speeches delivered by a string of conservative superstars to a crowd of about 150,000, the national rally originated as a grassroots cause. Some months before the D.C. rally, Seattle pastor Ken Hutcherson had organized a surprisingly well-attended pro-family rally at Safeco Stadium as a reaction to Seattle mayor Greg Nichols's issuing licenses to same-sex couples. Hoping to replicate Hutcherson's local success on a national stage, the Family Research Council joined forces with other conservative groups to stage a "distress call" aimed at Congress, highlighting how in their view the institution of heterosexual marriage was under threat from activist judges determined to overturn same-sex-restrictive "marriage protection" laws.[12] The rally's aim, therefore, involved demonstrating popular support for the proposed Federal Marriage Amendment, which would install a heterosexuals-only definition of marriage into the U.S. Constitution.

At first glance, the Mayday Rally seems like a nightmare of bigotry dedicated to a narrow-minded mission of excluding a whole class of people from the equality of regard due to them as human beings. Yet again and again, rally speakers and publicity materials stressed that theirs was not an anti-gay cause.[13] Indeed, the rally's predominant rhetoric consisted not of anti-gay diatribes but of a repeated invocation of a prime democratic value: the sovereignty of the people to determine the operation of government. The people's will, so went the rally's narrative, had been clearly established and enshrined in bill after bill, state amendment after state amendment: marriage is by definition for heterosexual couples alone. By overturning these laws, by listening to an elitist minority, the "imperial judiciary" had declared war on the sovereignty of the people. More than one speaker cited the dramaturgy of the Mall itself (not excluding the 1963 March on Washington) to animate the idea of "the people" to whom the government whose very capitol the crowd confronted was accountable.[14] In the rally's staging of the national debate, it was "the people" who were locked out of the circuits of political power, "the people" whose rights were being ignored, and "the people" who were in need of justice. And, suggested speaker James Dobson, it would be "the people" who would act in upcoming elections to make sure that pro-"people" (i.e., pro-family) politicians got elected.[15]

Concomitant with the rally's staging of (heterosexual, pro-family) people as true inheritors of democratic legitimacy was its critique of gay and lesbian claims that theirs was a civil rights cause. Rally organizers made sure that their lineup included an ethnically diverse group, many of whom referenced the race-and-only-race dimension of historic civil rights struggles. Ken Hutcherson, the NFL-linebacker-turned-pastor whose activism had inspired the rally, particularly helped to refocus the civil rights issue. In his speech recounting his organization of the Safeco event, Hutcherson foregrounded his race, establishing his bona fides as an arbiter of civil rights legitimacy. "Every time I turned around for several months," he told the crowd, "I kept hearing how same-sex issue is a civil rights issue. Now, if you haven't noticed, I'm black. [*Laughter from the crowd*] I know something about civil rights. It's not homosexuals that's having a problem with civil rights."[16] His contribution, capitalizing on his sports fame and grassroots organizing cachet as well as his race, operated on two levels: trivializing the pro-gay movement's claims to civil rights discourse, while also strengthening the power of other speakers' references to King's 1963 rally. Hutcheson's performance of himself as stand-in for the otherwise ghosted black civil rights tradition, his assurance that the pro-family stance was in line with rather than opposed to an authentic tradition of civil rights, added an additional level to the moral high ground of the rally's pro-democratic rationale.

Of course, considering the rally's invocation of democratic and liberatory concepts, its tapping into the spectral power of civil rights rallies past, and its disqualifications of gay and lesbian access to civil rights legacies, an obvious riposte suggests itself: *hogwash!* Of course "pro-family" groups claim to be democratic, one could say; no one would listen to them if they advertised themselves as homophobic bigots. That doesn't mean that their claims to democratic ideals carry any weight.

But then, what does it mean for a concept like *democracy* or *liberty* to "carry weight"? What is the criterion here? Perhaps some broad standards are possible: if a military dictatorship were to label itself a democracy, the absence of elections under its rule would undermine its claim. The Mayday Rally's claims, though, offer no such clear-cut mendacity. The rally's speakers did not lie, for instance, when they stated that anti-gay-marriage statutes in various states passed with populist majorities, and they were technically correct to point out that court challenges to those statutes effectively seek to overturn the will of the people. A progressive counter-point, of course, would argue that liberal democracies balance a protection of minority rights with recognition of majority will; as was the case with *Brown v. Board of Education*, the former can legitimately trump the latter. But such a point-counterpoint debate plays out on a field presupposing the mutual legitimacy of competing claims, a field removed from the obvious dissonance of the dictatorship-democracy example mentioned earlier. The rally's "will of the people" rhetoric may not win the debate, but neither can it be disqualified as inappropriate.

Understand: I do not endorse the rally's claims that its stances embody a democratic or civil rights tradition. Nor do I believe in the equal validity of pro-gay and pro-family claims to liberatory discourses. I consider pro-gay goals not just *different* from pro-family stances but *better*, more solidly in line with discourses of liberty and justice for all. But pro-family advocates feel exactly the same way about the superiority of their claims to the democratic tradition. I can argue against these claims, but what I cannot do is win the debate once and for all by holding up some clear, unambiguous standard for defining democracy or social justice just as I do. This reality, however, gets occluded by an obligatory critical generosity toward progressive activism. If the words I use to describe Tim Miller's performances situate him automatically into the warp and woof of True Democratic Good, I miss the fact that the democratic fabric contains other threads, other patterns that pull against my own beliefs.

As an intervention, then, I recommend seeing progressive watchwords not (only) as approving descriptors of progressive activist performances but (also) as essentially contested concepts. Long a staple of political science discourse, the notion of essentially contested concepts comes from the work of midcentury historian W. B. Gallie. After studying debates around concepts like *social justice, the Christian tradition, work of art,* and *democracy,* Gallie grew dissatisfied with the assumption that such terms had only one proper definition or that such terms were practically useless due to terminal imprecision. What if, he argued, perpetual debate over a term's meaning might itself form an intrinsic aspect of its identity? Thus, he offers essentially contested concepts: ideas for which "there is no clearly definable general use . . . which can be set up as the correct or standard use."[17]

Gallie specifies a number of criteria by which an essentially contested term may be distinguished from complicated or misunderstood terms, on the one hand, or from a term whose meaning has changed slowly over time, on the other.[18] First, essentially contested concepts are *appraisive* as well as descriptive. That is, they refer to a vaguely identifiable core of meanings (e.g., democracies are not autocratic dictatorships), and they impart some value judgment on the object, event, or person to which they are linked.[19] This value may be generally positive (*social justice*), negative (*totalitarian*), or either depending upon context (*socialism, communism, capitalism*).[20] Second, essentially contested concepts encompass a complex ensemble of component meanings, the arrangement and ranking of which will vary.[21] An array of moving parts contributes to the total meaning of a concept like *democracy* (elections, bureaucracy, civil rights, and popular sovereignty, just to name a few). The eponymous contests that redefine the concept in question consist of perpetual struggles over the relative arrangement or significance of those components. Finally, since the concept's internal components remain open to rearrangement, the concept itself is persistently and passionately contested. Gallie describes contestants wielding essentially contested concepts both aggressively and defensively.[22] Such contestation appears to take place both diachronically (between one historical moment and another) and synchronically (within any single moment).[23]

How might activist performance historiography change were it to incorporate a framework of essentially contested concepts? I do not believe, first of all, that historians would need to relinquish the idea of critical generosity altogether. I am convinced that terms like liberty, democracy, and community function as essentially contested concepts; nevertheless, I continue to use those words (and the activist models and theories built on them) to describe and contextualize—and at times endorse and affirm—performances of queer artists like Miller. To acknowledge that certain terms are essentially contested does not invalidate Román's critique of objectivist historiography. Historiography does not consist of soulless data collection and reportage, nor can the historian pretend to write from a political no-space (*utopia*). I endorse arguments by Román and Dolan that scholarship can and should participate in larger initiatives for social change. As a historian of activist performance, I participate in building, constructively criticizing, and strengthening a legacy of change that I as a progressively minded gay man pursue.

What does change with the added framework of essentially contested concepts, however, is the degree of awareness I as a scholar must practice when historicizing the stances toward which I display critical generosity (or, indeed, those toward which I feel critical animosity). Representing Miller's historical context, for example, cannot consist of naming the faceless forces of oppression-intolerance against which Miller fights, assuming the pure "rightness" of Miller's causes and of my support for them. Historicizing Miller's performances must instead consist of relating, in synchronic and diachronic dimensions, the dynamic field of contested and contesting configurations of *democracy-rights-community-sexuality*. Recognizing this contested field, for instance, might move me to ask questions of Miller other than simply, "What are his strategies for advancing the same-sex marriage cause?" and "Are those strategies effective?" I might also ask, "When in the history of gay activism did 'same-sex marriage' become thinkable at all as a political goal for GLBT people?" or "How did same-sex marriage become the cause par excellence of U.S.-based GLBT activism given that previous generations of GLBT activists rejected marriage as a heteronormative practice incompatible with gay liberation?"[24] Viewing power words like *democracy* or *community* as essentially contested also reminds me that my encounters with nonprogressive activisms must (despite the title of this article) avoid demonizing such viewpoints. Flattening the complexity and heterogeneity of movements opposed to GLBT rights through the use of terms like *anti-gay*, *bigoted*, or *homophobic* (or, indeed, even *nonprogressive* or *conservative*) certainly reinforces the moral authority of activists I represent as opposing such movements. But such a representation would also stray from critical generosity toward GLBT activism into the mire of bad scholarship. Opposition to same-sex marriage takes on many forms, many of which are themselves mutually antagonistic. To lump into one category the "ex-gay" movement's understanding of homosexuality as a mental disorder and more radically fundamentalist "gays are reprobate pedophiles" rhetoric, for example, is not to practice critical generosity toward pro-gay causes but to spread progressive propaganda.

Acknowledging that the configurations of liberty, democracy, and community Miller and I espouse are not the only such configurations active on the political field does not, however, mean that I portray that configuration as no better or worse than alternatives from history or contemporary society. Using Gallie's framework does not condemn critics and activists to impotent relativism. As Mouffe argues, liberal democracy operates via paradox.[25] The condition sine qua non of democratic politics is contestation over the meaning and application of core values and assumptions (e.g., rights, sovereignty, justice, fairness, distribution of resources). A system without disagreement about the meaning of core concepts would be definitionally undemocratic. But democratic partisans aim for the eventual *decontestation* of the issues they fight for. That is, activists strive to ensure that their "take" on a particular configuration of democratic values (e.g., adult women should enjoy the right to vote, or marriage should be open to same-sex couples) achieves so thorough a level of acceptance that the issue ceases to become contested at all.[26] Democracy demands that the reality of contestation among parties and the single-mindedness of parties to decontest issues both obtain. Using essentially contested concepts allows historians to balance an acknowledgment of disagreements about an issue or concept with a generosity (or antipathy) toward the causes of the activist performances they study.

I should mark, in closing, that my commitment to critical generosity in scholarship is itself open to contestation. Not all historians subscribe to a practice of indicating relationships between scholar and subject, advocating instead a more objective, less personal model of scholarship to uphold as a guiding ideal for researchers. Nor is the line between "soulless reportage" and "gossipy memoir" always as clear as I may have suggested here; past a certain point, judgments about where a critically generous discourse strays into purely subjective reflection vary from reader to reader. Scholarship—or at least the idea of "good scholarship"—operates to a degree as an essentially contested concept itself, defined in part by ongoing debates, divergent practices, and ever-shifting trends. Within this contested field, however, I stand by my own preference for critically generous scholarship of activist performance, a preference that stems from my commitment to radical democratic philosophies. These move me to extend liberal democratic considerations—to treat seriously as equal participants—those viewpoints with which I disagree both in life and in my scholarship.[27]

Filtering activist scholarship through the perspective of essentially contested concepts enhances critical generosity. It reminds scholars that the political tasks of contestation (and, perhaps, decontestation) embodied in activist performances are in fact *work*—hard, long, self-questioning, and uncertain—rather than the sure-and-right march of justice. It forces scholars to treat allies and opponents carefully, reimagining the democratic field as one on which contestants are often devils to each other. In such a field, surrender is not an option. But sympathy for a fellow devil might make the contest more productive.

NOTES

1. David Román, *Acts of Intervention: Performance, Gay Culture, and AIDS* (Bloomington: Indiana University Press, 1998), xxvi.

2. Román, *Acts of Intervention*, xxvi–xxvii. Román clarifies that critical generosity does not mean uncritical propaganda, heaping praise on the performances one studies without investigating instances in which the performances did not succeed (xxviii).

3. Ernesto Laclau and Chantal Mouffe introduce this term in their 1985 *Hegemony and Socialist Strategy*, identifying equality for all and rights for all as the twin guarantees that underwrite the legitimacy of liberal democratic regimes. Actual democratic governments, however, fail to realize these guarantees as fully or deeply as they ought. Democracies must thus be radicalized and pluralized, pushed to live up to the ideals they espouse (*Hegemony and Socialist Strategy: Towards a Radical Democratic Politics*, 2nd ed. [New York: Verso, 2001], 176). Mouffe's subsequent work expands upon this notion (see Chantal Mouffe, *The Democratic Paradox* [New York: Verso, 2000]). See also my work on the "God Hates Fags" protest of the Reverend Fred Phelps (John Fletcher, "Ten-Foot Pole Historiography: Liberal Democracy, Ideological Difference, and Despicable Acts," in *Querying Difference in Theatre History*, ed. Scott Magelssen and Ann Haugo [Newcastle upon Tyne: Cambridge Scholars Publishing, 2007]).

4. One such exception would be the "Vanguards of the Right" seminar session in the 2008 meeting of the American Society for Theatre Research.

5. Kathleen M. Blee, "Ethnographies of the Far Right." *Journal of Contemporary Ethnography* 36, no. 2 (2007): 119–28, 120.

6. Specifically, Miller uses the metaphor of the "glory box" (the Australian equivalent of a hope chest) to "discover" and reenact treasured moments from both his romantic past (charming stories of crushes and boyfriends) and his romantic future (a fictional narrative about flying to the United States with his real-life Australian partner, Alistair). See John Fletcher, "Identity and Agonism: Tim Miller, Cornerstone, and the Politics of Community-Based Theatre," *Theatre Topics* 13, no. 2 (2003): 189–203.

7. See Jill Dolan's *Utopia in Performance: Finding Hope in the Theatre* (Ann Arbor: University of Michigan Press, 2005) for her full argument about the utopian performative.

8. Of course, my article does not simply heap praise upon Miller. The political, cultural, and performance studies frameworks I invoke and define establish a critical field on which I can position and evaluate Miller's work by a set of standards that I suggest are appropriate to it. For instance, within that field I can and do suggest instances where *Glory Box*'s aspiration as community-based theater falls short of representing particular parts of the queer community. But such criticism is still a far cry from arguing that Miller is anti-democratic or fascist. Miller may not cover every base at once (no one performance could), but he's at least playing in my ballpark.

9. Given popular stereotypes of people who hold such beliefs (fostered in part, it must be said, by certain prominent conservative spokespeople), it's difficult even to picture someone who is both anti-gay and an active social change scholar, let alone anti-gay and interested in historicizing a queer solo artist's activist performances. This imaginative roadblock itself bespeaks the degree to which the field of activist performance scholarship silently presumes a certain set of (progressive) political beliefs, as well as attesting to the rarity of straying outside of one's own political framework to study activist performers opposed to that frame.

10. I trust I need not wade into grand debates about the ontological status of historical events and their representations to assert that a partisan screed (pro-gay, anti-gay, or otherwise) does not qualify as scholarship. I appeal here to a present-

day critical consensus in the humanities that expects historians, at minimum, to refrain from misrepresentation or calumny and to strive for accurate, complete contextualization. Meeting such expectations, I argue, constitutes a base-level criterion of acceptable historiographic work, not critical generosity.

11. Most of the information on the Mayday for Marriage Rally's history, backing, and lineup was available from the event's Web site, now defunct: http://www.maydayformarriage.com. The Internet Archive's "Wayback Machine" helpfully archives the Web site's contents. I also reference the three-disk DVD of the event, containing all of the speakers' contributions.

12. "Pastor's Resource Guide," Mayday for Marriage, http://www.maydayfor marriage.com, 2 Nov. 2005, accessed 19 Mar. 2009; archived at http://web.archive .org/web/*/ http://www.maydayformarriage.com.

13. Indeed, many speakers at the rally (notably Alan Chambers and Anne Graham Lotz) detailed—and professed grief over—the ways that pro-family forces had unfairly demonized gays and lesbians (when what they really needed was compassion and healing) (*Mayday for Marriage Rally*, 15 Oct. 2004, DVD [Dove Cassettes Conference Recording and Duplication, 2004]).

14. In his speech, Southern Baptist Convention president Richard Land referenced the "hallowed ground" on which the rally took place, characterizing (inaccurately) the Mall as a "liftoff point" for the civil rights movement and expressing hope that this rally would also be a "liftoff point" for the pro-family justice movement (Richard Land, speech, *Mayday for Marriage Rally*, 15 Oct. 2004).

15. James Dobson, speech, *Mayday for Marriage Rally*, 15 Oct. 2004.

16. Ken Hutcherson, speech, *Mayday for Marriage Rally*, 15 Oct. 2004. Hutcherson had previously established himself as a critic of the gay and lesbian rights movement's claims to civil rights discourse in an editorial published in the *Seattle Times*: "Gays Are Not the Nation's New African Americans," 29 Mar. 2004 (http://archives.seattletimes.nwsource.com/cgi-bin/texis.cgi/ web/vortex/display?slug=hutcherson29&date=20040329&query=hutcherson, accessed 18 Apr. 2005).

17. W. B. Gallie, "Essentially Contested Concepts," *Proceedings of the Aristotelian Society, New Series* 56 (1955–56): 167–98,168.

18. Gallie's seven criteria (in his original order, which I did not replicate in my text and which are not understood to be ranked) are (1) apprasiveness, (2) internal complexity, (3) diverse describability, (4) persistent openness, (5) reciprocal recognition of the concept's contestedness by parties, (6) reference to an exemplar or core that anchors the concept, and (7) the progressiveness (i.e., productivity) of continued contestation ("Essentially Contested Concepts," 171–80). David Collier, Fernando Daniel Hidalgo, and Andra Olivia Maciuceanu provide a detailed overview of both Gallie's original conception and its key interlocutors and critics ("Essentially Contested Concepts: Debates and Applications,'"*Journal of Political Ideologies* 11, no. 3 [2006]: 211–46).

19. Gallie, "Essentially Contested Concepts," 171.

20. Collier, Hidalgo, and Maciuceanu, "Essentially Contested Concepts: Debates," 216.

21. Gallie, "Essentially Contested Concepts," 171–72.

22. Gallie, "Essentially Contested Concepts," 172.

23. This dual (synchronic and diachronic) dimension of contest, as well as Gallie's other criteria, moves me to prefer his framework over related models of complicated or debatable terms, such as Anthony Cohen's "hurrah words" or Raymond Williams's "keywords." See Anthony Cohen, *The Symbolic Construction of Community* (New York: Tavistock, 1985); Raymond Williams, *Keywords: A Vocabulary of Culture and Society*, 2nd ed. (New York: Oxford University Press, 1983).

24. Some GLBT activisms, such as the "Gay Shame" movement, still do reject marriage. See Mattilda (Matt Bernstein Sycamore), ed., *That's Revolting! Queer Strategies to Resist Assimilation* (Baltimore: Soft Skull Press, 2004).

25. Here Mouffe's arguments about what she calls "the democratic paradox" parallel arguments by Jacques Rancière about dissensus or disagreement as the prime criterion of democratic politics. See Mouffe, *Democratic Paradox;* Jacques Rancière, *Disagreement: Politics and Philosophy*, trans. Julie Rose (Minneapolis: University of Minnesota Press, 1997).

26. As Collier, Hidalgo, and Maciuceanu point out, such decontestation does occasionally occur. Woman suffrage in the United States provides one such example; this was once a contested issue, but now no one in the United States seriously debates the notion of whether adult women should enjoy the right to vote. We might call such a shift from political contestedness to political common sense the achievement of hegemony in Antonio Gramsci's sense.

27. A more radical brand of activism, however, might espouse wholly different modes of identifying, interacting with, or ignoring political opponents, practicing a politics—and a scholarship—in which critical generosity plays no part.

PART III

Historiography for a
New Millennium

Theater History and Digital Historiography

SARAH BAY-CHENG ◞

In a blog post from December 1, 2008, director Anne Bogart notes a recent trend in museum behavior: people taking pictures of art with their mobile phones. Disturbed, she observes: "The phone seems to act as a medium between the observer and the observed, cutting off direct experience. Perhaps the phenomenon of cell phone photos speaks to a certain lackadaisical attitude towards both making and 'consuming' art. And so I have decided to give thought and words to what troubles me."[1] After reflection, Bogart concludes that what bothers her most is a lack of engagement between the viewer and art experience, and the ultimate act of possessing or consuming the art as a personal object. As she puts it, "the impulse to take these photos is an attempt by the viewers not only to distance themselves from the potential danger and violence of the present moment but also it allows them to store the experience for a safer moment in an uncertain future."[2]

In her concern about mobile-phone art photography (not to be confused with mobile-phone capture *as* art photography), Bogart articulates some of the core issues in contemporary debates over theater, performance, and documentation. She regards the mediating effect of technology as an interruption that cuts the viewer off from the direct experience of the artwork, what performance and theater studies have often identified as "presence." But she also objects to the viewer's experience of the artwork on the viewer's own terms, one Bogart pejoratively identifies as safer, and though she doesn't say so explicitly, Bogart's use of the verb "store" suggests the "consumption" of an experience that ought not to be absorbed as such. By storing the image for later, safer viewing, the viewer trades the lived, potentially violent moment in front of the artwork for a souvenir. Implied in Bogart's description is the ignorance of the camera-phone-wielding viewer who sees only the object for reproduction later, not the experience unfolding in time, and who, perhaps unwittingly, violates the ephemerality of the moment.

Diana Taylor has argued that "writing has paradoxically come to stand in for and against embodiment. . . . Now, on the brink of a digital revolution that both utilizes and threatens to displace writing, the body again seems poised to disappear in a virtual space that eludes embodiment."[3] Certainly "the virtual" troubles embodiment, but we must remember that digital technology is itself an embodied practice.[4] Taylor herself acknowledges the possibility that the digital may offer a different vision of the archive, though she approaches the topic with calculated wariness: "Other systems of transmission—like the digital—complicate any simple binary formulation [between archive and repertoire]. Yet it too readily falls into a binary, with the written and archival constituting hegemonic power and the repertoire providing the anti-hegemonic challenge."[5] Rather than contest Taylor's statement, I would like to trouble it by suggesting that the digital neither eclipses nor negates embodiment, but changes our relationship to the archive and thus constitutes a kind of digital repertoire that is closer to Taylor's formulation (both formally and politically) than prior documents.

Accepting that we are now in the "digital moment" of an "information age," what is the relation of digital documentation to theatrical performance? To what extent does digital documentation change the way we approach theater history and performance's ephemerality? And, perhaps more significantly, what effect do these digital records have on the performances themselves? In this essay, I'd like to sketch some of the key issues confronting theater historians of the future and to outline an approach to digital historiography today. We cannot, I argue, simply dismiss the digital records as inadequate and hegemonic, nor should we rely on documentation so "bad" that it makes us wish we had seen the "real thing." Indeed, as digital technologies infiltrate time-based performance, it may be that the best seat in the house will be from behind a computer screen. Do we really lose the essence of theater in this digital transfer, or are we simply differently positioned as theater historians?

Since Walter Benjamin's celebrated essay "The Work of Art in the Age of Mechanical Reproduction" (1936), historians have wrestled with the relations between emerging technology and its implications for history. Perhaps the most widely cited essay on the relations between culture and technology, Benjamin's considerations of presence, aura, and authenticity in the mechanically recorded document (namely, photography and film) have assumed particular relevance in the digital age. Advances in digital recording devices (DV cameras, smartphones with video), methods of distribution (YouTube, Flickr), and digital performance archives (Brunel University's Digital Performance Archive, rhizome.org, Brockett's Digital

Bibliography) have made the digital presence of theater and performance more widely accessible to an online audience. Recording technologies are quickly growing alongside textual records of performance and eventually may replace them. In place of script marginalia and first-person descriptions, theater scholars can increasingly turn to video documentation, now available not only on expensive DVDs and rapidly deteriorating bootleg videotapes but through online streaming archives and YouTube. Given the sheer volume of material regularly produced and disseminated, it is not difficult to imagine that moving images, over time, may come to eclipse or even to replace other documents of performance: photographs, individual accounts and reviews, even play scripts themselves. Consider Suzan-Lori Parks's national theater project "365 Days/365 Plays," which required participants to record and upload documentation of the work for which the festival (and Parks, individually) retained copyright ownership.[6] Such developments require new attention to the digital records of performance and to their deployment as artifacts of historical performance, or "videocy," as termed by Denise Varney and Rachel Fensham.[7] In my own work, I've noted some ways we might attend to the moving image as a distorted but nevertheless effective or thick record of performance.[8]

These recording technologies have caused, however, a kind of anxiety as the documentation threatens to replace the event or even, as Philip Auslander suggests, to undermine the very ontology of the live performance as such. While some critics, most notably Auslander and Roger Copeland, have criticized the privileging of live performance over mediated reproductions as "sheer bourgeois sentimentality," many others have defended and defined the essence of performance by its ephemerality.[9] Often, recordings of any kind are perceived as an essential threat to the performance itself. As Nick Kaye contends, documentation "invariably presents itself as threatening to reinstate those stabilities and terms this very move toward 'performance' challenges."[10] Eugenio Barba makes it even clearer when he explicitly pits theater performance as a defense against the tyranny of digital records: "In the age of electronic memory, or films, and of reproducibility, theatre performance also defines itself through the work that living memory, which is not a museum but metamorphosis, is obliged to do."[11] In this assessment, theater is theater because it changes, because it lives and dies. To create an unchangeable, immortal document (a monument, as Foucault suggests) is to violate the living memory that is theater.

But why this resistance to the digital in theater and performance studies, especially when so many digital records are available to theater scholars? Is it only sentimentality, or are there other deeper concerns? One possible answer is the traditionally hegemonic power of the archive to shape the perpetual reception of performance over time. What happens if we accept that the digital record offers us a unique insight into theater history rather than an obscured view of a moment passed?

To address such a question, I posit that Taylor's repertoire articulates the potential for theater's digital historiography. Although Taylor approaches the digital cautiously, her formulation of the repertoire, with its emphasis on networks, mutability, social contexts, and embodiment, may (ironically) provide a useful model for digital theater historiography. Taylor describes a dynamic, responsive, and evolving repertoire as embodied memory in contrast to the disembodied archive. Whereas the archival memory "exists as documents, maps, literary text, letter, archeological remains, bones, videos, films, CDs, all those items supposedly resistant to change," the repertoire "enacts embodied memory: performances, gestures, orality, movement, dance, singing."[12] If we follow Taylor's and others' archival critiques, then, ideally theatrical performance will be preserved not as "dead texts" or documents, but as a kind of a organism: "a living memory," "a living history," a "tissue of quotations," and a "body-to-body transmission."[13]

At first blush, it would appear that documentation of any kind, be it text, photograph, or moving image, would infringe upon this living history of theater. But if we look closely at either Joseph Roach's surrogation of performance or Taylor's repertoire, we find resonances of the moving image and, more significantly for historiography, the echoes of the digital as it becomes assumed into daily life. The relations between people and their technologies have never been clearly divided, and while the online virtual community Second Life continues its popularity, bioartists like Stelarc and Eduardo Kac continue to integrate new media transmissions into their work and even their own bodies (cf. Stelarc's 2007 "third ear," an electronically functional ear surgically implanted with living tissue in his forearm). The extensive relations between embodied engagement and digital technologies are beyond the scope of this essay, but one can certainly point to writing by N. Katherine Hayles and Donna Haraway for nuanced considerations of evolving dynamics between bodies and technology. Among digital archivists, the question of electronic art or "net-art" ephemerality is as potent in digital domains as in theatrical ones.[14] The events of electronic interactive literature, as well as massive amounts of digital data, are constantly under threat of technological obsolescence, erasure, and other forms of loss. Taylor herself acknowledges the potential of the digital to disrupt the binary of archive and repertoire, although she asserts the necessity of presence in apprehending the work: "the repertoire requires presence: people participate in the production and the reproduction of knowledge by 'being there.'"

But what does "being there" mean in a digital context?

While some art historians and cultural critics argue that one must have been present to fully appreciate (and to write about) performance art, few theater historians apologize for missing the premiere of *Hamlet*. Theater history has become accustomed to, even celebratory of its ephemerality, our lack of being there. For some, there is a political power in this impermanence, as in Peggy Phelan's oft-cited ontological definition of performance as "that which disappears."[15] For others, the ephemerality allows for a different, more fluid sense of theater and performance history, contained not only in the concrete material traces but also in the reiterations of performance, including "restored behavior," ritual, and "surrogation," and even from the dramatic text as "a site of agency."[16] The necessary reiteration of performance to exist in and as history affects the construction of the archive and the historian's relationship to it, as Rebecca Schneider argues in "Archive: Performance Remains" and as David Román argues in his reading of Taylor's repertoire "not as the archive's antagonistic opposite, but as a separate repository of cultural memory, [that] allows for that memory to be reembodied, reperformed, and thus restored."[17]

We need not separate digital archives from these forms of reembodied performance archives. Indeed, unlike the models provided by film, television, and video documentation, digital archives may ironically get us closer to the preservation of cultural performance and memory that historians such as Roach, Taylor, and Román articulate. If film and video are of the archive, then the digital is more closely related to the repertoire. Unlike these earlier forms of media that are fixed, didactic, and linear, digital technologies are fundamentally constructed as mobile, interconnected, and pervasive. If, as Matthew Causey argues, "performance has taken on the ontology of the technological," then current performance not only admits but also *requires* a mode of theater historiography that takes a digital approach to performance, rather than an archival one.[18]

What might this digital historiography look like? Despite Taylor's stated discomfort with the uses of the digital and its easy slip back into hegemonic practices, digital technologies may have more to offer progressive cultural practices and the repertoires of performance and theater history than first appears. One important difference between emerging digital networks and past formulations of the archive is its potentially open access to the many needed to create it. One of the objections to the archive as such has been not the collection, per se, but the way its formation is determined (i.e., the choice of materials to include and to exclude); such determination makes up an archive that necessarily determines singular and potentially exclusionary visions of the future. Most existing performance archives, such as the Billy Rose Theatre Collection, work on a similar model. However, digital technologies that intersect emerging social network theory and cybernetics (e.g., Web 2.0) offer new models of distributed intelligence for information collection, distribution, and preservation.[19] The term "Web 2.0," referring to the proliferation of interactive Internet sites and social networking, was first articulated by Tim O'Reilly in 2004 and widely disseminated through his blog in 2005. O'Reilly's vision of Web 2.0 hinges on the possibility of "creating network effects through an 'architecture of participation,' and going beyond the page metaphor of Web 1.0 to deliver rich user experiences."[20]

Let's consider for a moment the "architecture of participation" alongside Taylor's repertoire. Taylor's repertoire "requires presence: people participate in the production and reproduction of knowledge by 'being there,' being a part of the transmission."[21] This might seem to preclude the relevance of digital records that, after all, mediate at best and may even prohibit our presence. And yet, in the digital sphere, presence is defined not by physical touch but through avenues of participation. In a digitally connected and networked world, participation creates presence. In a digital context, people do not participate by being there; people are "there" by participating.

A quick glance at popular literature reveals that this sense of presence has already penetrated our cultural sense of the digital. The term "online presence," for instance, generates more than four million results from a Google search. If we shift our thinking away from exclusively physical presence, we find that digital technologies offer different yet complementary ways of "being there," of being part of the transmission and reproduction of knowledge. For example, virtual reality strives to foster a sense of presence in the user, a sense of being there in the digital world that has become the sin qua non of interactive fiction, online gaming, and social media sites.

Within a larger rubric of digital presence, we can apply Taylor's being there both to the embodied performances and to the digital traces left by mobile, digital technologies. Such works can blur the boundary between creator, participant, and digital presence, as in Iraqi artist Wafaa Bilal's *Domestic Tension* (2008). In this interactive digital installation, Bilal confined himself to a gallery space outfitted with living accommodations and surveillance cameras. To draw attention to the lack of privacy in times of war, Internet viewers had twenty-four-hour video access to Bilal as he lived in the space with only a bed, a computer, and a few tables. Also included in the space was a paintball gun that online viewers could control, choosing if they wished to shoot at Bilal. While in the room for thirty-one days, Bilal kept a video weblog, or vlog. Watching the videos, one can see the conditions in which he lives and hear the oppressive, repetitive, but unpredictable sound of the paintball gun firing. As Bilal's installation makes disturbingly clear, digital access *is* digital presence. With a globe wired for rapid data transfer, all digital presence has material consequences, even (perhaps especially) among those without digital access themselves. Bilal's performance was only visible through the Internet, and the participation was only possible at a digital distance. But, watching the video and the physical impact of the paintballs as they pound his body, one cannot deny the presence of this performance for either performer or viewer.

Elsewhere, Taylor notes that "actions that are repertoire do not remain the same. The repertoire both keeps and transforms choreographies of meaning."[22] So too do digital records. In addition to the most concrete examples of digital ephemera, such as obsolete technologies, incompatible operating systems, and any number of technical problems involved in maintaining digital records (problems that are striking similar to performance), the experience of digital engagement changes over time. In their *Remediation*, Jay David Bolter and Richard Grusin articulate a definition strikingly similar to Taylor's notion of the repertoire. Bolter and Grusin note that contemporary media operates according to a bifurcated structure that vacillates between "the transparent presentation of the real and the enjoyment of the opacity of media themselves."[23] The digital, like the repertoire, is always in tension between its fixed and fluid qualities. In part because new modes of technology are always developing, our sense of a particular digital interaction necessarily changes over time even as some of the formal devices (e.g., the keyboard) remain the same.[24] The device, game, or software that appears so new may, in only a few years, feel sluggish, outmoded, obsolete. While this planned obsolescence of new technology fits perfectly into capitalist business models, such shifts in our participation with the digital record also affect our relation to the digital experience itself. Taylor includes sports and dance as examples that preserve and evolve form and meaning through reenactment, but we could perhaps add digital performances and even online and pervasive games to this dynamic.

The development of new modes of digital exchange, like the repertoire, has a reciprocal impact on theater and performance. Although first used simply to record and preserve performances, video rapidly became assimilated into theatrical performance. Early experiments in this, such as the Wooster Group's use of video (a familiar touchstone for digital media and theater studies), began to record and replay the recordings within the space of the theatrical production. Videos of Ron Vawter, for example, came to function as both archival footage (the video record of his performance, particularly after his death) and as material in the "live" performance. As they branched out into digital contexts (including their collaboration with media artist Zoe Beloff in 1999), the records of performance became as dynamic as the evolution of the performance itself.[25] The fluidity and random access of digital technologies allow for the recording devices to become responsive to the performance just as the performance may respond to digital devices. Once absorbed within distributed social networks and digital networked technology, these records take on lives of their own as they are reworked, remixed, and remediated from one viewer to the next. Take any one of thousands of mash-ups from YouTube to see just how digital content may become part of a larger performance landscape.[26]

What impact might this have on theater historiography? Often, when we talk about performance and theater, we are discussing very different things. After all, most of what that which we think of as theater still happens in buildings exclusively defined for that purpose. Theatrical performances draw on established, written texts and are often performed without overt media influence. While we might accept much of this definition, parts are becoming incomplete and inadequate. Auslander's *Liveness* points in many ways to the media saturation of even the most traditional Broadway theaters (e.g., the ubiquity of microphones), and David Saltz points to interactive technology as similar in its goals to the creators of Happenings and environmental theater in the 1960s.[27] I was curious to see the most recent revival of Sondheim's *Sunday in the Park with George* at the Roundabout Theatre in New York, performed with a mostly electronic orchestra positioned in such a way that the actors required a monitor to see the conductor for essential cues. Such configurations are hardly unique, as digital scores have become increasingly popular, just as more seats and fewer musicians have become more profitable. If one were commenting on such productions in the future, would not the recording of this monitor be useful?

Theater history has much to gain from the diversity of digital records, and it has much to offer in return. Current debates among those concerned with new media preservation are similarly centered on questions of ephemerality and disappearance. How will events, performances, installations, net-art, and so on, be preserved when the technologies become obsolete? Theater history has a long tradition of "not being there" as we piece together images, records, and remembrances of the past. If we attend to the wider context, as Roach and Taylor advocate, then we must note the ways in which performances are passed down, reiterated, and performatively remembered, literally pieced back together by new performing bodies (as in Román's "archival drag"). This is little different from Bolter and Grusin's observation, derived from Marshall McLuhan's insights, that all new media contains and remediates prior media forms, and by no coincidence do they describe a "genealogy of media" in much the same way that Roach defines a "genealogy of performance." The genealogical construct in digital media is deeply and intrinsically related to Marvin Carlson's argument that theater is always haunted by the theatrical past. Our memories of the theater, the performances on stages and screens, *and* our relations to new media forms, both participatory and not, are always informed by their individual pasts *and by each other.* We can no longer hold theater history to the side without taking into account the digital records of past performances and the digital circulation of images in the present.

I'll conclude by revisiting the example Bogart raises in her disdain for image-catching in the museum. Let's imagine that instead of being lackadaisical about the unnamed artwork, the person taking the picture on her phone does have an engaged, even profound experience while looking at the artwork. So moved, she takes a picture on her phone and instantly uploads it to her weblog with a brief comment about her experience. She then links this to her Facebook page so that all of her 208 friends can see the image. Several of these friends download the image for themselves; one posts it on his own blog with a witty bit of text that recontextualizes and transforms the meaning of the image, in part as a response to his friend's original response. Someone following this blog sees the picture and compares it to her own experience of looking at the artwork last week when the exhibit first opened; she notes this in a review of the work that she's writing for an online journal. Someone else sees this link and copies it into a video project that remixes webcontent for a new installation opening at the same museum the following month. At that later exhibit, our original viewer recognizes the image and takes another picture.

Though fantastic and condensed for dramatic effect (and assuming a creative commons copyright license), all of these are common, everyday occurrences as those with digital access experience, record, and transmit images, impressions, and experiences. All of the actions described have clear parallels and histories in print culture (diaries, letters, adaptations, appropriations), but the speed and random access of digital technologies make not only the objects (in this example, the artwork) transferrable, but also the lived and embodied experiences recorded and transmitted in real time across space. Although we might be tempted to siphon off theater from such circulation, it will not be for long. As theaters upload images, videos, and texts; as theater-goers take pictures of theater performances; as theater includes digital content that can be perceived and preserved only in digital form; as theater streams performances "live" via Web technologies, theater history will need to take into account a greater range of moments in the theater than a seemingly uniform seat positioned eighth row, center. In the movement of images, the circulation of performances, and the haunting of media as we attend the theater, digital historiography takes on the characteristics of the repertoire and thus provides a way of looking at theater anew. Perhaps no single view is ever complete. Something is indeed lost in every record, just as memory itself is incomplete. But digital historiography allows for both a fuller understanding and a clearer articulation of those performance memories, including multiple forms of presence, all of which offers us a diversity of knowledges and perspectives that may extend our sense of being there.

NOTES

1. Anne Bogart, "December 1st, 2008 | Anne's Blog—Blog | SEE | siti.collectivex.com," group blog, *SEE—Siti Extended Ensemble*, Dec. 1, 2008, http://siti.col lectivex.com/post/december-1st-2008.

2. Bogart, "December 1st, 2008."

3. Diana Taylor, *The Archive and the Repertoire: Performing Cultural Memory in the Americas* (Durham: Duke University Press, 2003), 16.

4. Steven E. Jones, e.g., notes that video-game play "is necessarily a hybrid experience, bodily as well as mental" ("Second Life, Video Games, and the Social Text," *PMLA* 124, no. 1 [2009]: 270), and N. Katherine Hayles argues for an understanding of digital interactivity as a mutual engagement of text, technology, and human participation in which "people and machines are both embodied" (*Electronic Literature: New Horizons for the Literary*, Ward Phillips Lecture [South Bend: University of Notre Dame Press, 2008], 129).

5. Taylor, *Archive and the Repertoire*, 22.

6. 365 National Festival, "Participant Letter of Agreement," email to participants, Nov. 29, 2006. The actual language of the document stipulated the required documentation as a work-for-hire, although some groups were able to retain some limited rights to the images: "Further, Participant agrees to provide documentation (in the form of digital or conventional photography) of performances from all designated plays within the assigned Production Week. These photos are to be, sub-

ject to any union requirements, uploaded onto the 365 National Festival website and used in other 365 Festival publicity. All such photographs shall be a 'work for hire' by the 365 Festival, and the 365 Festival shall control all rights therein. Participant agrees to execute, or cause to be executed, any documents needed to secure 365 Festival's ownership of said photographs."

7. Denise Varney and Rachel Fensham, "More-and-Less-Than: Liveness, Video Recording, and the Future of Performance," *New Theatre Quarterly* 16, no. 1 (2004): 88–96.

8. I take this notion of a "thick description" from Patrice Pavis, who cites anthropologist Clifford Geertz. See Patrice Pavis, *Analyzing Performance: Theater, Dance, and Film*, trans. David Williams (Ann Arbor: University of Michigan Press, 2003), 294; Sarah Bay-Cheng, "Theatre Squared: Theatre History in the Age of Media," *Theatre Topics* 17, no. 1 (2007): 37–50.

9. Roger Copeland, "The Presence of Mediation," *TDR: The Drama Review* 34, no. 4 (1990): 42.

10. Nick Kaye, "Live Art: Definition and Documentation," *Contemporary Theatre Review* 2, no. 2 (1994): 6.

11. Eugenio Barba, "Efermaele: 'That Which Will Be Said Afterwards,'" *TDR: The Drama Review* 36, no. 2 (1992): 78.

12. Taylor, *Archive and the Repertoire*, 19, 20.

13. Barba, "Efermaele," 78; Joseph Roach, *Cities of the Dead: Circum-Atlantic Performance* (New York: Columbia University Press, 1996), 25; Marvin Carlson, *The Haunted Stage: Theatre as Memory Machine* (Ann Arbor: University of Michigan Press, 2003), 5; Rebecca Schneider, "Archives: Performance Remains," *Performance Research* 6, no. 2 (2001): 105.

14. In 2009, e.g., the listserv empyre invited discussion on "Participatory Art: New Media and the Archival Trace." See Roach, *Cities of the Dead*, 25.

15. Schneider, "Archives," 105.

16. Richard Schechner, *Essays on Performance Theory* (New York: Routledge, 1988); Roach, *Cities of the Dead*; Taylor, *Archive and the Repertoire*; W. B. Worthen, "Antigone's Bones," *TDR: The Drama Review* 53, no. 3 (2008): 10–33.

17. David Román, *Performance in America: Contemporary U.S. Culture and the Performing Arts* (Durham and London: Duke University Press, 2005), 139.

18. Matthew Causey, "The Screen Test of the Double: The Uncanny Performer in the Space of Technology," *Theatre Journal* 51, no. 4 (1999): 394.

19. This concept of networked social production (as defined by Yale Law professor Yochai Benkler in 2006) or collective intelligence (as coined by digital theorist Pierre Lévy in 1997) has most prominently appeared in business- and new media–focused literature.

20. O'Reilly's "compact definition" is worth quoting in full:

Web 2.0 is the network as platform, spanning all connected devices; Web 2.0 applications are those that make the most of the intrinsic advantages of that platform: delivering software as a continually-updated service that gets better the more people use it, consuming and remixing data from multiple sources, including individual users, while providing their own data and services in a form that allows remixing by others, creating network effects through an "architecture of participation," and going beyond the page metaphor of Web 1.0 to deliver rich user experiences.

See Tim O'Reilly, "Web 2.0: Compact Definition?—O'Reilly Radar," http://radar .oreilly.com/archives/2005/10/web-20-compact-definition.html.

21. Taylor, *Archive and the Repertoire*, 20.

22. Taylor, *Archive and the Repertoire*, 20.

23. Jay David Bolter and Richard Grusin, *Remediation: Understanding New Media* (Cambridge: MIT Press, 1999), 21.

24. For how many decades now has the qwerty keyboard been in use (a device with a distinct political, economic, and gendered history), even as its specific role in new media forms evolves?

25. I'm thinking particularly of Beloff's CD-ROM game "Where Where There There," based on the Wooster Group's production *House/Lights*. Since the CD-Rom was released in 1999 (sold both online and at performances), the Macintosh OS needed to play the game has become obsolete. Although I still have my original copy of the game, I no longer have a computer on which to play it, making this particular digital record as impermanent as the performance itself and turning the disc itself into a kind of a fetish object.

26. We might also consider digitally connected pervasive games such as Jane McGonigal and Ian Bogost's "Cruel 2 B Kind," in which players sign up via their cell phones to "assassinate" rival players with seemingly random acts of kindness. Another useful example of performance responding to the digital is the motion-capture project *Ghostcatching* (1999), by digital artists Shelley Eshkar and Paul Kaiser. In this project, Bill T. Jones and other HIV+ dancers were connected to a motion-capture device in which their movements were recorded as digital, abstract images. The goal of the project was very much one of preservation: "a project designed to preserve the choreography and performances of dancers who have been diagnosed with AIDS or are H.I.V.-positive." See Zoe Ingalls, "Using New Technology to Create 'Virtual Dance,'" *Chronicle of Higher Education*, Jan. 29, 1999, http://chronicle.com/weekly/v45/i21/21a02901.htm. For an extensive discussion of digital technology and its impact on how performers conceive of and make new work, see also Susan Kozel, *Closer: Performance, Technologies, Phenomenology* (Cambridge: MIT Press, 2007).

27. See David Z. Saltz, "The Art of Interaction: Interactivity, Performativity and Computers," *Journal of Aesthetics and Art Criticism* 55, no. 2 (1997): 117–27.

Writing with Paint

HARVEY YOUNG ❧

Historians, especially within the disciplines of theater and performance studies, tend to lean heavily on the written word. As stage props are repurposed for future productions and sets are razed following the end of a particular run, the only element that seems to *remain* are recorded words: a play script, a stage manager's rehearsal notes, critical reviews and personal accounts/memoirs of a performance encounter. As a result, the bulk of our present-day knowledge of theater and performance practice reflects the source material: textual traces of past events. Samuel Pepys's diary, a resource frequently cited by Joseph Roach, grants that esteemed professor multiple opportunities to re-create, through literary analysis, the experience of attending a prior production or encountering an object of history (such as the bones of a deceased monarch).[1] More generally, the emphasis on the written word has resulted in the prioritization of the experiences of individuals whose voices and memories were deemed worthy of preservation within archives and special collections. Historical accounts premised upon the surviving remains of the socially privileged frequently fail to represent the experiences of those who were relegated to lower social strata and whose stories may have been considered not worthy of preservation.

In separate essays that appeared within a 2004 special issue of *Theatre Survey* dedicated to exploring the relevance of theater history in the twenty-first century, Marvin Carlson and Harry Elam urged the journal's readers not only to broaden their definitions of theater but also to consider the process by which they write theater history. Responding to the following question: "What is the single most important thing that we can do to bring theatre history into the new millennium?" Carlson replied, "I would propose a simple, three word response: Become Less Provincial."[2] He contended that the "focus upon high culture, especially literary culture," in historical scholarship, coupled with an emphasis on the writings of Westerners, creates "constraints" that prevent theater scholars from scripting inclusive and diverse histories.[3] Citing similar concerns, Elam asserted that theater historians need "to work against conventional historical narratives and the ways in which history has been told in the past."⁴ Acknowledging the difficulty of accessing the artifacts of African American cultural experiences, he called for a "commitment to an imaginative archeology where one endeavors not only to uncover the past but also participates in its construction in the present."⁵

This essay makes that commitment and ventures outside of the province (or discipline) of conventional theater studies in order to better spotlight a reading strategy that restores the presence of those who were "disappeared" by less imaginative histories. In a manner similar to Roach's engagement with Pepys's diary, I offer a brief biography of landscape painter Robert S. Duncanson (1817–72), a free black artist who worked in the mid- to late nineteenth century, and an analysis of several of his artistic projects. Unlike Roach, who privileges seventeenth-century memoir, I center on nineteenth-century landscape painting, which is a visual trace of performance (the act of painting), the actual performance itself, and a form of life writing. While an essay about a landscape painter may at first blush seem out of place in a theater historiography collection, and perhaps even in theater studies in general, I argue that it is precisely this kind of move that can open traditional historiographic discourse in our field to new and necessary questions: here, the emphasis on a visual artist provides an example of a research model that could be used not only to rediscover other visually oriented performers (including designers) but also to acknowledge the subjective positioning of the historian in the interpretation of the remains of a performance event. In this manner, I introduce a way of using the study of nontextual remains as the basis for writing performance history.

Though he kept no written memoir, Duncanson recorded the story of his lived experience by mapping it onto his paintings. Through an examination of his landscapes, we can hear the artist testify to the legacy of captivity that ghosted him throughout his life. We can learn about his experience of being confined and spatially marginalized. To look at one of his paintings is to enter a world of relative isolation in which the viewer feels trapped or hemmed in by a variety of natural elements (a wall of trees, a body of water, etc.). When the artist depicts the black body within this environment, the irony of a claustrophobic landscape becomes even more apparent. Thus in privileging the story and artistry of Duncanson, I provide an introductory example of a method—blending biographical, phenomenological, and visual analysis—that I suggest should be employed more consistently within theater and performance studies.

Philosopher Maurice Merleau-Ponty asserts that experiences of the body can be shared through communication. When two or more bodies are exposed to a third body and are allowed to discuss their impression of this third figure, the conversing bodies will share with one another their reactions and will gain a better understanding or insight into how the other person views the conversant body. Within this framework, the third body, which remains constant and accessible to each person, enables each to decipher the experiences of the other. Figuring landscape painting as his common text, Merleau-Ponty writes:

> It suffices to say that I look at a landscape, that I speak of it with someone. Then, through the concordant operation of his body and my own, what I see passes into him, this individual green of the meadow under my eyes invades his vision without questioning my own, I recognize in my own green his green, as the customs officer recognizes suddenly in a traveler the man whose description he had been given.[6]

Discussion of a common body—artwork, the black body or artist/author—encourages comprehension of the experiences of others. While we can never know the full experience of any given person, we can gain a glimpse of it by observing how she reacts to (or engages with) an object (or person) to which we also have access. Our ability to encounter a conversant body offers us the chance to imagine what the other person may have experienced in order to generate the reactions she has. In Merleau-Ponty's example, the fact that he can both see the color green and hear another person's reaction to that same color allows him to better understand the person with whom he is speaking. Merleau-Ponty's lens proves useful to my ongoing effort to comprehend similar expressions of black experience within and across a variety of performance media. To paraphrase the French philosopher, it is possible to recognize in one's own blackness another's. Applied to Duncanson's landscapes, this analytical framing helps us to see how his paintings exist as texts in common with both the painter and the viewer of the artwork. These images invite us to peer into his experience of the body and to witness his life situation.

Contrary to rumors that Robert Duncanson was the son of a Scotch-Canadian father and a free black mother and was raised in Scotland, recent evidence suggests that he was born in the Finger Lakes region of New York State to former black captives.[7] According to Joseph Ketner, author of the only book-length study of the painter, Duncanson's genealogy can be traced to his paternal grandfather Charles, a mulatto captive who lived and worked on a Virginia plantation. Charles, who was the illegitimate child of a black female captive and her (white) "master," acquired the skills to become a house painter and, upon receiving his freedom in 1790, relocated his family to upstate New York, where he established a house painting business.[8] Following Charles's death in 1828, his son John Dean moved to Monroe, Michigan, where he apprenticed Robert alongside his four other sons in the family trade. A decade later, Robert, at the age of seventeen, briefly operated his own house painting business. The venture lasted less than a year.

Duncanson's early career as a house painter informs our reception of his artistic work. While other successful, white American landscape artists of the period (such as William Sonntag and T. Worthington Whittredge) began by similar means, the foundation of their artistic projects was not haunted overtly by a legacy of captivity.[9] Duncanson's was. Ketner writes: "Perhaps because he was the illegitimate offspring of his master, Charles Duncanson had been permitted to learn a skilled trade and later to earn his release from bondage. . . . It was a common practice for masters to award their illegitimate offspring preferential positions, to provide them with education, and to teach them skilled trades."[10] The Duncanson family's association with the painting industry derived not only from an experience of black captivity but also from the experience of sexual assault on a Southern plantation. Although it is possible that Duncanson's great-grandparents may have been involved in a loving, consensual sexual relationship, it is crucial to note the difference in social standing and status between the captive and her "master," which, according to performance artist Robbie McCauley among many others, is more akin to sexual assault and rape.[11] If Charles Duncanson learned the trade of house painting as a result of the circumstances of his conception, and he passed his artistic knowledge on to his children, who in turn shared it with their children, then it follows that Robert Duncanson's paintbrush alongside Duncanson's own body could be read as ghosted not only by the captivity of his grandfather and great-grandmother but also by the sexual assault of his great-grandmother by his great-grandfather. Furthermore, if guilt—more about creating a mulatto child than, perhaps, about committing the assault—resulted in the early patronage of Charles Duncanson, then we can see a parallel with the white, abolitionist patronage that fostered the career of his great-grandson.

Shortly after moving to Cincinnati and opening his studio in 1848, Robert Duncanson gained the attention of abolitionist art patrons who were looking for a body, and indeed, a body of artistic work, to present as evidence that blacks were more than mere chattel. The abolitionists commissioned paintings from the artist and displayed his portraits as proof that the institution of slavery should be banned. In addition to the quality of the artwork, the geographical setting of Cincinnati supported their claims. Separated from Kentucky, a "slave state," by only one thousand feet—the expanse of the Ohio River—this same body (Duncanson), within that setting (Kentucky), abolitionists asserted, would be denied his freedom and the possibility of realizing his artistic talents.[12]

Duncanson could not have been unaware of his status as a black body within the society in which he lived. In addition to the fact that his grandfather, father, father-in-law, and wife were former captives, we cannot ignore the daily living situation within which Duncanson and his family dwelled. Despite his "fair" complexion, which afforded him "the same legal protection accorded to whites, while darker 'free colored persons' were not permitted the basic liberties of owning property, voting, and obtaining legal representation," Duncanson's everyday reality of living in a segregated community and across the river from a slave society necessitated an awareness of the spatial limitations associated with having a skin color other than white.[13] In addition, his patronage by abolitionists and their desire to uphold Duncanson as a model of his race further urges us to see him as a man grounded and delimited by his racial status. These experiences appear within his artistic creations. Duncanson's paintings depict the American landscape not as a wilderness but as a bounded, perimetered space. In *Mt. Healthy, Ohio* (1844), he literally constructs a perimeter in the form of a fence that runs along the bottom third of his canvas. The painting, which bears a strong resemblance to images of Southern plantations, features a large white house on a hill that looks down on its property. Established within a simple hierarchy, the height of the house and its (white) color signify a colonial authority that governs all that exists below it. It metaphorically tames the seen nature and the unseen "nonwhite." The perimeter again appears in *View of Cincinnati, Ohio from Covington, Kentucky* (1851). In the painting, the Ohio River divides the foreground naturescape of Covington from the background cityscape of Cincinnati. In this foregrounded area (Covington), a black male captive leans against a scythe and listens to a couple of white children, likely his young "masters," as a black female captive hangs laundry on a nearby clothesline. Here, the naturescape exists as a space of white leisure and black labor.

Duncanson's spatial limitations can be seen by tracking his movements. Despite the fact that he painted over a dozen landscapes of the Ohio River Valley, covering areas that extended as far south as North Carolina, there are not any official records to suggest that he traveled south to any of the states where captivity was legal. Nevertheless, the presence of the land-scapes, which have been authenticated as painted by Duncanson, give the impression that the artist, like other "free persons of color," traveled into "slave states," presumably with documentation that testified to his "free" status. History does not record whom he visited, where he stayed, or what he did when (and *if*) he journeyed to the places where black captivity remained legal. Did he visit extended relatives who still labored as/on someone else's property? Does the fact that his Southern landscapes are limited to North Carolina imply an inability or an unwillingness to explore the "Deep South," where racial tensions could have been elevated? In contrast to the uncertainties that relate to his Southern expeditions, more is known about Duncanson's fugitive-like ventures to Canada and Europe. The painter fled to Canada and from there went to Europe during the most heated years of the Civil War. His residency abroad implies an awareness of the decreasing space that was available for people of color within the United States at that time.

While it is tempting to say that a person who is spatially restricted yet paints expansive landscapes probably does so in order to flee into the image, such a contention does not apply to Duncanson in either his pastoral landscapes or his literaryscapes, paintings of fictional places described in novels. In both forms, the landscape painter highlights the feelings of entrapment and confinement that may have haunted him in real life. His occluded landscapes present obstacles, often bodies of water, which succeed in leaving the spectator stranded on the foregrounded shore and unable to access the seeming infinity of the horizon. In *Blue Hole, Flood Waters, Little Miami River* (1851), *Pompeii* (1855), *Italianate Landscape* (1855), *Vale of Kashmir* (1864), and *Dream of Italy* (1865), among others, Duncanson deploys water as a spatially divisive element. It separates the viewer from (the promise of) the horizon in a way similar to the way the Ohio River kept black captives from freedom. Rendered static and immobile by a lack of space, we find ourselves confined in and by the landscape.

Duncanson's ability to landscape claustrophobia appears best in his 1850–52 murals commissioned by Nicholas Longworth Belmont. The artist spent an estimated two years sketching the various Belmont holdings in order to re-create them across the walls of the patron's mansion. Measuring 110 × 77 inches each, the eight Belmont murals are the largest of Duncanson's landscapes. Adorning the hallway walls, they map the property that resides outside the dwelling. As an interiorized exterior, the landscapes indeed are confined and restricted spaces. In each of the murals, the spectator finds himself separated from the background via the presence of

Figure 11.1. Taft Museum, formerly Nicholas Longworth Belmont's estate. Photograph by Harvey Young.

a body of water and in one instance a mountain range. Relegating the viewer to a small patch of foregrounded land, the paintings offer the impression of spatial deprivation within an environ of excess. Unable to cross or bridge the various obstacles presented, the spectator of the painted text must accept the small parcel of land allotted him

It requires little imagination for a person to feel that he has become a part of the picture. Each mural, nearly nine feet tall, towers over the spectator. Its height and width expand beyond the limits of peripheral vision and, in so doing, envelop the viewer. Duncanson's skillful inclusion of a trompe l'oeil frame, a painting of a frame designed to evoke the sense of an actual, three-dimensional one, only adds to this illusion. Standing before the landscape, the viewer feels that he is looking at and housed within an environment both created and tamed by the painter's brush. In the only published mural image that the Taft Museum, formerly Belmont's estate, has approved for circulation (as a postcard), spindly, crooked, and wind-blown trees tower over both the spectator of the landscape painting and the white figures featured within, who are presented standing on the edge of the Ohio River's bank. The majority of the other, nonreproduced murals repeat this style, coupling a rugged but perimetered landscape with white leisure. The exception appears in the mural closest to the corner, nearest the doorway in Belmont's foyer and therefore easiest to overlook. In this painting, the winding river similarly bisects Cincinnati and Covington, but the difference is that the featured bodies, who are stranded on the other side of the river, the slavery side, are all black. Duncanson paints a baptism scene in which a handful of bodies stand still in shallow water and witness the baptism of another. In contrast to the white figures who loiter or appear at leisure in the other murals, the presence of these black figures, coupled with the realization that they are someone's property, offers a glimpse of the spirit of faith and, perhaps, hope that survived within black captive communities during centuries of legalized captivity. In addition, it suggests that the presence and the experiences of black captive bodies were visible to Duncanson even as he resided in a free state as a "free person of color" and that their religious/cultural performances were important to him.

The Belmont murals as signifiers of claustrophobia also promote a reading of racialized space deprivation when read as interior decoration. Indeed, it appears that Duncanson's background as a house painter as much as his acclaim for being a successful portraitist and landscape painter led to his commission.[14] Seeing that Duncanson's largest and arguably some of his most important landscapes are the Belmont murals, it is crucial for us to ask what effect Duncanson's return as a "decorator" at the pinnacle of his career had on his artistic legacy. If painting, and house painting in particular, can be read as ghosted by his family's former captive history, then it seems ironic that Duncanson, undoubtedly the most important black landscape painter of his time, would in a sense reenact the role of his grandfather Charles. Duncanson must have seen the doubled nature of his commissions by abolitionists as both a sincere effort to support black artistry and a reinforcement and reinscription of a preexisting racial prejudice that declared that black artistry is more trade than art. Despite oral histories that suggest that Belmont actively praised the artwork, the more tangible evidence that all eight murals were wallpapered over within twenty years of their commission suggests that the decorative value of Duncanson's work must have been heralded more than its artistic durability.[15]

In assessing Duncanson's career as a landscape painter, we can see that his lived experience differed from that of his artistic contemporaries. Although he may have shared similar influences and even similar occupations with white landscape painters, Duncanson incorporates within his landscapes a feeling of racially rooted claustrophobia not found in the work of

OHIO
HISTORICAL
MARKER

ROBERT S. DUNCANSON

The first African American artist to achieve international
acclaim. painter Robert S. Duncanson (1821-1872) was born in
New York and settled in Cincinnati in 1840.   He pursued his
artistic career during a time of tremendous racial prejudice
and was acknowledged as the "best landscape painter in the
West." Arts patron Nicholas Longworth commissioned murals
from Duncanson around 1850 for his home Belmont,   now the
Taft Museum of Art;   these paintings are regarded as one of
the finest pre-Civil War domestic decoration schemes in the
United States.   Sponsored by anti-slavery groups, he traveled
widely during the 1860s in Europe.   Duncanson rose above
oppression to create expressions of African American cultural
identity. leading the way for other people of color to pursue
careers in the arts.

THE OHIO BICENTENNIAL COMMISSION
CINERGY
THE OHIO HISTORICAL SOCIETY
2003   35-31

Figure 11.2. Historical marker. Photograph by Harvey Young

others. In his paintings, the viewer encounters specters of captivity that
cannot be dissociated from his brush: the segregated environment of
Cincinnati; the relative confinement of living in a border state in an era of
black captivity; the self-imposed exile during the most heated years of the
Civil War; and the threat of the return of tradesmanship over artistry.

Despite the fact that we no longer can speak with Duncanson, we can
piece together biographical fragments with our interpretations of his
paintings to develop an approximation of his perspective and life situation.
It is Duncanson, as imagined, who engages and, indeed, converses with us
as we read his images. His landscapes, which exist as recordings of his experiences, enable an intimate encounter with the artist that rivals a memoir. They envelop the viewer and invite him to share Duncanson's perspective. They place him in the stead of the artist, standing where he stood as
he created his performances, his landscapes. Just as Merleau-Ponty understood his companion's "green" through the shared act of gazing at a landscape painting, we develop an understanding of Duncanson's life situation
by collectively looking upon the body of his work and remembering the

many bodies who surrounded and enabled the creation of his paintings: Duncanson and his ancestors, the black captives who participate in a baptism ritual, and Nicholas Longworth Belmont, among others. This process, which privileges the subjectivity of artists, renders both Duncanson himself and the many lesser-known figures who touched his life and, in turn, touched his canvas present within history. Similar to Duncanson, other artists wrote their stories and memoirs in a nontextual format. If historians, especially theater and performance historians, become "less provincial" and embrace "imaginative archeology" by more closely reading visual remains of past performances, then previously unknown (and neglected) histories, experiences, and perspectives may present themselves. Although painting may appear to be far afield from theater, there are plenty of examples within theater history, particularly African American theater history, of their kinship. For example, playwright Lorraine Hansberry majored in painting at the University of Wisconsin at Madison and likely developed her narrative voice through the use of her paintbrush. August Wilson found the inspiration to write several of his plays, including *The Piano Lesson*, by looking at the paintings of Romare Bearden. Reflecting upon the profound influence of Bearden on his work, Wilson once noted, "I try to make my plays the equal of his canvases."[16]

NOTES

1. See Joseph Roach, "History, Memory, Necrophilia," in *The Ends of Performance*, ed. Peggy Phelan and Jill Lane (New York: New York University Press, 1998), 23–30, and *It* (Ann Arbor: University of Michigan Press, 2007).

2. Marvin Carlson, "Become Less Provincial," *Theatre Survey* 45, no. 2 (2004): 177.

3. Carlson, "Become Less Provincial," 177.

4. Harry J. Elam, Jr., "Making History," *Theatre Survey* 45, no. 2 (2004): 219.

5. Elam, "Making History," 219.

6. Maurice Merleau-Ponty, *The Visible and the Invisible* (Evanston: Northwestern University Press, 1986), 142.

7. See Romare Bearden, "Robert S. Duncanson," in *A History of African-American Artists: From 1792 to the Present*, ed. Romare Bearden and Harry Henderson (New York: Pantheon Books, 1993), 19–39; Guy McElroy, "Robert S. Duncanson (1821–1872): A Study of the Artist's Life and Work," in *Robert S. Duncanson: A Centennial Exhibition* (Cincinnati: Cincinnati Art Museum, 1972).

8. Joseph Ketner, *Robert S. Duncanson: The Emergence of the African-American Artist* (St. Louis: University of Missouri Press, 1993).

9. Duncanson, Sonntag, and Whittredge painted in the style of the Hudson River School, a movement popularized by Thomas Cole that featured landscapes of

an American frontier that felt settled, tamed, and closed. See Anthony F. Jansen, *Worthington Whittredge* (Cambridge: Cambridge University Press, 1990); Nancy Dustin Wall Moure, *William Sonntag: Artist of the Ideal, 1822–1900* (New York: Goldfield Galleries, 1980).

10. Ketner, 12.

11. Robbie McCauley, in the preface to her play *Sally's Rape*, writes, "I'm going against the myth of the romance of the slave master and the overseers with the slave women, . . . because it was a power thing, so we call it rape" (*Sally's Rape*, in *Moon Marked & Touched by the Sun*, ed. Sydne Mahone [New York: Theatre Communications Group, 1994]), 215.

12. History demonstrates the validity of their argument. While the condition of captivity afforded Charles and John Dean the opportunity to learn how to skillfully use the brush, the Duncanson family's association with painting did not become "artistic" until after they had secured their freedom and moved to a "free state."

13. McElroy, "Robert S. Duncanson," 33.

14. McElroy, "Robert S. Duncanson," 50.

15. The Belmont estate is currently a private museum, the Taft Museum of Art. Within the museum, the wallpaper has been removed, and Duncanson's paintings have been restored. Museum docents and even security guards willingly recount the restoration process.

16. Bonnie Lyons and George Plimpton, "The Art of Theater: Interview with August Wilson," *Paris Review* (Winter 1991): 16.

Beyond the Nature/Culture Divide

Challenges from Ecocriticism and Evolutionary Biology for Theater Historiography

WENDY ARONS ∾

Some of the most recent scholarship from the field of literary studies emphasizes the advantages to be gained from critical approaches that incorporate new knowledge and theories from the biological sciences, in particular from evolutionary biology and ecological science.[1] Recently, several theater historians have put forward arguments in favor of incorporating findings from cognitive neuroscience into our work as theater critics and historians.[2] In many of these cases, post-structuralist assumptions about the social construction of identity, gender role, and cultural priorities are directly challenged by scientific evidence of the genetic basis for, and evolutionary function of, human behaviors—including our unique ability to create literature and art.[3] In other words, some of the newest work in the area of both literary criticism and theater criticism is reopening the question of the extent to which, and how, cultural production is linked to our evolution and adaptive survival as a species.

What are the ramifications for theater historiography if we take seriously the biologically grounded theoretical proposition that the arts—and here, specifically, theater and performance—have been part of our evolutionary heritage and have helped humans adapt to and thrive in our ecological niche? One answer is that we may need to rethink the significance of the "nature/culture" divide that animates both the history of Western theater and a majority of contemporary performance practices. My argument will proceed with an overview of recent work in literary ecocriticism and of theories that seek to explain the development of literature and culture in terms of Darwinian evolution. I conclude with speculations about the challenges these theories pose to us as theater historians to recast our interpretation of the theatrical past and reimagine our theatrical future.

Ecocriticism concerns itself with the study of the relationship of literature to the natural world. In the past fifteen years, ecocriticism has been a steadily growing field of inquiry within literary studies, spawning a foundational text (*The Ecocriticism Reader*), a professional organization (the Association for the Study of Literature and the Environment [ASLE]), and a number of articles and books.[4] While there is no one single perspective or philosophy that unites literary scholars who engage in ecocriticism, in general the ecocritical enterprise seems to take one of two forms: either analysis of the depiction or figuration of nature and the land in "canonical" works of fiction, or studies of nature writing.

Oddly, the growth of interest in ecocriticism among literary scholars has not been paralleled by an interest in the subject among their colleagues in theater departments. This may be due to the fact that the ecocritical wave coincided chronologically with the explosive growth of performance studies as a central area of theoretical and research interest among theater scholars. Whatever the explanation, the fact remains that only a handful of theater scholars and historians to date have attempted similar studies of the relationship of theater to the environment. In a 1994 special issue of *Theater*, Una Chaudhuri and Erika Munk were among the first to make an urgent plea to the profession to undertake such studies, a plea that went largely unheeded until recently, when a smattering of articles and books appeared on the subject.[5] But as of this writing, the number of theater scholars writing about the relationship of drama and theatrical performance to the natural world amounts to less than a dozen.

The need for theater scholars to investigate the ways in which theater and performance have shaped and/or might reshape our orientation to the natural world has not become any less urgent as the threat of global warming (and its attendant ecological and social catastrophes) looms ever nearer. As creators and interpreters of the arts and humanities, we play a role (however marginal it may seem at times) in helping to shape social attitudes about the natural world. Biologist Neal Evernden reminds us that "an involvement by the arts is vitally needed to emphasize . . . the intimate and vital involvement of self with place. . . . Environmentalism involves the perception of values, and values are the coin of the arts. Environmentalism without aesthetics is merely regional planning."[6] In her essay "Greening the Theater: Taking Ecocriticism from Page to Stage," Theresa May describes and models methods for incorporating ecocriticism into both theater criticism and stage production. Echoing the strategies of feminist and Marxist literary criticism, May's methodology demonstrates how an ecocritical approach can, on the one hand, reveal the ways that anthropocentrism (or eco-hostility) is inscribed and naturalized in dramatic literature and, on the other, provide insights into staging such plays in ways that make their "eco-hostile" attitudes available for scrutiny as a first step toward changing them (just as progressive theater artists have done with plays that re-present class, race, and gender difference as "natural" and "invisible").

While such an ecocritical approach promises to yield fresh insights into both theater history and current theater practice, one drawback of ecocriticism as currently practiced is that it remains rooted in social constructionist theories that, paradoxically, assert that the nonhuman environment that requires our attention and care is discursively constructed in the first place.[7] As Glen Love argues in his book *Practical Ecocriticism*, "ecological thinking about literature requires us to take the nonhuman world as seriously as previous modes of criticism have taken the human realm of society and culture."[8] What "nature" is, and how we relate to it, may be discursively constructed, but no matter how we apprehend that nature, there are in fact real ecological systems that are affected by material action (or nonaction) on the part of the one species (human) that has evolved the capacity to shape and, in some cases, dominate the natural environment, for both better and worse. In order to truly think ecologically, we need to have the clearest possible understanding of the human species as a species of both nature *and* culture; and to come to that understanding, we need to take seriously the understanding of human nature produced by the latest research in the biological and social sciences.[9] Indeed, we may find that because scientific theory reminds us that, like every other living organism on this planet, we have evolved and continue to evolve within a changing natural environment, it may help us to find ways to use our great adaptive advantage—culture, language, literature, and art—to avert the impending ecological catastrophe.

I should emphasize here that we are about to wade into contested territory. Our hominid ancestors in the Pleistocene era obviously did not leave detailed records, so theories about why and how aspects of culture evolved, in what order, and to what purpose may never be fully proven true or false based on physical or biological evidence. My aim here is not to adjudicate among competing views, but rather to provide a brief representative snapshot of the most current thinking about the question of the adaptive function of culture, which in general is grounded in the principle that the reason human culture exists at all is because, at some point in our prehistory, it conferred an adaptive advantage on us as a species.[10] The implication of this foundational notion is clear: evolutionary theory locates the origin of culture (which includes language, tool-making, parenting, religion, kinship structures, and social relations, as well as literature, art, music, and theater) in natural, biological processes.[11] Those of us who cut our scholarly teeth on literary and cultural theories grounded in social constructionism (i.e., Marxist, feminist, post-structuralist, queer, etc., theory) may have a knee-jerk negative reaction to the universalism and essentialism that such biological determinism implies. But rather than dismissing out of hand theories that find validation in scientific reasoning and empirical evidence because we find them politically unpalatable, we should instead take up the challenge of integrating an understanding of literature and culture as a biological adaptation with the political and social insights gained from half a century of literary and cultural criticism influenced by social construction theory.[12]

Scholars who turn to evolutionary theory to understand human cultural products seek not only to explain why humans began to produce art in the first place but also to analyze and interpret our continued production of (and response to) art in terms of the adaptive advantage it may have originally conferred. So, for example, Joseph Carroll (who pioneered the field of "adaptationist literary studies") finds a compelling answer to the question of why the human mind began to produce culture in a hypothesis proposed by biologist E. O. Wilson.[13] Wilson suggests in his book *Consilience* that fiction-making and the arts represent an adaptation that enabled humans to cope with the bewildering array of information our large and flexible brains needed to process: "Early humans invented [the arts] in an attempt to express and control through magic the . . . forces in their lives that mattered most to survival and reproduction."[14] Carroll builds on this premise, and on recent research into cognitive behavioral systems, to argue that literature and culture would consequently find basis in, and derive from, cognitive motives and behaviors fundamental to our survival and reproduction as a species.[15] He groups these universal motives and forces into seven basic "behavior systems"—survival, mating, parenting, social networking, tool building, kin system maintenance, and cognition—all of which subserve the two primary biological imperatives of somatic growth and reproduction.[16] The literary critic's task, according to Carroll, is to identify, explain, and analyze the fundamental motives and cognitive dispositions that authors weave into literature as part of our naturally selected coping mechanism against a bewildering, confusing environment.

Carroll's theorization of literature in evolutionary terms finds echoes in other cultural fields as well. For example, in his book *The Art Instinct*, Denis Dutton puts the focus on art's social function and proposes that the development of art was crucial to our success in living together socially. Dutton's hypothesis is that art (and fiction, in particular) gives us access to other minds. He notes:

> Stories not only take their audiences into fictional settings but also take them into the inner lives of imaginary people. . . . For an intensely social species such as *Homo sapiens* there was an advantage in the ancestral environment in honing an ability to navigate in the endlessly complex mental worlds people shared with their hunter-gatherer compatriots.[17]

Dutton's theory of fiction might easily be extended to explain the evolution of acting as both an evolved skill and a pleasure to watch: early humans who mastered the ability to embody another's subjectivity might not only be more adept at forming and maintaining social groups but might also confer an adaptive advantage, in terms of group understanding and cohesion, to the social group as a whole.

Dutton's focus differs from Carroll's in his claim that a crucial aspect of evolutionary theory inheres in its ability to explain the *emotional* impact of art. Dutton hypothesizes that the adaptive advantage of gaining access to other minds was so strong that we evolved to derive deeply pleasurable emotion from it. Dutton observes (in a passage that could do well to describe our fascination with actors) that the "intense interest in art as emotional expression derives from wanting to see through art into another human personality: it springs from a desire for knowledge of another person."[18] While the pleasures induced by art in our Pleistocene ancestors no longer serve the same adaptive purpose today as they did in our ancestral environment, the instinct for (and impact of) art survives.[19]

In the field of theater studies the adaptationist literary argument has recently been taken up by Daniel Nettle in his essay "What Happens in Hamlet? Exploring the Psychological Foundations of Drama." Like Dutton, Nettle locates the hypothetical origin of the dramatic mode in the adaptive advantage conferred by social success, in this case, the ability to engage in good conversation. Nettle hypothesizes that drama may have originated as "a contrived conversation that stimulates the mechanisms of reward that evolved for natural conversation."[20] Like Carroll, moreover, Nettle seeks to identify deep structures in drama that map onto inherent motives in human psychology.[21] Nettle's analysis then proceeds to attribute the enduring impact of a play like *Hamlet* to its successful activation of features that appeal to our innate psychology. Nettle's methodology seems at first glance circular and unrewarding—once we have posited that drama will be successful if it fulfills identified inherent psychological needs, the analytical task is reduced to finding (or failing to find) those features that we seek. Nevertheless, it stands as a first step toward grounding our understanding of the development of theater and dramatic literature in scientific knowledge about human evolution and cognition.

Moreover, adaptationist literary theory is not a priori limited to circular, closed analysis. The three approaches to adaptationist literary theory that I have outlined find support in arguments advanced in recent works by social scientists that seek to understand the origins and development of culture in terms of a *reciprocity* between genes and culture, which leaves ample room for a consideration of humans as "unusually active agents in our own evolution."[22] For example, in *Not By Genes Alone* social scientists Peter J. Richerson and Robert Boyd propose that once genes produce individuals disposed to culture, those individuals become an "environment" that exerts selection pressures on genes.[23] Using as an example the evolution of cooperation as a cultural trait, they hypothesize how this mutual influence might work:

> The phenomenon of group selection on cultural variation . . . could have produced institutions encouraging more cooperation with distantly related people than would be favored by our original evolved psychology. These cooperators would have discriminated against individuals who carried genes that made them too belligerent to conform to the new cooperative norms.[24]

Richerson and Boyd's argument about the evolution of culture uses population-level modeling to demonstrate that humans are genetically predisposed to select cultural variants on the basis of the frequency with which they appear among the group—thus, they argue, while our genes may not directly determine cultural adaptations, as a cultural trait begins to appear with greater frequency within a group, it will be more likely to be adopted by other members of the group.

In *The Imagined World Made Real*, Plotkin takes up Richerson and Boyd's hypothesis and extends it to suggest an explanation for the process through and by which the imagined world—that is, the social rules and conventions of a given culture—are made "real":

> If culture is imagination made real, one of the forces that compels each of us to believe in and adhere to extraordinary imaginings is sheer weight of numbers of others believing in them. This does not mean we are all enslaved to the majority all of the time. It merely means that most of us are so predisposed some of the time.[25]

The implication of these two arguments for any theory of art or literature that seeks grounding in evolutionary theory is that scientific thinking does not necessarily land us in positivist territory. Rather, if a scientific theory that describes a reciprocal process of influence between genetic and cultural evolution can be tested and proven—and Plotkin proposes that just such scientific evidence will eventually emerge with developments in neuroscience and neurobiology—then an adaptationist approach to the study of literature, art, and theater does not have to reduce down to discovering "universal" themes, motives, and desires but can take into account the ways in which culture both expresses and shapes the mental and social life of the human species.

It is precisely such an integration of the evolutionary and social constructionist approach that David Sloan Wilson argues is necessary in his essay "Evolutionary Social Constructivism." For Sloan Wilson, what bridges the gap between genetic evolutionary theory and social constructivism is the fact that stories serve as guides for human action and behavior from one person or generation to another. His notion that stories themselves can "play the role of genes in nongenetic evolutionary processes" brings us to the doorstep of the other current approach to integrating evolutionary theory and culture: meme theory.[26]

The term *meme* was first coined by biologist Richard Dawkins in the final chapter of his 1976 book *The Selfish Gene*. Dawkins's argument in the book is that the gene is the primary unit of natural selection and that the organisms that genes "build" should be thought of as survival machines that allow genes to replicate. Toward the end of his book, Dawkins floats the hypothesis that culture might be a similar "replicating entity" that uses living organisms as its means of transmission and evolution. He called this replicator a "meme":

> Examples of memes are tunes, ideas, catch-phrases, clothes fashions, ways of making pots or of building arches. Just as genes propagate themselves in the gene pool by leaping from body to body via sperms or eggs, so memes propagate themselves in the meme pool by leaping from brain to brain via a process which, in the broad sense, can be called imitation.[27]

In the three decades since Dawkins proposed the idea of the "meme" as a unit of cultural evolution, a number of writers have attempted to theorize what memes might be and how they might operate. Meme theories seem to fall into roughly two categories. The first, which I'll label the "soft" approach, uses the notion of a "meme's eye view" as a useful explanatory metaphor for explaining how culture evolves over time and between populations.[28] While this approach can certainly yield a fresh perspective on cultural history, many critics of meme theory object that it is methodologically similar to a semiotic or structuralist approach.[29]

The second approach, which I'll call the "hard" approach, gives memes an agency akin to that of genes. In *The Meme Machine* Susan Blackmore summarizes the theoretical shift in perspective: "Instead of thinking of our ideas as our own creations, and as working for us, we have to think of them as autonomous selfish memes, working only to get themselves copied. We humans, because of our powers of imitation, have become just the physical hosts needed for the memes to get around."[30] Memes are, according to this approach, like "viruses of the mind" (to take a cue from the title of another elaboration of the theory).[31] Critics of this "hard" version point to a number of problems with the theory, the most serious of which are (1) the lack of precision and rigor with which a "meme" is defined; (2) the fact that brains generally do not faithfully "replicate" received ideas and thoughts, but rather engage in a constant process of unmaking and remaking; and (3) the fact that, taken at face value, such a theory seems to rob humans of agency, creativity, and free will.[32]

In her recent book *The Selfish Meme* Kate Distin takes this criticism head on and develops a theory of the meme that incorporates the same reciprocity we saw in theories of evolutionary psychology. Thus she concludes that

> a human mind . . . is partly the product of the memes that bombard it, but only because it has the innate potential to interact with and develop in response to those memes. Culture, in turn, is ultimately the product of human minds, but the preservation of information in representational content ensures that the culture we encounter today is largely composed of memes produced by human minds of long ago.[33]

Distin's emphasis on the meme's governance by natural selection puts focus on the ways in which cultural change is dependent upon both what has gone before and the environment in which change is taking place. Such an emphasis does not ask for a repudiation of human will and creativity, but rather for a more rigorous tracing of cultural stability and mutation over time.

Ecocriticism, adaptationist literary theory, and meme theory challenge the practice of theater historiography in different ways. Some of the suggestions that follow are contradictory; I offer them all in the spirit of scientific inquiry and with the assumption that some may prove to be theoretical or methodological dead ends after testing.

(1) We cannot simply ignore or dismiss out of hand evidence from the sciences and social sciences that demonstrates that much of human behavior and response is "hard-wired" as a result of evolutionary pressures on early hominids simply because the ramifications of such findings contradict the social constructionist theory that has dominated literary and cultural criticism for the last half century. Instead, we need to find ways of integrating an understanding of the evolutionarily adaptive function of literature and the arts in the Pleistocene environment with the political gains and social insights gained as a result of socially progressive theory in our own environment.

In fact, social scientific theories that describe mechanisms by which genetic information and environmental/cultural information mutually influence each other will enable us to articulate more clearly in what ways drama and theater are part of the human animal "instinct" and in what ways they allow us to define our social world, aside from or in spite of genetic determinism. But in order to do that, we will need to take up the challenge of understanding and articulating the precise mechanisms and processes that govern those mutual influences, so that, for example, we can come to a more scientifically grounded explanation of why people respond emotionally to certain themes or plots or whether and why certain representations seem to have "universal appeal."[34] Moreover—and here is one way that evolutionary theory may intersect with ecocriticism—integrating a more biologically grounded understanding of the human animal into the study of culture may give us insights into how the arts can help us evolve into more ecofriendly inhabitants of our environment. That is, a more precise understanding of the ways in which our culture *is* part of our nature might also help artists and writers make culture that brings us back into consilience with the natural world.

(2) Many theater historians (and theater history textbooks) describe drama as an art form that evolved out of early ritual.[35] But evolutionary theory demands that we think more rigorously about the evolutionary function of both ritual and drama, and the adaptive purposes each may have served for early humans. Social scientists Richerson and Boyd theorize that the ability to imitate, and to learn through precise imitation, may have conferred an evolutionary advantage on early members of the human species, in particular once that ability had evolved in a critical mass of the population: "when lots of imitation is mixed with a little bit of individual

learning, *populations* can adapt in ways that outreach the abilities of any individual genius."[36] Theater historians can look to such evolutionary theory to come to more precise descriptions of the origins of ritual, drama, and acting or impersonation. To do so, we need to ask questions like: What survival or somatic advantages were gained by groups of hominids who practiced ritual? What are the selection pressures that might have nudged ritualistic behavior toward dramatic behavior? If drama did indeed evolve from ritual, is it an example of the kind of gene-culture interaction described by Plotkin, or Richerson and Boyd, or does it represent a form of "meme" evolution? And even more fundamentally, if *imitation* is an evolved trait, then might there be an "instinct" for drama—rooted in the survival advantages conferred by the ability to mimic—antecedent (or even unconnected) to ritual? In other words, might we need to overhaul our assumptions about where drama and theater come from in light of evolutionary theory?

(3) As Una Chaudhuri noted in her 1994 essay "There Must be a Lot of Fish in That Lake," the vast majority of dramatic literature foregrounds human conflict against a backdrop of—and often at the expense of considering—the natural world. Indeed, one hypothesis about the development of drama as a genre and art form might be that it instantiates an adaptively advantageous anthropocentric turn in culture and has thus contributed to the human species' ability to (psychologically, if not physically) dominate and master the natural environment. An ecocritical perspective would lead us, as theater historians, to adopt a methodology analogous to that of feminist critics confronted by a history of patriarchal literature. This might call for a theater history that traces the development of "ecohostile" anthropocentrism in over two millennia of dramatic literature; conversely, we may wish to look for those contestations of anthropocentrism that have been left out of the canon. The stakes are high in this endeavor: Joseph Meeker suggests that the ways of thinking about our relationship to the natural world that we inherited from Greek tragic drama may confer upon us "the distinction of being the first species ever to understand the causes of its own extinction."[37] As was important to feminist criticism, recovering the history of anthropocentrism in theatrical literature will be a first step toward redressing the effects of that history.[38] Reframing that literature through imaginative stagings that reveal why such attitudes are problematic will be a second step, and writing new theater and performance that inscribes humanity within the human animal's ecological niche in ways that might prolong rather than shorten our existence within it—in other words, finding ways to "perform" humanity in new concert with the nonhuman world—will be a third.

Such an ecocritical perspective can be integrated with a theoretical approach grounded in evolutionary theory. To keep the focus more squarely on the evolutionary advantages conferred by literature and drama, a theater history concerned with tracing the development of anthropocentrism in theatrical literature could follow Carroll's lead and center on how a particular form of drama or performance (or literary theme) might have suited the psychological and cognitive needs of hominids evolving in the Pleistocene era and then (moving beyond Carroll) analyze how those forms and themes have evolved during the ten thousand years humans have existed in their evolved form. What was once adaptive (anthropocentric drama and literature) may have become maladaptive over time. Thus perhaps even more crucial to the ecocritical project would be a new form of theater that draws on an evolutionary approach to reorient our relationship to the natural world. We might model that reorientation on the strategy adopted by Michael Pollan, who, in his book *The Omnivore's Dilemma*, rewrites the history of agriculture in terms of corn's maximization of its utility to a human-centered ecology.[39] Such a shift in perspective—one that understands ecology as a system in which humans are not the only "manipulators" of the environments and ecosystems we inhabit—helpfully reminds us that despite the culture that allows us to shape and understand our environment, we remain subject to the same evolutionary forces that drive all biological processes and cannot survive as a species as long as we continue to divide culture from nature.

NOTES

1. See, e.g., Bryan Boyd, *On the Origin of Stories: Evolution, Cognition, and Fiction* (Cambridge: Harvard University Press, 2009); Denis Dutton, *The Art Instinct: Beauty, Pleasure, and Human Evolution* (New York: Bloomsbury Press, 2009); Jonathan Gottschall, *Literature, Science, and a New Humanities* (New York: Palgrave Macmillan, 2008); Laura Walls, "Seeking Common Ground: Integrating the Sciences and the Humanities," and Michael P. Cohen, "Reading after Darwin: A Prospectus," both in *Coming into Contact: Explorations in Ecocritical Theory and Practice*, ed. Annie Merrill Ingram, Ian Marshall, Daniel J. Philippon, and Adam W. Sweeting (Athens: University of Georgia Press, 2007); Jonathan Gottschall and David Sloan Wilson, *The Literary Animal: Evolution and the Nature of Narrative* (Evanston: Northwestern University Press, 2005); Joseph Carroll, *Literary Darwinism: Evolution, Human Nature, and Literature* (New York: Routledge, 2004); Glen A. Love, *Practical Ecocriticism: Literature, Biology, and the Environment* (Charlottesville: University of Virginia Press, 2003); and Brett Cooke and Frederick Turner, *Biopoetics: Evolutionary Explorations in the Arts* (Lexington, KY: ICUS, 1999).

2. Some key works include Bruce A. McConachie, *Engaging Audiences: A Cognitive Approach to Spectating in the Theatre* (New York: Palgrave Macmillan, 2008); Rhonda Blair, *The Actor, Image, and Action: Acting and Cognitive Neuroscience* (New York: Routledge, 2008); Bruce A. McConachie, "Falsifiable Theories for Theatre and Performance Studies," *Theatre Journal* 59, no. 4 (2007); C. B. Davis, "Cultural Evolution and Performance Genres: Memetics in Theatre History and Performance Studies," *Theatre Journal* 59, no. 4 (2007); Amy Cook, "Interplay: The Method and Potential of a Cognitive Science Approach to Theatre," *Theatre Journal* 59, no. 4 (2007); Tobin Nellhaus, "From Embodiment to Agency: Cognitive Science, Critical Realism, and Communication Frameworks," *Journal of Critical Realism* 3, no. 1 (2004); and the essays in Bruce A. McConachie and F. Elizabeth Hart, eds., *Performance and Cognition: Theatre Studies and the Cognitive Turn* (London: Routledge, 2006).

3. Post-structuralist theorists would argue that scientific discourse itself is socially constructed; for one example of such argument, see the first chapters of Sue-Ellen Case, *Performing Science and the Virtual* (New York: Routledge, 2007).

4. A Worldcat subject search on the keywords "ecology and literature" returns over 500 entries; a search on the keyword "ecocriticism" returns over 150. Contributions to the field in just the last decade include Karla Armbruster and Kathleen R. Wallace, *Beyond Nature Writing: Expanding the Boundaries of Ecocriticism* (Charlottesville: University Press of Virginia, 2001); Lawrence Buell, *Writing for an Endangered World: Literature, Culture, and Environment in the U.S. and Beyond* (Cambridge: Harvard University Press, 2001); Laurence Coupe, *The Green Studies Reader: From Romanticism to Ecocriticism* (New York: Routledge, 2000); Greg Garrard, *Ecocriticism: The New Critical Idiom* (New York: Routledge, 2004); Ingram et al., *Coming into Contact*; Love, *Practical Ecocriticism*; Bill McKibben, *American Earth: Environmental Writing since Thoreau* (New York: Penguin Putnam, 2008); Bryan L. Moore, *Ecology and Literature: Ecocentric Personification from Antiquity to the Twenty-First Century* (New York: Palgrave Macmillan, 2008); and Dana Phillips, *The Truth of Ecology: Nature, Culture, and Literature in America* (Oxford: Oxford University Press, 2003).

5. A representative (but not comprehensive) list would include Gabriella Giannachi and Nigel Stewart, eds., *Performing Nature: Explorations in Ecology and the Arts* (Oxford: Peter Lang, 2005); Bronislaw Szerszynski, Wallace Heim, and Claire Waterton, *Nature Performed: Environment, Culture and Performance* (Oxford: Blackwell Publishing, 2003); Wendy Arons, "Introduction to Special Section on 'Performance and Ecology,'" *Theatre Topics* 17, no. 2 (2007); Downing Cless, "Eco-Theatre, USA: The Grassroots Is Greener," *TDR* 40, no. 2 (1996); Theresa J. May, "Greening the Theatre: Taking Ecocriticism from Page to Stage," *Interdisciplinary Literary Studies: A Journal of Criticism and Theory* 7, no. 1 (2005); Theresa J. May, "Frontiers: Environmental History, Ecocriticism and *The Kentucky Cycle*," *Journal of Dramatic Theory and Criticism* 14, no. 1 (1999); Theresa J. May, "Beyond Bambi: Toward a Dangerous Ecocriticism in Theatre Studies," *Theatre Topics* 17, no. 2 (2007); Cindy Rosenthal, "The Common Green/Common Ground Performance Project: The Personal, the Political, the Gardens, and NYU," *The Drama Review* 46, no. 3 (2002); Shelly R. Scott, "Conserving, Consuming, and Improving on Nature at Disney's Animal Kingdom," *Theatre Topics* 17, no. 2 (2007); Jennifer Spiegel

and Annalee Yassi, "Theatre of Alliances? Role-Play, Representation, and Ecosystem Health in Ecuador," *Theatre Topics* 17, no. 2 (2007); and several of the articles included in Elinor Fuchs and Una Chaudhuri, eds., *Land/Scape/Theater* (Ann Arbor: University of Michigan Press, 2002).

6. Neil Evernden, "Beyond Ecology: Self, Place, and the Pathetic Fallacy," in *The Ecocriticism Reader: Landmarks in Literary Ecology,* ed. Cheryll Glotfelty and Harold Fromm (Athens: University of Georgia Press, 1996), 102–3.

7. Cf. Carroll, *Literary Darwinism*, 85.

8. Love, *Practical Ecocriticism*, 47.

9. Cf. Love, *Practical Ecocriticism*, 51.

10. As Henry Plotkin notes: "Human extragenetic information transmission is a major systemic change in how life works. Something changed in our brains and our cognition, and that change was the crucial trick that gave rise to human culture" (*The Imagined World Made Real: Towards a Natural Science of Culture* [New Brunswick: Rutgers University Press, 2003], 142).

11. Edward O. Wilson puts it bluntly: "That there is a human nature is no longer in doubt. . . . Human behavior is determined by neither genes nor culture but instead by a complex interaction of these two prescribing forces, with biology guiding and environment specifying" ("Forward from the Scientific Side," in Gottschall and Sloan Wilson, *Literary Animal*, viii).

12. Cf. McConachie, "Falsifiable Theories," esp. 554–56, for similar reflections on the need to integrate a scientific approach with theatre historiography and theory.

13. Carroll's understanding of the relationship between evolution and culture takes off from the premise of evolutionary psychology, which proposes that the human mind evolved to adapt to its ancestral environment, and this adapted mind produces literature (*Literary Darwinism*, xii). See also David Sloan Wilson, "Evolutionary Social Constructivism," in Gottschall and Sloan Wilson, *Literary Animal*, 21. A standard reference in the field of evolutionary psychology is Jerome H. Barkow, Leda Cosmides, and John Tooby, *The Adapted Mind: Evolutionary Psychology and the Generation of Culture* (New York: Oxford University Press, 1992). On cognitive behavior systems, see Lawrence A. Hirschfeld and Susan A. Gelman, *Mapping the Mind: Domain Specificity in Cognition and Culture* (Cambridge: Cambridge University Press, 1994).

14. Edward O. Wilson, *Consilience: The Unity of Knowledge* (New York: Knopf, 1998), 225. See also Carroll, *Literary Darwinism*, xxi.

15. Carroll, *Literary Darwinism*, 193.

16. Each behavioral system has certain specific actions that pertain to it; so, e.g., under "mating" Carroll lists, "Assess and allure sexual partners / Overcome competitors / Avoid incest." Cf. Carroll, *Literary Darwinism*, 201.

17. Dutton, *Art Instinct*, 118.

18. Dutton, *Art Instinct*, 234–35. See also McConachie, "Falsifiable Theories" (esp. 561–70), for an explanation of the evidence from cognitive science that supports this hypothesis.

19. For a somewhat different argument about the adaptive advantage conferred by art, see Kathryn Coe, *The Ancestress Hypothesis: Visual Art as Adaptation* (New Brunswick.: Rutgers University Press, 2003).

20. To that end, he proposes a list of six features in drama that would have "high psychological appeal" to the adapted Pleistocene hominid mind. For example, Daniel Nettle's third criterion reads, "The protagonists should make attempts to maximize their biological fitness by . . . protecting themselves, protecting kin, enhancing their own status, and seeking mates" ("What Happens in Hamlet?" in Gottschall and Sloan Wilson, *Literary Animal*, 65).

21. Nettle, "What Happens in Hamlet," 67.

22. Peter J. Richerson and Robert Boyd, *Not by Genes Alone: How Culture Transformed Human Evolution* (Chicago: University of Chicago Press, 2005), 253.

23. Richerson and Boyd, *Not by Genes Alone*, 5.

24. Richerson and Boyd, *Not by Genes Alone*, 15.

25. Plotkin, *Imagined World Made Real*, 285. See also Robert Boyd and Peter J. Richerson, *Culture and the Evolutionary Process* (Chicago: University of Chicago Press, 1985); Henry Plotkin, "Culture and Psychological Mechanisms," in *Darwinizing Culture: The Status of Memetics as a Science*, ed. Robert Aunger (Oxford: Oxford University Press, 2000).

26. Sloan Wilson, "Evolutionary Social Constructivism," 35.

27. Richard Dawkins, *The Selfish Gene* (New York: Oxford University Press, 1976), 206.

28. This is the approach taken, e.g., by C. B. Davis in his essay "Cultural Evolution and Performance Genres." See also Plotkin, *Imagined World Made Real*, 146–59.

29. We might take as an example Propp's work on the folktale, which could in retrospect be described as a "memetic" approach to narrative.

30. Susan J. Blackmore, *The Meme Machine* (Oxford: Oxford University Press, 1999), 8.

31. Cf. Richard Brodie, *Virus of the Mind: The New Science of the Meme* (Seattle: Integral Press, 1996). Other key contributions to meme theory include Daniel Dennett, *Darwin's Dangerous Idea: Evolution and the Meanings of Life* (New York: Simon and Schuster, 1995); Robert Aunger, *The Electric Meme: A New Theory of How We Think* (New York: Free Press, 2002); and the essays in Aunger, *Darwinizing Culture*.

32. Cf. Richerson and Boyd, *Not by Genes Alone*, 82; Maurice Bloch, "A Well-Disposed Social Anthropologist's Problems with Memes," in Aunger, *Darwinizing Culture*, 198.

33. Kate Distin, *The Selfish Meme: A Critical Reassessment* (Cambridge: Cambridge University Press, 2005), 203.

34. See, e.g., the works cited in note 2.

35. One noteworthy exception is Eli Rozik, who locates the origins of theater in dreams, play, and myths. See Eli Rozik, *The Roots of Theatre: Rethinking Ritual and Other Theories of Origin* (Iowa City: University of Iowa Press, 2002).

36. Richerson and Boyd, *Not by Genes Alone*, 13.

37. Joseph W. Meeker, *The Comedy of Survival: Studies in Literary Ecology* (New York: Scribner, 1974) 5.

38. A project that has already begun: see Moore, *Ecology and Literature*.

39. Michael Pollan, *The Omnivore's Dilemma: A Natural History of Four Meals* (New York: Penguin Books, 2006), 15–31.

"Or I'll Die"

Death and Dying on Page and Stage

JONATHAN CHAMBERS ∾

Death is not life.
Death is nothing, less than nothing.

—Hecuba, *The Trojan Women*

At bottom no one believes in his own death.

—Sigmund Freud,
"Our Attitudes Toward Death"

And if one is not able to die, is he really able to live?

—Paul Tillich, "The Eternal Now"

When student actors are first introduced to the protocols of contemporary, realistic acting, they are frequently encouraged to weigh the effectiveness and value of their choices against the bold hypothetical, "I must achieve my goal, or I'll die." That is, the pursuit of the chosen objective and super-objective is configured so that the stakes become a matter of life and death. Clearly, in this configuration, death is situated as the outcome to be avoided at all costs. While this hypothetical has undoubtedly structured in-numerable compelling performances in the theater, I am nonetheless struck by the apparent unrecognized ontological assumption underpinning this approach; specifically, the notion that death is categorically terrible and that any reasonable person will undertake most any action in order to evade it unconditionally.

My thinking about this hidden assumption has led to two key questions: What ideological and sociocultural forces underpin this negative conception of death? And what is the effect (tacit though it may be), not only on the actor's process but also on the enterprise of theater more largely construed, when death is time and again situated as the outcome to elude? Using these questions as a point of departure, in this essay I consider both the twentieth-century, realistic acting process writ large (i.e., Stanislavski and Stanislavki-inspired approaches), as well as representative examples drawn from the field of Western dramatic literature, to argue that far from offering visions of death (and, for that matter, life) that are universal or innate, the representation of mortality in theater—on page and on stage—is always ideologically and contextually specific. In arguing this point, I hope to demonstrate that theater historians and theater artists should take care not to assume or assign universal conceptions of death when engaging with historical objects. Instead, scholars and artists must think critically about how notions of mortality embedded in those objects are at all times ideologically and historically informed and, moreover, recognize that such notions render and perpetuate particular viewpoints of how one should live and how one should die.

Live, or Else

While it is true that writers from across the globe have long ruminated on the so-called question of death—Schopenhauer's declaration that "without death there would hardly have been any philosophizing" is an apt summary of this tendency[1]—it is also true that the subject became particularly important to numerous post-Enlightenment/modern, European thinkers keen on exploring the vexed relation between existence and consciousness.[2] Though such views on death and dying are varied, complex, and often incongruous one with the other, in some respects Freud's thinking on the subject may be viewed as emblematic of those early twentieth-century moderns who held humanist visions of the world and its functions.

In sum, Freud held that the belief in life after death, and its coexistent, the Christian God or some other divine entity, was chief among humanity's myriad false hopes and illusions.[3] More specifically, he argued that humans too often held to the falsehood of life after death, imparted by all major religious systems, because the finality of absolute annihilation that accompanied biological death was too difficult to process psychically. Regarding the effect of this penchant, he remarked that we have shown "an unmistakable tendency to put death on one side, to eliminate it from life. We tried to hush it up. . . . It is indeed impossible to imagine our own death."[4] Thus, for Freud, one of humanity's base fears—the fear of death without the promise of immortality—led to its denial; funded illusory, preposterous, and untenable visions of the immortal soul, heaven, hell, reincarnation, and resurrection; and, in the end, hindered the logical pursuit of truth and retarded humanity's progress.[5]

Freud's ideas on death stand as a humanist counterpoint to traditional religious doctrines that professed the immortality of the soul and a belief in a better, heavenly world to come. Broadly construed, humanism, emphasizing as it does "the fulfillment of the potentialities of each human being in a happy, just, democratic and peaceful world," accentuates the view that each person has one life to live and that death amounts to "total annihilation."[6] As with Freud, humanists place emphasis on material existence, hold that the world is complete, maintain that humans are self-contained and self-determining and have the rational ability to understand (and, indeed, construct) the world's functions, and claim that "death is the end of life and . . . that there is nothing beyond it: immortality is a myth."[7]

Such thinking is not without consequence. Indeed, dependent as it is on the belief in humanity's promise and material progress, death under humanistic thinking is cast as "not a natural and necessary" part of existence, but as an unnatural embarrassment that amounts to failure. Moreover, because death rebukes the faith such humanists place in the future, its existence is denied.[8] Thus, to Johan Huizinga's claim that "no other epoch has laid so much stress as the expiring Middle Ages on the thought of death," one might add this coda: no other epoch like the modern has so tried to deny it.[9]

The view that death must be denied left its imprint on the modern, realistic acting process, developed by Stanislavski in the first decades of the twentieth century and subsequently interpreted by many others. Though his central concern for humans in "action" (which, in turn, leads to the humanistic interpretation of scripts), as well as his "essentialist vision of the human subject," are both clear indications of his alliance with humanism, a close reading of his work reveals that the strong opinions regarding mortality underscoring many of his ideas, specifically the glory of life and shame of death, also mark his work as fundamentally humanist in its orientation.[10] This particular view of mortality is, perhaps, most evident in *An Actor's Work*, which offers a lively description and passionate justification of the concept he terms "grip."[11] Ninety-five percent of our life is routine, Tortsov (Stanislavski's analogue) tells his students, and doesn't require continuous grip. These kinds of automatic functions have no place on the stage. But the other 5 percent is essential, especially in tragedy:

> There are other Bits in our lives, when moments of horror, sometimes short, sometimes long, or of great joy, of wild passion and other momentous experiences erupt into our daily routines. *They*

*summon us to fight for freedom, for an ideal, for our very existence, for jus-
tice. Those are the moments we need onstage.*[12]

This notion of grip (or "grasp," as it is called in the widely used Hapgood
translation/adaptation of Stanislavski's acting manual, *An Actor Prepares*) is
commonly regarded as the foundation for the concept of urgency, level of
importance, or, as it is often called by many acting teachers, "stakes."[13]
That is, in the course of determining the character's objective and super-
objective, the actor is asked to heighten, deepen, and strengthen the pursuit of those goals by investing them with a sense of profound risk and substantial consequence.

The importance of grip or stakes is emphasized, repeatedly, in modern
and contemporary acting manuals and likewise is consistently positioned as
a mortal struggle against death. Cuing off Stanislavski's assertion that the
actor must in the course of performing a role "fight . . . for [his/her] very
existence," the author of one such text notes that the actor's process of determining stakes begins by first asking, "What do I have to gain or lose,
should my character achieve or not achieve his or her objective?" The author then frames the suitable (if not ideal) terms for responding to that hypothetical, noting, "Stakes [should be] the highest anyone can have: life or
death. . . . If you can elevate your character's stakes to life or death, then
your scenes will never be boringly casual or low energy."[14]

The implication that the prospective death of the character must be fer-
vently resisted/denied may be linked to social historian Philippe Ariés's
conception of "modern death" (a concept that will be discussed in greater
depth in the second half of this essay) and echoes as well Freud's humanist
rendering of mortality. To be sure, the implication central to modern acting approaches—that death is unacceptable because it will bring about the
end of the individual's/character's pursuit of an objective and therefore
constitutes an utter collapse of the individual's/character's drive—are concomitant with humanistic visions of death as reprehensible, as an affront to
the natural order of things, and as failure. Thus, when considered in relation to the prevailing humanist assumptions about mortality, Stanislavski's
inclusion of "grip" or the question of existence in the acting process is not
at all surprising.[15]

From Faith to Failure

In my foregoing discussion, I focused on the ways that modern humanistic
attitudes regarding mortality shaped acting. It is important to recognize,

however, that views on death have also underscored the practice of theater more broadly construed. Indeed, just as Stanislavski's work bears the imprint of humanistic thinking that is neither universal nor timeless, but instead contextually specific, other historical objects from other periods also hold clues to the past's ever-changing relationship to and regard for death. In an attempt to better understand how various historical representations of death in the theater corresponded with various prevailing attitudes and assumptions regarding mortality, in this section I will look to the field of dramatic literature.

To support my contention that theater echoes and reproduces historically particular conceptions of life, I draw on the work of Philippe Ariés. Author of arguably the most significant recent histories of death, Ariés meticulously charts the advent of the modern attitude toward mortality. In doing so, he unsettles the universality of the common anecdote, "everyone dies and, moreover, everyone knows s/he is going to die."[16] While this anecdotal truism is on some level a valid and rational response to a biological certainty, it nonetheless obscures the complex sociocultural history of death, specifically the ways in which attitudes regarding mortality and the afterlife have shifted and, indeed, continue to shift.

According to Ariés, prevailing premodern/medieval conceptions of death constituted a more holistic, communal, and comprehensive vision of death, seeing it as an integral and inseparable part of life. This "tamed death," as termed by Ariés, "was both familiar and near, evoking no great fear or awe"; was regarded as "the collective destiny of the species"; and was guided by the ruling presupposition, "*Et moriemur,* and we shall all die."[17] Significantly, this traditional attitude, which was widespread within a variety of populations across Europe during the early and mid–Middle Ages, situated the loss of life not as a individual act but as one that was deeply embedded in the networks of family and community; hence, the operative word "we" in the phrase "we shall all die." Additionally, the distinction between life and afterlife was not neatly demarcated. Thus, when Ariés speaks of the "promiscuity between the living and the dead," he is highlighting the notion that the dead were not perceived as being especially distant from the living.[18] Death was not configured as an absolute end or annihilation, but was instead regarded as a passage into a resting or sleeping place where the soul would wait until judgment day.[19] Correspondingly, the attitude toward death was not one of hopelessness or fright, but of consent to the draw of collective destiny and abiding faith in a heavenly reward.

In theater history, this view of death is apparent in the miracle and mystery play traditions. Though an exhaustive overview of these traditions is beyond the scope of this essay, it is nonetheless fair to say that in these plays death is repeatedly established as the collective destiny of all believers; as a passing from this world into the afterlife; and as an event that, though perhaps uncomfortable and difficult, in no way constitutes complete annihilation. Thus, be it the passion and resurrection of Christ in the mysteries, or the martyrdom of pious saints in the miracles, the representation of death is guided by the presupposition *Et moriemur* and, as such, is established as familiar, accepted, and necessary.

Beginning in the twelfth century, the traditional suppositions of *Et moriemur* were slowly supplanted by an attitude focused more squarely on the individual. Forgoing the notion of "collective destiny," this new attitude "expressed the indiviudal's desire to assert his creative identity in this world and the next, his refusal to let it dissolve into some biological or social anonymity."[20] This emerging protohumanist attitude, championing a nascent modern awareness of the private self and property and termed by Ariés as *"la mort de soi,* one's own death,"[21] was initially the conceit of the economic and intellectual elite.[21] Nonetheless, it subsequently came to reflect the burgeoning bourgeoisie's emerging views regarding selfhood and the prospects and challenges of self-determination, as well as its growing anxiety about its own death, the heavenly afterlife, and its place in it. This anxiety, born from the increasing chasm separating individual from community, and earthly life from afterlife, was manifest most obviously in that population's newfound concern for its own mortality; its growing and impassioned resentment/fear of death; and its newly adopted attitude that death, though inescapable, was to be not to be yielded to, but instead struggled against.[22]

This attitude regarding death, which Kent Cartwright identifies with a protohumanistic impulse, became increasingly discernible in the late fifteenth-, sixteenth-, and seventeenth-century European theater and had a marked impact on Tudor drama.[23] This impulse is readily apparent in Norton and Sackville's tragedy *Gorboduc* (1561/65). When the title character of this play, a mythical king of England, foolishly divides his kingdom between his two sons to ensure their "profit and advancement," he sets into motion a series of events that will ultimately lead to the murder of not only the sons but also his wife, himself, and ultimately the citizens who rebel.[24] Despite warnings from his wise counselors that his decision to divide the kingdom will lead to the "ruin of this noble realm," Gorboduc—driven by anxiety about his own mortality and concerned about the continuancy of his family line and issues of inheritance—pushes ahead, exerting his individual will.[25] As the play unfolds, and as casualties mount, borne from this expression of individual will, death is variously configured as a "creeping" inevitability that is "cruel," "reproachful," and "graved."[26] Furthermore, the deaths represented in *Gorboduc* are never natural, but instead are the result of acts of humans who have disturbed the divine order of things. Thus, the play, in its blending of traditional medieval and protohumanist ideas, corresponds to the presuppositions of *la mort de soi*.[27]

On the heels of this attitudinal shift another occurred in the eighteenth century, when *la mort de soi* gave way to what Ariés dubs *la mort de to*, or "thy death."[28] Ariés offers a concise description of the character of this new mind-set: "The death of self had lost its meaning. The fear of death . . . was transferred from the self to the other, the loved one."[29] In brief, death, through the process of privatization, became an object and was perceived as no longer happening to the self, but only to others. As such, any emotional pain an individual experienced came not from facing one's own death, but was manifest only when someone else ("the loved one") died. For Ariés, this shift from a focus on self to a focus on others in relation to the end of life constitutes the birth of the conception of denial of death (i.e., death happens to others)—an idea that would continue to hold sway in the modern and contemporary West. This distancing of/from death was further symbolized in the moving of burial sites from the center of cities and towns to locations more remote. Thus, the living and the dead, as well as the self and death, were separated, one from the other. This separation of self from death had other important ramifications, principally the aforementioned objectification of death. Distanced from the self, death was readily sentimentalized, romanticized, beautified, even eroticized. As Ariés posits, during the late eighteenth and early nineteenth centuries, "man in western societies tended to give death a new meaning. He exalted it, dramatized it."[30]

While no single example from theater history embodies all of the wide-ranging presuppositions of *la mort de to*, in a number of ways the ubiquitous melodramatic form of the nineteenth century brought to innumerable Western stages this new vision of death. As noted earlier, whereas under the sway of *Et moriemur* death had been communal, by the nineteenth century it had become distinctly private. Moreover, with the shift away from the presuppositions of "one's own death" to those of "thy death," the character of mortality on stage altered as well, moving from a focus on the death of an individual to a focus on the grief process of the living. The nineteenth century was replete with melodramas that include emotionally wrought, sentimental scenes, where a still-living family member, sick with grief, is barely able to tolerate the recent death of a loved one. Such an event occurs in Act III, scene iv, of the wildly popular *Uncle Tom's Cabin* (1852), where the "dreadful" death of the innocent child Eva becomes secondary to the histrionic mourning of those who are also present: Uncle Tom, St. Clare, Ophelia, and Marie.[31] Moreover, there is an overriding sense that with the child's death, a brutal rupture will occur between life and death—one that cannot be spanned.[32] Thus, in a number of important ways, Aiken's script embodies the highly sentimentalized attitude toward death unique to this era.

Beginning in the second half of the nineteenth century and extending well into the twentieth, the impulses characterizing *la mort de to* were overstated, creating the modern attitude toward death. This modern conception of death, variously termed by Ariés as "forbidden death" and "invisible death," marks a complete volte face from the presuppositions of *Et moriemur*. Whereas in the Middle Ages death was ubiquitous, communal, and acknowledged, in the modern world it was cast as reprehensible, private, and concealed. And whereas it was once viewed as part of the natural order of things, death was now thought to be unnatural. In light of this, as Ariés claims, "death has become *unnamable*"; society has become "ashamed of death, more ashamed than afraid," and behaves "as if death [does] not exist."[33] Thus, the denial of death becomes almost pathological. As this attitude took root and flourished, and shame supplanted fear as the ruling emotion related to mortality, death was situated less and less as a natural occurrence that happens to all living things and increasingly as an irresistible and overwhelming tragedy and, perhaps most importantly for the purposes of my argument, as a symbol of defeat and ultimate failure. This shift to view death as failure is coexistent with the humanist belief in progress. Indeed, because it stops cold the faith placed in the future, death must become abnormal, dispensable, and a source of shame. Significantly, however, while death was becoming taboo and hidden from life, its absence in the modern world was not total. That is to say, "forbidden death" or "invisible death" did not equate with the disappearance of death.[34] In short, then, though hidden, death was also present, thus leading to the ruling presupposition of the modern attitude regarding mortality: Because death is failure, it does not exist. And yet, it is everywhere.

The first half of the twentieth century saw the staging of numerous plays that embodied the paradoxical presuppositions of forbidden death. However, it is likely that none was as popular as, or had the impact of, Arthur Miller's *Death of a Salesman*. Of course, the very title reveals that death looms large in the play.[35] And yet that death, though ever present, is also consistently denied. Time and again, when the discussion turns to mortality and the prospect of death, it is dismissed as something unspeakable that retards the march of progress and, therefore, is of no concern for the living. For example, near the end of Act II, and mere moments before Willy commits suicide, he adamantly denies his secret obsession with death and the possibility that it might occur. When Biff confronts him with the rubber tube he found in the cellar, Willy refuses to acknowledge or even look at it.[36] Dismissed out of hand, death is configured as an irrelevancy and symbol of failure. However, in the end, the pall of failure that has followed Willy through his life—his obsession with suicide, as well as his failure as a husband, a father, and a salesman—marks his death as well. To be sure, while many have argued that Willy's suicide is a final act of a tragic hero and stands as his way of triumphing over insurmountable odds by providing for his family, his death may also be viewed as merely the final failure in a long line of indignities.[37] This becomes readily apparent in the requiem that closes the play. There, standing beside his grave, Willy's family does not see his death as a triumph of any kind.[38] For them, Willy's death is neither natural and necessary, but a symbol of one individual's ultimate failure.

Coda

I distinctly recall instances from my own actor-training history when, as a student, I was encouraged to weigh the effectiveness, validity, and value of my chosen objectives and superobjective against life-and-death stakes by applying to my work the hypothetical, "I must achieve my goal, or I'll die." In particular, I remember very vividly one acting instructor asserting time and again with every role I played, "If the objective you have identified for your character is more than two or three steps removed from the possibility of death, it isn't strong enough." The prospect of death thus loomed as a great, disquieting prospect that was to be avoided at all costs.

While structuring a role in this way undoubtedly makes sense when dealing with certain texts—that is, when the dramatic text is also imprinted with the denial of death and the vision that dying constitutes failure—assuming this attitude as a default position is problematic, especially when actors are working on texts that carry with them different attitudes and assumptions regarding mortality. Indeed, to unconditionally impose the modern, humanist, Stanislavskian template of death (and, for that matter, acting) on a character that belongs to another time and place is historiographically suspect. As such, I would like to suggest the necessity of having an historically informed actor, one who will bring to the structuring of his or her role an awareness of the history and historiography of death. To be sure, an actor who holds a savvy understanding of death will not only enhance his or her understanding of the Stanislavskian emphasis on life-and-death stakes but will also build an awareness of how people in different times understood and represented death differently.

While having historically informed actors is an irrefutable benefit, I contend that all theater historians and artists should aim to never assume or assign universal conceptions of mortality when engaging with historical objects. To support this assertion, I return to the three quotes used in the epigraph of this essay. The first quote, spoken by the queen of the destroyed city of Troy, is decidedly similar to modern humanistic conceptions of death, that is, that it constitutes utter annihilation.[39] The second, by Freud, reiterates Hecuba and adds denial, another key characteristic of the modern conception of death.[40] Paul Tillich, however, points up the limits of such modern and humanist thinking: "And if one is not able to die, is he really able to live?"[41] In calling on all to face mortality, Tillich's question directs us out of the modern and humanistic state of mind and asks us instead to think differently about mortality. Tillich's call is an important one if we believe the oft-made claim that all plays written on some level deal with humanity's preoccupation with two occurrences basic to human existence: sex and death. Thus, if scholars and artists intend to interpret and present works that deal with the latter of these two issues with integrity, it seems vital to recognize how contexts and ideologies have structured attitudes toward this, one of the greatest of human events.

NOTES

1. Arthur Schopenhauer, "Our Death and Its Relation to the Indestructability of Our Inner Nature," in *The World as Will and Representation, Vol. 2*, trans. E. F. J. Payne (New York: Dover, 1966 [1819/1844]), 463. Also see Dale Jacquette, *The Philosophy of Schopenhauer* (Montreal: McGill-Queens University Press, 2005).

2. Jonathan Dollimore, *Death, Desire, and Loss in Western Culture* (New York: Routledge, 1998), 153. An incomplete list of post-Enlightenment/modern, European thinkers who ruminated on death would include Hegel, Schopenhauer, Nietzsche, Freud, Jung, Heidegger, Camus, Sartre, and Marcuse.

3. See, e.g., Sigmund Freud, *The Future of an Illusion*, ed. James Strachey, trans. W. D. Robson-Scott (Garden City: Doubleday, 1964 [1927]).

4. Sigmund Freud, "Our Attitude towards Death" (1915), in *The Standard Edition of the Complete Psychological Works of Sigmund Freud, Volume XIV (1914–1916)*, ed. and trans. James Strachey (London: Hogarth Press and the Institute of Psycho-Analysis, 1957), 289.

5. Robert Jay Lifton and Eric Olson, "Symbolic Immortality" (1974), in *Death, Mourning, and Burial: A Cross-Cultural Reader*, ed. Antonius C. G. M. Robben (Oxford: Blackwell, 2004), 33, 36.

6. Jeaneane D. Fowler, *Humanism: Beliefs and Practices* (Brighton: Sussex Academic, 1999), 21–22.

7. Fowler, *Humanism*, 38.

8. Alfred G. Killilea, *The Politics of Being Mortal* (Lexington: University of Kentucky Press, 1988), 4. Also see Vivian M. Rakoff, "Psychiatric Aspects of Death in America," in *Death in American Experience*, ed. Arien Mack (New York: Schocken Books, 1972). This abiding faith in the future underpins the view that "the dead and their concerns are simply not relevant to the living in a society that feels liberated from the authority of the past and orients its energies toward immediate preoccupations and future possibilities" (Robert Blauner, "Death and Social Structure," *Psychiatry* [1966]: 391).

9. Johan Huizinga, *The Waning of the Middle Ages* (Garden City: Doubleday, 1956), 138; Phillipe Ariés, *The Hour of Our Death*, trans. Helen Weaver (New York: Knopf, 1981), 124–29.

10. Colin Counsell, *Signs of Performance: An Introduction to Twentieth-Century Theatre* (London: Routledge, 1996), 26, 40.

11. Stanislavski refers to the concept variously as "continuous grip," "inner grip," "iron grip," and "mortal grip."

12. Konstantin Stanislavski, *An Actor's Work*, ed. and trans. Jean Benedetti (London: Routledge, 2008), 251–52, emphasis added.

13. Constantin Stanislavski, *An Actor Prepares*, trans. Elizabeth Reynolds Hapgood (New York: Theatre Arts, 1984 [1936]), 204–6.

14. Charles Waxberg, *The Actor's Script: Script Analysis for Performers* (Portsmouth, NH: Heinemann, 1998), 47–50. "The urgency of a life and death struggle" is indeed reiterated by many modern and contemporary authors as a hallmark of the modern actor's process (Robert Benedetti, *The Actor at Work*, 8th ed. [Boston: Allyn and Bacon, 2001 (1970)], 96).

15. In *Death, Grief, and Mourning: Individual and Social Realities*, John Stephenson writes that death in the modern West represents the ultimate failure—failure of science and, more importantly, failure of the individual, who is supposed to be in control of his or her own fate (Killilea, *Politics of Being Mortal*, 5).

16. Dollimore, 63 and 161.

17. Philippe Ariés, *Western Attitudes toward Death: From the Middle Ages to the Present*, trans. Patricia M. Ranum (Baltimore: Johns Hopkins University Press, 1974), 13, 55.

18. This overlapping and comingling of life and afterlife was symbolized most obviously in the placement of burial sites at the hub of social/religious life (i.e., in churchs and churchyards), visited every day by the living (Ariés, *Western Attitudes toward Death*, 25).

19. Ariés, *Western Attitudes toward Death*, 14.

20. Philippe Ariés, *The Hour of Our Death*, trans. Helen Weaver (New York: Alfred A. Knopf, 1981), 606.

21. Ariés, *Western Attitudes toward Death*, 52.

22. Dollimore, 120.

23. As Kent Cartwright argues in *Theatre and Humanism: English Drama in the Sixteenth Century*, the protohumanist impulse was a significant, shaping force on theater during the Tudor period and inspired the exchange of Christian moralistic polemics for nuanced discussions of human potential (*Theatre and Humanism: English Drama in the Sixteenth Century* [Cambridge: Cambridge University Press, 1999]).

24. Thomas Norton and Thomas Sackville, *Gorboduc*, in *Renascence Editions: An Online Repository of Works Printed in English Between the Years 1477 and 1799*, ed. Risa Stephanie Bear (2003 [1565]), https://scholarsbank.uoregon.edu/xmlui/bit stream/handle/1794/772/gorboduc.pdf?sequence=1 (accessed 6 Mar. 2009), Act I, scene ii, ln. 154.

25. *Gorboduc*, Act V, scene ii, ln. 182.

26. *Gorboduc*, Act I, scene ii, ln. 105; Act IV, scene i, ln. 27; Act I, scene i, ln. 66; Act IV, scene i, ln. 20.

27. Irving Ribner, *The English History Play in the Age of Shakespeare* (London: Routledge, 2005 [1965]), 47–49.

28. Ariés, *Western Attitudes toward Death*, 56.

29. Ariés, *Hour of Our Death*, 610.

30. Ariés, *Western Attitudes toward Death*, 56–57.

31. George L. Aiken, *Uncle Tom's Cabin*, in *"Uncle Tom's Cabin" and American Culture*, ed. Steven Railton (2007 [1858, Samuel French]), http://www.iath.vir ginia.edu/utc/onstage/scripts/aikenhp.html (accessed 1 Mar. 2009), Act III, scene iv.

32. Dan Meinwald, "Memento Mori: Death and Photography in Nineteenth Century America," in *Terminals* (1999), http://vv.arts.ucla.edu/terminals/mein wald/meinwald1.html (accessed 20 Feb. 2009).

33. Ariés, *Western Attitudes toward Death*, 106, emphasis in original; Ariés, *Hour of Our Death*, 613.

34. Ariès, building on the work of Geoffrey Gorer, cited the process of embalming, an attempt to keep the dead present but also to deny the natural decaying processes that follow death, as an example of this view.

35. In *"Death of a Salesman* and the Poetics of Arthur Miller," Matthew C. Roudané documents this presence, meticulously cataloging the "death saturated dialogues," as well as the numerous "death illusions" that "permeate the script" (*"Death of a Salesman* and the Poetics of Arthur Miller," in *Cambridge Companion to Arthur Miller*, ed. Christopher Bigsby [Cambridge: Cambridge University Press, 1997], 76–77). In so doing, he offers evidence that death is tacitly, though powerfully and consistently, present in Miller's script.

36. Arthur Miller, *Death of a Salesman* (New York: Penguin, 1986 [1949]), 130.

37. Midway through Act II, Charley claims, "Willy, nobody's worth nothin' dead" (Miller, *Death of a Salesman*, 98). While Willy takes from this assertion the belief that he is worth more in death than life, for other characters in the play it is evident that this is not so.

38. Despite Charley's warning that "Nobody dast blame this man," the family sees the suicide as a meaningless and empty act: Biff views it as one more failure of

a man "who didn't know who he was"; Happy sees it as a model of failure that will inspire him to "beat this racket"; and Linda "can't understand it" (Miller, *Death of a Salesman*, 138–39).

39. Euripides, *The Trojan Women*, trans. Brendan Kennelly (Newcastle: Blood-axe Books, 1993), 37. Richard Lattimore's popular, mid-twentieth-century translation of this line is very similar: "No life, no light is any kind of death, since death is nothing" (150). See *The Trojan Women*, in *Euripides III*, ed. David Grene and Richard Lattimore, trans. Richard Lattimore (Chicago: University of Chicago Press, 1958).

40. Freud, "Our Attitude toward Death," 289.

41. Paul Tillich, "The Eternal Now" (1963), in *The Essential Tillich: An Anthology of the Writings of Paul Tillich*, ed. F. Forrester Church (Chicago: University of Chicago Press, 1999), 122.

PART IV

Performance as Historiography

Corpsing Molière

History as Fiasco

MECHELE LEON ✺

> When you realize that you are not getting something—a joke, a proverb, a ceremony—that is particularly meaningful to the natives, you can see where to grasp a foreign system of meaning in order to unravel it.
>
> —Robert Darnton, *The Great Cat Massacre*

> That corpsing might have something to do with the unwanted irruption of the real amid the unreality of the stage fiction is suggested here. But nobody is laughing. Something is going wrong and no one is prepared to admit they find it funny.
>
> —Nicholas Ridout, *Stage Fright, Animals,*
> *and Other Theatrical Problems*

There are minor but provocative discrepancies in historical accounts of Molière's death. According to the entry in La Grange's company register for February 17, 1673, Molière died in his home on the rue de Richelieu at ten o'clock in the evening after having performed the role of Argan in the comédie-ballet *Le malade imaginaire*. He was "greatly discomforted by a chest infection and a violent cough."[1] A similar account is given by La Grange in the preface to the first edition of Molière's complete works (1682). A few years after this, however, a pamphlet about the life of Molière's wife, Armande Béjart, suggested that Molière never completed the performance. According to *La fameuse comédienne*, the actors had great trouble rousing Molière after the scene in which Argan fakes death as a ploy in order to test the sincerity of his spouse.[2] Although he managed to revive and play on, during the final *intermède*—the wildly burlesque medical initiation ceremony—as Molière spoke the words "rhubarb and senna," blood suddenly poured from his mouth. This caused "extreme fright in both audience and fellow actors," and Molière was rushed away.[3]

177

By 1697, the idea had taken hold that Molière expired on stage during the performance itself. Apparently this mistaken notion was so widespread that Pierre Bayle felt it necessary to correct it in his *Dictionnaire historique et critique* (1697):

> An infinite number of people have said that Molière died [while faking Argan's death]. When it was time to continue playing, it became clear that it was not an act and that he could neither speak nor arise; he was actually dead. This remarkable event, having something uncanny to it, has furnished poets with plenty of striking and ingenious ideas, which is apparently the reason the tale has come to be believed. . . . But the truth is that Molière did not die in this way. Suffering though he was, he had time to finish the performance.[4]

New details appeared in *La vie de Molière* (1705). As for many of the anecdotes in this early biography of the playwright/actor, Grimarest's source was most likely Michel Baron, the celebrated actor whose association with Molière's troupe began in 1665: "Moliere performed with much difficulty; half the spectators noticed that at the moment of pronouncing 'juro' ('I swear') during the ceremony in *Le malade Imaginaire*, he had a convulsion. Remarking that this had been noticed, [Moliere] roused himself and with a forced laugh covered up what had just happened."[5]

Piecing together these different stories, historians conclude that Molière undertook the performance while quite ill; he was probably roused with difficulty following Argan's deathbed scene and subsequently suffered a pulmonary hemorrhage during the final sequence of the play. As to the exact moment of convulsion, "juro" is as likely as "rhubarb and senna." However, Michel Baron's account, coming as it does from an actor who was onstage for *Le malade imaginaire* (probably in the role of Béralde), has the edge on credibility over the story offered by the anonymous author of *La fameuse comédienne*—a questionable work of history that sought to damage the reputation of Molière's widow.[6]

Molière's death did not occur on stage, then, but a stage death took place. A rupture in representation occurred that suspended the performance, unsettled the actors, and startled the audience. It subsequently fueled a fascination in cultural memory that initially provided contemporary poets with rich metaphors for their epitaphs and then went on to inspire biographical drama on stage and in film. Molière's last performance involved the kind of stage death referred to in theater slang as "corpsing." This particular corpsing with its subsequent historiographical performances suggests an intriguing relationship between theatrical fiascos and the disasters, curiosities, and unfathomable jokes that arrest the attention of historians. The case of Molière's last performance of *Le malade imaginaire* also illuminates the possibility that historiographical representations, like theatrical representations, derive value from their own undoing.

"Corpsing" in British slang refers to instances in theater in which the actor is the perpetrator or victim of a stage blunder (usually involving laughing or forgetting lines) that spoils the performance of the play. In *Stage Fright, Animals, and Other Theatrical Problems*, Nicholas Ridout offers a fascinating discussion of this phenomenon well-known to both actors and audiences. At its most basic, corpsing amounts to an embarrassing, surprising, shocking, and sometimes hilarious deviation (in the sense of both a departure and a detour) from the "proper route" of a rehearsed production. It is a phenomenon affecting both actor and audience, as well as the premise of stage representation itself. As an "unwanted irruption of the real amid the unreality of the stage fiction"—to recall this chapter's epigraph—corpsing is a malfunction of theatrical illusion, an enemy to representational coherency.[7] For the actor who finds himself at a loss for the next line of dialogue or seized with uncontrollable laugher, to be thus "corpsed" is to be suddenly exposed, embarrassed, *voire* mortified. "The actor is cut adrift from the play," Ridout writes, "dislodged from the vehicle of the part or role, dumped out of the textual fabric of the play to appear as just himself, not the character he is trying to represent."[8] "Corpsing" as a term to describe this representational failure has a correlate in the commonplace of "dying" onstage (as in "I died out there" or a performance "having died"). Ridout ponders why laughing actors and failed performances should be described in similar morbid terms and suggests that it has something to do with the actor coming out of character: "In that coming out, nothing is left behind. There is no character left on stage into which the actor can be put back. The moment of laughter annihilates the represented being, leaving the performer alone on stage, helpless, with nothing to fall back on, nothing to do, no one to be. The actor does not 'die' himself, but rather commits an act upon the illusionary character: 'corpsing' it."[9] "The moment of the corpse," Ridout later writes, "is the moment in which we see the character crumple, and in the same moment, or just after, see the actor in effect standing over the dead body of the character, smoking gun in hand and silly grin on face."[10] The face of an actor corpsed is a macabre sight, presenting "a fixed grin, an immobilization of the expressive features, a freezing of the face into a mask that might resemble death."[11]

A defining feature of the corpsed performance is the actor's battle to re-gain physical self-control. In corpsing, "the body becomes a helpless ob-ject, shaken and squeezed until it starts to burst all over, overflow, exceed its bounds, lose all coherence. . . . Self-control is both alienated (main-tained in the interests of external forces) and threatened (by aspects of the same external forces), in a double movement which issues in the combina-tion of outburst and cover-up, falling apart and pulling yourself to-gether."[12]

The demands of an irrepressible body paired with the opposite and equal necessity for composure produces a struggle so violent as to make re-counting it the basis of a unique historiographical genre: the stage-life anecdote. Ridout offers several examples from Kenneth Branagh's 1990 autobiography, *Beginning*. While performing in a West End production, Branagh and his group of scene partners regularly gave in to fits of giggles, provoking the censure of a senior cast member (which only led to "stifled whimpers"—that is, more failed efforts at self-control). In another in-stance, Branagh recounts how the entire cast of a television production filming of Ibsen's *Ghosts* suffered uncontrollable fits of hysteria: a carnival of actors bending double, tears rolling down cheeks, hands covering faces, napkins stuffed in mouths, convulsions of laughter.[13] For the spectators of corpsing, Ridout suggests that these events provide an "erotic charge," a special excitement brought on by theatrical fiasco and specifically "the con-noisseur's delight at seeing how the mechanism works at the moment of its breakdown."[14] This is a powerful affective experience. It is "the occasion of some of [theater's] most intense pleasures and discomfort."[15] In sum, Rid-out's exploration of corpsing situates it as part of a complex phenomenon involving not only corpsing but the fascination it invites, and the com-pelling narrative accounts it generates. In other words, there is complicity among corpsed event, witnessing, and recounting.

The performance of *Le malade imaginaire* on February 17, 1673, has all the markings of a corpsed performance—seizure, deviation, embarrass-ment, laughter, and especially the "irruption of the real amid the unreality of the stage fiction"—all brought to a tragic conclusion: an actual death. The sparse but provocative accounts of the event testify to a performance whose rehearsed progression was clearly, if fleetingly, subjected to a terri-ble irruption of the real. Molière as Argan was to rise up abruptly from his fake deathbed; instead, nothing happened. In moments of stage corpsing—as in those moments in life when we learn about the death of someone we love—the substance of time changes, becomes suspended. Did Molière's fellow performers gather in the wings and hold their breath? Did those on stage widen their eyes, steal glances at each other in that special way that actors silently communicate on stage about stage doings? Like an actor suffering from a strong desire to laugh, Molière was betrayed by irrepressible physical demands. His body wanted sleep instead of action, and blood poured from his mouth even as he intended to speak the words "I swear." While this corpsing was not a result of uncontrollable laughter, laughter was involved in Molière's attempt to hide the loss of control: *"Remarking that this had been noticed, [Moliere] roused himself and with a forced laugh covered up what had just happened."* This was the falling apart and pulling oneself together that Ridout suggests marks the laughing actor. Actors sometimes turn unwanted laughter into a cough; in this instance the opposite apparently occurred as Molière transformed coughing into laughter, perhaps turning a face contorted in pain into one contorted by clowning. It was the face of the actor corpsed: the frozen grimace, the immobilized face, the mask of death. Molière became exposed as the cover of character fell away. Argan was left in the dust and Molière emerged, himself and utterly alone.[16] The sudden solitude of the corpsed actor that Ridout speaks of eerily reminds me of a critic's response to the first biographical drama on Molière's death, *La mort de Molière*, by Michel Cubières-Palmézeaux (1789). Charnois, writing in *Le Mercure de France*, found the stage depiction of Molière's death simply too painful to bear. He writes:

> When one recalls the circumstances surrounding the death of Molière, one sees the contemplator *par excellence*, the apostle of morality, the denouncer of vices, one of the most ardent adherents of sane philosophy, one sees, in sum, an enlightened man, sensitive and generous, isolated in his last moments, beyond all assistance, abandoned by nature herself.[17]

Corpsing and its "mutual predicament" fiasco produce intense and vivid events for performers and audiences alike; these events endure in memory and call out for retelling. Like tales of corpsing in actor biographies, Molière's corpsing in 1673, once lodged in cultural memory, continued to excite popular imagination through historiographical repetition. With varying degrees of detail and accuracy, Molière's stage death (or near death) has been depicted from the eighteenth century to the present in biographical drama, historical films, biographical narratives, poems, and commemorative events. Some of these performances re-create the last moments of *Le malade imaginaire* or a fictionalized version of presumed backstage action; other representations focus on Molière's passing as it occurred following the performance. The depiction of his dying sometimes comprises only one episode in a larger biographical or historical drama; in other cases, the premise of the work is his death alone.[18] These representations are inspired by the same gripping event, the corpsed performance. Like the ubiquitous stage-life anecdote, this persistent retelling of the past points to a larger phenomenon: the historiographically generative quality of corpsing events. Not surprisingly, theater historiography thrives on stories of mishaps; disrupted performances; and other events in which actors and audiences are treated to the thrill of a disturbance in the representational apparatus, of a deviation in its "proper route." (Most typical of these are the stories of riots, for example, the premier of *Hernani* in 1830 or New York's Astor Place Theatre in 1849.)

Of the many historiographical performances concerning the death of Molière, two films in particular help illustrate something of this special interpenetration of corpsing and historiography. These films offer an account of Molière's death, and they do so in a way that captures the quality of the corpsed performance that defined the original event. In the famous ending to Ariane Mnouchkine's 1979 film *Molière*, Molière is rushed off stage following the final scene of *Le malade imaginaire* and then taken by carriage to his home. His company members carry him bleeding and half conscious up the stairs, but their climb becomes interminable. For every two or three steps forward the group falls back. It is the kind of stair-climbing that one experiences in a bad dream: striving but never making it to the top landing. This lengthy and disturbing sequence is scored with a halting sequence from Henry Purcell's semiopera *King Arthur*. Mnouchkine created a scene for the death of Molière that seems to capture the nature of a corpsed event as a disruption in the fabric of time, a *seizure* of representation. It focuses viewers on the moment: on those actors, that man, that staircase. The typical representational mode of film where time passes in realistic fashion becomes instead the suspended temporality of the corpsed staged. Historians corpse time in similar fashion, training attention on a moment, a period, or an era, until it slows to a crawl under the gaze of investigation.

Robert Wilson's 1994 film *La mort de Molière* goes further in this vein. The film's forty-seven minutes are focused entirely on those moments when Molière rests only seconds from death. Time for him has almost stopped. He lies silent, opening his mouth but without a voice. Like the actor gone up in his lines, no words emerge. As in Mnouchkine's depiction, Wilson gives us a nightmare—an actor's nightmare. History, meanwhile, continues on around Molière: Galileo watches a comet, Colbert boasts of the colonization of America, Racine recites his verses, and Louis XIV dances. Molière lays dying, immune to time, corpsed. This juxtaposition is captured in Heiner Müller's text, which is heard in voice-over:

> This is a poem about Molière
> The poem watches Molière dying
> The poem watches a dying man at work
> Who is called Molière The Poem is not a film
> The film watches an actor at work
> Who plays a dying man who is called Molière.
>
> Galileo watches the stars.
> The stars are not concerned
> With the chance of mankind, an experiment
> between angel and beast. The outcome
> depends on circumstances other than
> The orbits of the stars.
>
> Molière is dying.[19]

The Molière of Wilson's film is the naked actor, a mere "dying man." Molière's dying, as Charnois pointed out, is an image of utter isolation, of a man "abandoned by nature herself." Following the essence of corpsing as the unmasking of an actor, the text also exposes Wilson as "an actor at work who plays a dying man who is called Molière."

In the conclusion to his chapter on laughter, Ridout suggests that corpsing (and its partner fiasco) is not so much an unhappy detour in the progress of theatrical representation as the foundation, paradoxically, of the pleasure it offers spectators. Corpsings are inseparable from the performance they appear to spoil. Ridout suggests that actorly blunders such as fits of laughter are evidence of the unique value of theater as an indispensible and reliable medium for elusive outbreaks of presence. "Any moment," he writes, "which aspires to the grace of 'pure, punctual presence' must also live by its entanglement with repetition." That is, the longed-for experience of presence that is precisely *not* representation is found "right here, in the theatre of representation, by way of the gracelessness that fails, or the sheer pleasure of watching the wheels spin."[20]

Historiographical performance, like historiography, offers the special thrill that accompanies unmasking a mystery, revealing essence, the possibility of seeing the occluded, and the promise of finally getting the joke. Constructing history in ways salient and meaningful involves willing encounters with representations of the past while keeping a keen, spectator's eye trained for the events that trouble these representations. It means noticing those moments when imagined knowledges about history are challenged—as Darnton suggests, by the joke one does not get.[21] Theater is a powerful place to represent history precisely for this reason. If historiography feeds on those places where representations of the past fail (to be understood), where better to perform history than through an art whose affirming value is its tolerance for events that undermine its own form? In this, corpsing suggests to me an opportunity to take a methodological position that affirms theater, not merely as an object of study, but as an informing framework, a conceptual model, and an imaginative incitement, for historiography. I like my theater history to be stageworthy, by which I do not mean entertaining. I want it to accommodate not only meaningful representations of the past but the inevitable disruption—the corpsing—of those representations.

NOTES

1. Georges Mongrédien, *Recueil des textes et des documents du XVIIème siècle relatifs á Molière*, 2nd ed. (Paris: C.N.R.S., 1973), 2: 435.

2. There are two such instances of Argan playing dead in the play, and it is not clear exactly which one this account refers to. Argan fakes death at the start of Act III, scene xii. One or two minutes of dialogue ensue between Argan's wife, Béline, and Toinette, the servant, before Argan rises (abruptly, according to the stage direction) to surprise Béline. After she exits, Argan once again plays dead, this time to test his daughter Angélique. Another short sequence of dialogue occurs involving several more characters, until Argan wakes to greet his daughter.

3. Anonymous, *La fameuse comédienne, ou Histoire de la Guérin auparavant femme et veuve de Molière* (1688), ed. Etienne Wolff (Monaco: Rocher, 2001), 55.

4. Pierre Bayle, *Dictionnaire historique et critique* (Rotterdam, 1697), 4: 870. In referring to poets' ideas, Bayle had in mind the dozens of epitaphs to Molière that appeared immediately following his death, many of which were based on the conceit of Molière as an actor who played his part too well.

5. Jean-Léonor de Grimarest, *La vie de M. de Molière* (1705), ed. Georges Mongrédien (1955; repr., Geneva: Slatkine Reprints, 1973), 120.

6. For a discussion of evidence regarding Molière's final hours, see Pierre Bonvallet, *Molière de tous les jours: échos, potins et anecdotes* (Paris: Imago, 1995), 278–81; Virginia Scott, *Molière: A Theatrical Life* (Cambridge: Cambridge University Press, 2000), 256–57. The usefulness of *La fameuse comédienne* as a historical source is discussed in Etienne Wolff's introduction to the edition referenced earlier.

7. Nicholas Ridout, *Stage Fright, Animals, and Other Theatrical Problems* (Cambridge: Cambridge University Press, 2006), 132.

8. Ridout, *Stage Fright*, 133.

9. Ridout, *Stage Fright*, 134–35.

10. Ridout, *Stage Fright*, 147.

11. Ridout, *Stage Fright*, 135.

12. Ridout, *Stage Fright*, 142.

13. Ridout, *Stage Fright*, 136–37.

14. Ridout, *Stage Fright*, 148.

15. Ridout, *Stage Fright*, 158.

16. It is an unfortunate fact that nothing in the way of eyewitness accounts of Molière's death has been recorded, aside from the remarks quoted earlier. Judging from the material that has survived, attention seems to have been drawn immediately to the attempt to secure him a Christian burial.

17. Jean-Charles Levacher de Charnois, *Le Mercure de France*, June 13, 1789, 78.

18. Plays depicting Molière's death, dating from 1789 to 1922, include *La mort de Molière* (Michel Cubières-Palmézeaux, 1789); *La mort de Molière* (Théophile Marion Dumersan, 1830); *La mort de Molière* (M. Pinchon, 1873); *La fin de Molière* (G. Janelli); and *Le dernier soir de Molière* (anonymous, 1914). Maurice Rostand wrote a dramatic poem, *La mort de Moliere*, for the tercentenary of his birth in 1922. More recently, his death has been depicted in the films *Molière, ou Vie d'un honnête homme* (Ariane Mnouchkine, 1979); *La mort de Molière* (Robert Wilson, 1994); and *Le roi danse* (Gérard Corbiau, 2000). For a full listing of biographical plays about Molière, see W. D. Howarth, "The Playwright as Hero: Biographical Plays with Molière as Protagonist: 1673–1972," in *Molière and the Commonwealth of Letters: Patrimony and Posterity*, ed. Roger Johnson Jr., Editha S. Neumann, and Guy T. Trail (Jackson: University of Mississippi Press, 1975), 557–72. I discuss the earliest biographical plays about Molière in my study of his revolutionary-era reception, *Molière, the French Revolution, and the Theatrical Afterlife* (Iowa City: University of Iowa Press, 2009).

19. Heiner Müller, "Texts for the Death of Molière," *Performance Research* 1 (1996): 96–103. In quoting I have preserved the punctuation of this text.

20. Ridout, *Stage Fright*, 159.

21. Robert Darnton, *The Great Cat Massacre and Other Episodes in French Cultural History* (New York: Basic Books, 1984), 5.

The Ice

A Collective History of the History of Our Collectivity in the Theater

NICHOLAS RIDOUT ॐ

> We know the scene: there is a gathering, and someone is telling a
> story. We do not yet know whether these people gathered together
> form an assembly, if they are a horde or a tribe. But we call them
> brothers and sisters because they are gathered together and
> because they are listening to the same story.
> . . . .
> We also know that this scene is itself mythic.
>
> —Jean-Luc Nancy, "Myth Interrupted,"
> in *The Inoperative Community*

I.

We file upstairs to the studio of the Théâtre National in Bruxelles. This is
the national theater of Belgium's French-speaking community. In this
officially bilingual city of Brussels (Bruxelles/Brussel) there are two national
theaters: this and the Koninklijke Vlaamse Schouwburg (Royal Flemish
Theater). Once in the theater, we take seats in one of four blocks of seating,
arranged around a square playing space. Behind each of these blocks of seats
hang large photographs, in each of which people are embracing, lovingly, in
everyday situations: in a library, a supermarket, a swimming pool. In two
corners of the studio stand booths in which simultaneous interpreters will
do their work, translating the spoken language of the production (which
will be Latvian) into the two languages of the Belgian capital, Dutch and
French. Each member of the audience receives a set of headphones, and we
are collectively instructed (twice, once in each language) in their correct use
and informed as to which channel on the control panel we should select in
order to hear the language in which we wish to listen.

The performance begins, if it has not begun already, when the members of the acting company of the New Riga Theatre appear and start handing out large-format books for each member of the audience. There are not quite enough to go round, and many of us find ourselves sharing this reading material with our neighbors and in many cases, therefore, making modest negotiations of engagement across and between language communities. This performance is entitled *The Ice. A Collective Reading of the Book with the Help of Imagination in Riga.* It is based on *Ice,* by the contemporary Russian novelist Vladimir Sorokin. It is directed by Alvis Hermanis. Having handed out the books in an efficient, graceful, but uningratiating manner—a little like the crew of an airline with no investment in sycophancy—the actors sit down on chairs set up around the four sides of the playing space, facing one another, so that those closest to us have their backs to us. They carry copies of the Latvian translation of the Russian novel. Someone starts to read, rapidly, functionally, in Latvian. The simultaneous translation begins. It becomes clear that the action described in the spoken text is also represented in the books we have been given, not as text, but as photographic images.

What we are looking at, as we listen to the Latvian (and Dutch or French) spoken, is a kind of photo-novel, or a series of stills from a film that may or not have been made. In these action photographs we can see members of the very same acting company who are here in the theater tonight enacting the very scenes from the novel that we are hearing read to us. In the photographs they are on location, with real cars, buildings, and streets. Here, in the theater, the same actors start to enact the same scenes. They are scenes of abduction and violence, performed brusquely and adequately, but at first, at least, without intensity. What seems to be going on is that individuals are targeted and abducted by some kind of cult. Each abductee is pierced through the heart with a hammer made of ice. When they come round from the effects of this penetration, they experience a deep feeling of love for the group among whom they now find themselves. They become aware of their real names and acquire the ability to communicate with other members of the group in a twenty-three-word language of the heart. All members of the group are apparently blond and blue-eyed (although by no means do all of the actors match this description). The ice comes from the Siberian impact site of Tunguska, where in 1908 a meteor exploded above the surface of the earth. The cult is gathering its twenty-three thousand members together in anticipation of a collective effort to purge a corrupt world of its millions of parasites. Their leader is a young woman named "Khram," whose own induction into the cult was at the hands of a German SS officer in a labor camp.

The first section of the performance concerns the abduction and induction of three new members of the cult, Nikolaeva, Lapin, and Borenboim. At its conclusion the newly inducted members finally meet Khram herself, and it is at this point that her story, of transport and enslavement in the Third Reich, takes over as a kind of flashback. For this section our photo-novels are replaced by similar large-format books, which, again, we have to share among ourselves. In this second act of "collective reading" the books are graphic novels, depicting the events of Khram's narrative in lurid Nazi-fetish pornographic images: square-jawed men in leather ravishing pouting blond women with improbable lips, eyelashes, and breasts.

Thus an audience, so often a collection of individuals keen to imagine or experience themselves in some kind of collective, or even as a community, finds itself here divided by the very collective act that is supposed to be the point of its gathering: divided by languages and by modes of representation. In this state of uneasy collaborative division, the audience is presented with a fiction of community (the Aryan cult), imagined in the aftermath of the failure and waste of a historical vision of the collective (the Soviet Union). This is presented by a repertory theater company whose evident familiarity with one another and professional distance from the audience mark them out as yet another image, of a community of collective labor (reading, performance) to which the fractured audience might aspire. At least one of those individuals found the seductiveness of this last image of community so powerful that he decided he must turn at once to Plato's *The Republic*, in order to correct this dreadful desire.

2.

Here he discovered that acting things out is especially dangerous. In Book Three of *The Republic* Plato has Socrates explain to Adeimantus that it is not simply the question of what is said or represented in poetry that matters, but also how it is said. Socrates draws a particular distinction between reported and direct speech: "narrative consists of both speeches and passages between speeches, does it not?"[1] The poet then (whom we must imagine still as a speaker, rather than a writer) will "assimilate his manner of speech as nearly as he can" to what he imagines "the character concerned" to be like.[2] This, argues Socrates, is an activity to be avoided in the education of Guardians: "For have you not noticed how dramatic and similar representations, if indulgence in them is prolonged into adult life, establish habits of physical poise, intonation and thought which become second nature?"[3]

The Ice offers its audience a choice among hearing the story read, seeing it represented in a sequence of visual images, or watching its enactment. Or, more precisely, it offers the simultaneous experience of all three. It thus invites the spectator into a negotiation among three modes of apprehension, each of which may alternately reinforce or interfere with the communicative and affective consequences of the others.

In Brussels, of course, this situation was complicated further by translation: of a Russian text, read in Latvian, translated into French. It may have been this additional layer, not intrinsic to the production as conceived but certainly fundamental to the condition of its presentation in Brussels, that drew my attention so forcibly to the negotiation among these modes of apprehension, and to experience in that negotiation problems of sameness and difference. But this simply foregrounded a problem to which the production was in any case addressing itself directly. The form in which Hermanis chose to produce this work was designed to provoke its audience into a reflection upon the modes of representation and apprehension through which it operated and, in doing so, to reflect upon aspects of the history of theatrical representation itself. This act of historiography coincided, as I shall seek to show in the third part of this essay, with a process of reflection upon the history of Latvia and broader questions of how history itself gets made, written, and received.

Translation seeks to produce enough sameness out of difference to permit communication. In my encounter with *The Ice* it was not clear whether two or three languages were in operation. Was I making a mental translation into English from the French translation of the Latvian speech, or was I understanding the French translation in French? Was I, in other words, the same or different? Was I in my proper person, my English language, or was I other than myself, operating out there in French, which is not my language community? In Socrates's terms, was I assimilated to the speech, poise, and thought of another?

Similar questions are provoked by what I perceived as a gradual shift in the mode of acting used in the production. At the start of the performance the actors seemed to be doing a little more than going through the motions, but not a great deal. At some point this changed, however, and retrospectively I wish to assign this shift to the entry of Nikolaeva, Lapin, and Borenboim into full possession by the cult. Certainly as the production moved onward into a series of celebratory collective actions—in which members of the cult ice-skated together, embraced one another in a kind of mass love-in—a far stronger sense of the actors' "assimilation" to their roles emerged. This "assimilation" at the level of the individual actor also produced an interesting and troubling "assimilation" of the collective of the Riga repertory company to the cult itself: troubling because of the sequence of identifications it produced.

The initial indifference of the acting company to the audience (or, at least, the apparent absence on their part of any desire to make us "love" them) also contributed to the event a particularly strong sense of the acting company as a collective. The collective nature of their labor was made apparent, not only in the handing out of books but also in the fluid interplay among them, as readers, speakers, actors, people moving objects around the stage. In representing the Aryan cult community of *The Ice*, the company simultaneously represented to the audience a rather more benign (and desirable) image of a community. The cult—a community based upon the logic of the same (imagined racial identity)—is made seductive in this theater by means of its representation by a company whose logic, as an acting company, might be said to be a logic of difference in search of the same (through the act of impersonation). The seduction rests in the provocation of the audience's desire for interaction and collaboration with the actors: their work-life as the company that performs *The Ice* appears on stage as a highly desirable community of pleasurable labor and love.

This community (of the performance) was within touching distance of the audience but also resisted any move toward participatory assimilation of audience to acting company. At the end of the performance the acting company formed a circle, facing inward (thus, again, so that each actor stood with their back to their closest block of audience), and, as the lights fell, sharpened their ice skates, sending showers of orange sparks into the darkness. This closing image, in which "they" visibly performed an act of spectacularization for "us," both included and excluded: we were the "same" in that we all (perhaps) experienced a certain frisson of minor awe at the play of fire and darkness, but we were "different" inasmuch as "they" made the experience for whichever "us" it was that apprehended it.

Thus in the midst of an experience in which the audience was invited to become acutely vigilant about modes of representation, and in a work that addressed perhaps a topic over which the most particular care needs to be taken in avoiding the seductions of communitarian identification, the production worked to encourage the audience to disregard its own Platonic cautions and to succumb, by means of an affective identification of consumers with producers, to the power of theatrocracy: the terrifying idea of government by theater audiences. What was dangerous here, then, was the production of the desire to act things out, by the act of acting them out.

3.

The history of Latvia's experience of World War II, and of the Holocaust, is, I think, the other main anxiety explored by means of this adaptation of Sorokin's novel. It is the entanglement of these two anxieties that makes the production an act of theatrical self-reflection that is also a work of political historiography. It may be productively compared, briefly, to a parallel project in political historiography: the Museum of the Occupation of Latvia. This museum, established in 1993 (shortly after independence from the Soviet Union in 1991), declares that it has three purposes: "to provide information about Latvia and its people under two occupying totalitarian regimes from 1940 to 1991; remind the world of the wrongdoings committed by foreign powers against the state and people of Latvia; remember those who perished, who suffered, and who fled the terror of the occupying regimes."[4] The museum "collects and preserves documents, photos, written, oral and material evidence, artifacts and keepsakes, which document the occupation of Latvia from 1940 until 1991, as well as the events which led to and the consequences of Soviet and Nazi occupation."[5]

In just under a year of the first period of Soviet occupation it is estimated that "at least 7,292 people were arrested for 'political crimes,' [and] about 1,500 of these were executed."[6] In a single night in June 1941 the Soviet NKVD arrested more than 14,000 people for mass deportation, in an action which prefigured the more systematic deportations of the imminent Nazi occupation. Germany began Operation Barbarossa—its attempt to invade the Soviet Union—with three simultaneous eastward incursions on June 22, 1941. By July 1 they had occupied Riga, and had consolidated control over the entire territory of Latvia by July 5. In the remaining months of 1941 around 70,000 Jews were killed (alongside other supposed enemies of the Nazi regime).[7]

One of the most difficult questions for Latvian historians of this period has been the extent and nature of Latvian complicity in this part of the Nazi genocide. The foremost historian of this question, Andrew Ezergaidis, articulates his own project in familiar terms, thus: "In our journey through the mass of details, testimonies, court procedures, reminiscences, and archival materials we will see emerge a clearer picture of what actually happened in Latvia during the German occupation from 1941 to 1945."[8] This is the promise of historical work: that from perhaps conflicting and incommensurate materials, presenting evidence of differing types and in multiple representational forms, a truth of some kind, or at least "a clearer picture," will be obtained.

To engage in such a project might require the same kind of attention to the forms of representation as that solicited by Hermanis's theatrical production. The Museum of the Occupation of Latvia deals in just such a multiplicity of representational forms (including a virtual gallery), and its own publications reflect this.[9] The thirty-nine-page booklet entitled *Occupation of Latvia. Three Occupations: 1940–1991*, published by the foundation that established the museum and "based on the Museum's archival holdings, exhibition materials and publications," contains maps; photographs and reproductions of texts such as treaties and the secret protocol between Germany and the Soviet Union assigning the Baltic states to a Soviet sphere of influence; notes of protest; illegal leaflets; images of pages from the *New York Times;* bar charts showing shifts in the ethnic composition of the population of Latvia; and a drawing of deportees in a freight car by Aina Roze, daughter of a famous Latvian publisher who was herself deported to Siberia, along with her father, in 1941. The front cover bears an image of a barren tract of land covered in rubble. The back cover shows a map of Europe with Latvia highlighted in red. All of these resources—which we might usefully think of as rhetorical devices or, like the theatrical production under consideration here, as acts of historiography—are mobilized in the service of a particular "story" of the occupations. This "story," as the museum's leading aims have already indicated, will emphasize "wrong-doings committed by foreign powers."

It does not dwell on the activities of the Latvian killing squads led by the right-wing militant Viktors Arjas, who murdered around twenty-six thousand people, mostly Jews, in July 1941 and who also assisted German SS forces in the mass murder of some fifteen thousand Jews at Rumbuli, near Riga, in a single night in November of the same year. The idea of spontaneous Latvian participation in genocide is avoided. In Ezergaidis's more balanced version of the story, this Latvian participation in the murder of Jews was fundamentally different in character from the systematic genocide perpetrated by the Nazis: Ezergaidis argues that Latvian anti-Semitism was not itself a powerful cultural force, that the killing of Jews was primarily motivated by a conflation of Jews with Bolsheviks in the aftermath of Soviet oppression, and that Latvians were generally accomplices rather than instigators. Valdis O. Lumans is even more critical: "Evidently some Latvian commentators want to have it both ways. While arguing that Latvian fighters began spontaneously freeing Latvia before the Germans arrived, they deny the possibility of the spontaneous murder of Jews."[10]

What I want to suggest is that these questions of evidence and responsibility, feeling and representation all converge here upon the problematic of "community." Clearly this particular work of theater bears its own oblique relationship to the events of World War II and to Latvia's occupations. Although Latvia has no place as such in Sorokin's novel, its assimilation by Latvian theater makers draws it into the atmosphere, at least, of that historical problem. One might also incline to think that its presentation in Brussels, of which location the spectator with the simultaneous translation in his ear is constantly reminded, might also open its questions of community and color toward a historical resonance with the colonial Brussels of Joseph Conrad's *Heart of Darkness*, that "white" and "sepulchral city" from which an earlier act of European genocide had been launched. Thus implicated by multiple frames and representations, what might a singular theatrical spectator say now about the "collective reading" that might or might not constitute a "community"?

4.

In *The Inoperative Community* Jean-Luc Nancy inaugurates thus a line of thought about community in the context of the failures and hopes of communism:

> There is . . . no form of communist opposition—or let us say rather "communitarian" opposition, in order to emphasise that the word should not be restricted in this context to strictly *political* references— that has not been or is not still profoundly subjugated to the goal of a *human* community, that is, to the goal of achieving a community of beings producing in essence their own essence as their work, and furthermore producing precisely this essence *as community*.[11]

Nancy seeks to undo this notion of community—which for him is coercive even in its supposedly universalizing form, in communism, let alone in its essentializing, exclusionary, and particularizing form in various kinds of racist constructions—and to develop instead a mode of relation between singular beings, in which, rather than being fused into identifications with the same, we become exposed to the singularity of others and find our relation in the sharing of that exposure. The mythicness of myth is an enabling condition for the emergence of such relations. In the scene "we all know," in which the horde or the family (the community) gathers around the storyteller (like Homer's first admirers, like the audience in Brussels, like the newly inducted cult members around Khram's autobiography), the

community founds itself. But as long as we make and apprehend our theatrical experience of participation in this myth as myth, that is, as long as
we are not carried away or possessed in the event, then this myth is interrupted. As Nancy puts it:

> This does not mean only that community is a myth, that communi-
> tarian communion is a myth. It means that myth and myth's force
> and foundation are essential to community and that there can be,
> therefore, no community outside of myth. Wherever there has been
> myth, assuming there has been something of the sort and that we
> can know what this means, there has been, necessarily, community,
> and vice versa. The interruption of myth is therefore, also, necessar-
> ily, the interruption of community.[12]

What happens, I think, in *The Ice* is a staging of the simultaneous formation and interruption of myth and community together. That is to say
that myth and community appear simultaneously, and also that formation
and interruption do so too. The first is perhaps more obvious than the second: the myth of the cult is what binds the cult to itself. The second concerns the theatrical event itself. Here the audience is warned in no uncertain terms by the production's deployment of the representational devices
of historiographical rhetoric that they risk being caught up in the worst
kind of Platonic theatrocracy. The same audience is also seduced, over the
duration of the three or so hours of the performance, into a desire for precisely the promised community that has come bearing such obvious health
warnings. Perhaps salvation here lies in the absence of reciprocation.
Whatever this enchanted spectator might desire, he is not a member of the
acting company of the New Riga Theatre, any more than he is or would
wish to be a member of an Aryan ice cult. In the closure of the event (its
finitude and its turning of its back upon us) the production calls forth the
kind of passion that Nancy, talking of the exposure to the other that might
enable a community beyond community, suggests also constitutes the experience of the self itself: "The presence of the other does not constitute a
boundary that would limit the unleashing of 'my' passions: on the contrary,
only exposition to the other unleashes my passions."[13] Or, that what comes,
in place of community, is a being in common, in which we take our own being. Nancy himself puts it in the language of presence and appearance, inventing in the process a term—*compearance*—which seems to evoke precisely the conditions of theatrical togetherness and apartness that I have
been trying to describe here as a feature of Hermanis's *The Ice:*

Being in common means that singular beings are, present themselves, and appear only to the extent that they compear (*comparaissent*), to the extent that they are exposed, presented or offered to one another. This compearance (*comparution*) is not something added on to their being; rather their being comes into being in it.[14]

The performance of *The Ice* is, in large part, an exploration of one of the central questions of recent Latvian history: under what circumstances and around which understandings of "being in common" might a political community be established? At the same time it is also an exploration of theater's own capacity to inaugurate such a "being in common" and to make us experience it as a form of community. Theatrical performance is here both history, in that it makes and presents stories about the past, and also historiography, in that it calls into question the ways in which such stories might be made and presented, and with what political purposes. We "know the scene," and we "know that this scene is mythic," and it is theatrical performance that produces this particular form of double knowledge.

NOTES

1. Plato, *The Republic*, trans. and intro. Desmond Lee (London: Penguin, 1987), 92.

2. Plato, *Republic*, 92.

3. Plato, *Republic*, 95.

4. The Museum of the Occupation of Latvia, http://www.occupationmu seum.lv/eng/about_us/welcome.html (accessed Apr. 10, 2009).

5. Museum of the Occupation of Latvia. On Aug. 23, 1939, the governments of the Soviet Union and Nazi Germany concluded what has come to be known as the "Molotov-Ribbentrop Pact," after the two foreign ministers who signed it. The terms of this pact of nonaggression between Stalin and Hitler included a "secret protocol" according to which Latvia and its neighboring states of Estonia and Lithuania were assigned to a Soviet "sphere of influence" in a Europe divided between Germany and the Soviet Union. In June 1940 the Latvian government ignored an ultimatum from the Soviet Union to step down and allow the formation of a new government. Soviet troops moved into Latvia on June 17. By July an election process involving a single party—the Latvian Working People's Bloc—secured pro-Soviet domination of the Latvian parliament, which then petitioned for Latvia to join the Soviet Union. Latvia was admitted to the Soviet Union on Aug. 4, 1940.

6. "A Historical Introduction to Modern Latvia," in *The Baltic States: Estonia, Latvia and Lithuania*, by David J. Smith, Artis Pabriks, Aldis Purs, and Thomas Lane (London and New York: Routledge, 2002), 27.

7. See *Occupation of Latvia. Three Occupations: 1940–1991* (Riga: Occupation Museum Foundation, 2004).

8. Andrew Ezergaidis, *The Holocaust in Latvia, 1941–1944: The Missing Center* (Riga: Historical Institute of Latvia, 1996), xviii.

9. Museum of the Occupation of Latvia.

10. Valdis. O. Lumans, *Latvia in World War II* (New York: Fordham University Press, 2006), 161. Lumans goes on to refer to an incident during the aftermath of Latvian independence in 1991, when, in a speech at a ceremony to commemorate the fiftieth anniversary of the mass killings at Rumbuli, "the parliamentary president of the Latvian republic Anatolijs Gorbunovs spoke of the murder of innocent victims. But then he went on to suggest that these innocents had brought the tragedy on themselves through their pro-Soviet sympathies and actions in the year of Soviet occupation, a common yet baseless justification for anti-Jewish persecution also advanced by many Latvian exiles" (211). Clearly this is evidence that would support Lumans's claim about the impact of the events of World War II on contemporary Latvia: "Its repercussions as well as collective and individual memories of it inescapably and indelibly remain with all Latvians today" (211). It is to the inescapable and the indelible, as they appear to me as continuing repercussions, in the work of the New Riga Theatre, that I return in the remainder of the essay.

11. Jean-Luc Nancy, *The Inoperative Community*, ed. Peter Connor, trans. Peter Connor, Lisa Garbus, Michael Holland, and Simona Sawhney (Minneapolis and London: University of Minnesota Press, 1991), 2.

12. Nancy, *Inoperative Community*, 57.

13. Nancy, *Inoperative Community*, 32–33.

14. Nancy, *Inoperative Community*, 58.

Finding History from the Living Archives

Inscribing Interviews and Interventions

SUK-YOUNG KIM ❧

Comedian Ed Gardner once noted that "opera is when a guy gets stabbed in the back and, instead of bleeding, he sings."[1] I often feel that using traumatized subjects for theater research is like creating opera, since my research often entails searching for knowledge in someone's bleeding traumatic experience. My 2006 phone interview with the sixty-five-year-old choreographer of the musical *Yoduk Story*, Kim Young-sun, a North Korean expatriate, was just one of many. She narrated her life story in a calm and dignified voice from the other end of the phone line across the Pacific:

> I was a very successful dancer working for the army propaganda unit in Pyongyang before I was suddenly arrested and sent to Yoduk prison camp. No explanations were given upon my arrest, so I do not know to this day the official reason for my imprisonment. I can only suspect that I perhaps knew too much about the private lives of the high-ranking North Korean leaders. All of my immediate family members were also arrested at the same time. In the camp I lost my husband and my brother. My son went mad before drowning himself. My experience at the camp is practically what you see in *Yoduk Story*.[2]

Indeed, the musical *Yoduk Story*, which opened in Seoul in March 2006 and toured in the United States from October to November 2006, centers on a popular North Korean actress who is imprisoned in a penal labor camp when her father is deemed a spy. On her first day in the prison camp, she is raped by the captain of the prison and becomes pregnant. In a dramatic twist, her terrorizer becomes her attempted savior when he himself becomes a prisoner and tries to help the actress escape. In the end they both lose their lives, but their surviving child sends a Christian message of love and forgiveness to the audience.

Oftentimes, researching North Korean theater history becomes coterminous with exploring the very nature of state-sponsored terror. Theater historians interested in looking beyond the state-produced propaganda have no choice but to seek information from North Korean expatriates who have fled the country. In many cases, these are former political prisoners or economic migrants who survived unbearable hunger, physical and mental torture, and the excruciating pain of witnessing the death of their loved ones. Interviewing these human subjects inevitably conjures up painful memories of North Korea, yet their memories often serve as an invaluable resource for writing the theater history of that little-known country. Using my interviews with Kim Young-sun as a case study, this essay addresses the questions and situations theater historians face when using traumatized human subjects for research, in terms of ethnographic methodology as well as epistemological implication.

Many challenges and temptations arise during the interview process, some of which include journalistic sensationalism, the impulse to judge subjects, the impatient rush to draw conclusions even before the subjects are done with their stories, and the self-imposed desire to make the interviewees learn something about my own political agenda. How do I avoid my professorial habit of turning the interview subjects into captive audiences when my mission is to make them account for their own experience? More crucially, how do I legitimize someone's trauma as my research material? In the process of interviewing traumatized subjects, should I be content with the fact that "the value of ethnography," as Henry Jenkins has noted, "is not ultimately that it allows you to talk to 'the real' but that it introduces notions of dialogue and accountability"?[3] Should my attempt to engage in dialogue with North Koreans be enough to justify the potential ethical dilemma of interviewing traumatized subjects?

When extracting information from traumatized people's narratives, both compassion and neutrality can be problematic signals, potentially prompting interview subjects to tailor their stories. Kim Young-sun was idiosyncratic: she stood out from other North Korean defectors in that she initiated the reliving experience of trauma through art long before I started interviewing her. Her way of dealing with the aftermath of traumatic experience was a self-conscious performative reenactment of the original event, not a passive response to my questions. In this sense, the choreographer was consciously resisting what Diana Taylor terms the "anti-archival" nature of trauma.[4]

It is surprising, according to Taylor, to observe how performance studies scholars have paid little attention to the tenacious ways in which performance transmits traumatic memory, which she summarizes as follows:

> The individual focus of trauma studies clearly overlaps with the more public and collective focus of performance studies: 1. Performance protest helps survivors cope with individual and collective trauma by using it to animate political denunciation. 2. Trauma, like performance, is characterized by the nature of its "repeats." 3. Both make themselves felt affectively and viscerally present. 4. They're always in situ. Each intervenes in the individual/political/social body at a particular moment and reflects specific tensions. 5. Traumatic memory often relies on live, interactive performance for transmission.[5]

For the purpose of reflecting on the interviews with Kim Young-sun, what is particularly illuminating in Taylor's discussion is the trauma's repetitive impulse to be felt in the present moment, which is enhanced by the affinity between performance and trauma to exist as enduring ways of transmitting knowledge. The interview process often reveals substantial knowledge about North Korean theater practices that did not make it to the stage production and otherwise would have been lost. In this sense, interviews constitute a legitimate realm of knowledge-producing performance as much as the stage performance of *Yoduk Story*. But there is a thorny side of this process, in that the interviews inevitably force the interview subject to descend deep into dark corners of memory, often resuscitating the consciously forgotten memories of the past to become an active part of the present.

In a way, as a knowledge-producing performance, an interview can be seen as both an "archive" and a "repertoire" as Taylor defines them: "'Archival' memory exists as documents, maps, literary texts, letters, archaeological remains, bones, videos, films, CDs, all those items resistant to change. . . . Archival memory works across distance, over time and space,"[6] whereas "the repertoire . . . enacts embodied memory: performance genres, orality, movement, dance, singing—in short, all those acts usually thought of as ephemeral, nonreproducible knowledge."[7] Interviews belong to the archives once they are recorded and transcribed. And yet, if we think about how interviews are arranged and conducted before they become archives, they inherently demonstrate the traits of the repertoire: both interviewers and interviewees collaborate in the production of knowledge not only by means of verbal communication but also by nonreproducible "subtexts" such as body language, tonal variations, and the sociocultural context in which the interviewer and the interviewee interact. What happens to the ephemeral "subtext," which is an essential aspect of the repertoire but does not become a conspicuous part of the archive?

Interviews as an archive-producing process may embody various degrees of performativity for future researchers: archive-producing interviews may find ways to transcribe ephemeral oral statement into a semipermanent recorded text, while the act of conducting interviews also alerts us to see interviewees as "living" agents of archival potentiality, namely people who provide testimony to the production of archival knowledge. Both I, the interviewer, and Kim Young-sun, the interviewee, will invariably leave our idiosyncratic footprints on the archive, both through our verbal communication and through nonverbal punctuations of emotions and gestures. The latter part, which I term the "subtext" of the interview process, will ultimately find its way to the archive through discursive ways interviewers inscribe it. The context, contact, and code of communication that formulate the conversational dynamics between the interviewer and the interviewee might not be the primary elements inscribed in the archive, but they nevertheless may influence the way knowledge enters the archive.

This is to imagine the communication between the interviewer and the interviewee to be a flexible interaction whereby spontaneous accidents and surprises can take place, reaffirming that archive-producing performances are neither static nor permanent, but are subject to various outcomes depending on the interpersonal dynamics between the conversationalists. Of particular interest in this article are the various ways in which the interviewer may set the vocal and semantic tone for probing the interviewee's traumatic memory whereby the interviewee may respond in varying ways.

To complicate the dynamics of interviews even more, these archive-producing interview subjects are by no means immobile. They travel and can reach the interviewers by various forms of communication, thus providing an occasion to consider whether the archival materials should be "pawned" in one physical location only to increase the cultural and educational capital of the interviewer's host institution. Just as archive-producing subjects are mobile in nature, archives themselves could become mobile, after all. If Picasso's paintings can tour from museum to museum, why could the Folger Shakespeare Library collection not exit its holy shrine in Washington, D.C., and tour other cities for the benefit of livelier research, even though that tour might be limited to virtual format, such as granting full digital access to those who need the collection? Are we not fetishizing the immobile archive by alienating it from human contacts—both from the people who created the archive and from the users of the archive, who are distanced from the lively interaction between the interviewer and the interviewee involved in the archive-creating process?

This case study prompts me to consider the notion of "living archive." Interviewees are capable of providing knowledge, or what I would call "potential archival material"—thus rethinking Taylor's claim that "the live can never be contained in the archive; the archive endures beyond the limits of the live."[8] For the most part, the word *archive* conjures up a conventional image of dusty and dilapidated piles of manuscripts and rare editions, but let us for a moment think about the freshness of the archive, or the originating moment in which archive is created, such as interviews. In that moment of archival creation, knowledge arises out of human bodies and interactions as embodied experience. In my particular case, interviewees' painful memories become sutured into the oral narrative and find their way into the archive as visualized images or inscribed sounds, affectively carrying the emotion and aura that were present at the moment of face-to-face interviews.

This is to acknowledge the inherent danger that ethnographers, who eventually transcribe the interview material, may intentionally or inadvertently manipulate the interview subjects as well as the transcription process to fit their research mission. While it is my position that the interviewee's voice, knowledge, and conviction—not mine—should be embodied as an archive, I am nevertheless aware that I as an interviewer undoubtedly play a key role in creating and mediating the living archives by prompting the interviewees to speak and thus to suture their live emotions to the archives. How do I turn traumatic memory, which is pregnant with potential for the distorted production of knowledge, into a tangible archive through a tricky performance called the interview?

Traumatic neurosis, as Cathy Caruth explains it, is a reaction not just to the initial event but also to "the peculiar and perplexing experience of survival."[9] The survival of the event itself, and the difficulty comprehending and assimilating it, are themselves unbearable to the trauma victim: "the survival of trauma is not the fortunate passage beyond a violent event, a passage that is accidentally interrupted by reminders of it, but rather the endless *inherent necessity* of repetition, which ultimately may lead to destruction."[10] For many silent traumatized subjects, Caruth's warning about the possibilities of destruction may hold true, but based on my experience with North Koreans, when traumatized subjects emerge out of silence and choose to talk, they have a very strong mission statement to make. In many cases, rather than relating to trauma as stigma, they instead valorize their experience and transform personal trauma into something of a collective ritual. Frequently I have encountered moments when the speaking subject transforms from an individual to a political authority embodying the collective persona of a dissident-martyr.[11]

Such a tendency can help facilitate the interview process because the subjects are willing to share their stories, but it could also prove challenging because they have a preferred angle from which they narrate those stories. For the most part the proactive individuals are very eloquent, because they have been subject to North Korea's systematic training in public speech used for recurrent criticism of oneself and others. But on the other hand, they have also lived in a place where dissent equals treason and therefore are trained to constantly filter their language.

My goal in interviewing Kim Young-sun was to identify what she left out in her previous stories and to bring that significant absence back into conversation. Having read all the choreographer's previous interviews with major Korean press and other Western media, such as Reuters, the *Wall Street Journal*, the *New York Times*, the *Los Angeles Times*, and the *Washington Post*, I identified two points that were missing in them.

First, why did the creators of *Yoduk Story* choose overtly Christian language or iconography to address questions of human rights? In addressing this issue, I had to eradicate my bias as a nonreligious person and present the question with what Soyini Madison terms "positive naïveness"—a humble acknowledgment that I should rely on the knowledge of the interviewees.[12] Christianity as the chosen language to organize the condemnation of North Korea in the musical was a conspicuous issue from the beginning of the production, but once again it begged for intellectual scrutiny when I opened the program notes for the U.S. tour of the musical. The main sponsors of the U.S. tour were right-wing Christian organizations, such as the Defense Forum Foundation, Freedom House, and Liberty in North Korea: all of them in 2006 were Washington, D.C.–based activist groups aiming to lead a grassroots-level movement to bring down the North Korean regime. The Defense Forum Foundation's president, Suzanne Scholte, told a journalist that "the play is a cultural nuclear bomb against Kim Jong Il."[13] As if reflecting these sponsors' vision, the original lyrics of the musical, "God, do not only go to South Korea. Come to North Korea as well," were modified for the U.S. tour: "God, do not only go to South Korea and America. Come to North Korea as well."[14]

The second point I wanted to explore through the interviews was the production team's aggressive promotion of the musical as a real documentary of the North Korean gulag, dismissing the dramatized nature of the subject material. After the U.S. premiere, the director came up on stage and noted: "Today's show is not a show. It is reality in North Korea." In the program, there were satellite pictures of gulags scattered around North Korea and short testimonies of the camp survivors that paralleled the synopsis of the musical—an attempt to authenticate the performance as transmitting not only traumatic memory but also historical truth.

Both questions presented potential paradoxes, since they initially pointed to the striking affinities between the official North Korean propaganda and its counterpropaganda, which is the musical in this case. Both propaganda and counterpropaganda seem to have absolute religious centers—the Kim family leadership and Christianity—while they both blurred the boundaries between illusion and reality so as to claim that their version of reality was the genuine reality.[15]

Once I identified what to ask, I had to decide how to ask the questions. No doubt interviewers are performers as well as directors. Various styles of conducting interviews can bring out various results, and the interviewer has to be savvy in choosing from a variety of styles, ranging from intrusive to impersonal.

On the one extreme there is Italian journalist Oriana Fallaci's wrathful style of interviewing people, a confrontational approach that includes aggressive statements, provocative questions, and even name-calling.[16] Fallaci's approach produced insightful and award-winning results, but she showed her warrior attitude when interviewing tough dictators and warmongers rather than traumatized subjects.

On the other extreme of interviewing styles, there is David Boder, the former psychology professor at the Illinois Institute of Technology, who dragged primitive recording devices around Europe in 1946 to interview Holocaust survivors before the term was even coined to designate the Nazi-led genocide. Listeners marvel at Boder's impersonal style of asking obviously painful questions, such as what kind of razor the Nazis used to shave the inmates, while the subjects broke down in tears.

Then there is Bob Edwards, the former anchor of NPR's *Morning Edition*, who has recommended a minimalist approach. He once told a journalism professor that his two favorite interview questions were "Oh?" and "No!"[17] I also benefited much from talking to Neil Smelser, professor emeritus of sociology at U.C. Berkeley and a seasoned psychiatrist. He noted in an email correspondence:

The general wisdom emerging from psychiatric and interviewing cultures is that indirection is a valuable approach. You might first raise questions about positive memories and nostalgia that your subjects might have had about their past life. This alone might evoke negative memories. If not, then you might follow with a question, "Were there any memories that were less positive?" but go no further than that. This leaves the decision of what kinds and how much disturbing material the interviewee might wish to bring up.[18]

After some deliberation I decided to begin with David Boder's interview strategy, and if that did not yield insightful revelations, I would increase the level of intensity to lean toward Oriana Fallaci's aggressive style. The ideal image of an interviewer I had in mind was someone who had compassion yet was able to maintain a critical distance.

In order to get into the right mind-set, I tried to imagine how somebody like the late Dwight Conquergood might have talked to these North Korean people. In his seminal essay "Performance Studies: Interventions and Radical Research," he turns our attention to the hierarchal order between knowledge-producing modalities: "Between objective knowledge that is consolidated in texts, and local know-how that circulates on the ground within a community of memory and practice, there is no contest. It is the choice between science and 'old wives' tales' (note how the disqualified knowledge is gendered as feminine)."[19] Ethnographers, in a way, are the ones to mediate such dichotomized modalities of knowing, and yet, they may fall into the trap of disparaging "old wives' tales" (repertoire) over published (already archived) sources. With this potential pitfall in mind, I decided not to be influenced by what I had already read about North Korea and the production, and to move toward the interviews.

When the interviews began on October 2, 2006, I introduced my project and asked about the subject's background and current activities to warm up and build rapport. Since it was the first intensive contact I had with Kim Young-sun, and the method of contact was over the telephone, which is less preferable than in-person interviews, establishing a sense of safety and trust was important. When it came to the two important questions I had in mind (namely, "What does Christianity mean in this musical?" and, "Where does the boundary lie between reality and fiction in this musical?"), I expected to hear something new, because to my knowledge these questions had never before been asked. But I soon found myself somewhat disappointed that Kim Young-Sun was answering these questions the same way she had answered journalists—her responses were synoptic rather than descriptive, factual rather than insightful, short rather than elaborate. Even worse, I sensed that the choreographer seemed to have taken my second question as a mild challenge to the veracity of the events presented in the musical. She replied that the events presented in *Yoduk Story* were based on the testimony of the camp survivors, who had given lectures to help others understand the realities of the North Korean gulag. She replied to the first question as the best way to express the message of love and forgiveness, which were the two most frequently cited words throughout the musical. She also reiterated that the reality in the musical is actually a truthful reflection of what happened in the camps. After the initial interview, I thought about why I ended up not getting more in-depth answers. The questions posed in Boder's style—fact-orientated and impersonal—might have contributed to this outcome. I thought about the other extreme of interviewing styles, which would convert the two questions into:

1. Let's talk about Christianity. You extensively use Christian expressions because of the financial support you get for your production, don't you?
2. Why is your musical so much like the official North Korean propaganda in promoting illusion as reality?

Such questions promised to offend the interviewees and turn them against me, so I had to find ways to increase the level of intensity while making the questions not so offensive or invasive. I decided to use so-called quotation questions (e.g., "Somebody said this. What is your response to that?") in order to depersonalize the target toward whom they may feel hostile. So instead of designating myself as someone raising these questions, I made the questioning subject impersonal and turned these questions into: "Some people might say that the overtly Christian expressions in your musical have to do with the financial support you are getting from the Christian community. What would be your response to that?" And, "Some audience members might have noticed that your musical is much like the official North Korean propaganda in promoting illusion as reality. What would you say to these people?" These questions—which I see as a good middle ground between Boder's and Fallaci's styles—definitely brought more results than the first set of questions. During the second interview, conducted on October 4, 2006, the choreographer revealed new information that I had not previously encountered. The interview subject was more engaged in her answers, which revealed some key information about the creative process of the musical. On Christianity and recurring tropes of martyrdom, she specifically mentioned the name of a former inmate who was imprisoned for having brought back the Bible to North Korea from China, noting that it was this figure who inspired her to speak of the North Korean people's suffering through Christian language. This opened up a new dimension in the next question, of reality versus illusion (and provided me with another potential interviewee).

The most interesting moment of the second round of interviews came when Kim Young-sun answered the question about the boundary between reality/illusion: "Musicals are so much better than giving hours of political lectures about the North Korean gulag." Promoting performance, which is an interpreted version of reality, to make people understand reality is precisely what the official North Korean propaganda does, thus proving that there is a great affinity between propaganda and counterpropaganda, at least in their strategy to employ a certain vision of reality. Can counterperformance not escape the shades of the original performance it strives to oppose? The choreographer's answer opened an unexpected possibility of looking at the musical as something of a "Stockholm syndrome," where captives come to identify with and even mimic their captors. Can a dissident performance that represents trauma unconsciously endow power to the performer's aggressor?

Various ways to address this question will inevitably produce different types of documentation, which cautions researchers to patiently probe various degrees of trauma in the interview subject. Kim Young-sun as a living archive provided me with discursive potential for producing archival materials, ranging from unadulterated transcription of the interview to eclectic adaptation of the interview for larger research projects. I, as a mediator of the living archive, could never be an objective interpreter of Kim Young-sun's stories, but at the same time, I should not forget that my intervention should not turn into invention. I try to be faithful to the voice I hear and scrupulously inscribe its liveliness in my writing.

After all, ethnographers should not only be satisfied with the mere fact that ethnography brings the idea of dialogue and accountability to knowledge production, but also warrant that their research subject's knowledge is transmitted in the liveliest form of performance—that is, the interview—with all its embodied gestures and emotions making their way into the archive. Only then does ethnography become a reliable terrain of memory keeping and reenacting performance, which allows us to deal with the living archives more responsibly. History may best be found on the dusty pages of archives, but I also hear history speaking in an equivocal voice when I encounter North Korean refugees.

NOTES

1. Elizabeth Knowles, ed., *The Oxford Dictionary of Quotations*, 5th ed. (Oxford: Oxford University Press, 1999), 329.

2. Suk-Young Kim, "Gulag, the Musical: Performing Trauma in North Korea through Yoduk Story," *TDR: A Journal of Performance Studies* 52, no. 1 (2008): 118–19.

3. Henry Jenkins, *"Intensities* Interviews Henry Jenkins," *Intensities: The Journal of Cult Media* 2 (2001); quoted in Jonathan Gray, Cornel Sandvoss, and C. Lee Harrington, eds., *Fandom: Identities and Communities in a Mediated World* (New York: New York University Press, 2007), 182.

4. Diana Taylor, *The Archive and the Repertoire: Performing Cultural Memory in the Americas* (Durham and London: Duke University Press, 2003), 193.

5. Taylor, *Archive and the Repertoire*, 166–67.

6. Taylor, *Archive and the Repertoire*, 19.

7. Taylor, *Archive and the Repertoire*, 20.

8. Taylor, *Archive and the Repertoire*, 173.

9. Cathy Caruth, *Unclaimed Experience: Trauma, Narrative, and History* (Baltimore: Johns Hopkins University Press, 1996), 60.

10. Caruth, *Unclaimed Experience*, 62–63.

11. This point became most obvious during my interview with Kim Yong, who is the first known survivor to have escaped the notorious North Korean death camp No. 14. The result of this interview is published in Kim Yong, with Kim Suk-Young, *Long Road Home: Testimony of a North Korean Labor Camp Survivor* (New York: Columbia University Press, 2009).

12. Soyini Madison, *Critical Ethnography* (New York: Sage Publication, 2005), 32.

13. Quoted in Jay Solomon, "New Script on North Korea? Groups Hope Stark Prison Play Spurs Pressure on Pyongyang Regime," *Wall Street Journal*, Sept. 30, 2006.

14. A live performance of *Yoduk Story* I attended at the Strathmore Music Center in Maryland, on Oct. 4, 2006, featured the modified lyrics.

15. This issue has been thoroughly analyzed in Kim, "Gulag."

16. As Margaret Talbot notes in a profile published shortly before Fallaci's death, "Let's Talk about War," she challenged Henry Kissinger in their 1972 interview: "You are not a pacifist, are you?" When the subject refused to cooperate, he became a "a bastard, a fascist, an idiot." Naturally, Kissinger later admitted that the interview was "the single most disastrous conversation I have ever had with any member of the press" ("The Agitator: Oriana Fallaci Directs Her Fury towards Islam," *New Yorker*, June 5, 2006).

17. Joe Feiertag, Mary Carmen Cupito, et al., eds., *Writer's Market Companion* (Cincinnati: Writer's Digest Books, 2004), 74.

18. Email correspondence, Nov. 13, 2006, cited with permission of the author.

19. Dwight Conquergood, "Performance Studies: Interventions and Radical Research," *Drama Review* 46, no. 2 (2002): 146.

Performance as Learner-Driven Historiography

SCOTT MAGELSSEN ❧

You're teaching a section of graduate or undergraduate theater history and are looking for ways to amp it up. But also, on a deeper level, you are troubled by the limitations you perceive in your own history sequence, as it has traditionally been imagined, and you wish that the experience in the classroom could catch up to the ways our art is witnessing to the past in our practical theater classrooms, on our stages, and in the community. Well, you're about to read a call for performed/embodied experience to be used in the theater history classroom in order to grant learners more agency in constructing historiographic understandings of theater and performance. The following pages demonstrate how we can shift some of our emphasis away from received, archive-based chronological narratives of theater history toward modes where the past is remembered affectively and witnessed to effectively. Such performance practices in the theater history classroom can foment "deep" or "significant" learning, in which the learners experience what teaching guru Ken Bain calls a "natural and critical learning environment," one that the learner already finds intriguing.[1] In this way, students can not only acquire knowledge but learn how knowledge is produced in that subject area.

"Give me a break," you're saying. "This is nothing new. I've been using performance in the theater history classroom for years. The texts we teach are performance scripts, after all, and staging scenes—or designing models for them, and so on—are logical ways of getting at the modes of knowledge production that we wouldn't get if we were limited to simply reading dramatic literature. You're preaching to the choir. Students love these exercises. They break up the lecture-discussion routine, and I consistently get good marks in this area in my students' and colleagues' evaluations of my teaching." Excellent. But this is about something different: Rather than simply rehearsing the (already largely accepted) model of learning-by-doing in the academic theater community—that is, learning the conventions of theater history by staging historical drama—I'm going to survey some recent shifts in pedagogy and museum-user studies that offer paratheatrical programs that immerse learners in a historic persona, equip them with a delimited body of historical information, confront them with a historically based dilemma, invite them to address the dilemma by making decisions grounded in what their character "knows," and allow them to compare their choices with those of their historic referent and even to correct "mistakes." By looking to these case studies, and engaging the pedagogical strategies they model, we can offer theater historiography some possible tools for using performance as a way to make historical meaning in theater studies.

You very well may have heard about or experienced these programs. They include the staging of historic court cases at living museums, in which visitors are invited to issue a verdict based on the evidence that would have been available to the past juries. This happens at Conner Prairie living history museum in Indiana, where James Hudson is seasonally put on trial for the brutal massacre of nine Seneca Indians on March 22, 1824. Visitors, as jurymen, hear both sides of the case before making their recommendation to the judge.[2] It happens at Colonial Williamsburg, where a young woman breaks into a 1776 courtroom to demand action from the assembly of visitors because the Committee on Public Safety has been violating her right to privacy by intercepting and reading her correspondence.[3] The Constitution Center in Philadelphia allows visitors to sit on a simulated Supreme Court bench to hear famous or contentious cases and try their hand at making a decision. The museum even allows them to sign their name to the Constitution . . . or dissent and write their reasons why.[4] And the Chicago Museum of Science and Industry (MSI) predates these programs by almost a decade and a half with its "goal-based-scenario" exhibit "Sickle Cell Counselor," in which museum visitors consult physicians, run tests, collect data, and advise clients who are at risk for sickle cell disease on actions they should take.[5] The Sickle Cell Counselor experience has closed, but visitors to MSI since 2002 have participated in the "Genetic Counseling Experience," loosely modeled on Sickle Cell Counselor. If you do this program, you might run into the following scenario: a young African American couple with a family history of sickle cell disease seeks your advice about whether to try to have children and asks you about the attendant difficulties in raising a child with the disease. You need to give them frank and honest answers. If you're less than helpful with your response, your clients will let you know by exchanging glances with

each other and, with a tinge of impatience, give you something like, "Well
. . . that's interesting, but it doesn't really answer my question."[6] In all of
these cases, you listen carefully to information that equips you to make a
decision with high-stakes consequences. Will you condemn a man to
death? Will you amend the Constitution? Will you advise a couple with the
propensity for a debilitating disease to try for children?

Such programs are understandably limited: they must get several points
across in only a few minutes, so there can be only a handful of conversation
trajectories, and the user often chooses among a set of predetermined,
scripted responses. Yet visitors, as Supreme Court justices and genetic
counselors, are allowed to make choices based on information given to
them and in many cases, after debriefing, can correct their mistakes in a
second run. Thus visitors, as Ken Bain would have it, not only acquire
knowledge but learn about how knowledge is produced in these areas—a
historic courtroom, a counseling center, and so on. When this works, it
gives learners deeper and longer-lasting knowledges. As the designers of
the Sickle Cell Counselor program put it, the formula is simple: substitute
the traditional museum and classroom model of giving learners "isolated
facts that cannot be reliably recalled and used in solving future problems"
(what the designers call "inert knowledge"), with a model that "enables the
student to relate the knowledge to significant problems to be solved and
also to his or her pre-existing knowledge."[7] In an ideal museum learning
environment, the whole visit for the learner, not just one or two experiences, would be driven by his or her own inquiry. The producers of the environment would provide resources for the learner to draw upon but would
have a very hands-off role in conditioning the learner's movement through
the space, the order in which he or she assimilates information, or the reception of any linear and nonmutable text (as the museum visitor finds in
the curator-scripted labels that mediate the exhibited items). In this model,
the museum visitor, or *user*, in David Carr's terms, becomes the active agent
of knowledge production by performing as a protagonist equipped with the
necessary information and active experiences to make informed conclusions about the subject of the program or exhibit, rather than passively receiving it from the curators.[8]

The promise of these performative programs is a challenge to the institution's traditional custodianship and policing of learning that happens in
its space, empowering the learner (for our purposes the spectator, the student) to choose what they want to learn and to "authentically" cocreate and
actualize historic meaning, rather than solely taking the institution's word
for it. In other words, learner-driven performative historiography is user-

policed and thereby unmoored from the traditional centers of knowledge production that otherwise steer, check, and legitimize the learning taking place. This is the kind of learning environment I'm advocating for the theater history classroom.

"Now, hang on," you're saying. "Slow down. Is this a slippery slope? Can learner-driven historiography be trusted? What if the learner's experience of the past does not match the institution's or the archive's account? Can the performer's learning 'authentically' bear witness to the experiences of past individuals while being historically 'incorrect?'" You're right to ask. When it comes right down to it, the learner in such environments can come away with anything, and there's really no "reliable" way to assess (by traditional means such as testing) the learning that does happen. For our purposes, then, let's say that this is not about fidelity to the "lived past." In fact, such fidelity doesn't matter because we've been taking it for granted already that such accuracy will never be graspable, even by the most rigorous historiographic detective work. On the other hand, and more importantly, the one-to-one correspondence between the lived past and the present-day representation of it need not be the criterion for success for pedagogical experiences. In other words, we're not out to recover a concrete ontology from days gone by. We're producing meaning in the present with recourse to an imagined past.

"Tell that to my tenure and promotion committee (or my faculty supervisor). If they get wind that I'm privileging the experiential over the archive in the history classroom, they'll accuse me of the worst kind of solipsism and relativism. Worse, I'll lose my job." Well, maybe you're safer from your administrators than you think. In fact, this is the very kind of pedagogical experimentation worthy of tenure candidates at most colleges and universities: if you look at your institution's set of learning outcomes for its gen ed curriculum, you'll probably find language about critical and constructive thinking, inquiry and creative problem solving, effective skills in communication, and maybe something about knowledge in general and specific content areas (though that language is most likely silent on the subject of whether what your students learn is "right" or "true" or measurable by any other purportedly objective criteria).[9] This is about engaging in learning dispositions—that is, learners can be more affectively disposed toward theater history if they are given the agency to determine a fulfilling way to bear witness to the past. Institutional requirements aside, you know better than anyone that performance offers, as Diana Taylor reminds us, different or more accommodating ways of knowing than more traditional (text-based) historiographic practices.[10] Most of the other essays in this collection, in fact, speak to that very idea. You're a theater person. You know this intuitively.

"What would this actually look like in the theater history classroom?" The nice thing is, you've done some of this already. All of us, at one time or another, have put Medea (or Jason) on trial. We've decided, as the Academie française, whether to censure the author of *Le Cid* after examining Scudéry's complaints and Corneille's own defense. We've debated whether to skip out on Goldoni's latest *commedia* and catch Gozzi's new *fiabe* instead. We've weighed in on the Wilson-Brustein debate concerning color-blind versus race-specific theater practices. All are examples in which our students have been equipped through their reading, our lectures, each other's presentations and discussions, to enact informed choices and then hash out the attendant consequences.[11] Now, try this on for size: assign your students themselves the task of using performance in small groups to create an environment that bears witness to a past moment in theater and performance history. Don't give them a script. Have them devise the contours of the environment based on documentation they can access themselves. Tell them that they must find room in the simulation for the rest of the class to actively engage, respond to, and thereby coproduce the representation. Equip them from day one of the course with examples of such performances of the past, and make yourself available as a resource. Don't patrol their choices. What might result?

Here are some possible examples based on my own students' work: A group leads the class through a "museum exhibit" treating historic performances of blackface minstrelsy, then confronts their fellow students as actual blacked-up caricatures, in order to determine whether they will provoke visceral reactions, even when mediated by an academic display that contextualizes such performance as a product of the time. After a couple of uncomfortable numbers, the performers stop and ask the spectators, and themselves, whether the performance can go on. Another group posits that the surrounding academic institution is, in the moment, a living museum only representing the lived experiences there, based on the physical evidence available but distorted through the ages since. The experience culminates on the empty site of what was to be a new theater arts building (never actualized for reasons that are unclear), and the group places the bodies of its classmates in a tableau that "remembers" the experiences of those who may or may not have occupied that space: a precontact Native inhabitant, a balloonist, a young local resident who will one day become a famous figure skater, a potential school-shooter, and others. A third parades a number of sideshow acts, their bodies in various states of abjection or exoticization, in front of their fellow students—a fat lady, a strong man, a bearded lady, and a Tom Thumb. Each body presented is first accompanied by a version of its identity based on period accounts. Then comes an appeal from the individual to listen to her or his own stories from memoirs or correspondence, unmediated by the carnival-barker-style poster copy (if no first-person account is available, the performer only silently fixes the audience with her gaze). Yet another group treats its audience as U.S. government witnesses to oral testimony of the Holodomor forced famine in the Ukraine (1932–33), supplemented with scenes from Les Kurbas's White Sea Prison Camp production of Pogodin's *The Aristocrats*, and demands action from the listeners, ostensibly the only ones who can bring their story to light.[12]

In each case, the student groups assess their own performances in a debriefing with the rest of the class and in subsequent reflective writing. In the debriefing session, both performers and spectators reflect on what choices they made, how they might have chosen differently, and the consequences of their actions in the performance. In cases where the historical characters are based on documented individuals (blackface performers, Holodomor survivors, human sideshow attractions), the choices in performance are compared to the historically available choices the students are able to infer from period accounts. Evaluating the success of each project, and assigning it a grade, accordingly hinges not on accuracy, but on the complexity and rigor with which the group engages in the performance, as well as the thoroughness of their critical reflections. (Longer-term significant learning may be measured anecdotally: some of the students in the examples here went on to demonstrate their continued engagement with these topics after the course. So far, one of the projects has been developed into a fully realized production, and other ideas that emerged from the performance have been taken up as conference papers and thesis projects).

You may choose to measure complexity and rigor in performance and reflection as indicators of success as determined by your own institution's or department's statement on learning outcomes. But as a discipline, we have many usable rubrics for evaluating performances of the past. Diana Taylor's work, again, is a helpful resource here. If you take up Taylor's emphasis on the *repertoire*, you can ask whether the performances engagingly use embodied practice as a means to transmit knowledges in ways that are restricted by the print media (especially since those media have been controlled by a privileged hegemony).[13] Similarly, Charlotte Canning writes that "performance can demonstrate aspects of and ideas about history that are less possible in print." Based on Canning's invitation, you can evaluate a performance project according to whether it "encourage[s] considerations of the gestural, the emotional, the aural, the visual, and the physical in ways beyond print's ability to evoke or understand them."[14] Following Della Pollock's use of "historicity," you might gauge whether each of your students is explicitly voicing and reflecting on the manners in which her or his own body is "practicing history": whether it "incarnates, mediates, and resists the metahistories with which it is impressed," and "wrestles with the totalizing and legitimizing power of such historical tropes as *telos* and progress."[15] You can ask, with Harry Elam (drawing upon the work of Suzan-Lori Parks), whether the students show a "commitment to an imaginative archaeology where one endeavors not only to uncover the past but also actually participates in its construction in the present."[16] Or you can ask, with Freddie Rokem, whether the performance "forcefully" participates in the historiographic process by either inventing or shoring up historical and cultural identities and ideologies, or by resisting and challenging those identities and ideologies as they have been constructed and perpetuated by dominant discourses.[17]

"Wait a minute. This sounds very similar to the Theatre of the Oppressed workshop I did at my last conference. Is this really any different from what Boal advocates with Forum Theatre?" You're right that the connections are there. In the interest of full disclosure, the germ of this call to action can probably be traced back to my own work a few years ago in pushing museums to apply Boalian spect-actor technique to living history simulations in order that these institutions more adequately bear witness to the past.[18] Well, if I didn't turn the mandate back on my own classroom practices, it would be an instance of the pot talking to the kettle. This is one way I've found, then, to successfully link my own scholarly inquiry and research to my pedagogical practices. It allows me to do the kind of performative historiography I charge my research subjects to do, and at the same time it gets me out from behind the lectern or the seminar table to teach history in a more fulfilling and responsible manner, drawing upon what I find most compelling from the theories of Freire and Boal.

So, yes, if you've had some Boal training, you've been excellently equipped to push into this classroom model. TO (Theatre of the Oppressed) technique, based in Freire's Pedagogy of the Oppressed, already privileges the learner-driven mode of knowledge production, and the case can be made that performance exercises in the theater history classroom rehearse the students for real life—the major goal of Forum Theatre and other TO practices as they've traditionally been understood, though it's not within the scope of this essay to go into detail.[19] For now, let's agree that the modest goal for these exercises is to generate affective and embodied knowledges about the past that do not necessarily have immediate applications in real life, other than to foster a humble and responsible scholarly approach to the subject of inquiry, grounded in the desire to listen and give voice, rather than to salvage, condemn, or celebrate. To do otherwise, and to claim that problem-solving in the past rehearses for the present, would be to inscribe a kind of reductive comparative anthropology, with the problematic (and arrogant) conclusion that "they were just like us." By the same token, this should not necessarily be an exercise in adding another "prosthetic memory," Alison Landsberg's term for a performatively produced representation of an event that the spectator did not actually experience, but that becomes, through simulation, part of that spectator's mediated identity.[20] Aside from learning outcomes, this exercise should be about more than simply making ourselves better through studying others. As Jean Graham-Jones advised graduate students in the audience during her response to the Theatre History Symposium of the 2009 Mid-America Theatre Conference, in order for our discipline to become less insular, "you ought to look at sites in which you *don't* see yourself reflected."[21]

"All well and good," you say. "But remember, I'm teaching a history course. When it comes right down to it, is this *real* history?" That's the question, isn't it? Frankly, if what you're being asked to do is perceived as fake or unhelpful by your students, the most important stakeholders in good pedagogy (if not always the most reliable arbiters), it's not going to "sell." We've already established that the criterion for authenticity does not lie in fidelity or accuracy in relation to the lived past. And while it's a no-brainer for a lot of the students (even without having read Michel de Certeau) that legitimate narratives of history are no longer just those that have been corroborated by the state or the institution as the site of power from which the historian speaks,[22] some of your students likely will not see beyond traditional criteria for success. For them, but also for the others, diversify your pedagogical activities. Assign and make them accountable for textbook readings, plays and performance scripts, period accounts, and critical theory as well, and give these equal playing time. Put these discourses into circulation with the performance projects as a way to make the performances nuanced and more complex, but do not grant one kind of discourse more legitimacy than the other by treating it only as the "fun" component on the syllabus. This is not the "practical application" of received knowledge. This is the *production* of knowledge as much as is any other component of the course.

"Well . . . that's interesting, but it doesn't really answer my question." Okay, is it real history? B. Joseph Pine II and James H. Gilmore grapple with the same question put to the experiential museum programs that are becoming increasingly prevalent as alternatives to traditional, "real" museum collections. For Pine and Gilmore, and many others, realness and authenticity are not ontologically measured from the outside but are determined inside of us. Therefore, the goal of museums ought to be to *"render authenticity"* for the visitor by creating the *"perception"* of it in their minds "phenomenologically."[23] Whether dealing with "artifacts, edifices, or encounters," museums can negotiate visitor perception of realness by asking two basic questions: "(A) Is it true to itself? (B) Is it what it says it is?"[24] Drawing upon everything from the Shaker motto ("Be what you seem to be, and seem to be what you really are") to consumer studies, they advise, "The easiest way to be perceived as a phony here is to advertise things you are not."[25] You are not promising accuracy and fidelity. You are not promising coverage of the canon. Don't try to convince your students that these exercises fulfill these ends. The real history lies in *rendering the perception of authenticity* in your students' minds, in showing them that they can affectively generate modes of knowing that they will not encounter in their textbook.

Enough. Now go out and make some choices. You've been given the beginning of a mode of inquiry and equipped with enough advice from the "experts" to get you started. Is this equipage incomplete? Yes. Does its focus on museum education as a model replicate some of the work going on in community-based theater, arts activism, and critical pedagogy? Most likely. Here, though, is where you come in. If you see some success with what this essay proposes (or if you've got a background in activist or critical pedagogy and have already been doing this kind of thing), and you're so inclined, share your project prompts and syllabi with us and with others. Using performance as a learner-driven mode of historiography in the theater history classroom need not be based on a singular model. On the contrary, just as with a museum exhibit, it will benefit if its custodianship belongs to, and is informed by, a multiplicity of voices, discourses, and experiences. It is vital that we look to performance practices in our history courses for learner-driven modes of historiography. Not only will these practices close the gap between our learning experiences and those in the practical theater classrooms or on our stages, but they will equip the next generation with tools for more effectively witnessing to the theatrical past.

NOTES

I workshopped this essay at Bowling Green State University's Institute for the Study of Culture and Society's Visual and Cultural Studies Research Cluster and the Center for Teaching and Learning's Publication Learning Community. I am grateful for each group's enthusiasm and guidance.

1. Ken Bain, Augustana Faculty Fall Workshop, Rock Island, IL, Aug. 2006.

2. "Past Times," *Conner Prairie Guide* (Summer 2004): 18.

3. See my review, "Revolutionary City" (Colonial Williamsburg), *Theatre Journal* 59, no. 1 (2007): 117–19.

4. "High-Tech Meets History in a More Perfect Union: A New Museum Brings the Constitution to Life," *Chicago Tribune*, 13 July 2003; "1787 and All That: Walking through Amendments and Rubbing Elbows with Founding Fathers at the New Constitution Center," *New York Times*, 17 Aug. 2003.

5. Benjamin Bell, Ray Bareiss, and Richard Beckwith, "Sickle Cell Counselor: A Prototype Goal-Based Scenario for Instruction in a Museum Environment," *Journal of the Learning Sciences* 3, no. 4 (1993–94): 347–86.

6. On-site visit, "Be a Genetic Counselor," Museum of Science and Industry, Chicago, 24 Apr. 2008; Patricia Ward, administrator and program developer for MSI, telephone interview with author, 17 Apr. 2008, and personal interview with the author, 24 Apr. 2008.

7. Bell, Bareiss, and Beckwith, "Sickle Cell Counselor," 347–48.

8. David Carr, *The Promise of Cultural Institutions* (Walnut Creek, CA: AltaMira, 2003), xiv, 3–4.

9. Marcia Baxter Magdola writes, "Educators, legislators, and the American public concur that learning outcomes of higher education should include effective citizenship, critical thinking and complex problem solving, interdependent relations with diverse others, and mature decision making" ("Self-Authorship: The Foundation for Twenty-First Century Education," *New Directions for Teaching and Learning* 109 [Spring 2007]: 69). Thanks to J. L. Murdoch for bringing my attention to this study.

10. See Diana Taylor, *The Archive and the Repertoire: Performing Cultural Memory in the Americas* (Durham: Duke University Press, 2003).

11. James Peck reciprocally infuses theater history into the directing classroom by assigning student groups directing scenes in which they need to make choices based on historical conventions, theory, and aesthetics ("History in the Directing Curriculum: Major Directors, Theory, and Practice," *Theatre Topics* 17, no. 1 [2007]: 33–36).

12. These performances were devised by students in my THFM 668 Performance Studies course at Bowling Green State University in Spring 2008.

13. Taylor, *Archive and the Repertoire*, xvii.

14. Charlotte Canning, "Feminist Performance as Feminist Historiography," *Theatre Survey* 45, no. 2 (2004): 230.

15. Della Pollock, "Introduction: Making History Go," in *Exceptional Spaces: Essays in Performance and History*, ed. Della Pollock (Chapel Hill: University of North Carolina Press, 1998), 4.

16. Harry Elam, "Making History," *Theatre Survey* 45, no. 2 (2004): 219–25.

17. Freddie Rokem, *Performing History: Theatrical Representations of the Past in Contemporary Theatre* (Iowa City: University of Iowa Press, 2000), 3.

18. I discuss this in *Living History Museums: Undoing History Through Performance* (Lanham, MD: Scarecrow Press, 2007) and elsewhere.

19. See Augusto Boal, *Theatre of the Oppressed* (New York: Theatre Communications Group, 1993); *Games for Actors and Non-Actors*, 2nd ed. (New York: Routledge, 2002); *The Rainbow of Desire: The Boal Method of Theatre and Therapy*, trans.

Adrian Jackson (London and New York: Routledge, 1995); and "The Cop in the Head: Three Hypotheses," *TDR* 34, no. 3 (1990). See also Mady Schutzman and Jan Cohen-Cruz, eds., *Playing Boal: Theatre, Therapy, Activism,* (London: Routledge, 1994); Susan Kattwinkel, ed., *Audience Participation: Essays on Inclusion in Performance* (Westport, CT: Praeger, 2003).

20. Alison Landsberg, *Prosthetic Memory: The Transformation of American Remembrance in the Age of Mass Culture* (New York: Columbia University Press, 2004).

21. Jean Graham-Jones, MATC Theatre History Response Session, Chicago, 8 Mar. 2009. To be sure, as E. Patrick Johnson pointed out in his keynote address at the same conference the day before (making an assertion with which Graham-Jones readily agreed), one's lack of experience with another culture, population, or historical moment means one does not have the "tools for reading" performances by those groups, and thus, academics must approach this terrain with a degree of scholarly humility. And as Patricia Ybarra's essay in this volume reminds us, the institutional and economic structuring of our degree programs and departmental expectations does not allow adequate time for thorough labor in language acquisition, archive work, and site visits.

22. Michel de Certeau, *The Writing of History* (New York: Columbia University Press, 1988), 6ff.

23. B. Joseph Pine II and James H. Gilmore, "Museums and Authenticity," *Museum News* (May–June 2007), http://www.aam-us.org/pubs/mn/authenticity .cfm?renderforprint=1 (accessed 22 Jan. 2008), n.p., emphasis in original.

24. Pine and Gilmore, "Museums and Authenticity," n.p.

25. Pine and Gilmore, "Museums and Authenticity," n.p.

PART V

Theater History's Discipline

Interdisciplinary Objects, Oceanic Insights

Performance and the New Materialism

MARGARET WERRY ❧

Sea is History.

—Derek Walcott

The institutional rapprochement of performance and theater studies is said, at least by its protagonists, to have accomplished much for the practice of theater historiography. It is said to have led to greater interdisciplinarity in both motive and method and to have opened the field to new objects—those lying beyond its formerly, if broadly, Western remit and those outside the institutional precincts of theater, such as performances in popular culture, ritual, everyday life, or other artistic disciplines. Together with the theoretical turn that accompanied theater and performance studies' congress, these changes are often argued to have politicized scholarship and teaching in the newly expanded field. No longer limited by purely aesthetic, literary, or empirical concerns, we were freed to ask: to what ends, and in whose interests, does performance's action act? My goal in this offering is not to debunk this narrative of theater historiography's history—of new interdisciplinarity, new objects, and politicization (which like any such narrative is not so much either true or false as useful or not to particular actors in the present). It is rather to put some pressure on the limits of theater historiography as currently constituted by asking of this narrative: Which disciplines? What objects? What kind of politics?

My own research at the cusp of theater and performance historiography has led me to wonder whether certain default assumptions about theater that are the legacy of the former—in particular, its construal of theater as a representational practice—have stalled some of the more radical trajectories of the latter, delimiting the political imagination of the field, its capacity to address culturally different practices, and distancing it from the current theoretical ferment in the experimental social sciences and humanities centered on performance as a *non*representational process. Instead I ask, what could come of joining these interdisciplinary allies to ask how performance history might imagine a politics-to-come? As performance and theater scholars, we are uniquely equipped to contribute to this project, but we cannot do so on the basis of unexamined terms, categories, and habits of thought—our imagination necessarily needs to include Other voices and Other ways of knowing.

I come to this from trying to write about the performance culture of the Polynesian Pacific, with the goal of producing not a history of Oceanic performance, but an Oceanic history of performance. That is, I am interested in the historical consciousness of the Oceanic world; in the contribution that indigenous theory of the Oceanic region might make to understanding performance history more broadly; and in the ways in which *thinking Oceanically*—thinking with and through the phenomenological, material realities of Oceanic life—can draw fundamentally into question the shape and character of those macro-objects that provide the explanatory background for much of what we do in performance analysis (such as geopolitics, modernity, globalization, the social, agency, subjectivity, indeed performance itself). Taking an Oceanic approach means being alive to the radical alterity of Polynesian epistemology, being able not just to entertain, but to take as foundational, precepts such as the symmetry and continuity between object and human worlds or the principle of genealogy as the foundation of all knowledge, connecting the material substance of human, natural, and cosmological history. It means understanding that time and thus history do not travel inevitably forward in regular momentum that leaves the past behind and propels us into the future, but rather that the past appears before your face to lead you (spatially and temporally) into the future. It means believing that objects act with a will that is also a destiny and that as agents we don't invent our actions so much as discover and honor their historical essence in performing them.

Consider the following examples:

A carved pendant of pounamu (nephrite jade, from New Zealand) worn during a ritual of welcome by a traveling diplomat or sportsperson is an actor—not a costume, not a symbol of rank and affiliation, but literally the bones, and thus the incarnation, of an ancestor. (The earth, Papatūānuku, is the first living ancestor, and the bodies of all subsequent progeny, the forbears of contemporary

Māori, are returned to the earth, becoming part of its substance). Its journey is undertaken in support of the kaupapa (the mission) of its custodian, but were that pendant lost on the voyage, the loss might be interpreted as the pendant expressing a will to take a path of its own. Were it gifted, to a museum, say, or to another dignitary, it would become a political and historiographic agent in its own right: drawing a thread through the fabric of another history, place, and people and, on its inevitable (and propitious) reappearance in its community and place of origin, linking the two in a narrative (and implicitly political) bond.

A public art project is organized around the reclamation and conservation of a wetland area that had once been the subsistence-gathering grounds of a whānau (extended family) whose descendants still live in the area. Drained for industrial agriculture during the colonial era, polluted and depleted, "the wetlands remember how to be wetlands" in concert with the performers, whose artistic work documents the land's remembering and listens to its echoes in the memory of the living and the dead. As the wetlands recover, so does the knowledge base of the land: the old names and rhythms of the place return and with them old ways that humans and nonhumans lived entwined lives—ancient midden pits reveal themselves, the resurgence of plant species prompts the recollection of harvesting and preparation techniques, not so much forgotten as latent, awaiting return. The reclamation project is practice-based historiography and public pedagogy: the land is both scholar and pupil, as are the artists and the residents of the area, together inventing a new-old political ecology, a hybrid assemblage.

A Māori director works as a cultural consultant to the film industry. When questioned about the politics of Māori representation in cinema, he turns not to questions of casting, authenticity, or typification, narrative outcomes or authorship (although these indices of representational legitimacy are also on his mind). Instead, he talks about the tikanga (protocols) any production with Māori content or actors needs to observe. When you truly assume a role, you are calling on the mana from another epoch, and you have to have safeguards: ensure respect is given to elderly actors; guarantee that the language, te reo—a living treasure—is absolutely correct; bless the location or space in which the performances will take place

("The walls and the floors are the ears and eyes—you make sure that they're happy with your performance"). These measures secure the cornerstones of performance philosophy: the principles of ihi, wehi, and wana—the ability to draw in energies, forces; to create a sense of awe; to exude presence, affecting someone to the point of engendering a physical reaction in them (trembling, goosebumps, excitement). Ultimately, he explains, this power to generate and circulate affect emanates from the ground—literally—on which the performances take place, with its history, its ancestry: "At the end of the day, it's all about Papatūānuku. It's that that dictates the mana of the stories." This is political.

The art/science of instrument-free navigation, by which Polynesians peopled the island Pacific, is enjoying a renaissance as vessels such as *Hōkūle'a* criss-cross the ocean, training their Hawaiian crews in navigation's viscerally embodied epistemology. To discern a path, the navigator forges a bond between the self and a given star, an ancestor—a bond that is both ontological and perceptual—reading the movement of islands, ocean streams, and star systems around that fixed axis. To do so, she must not only see but also hear, smell, touch the ocean, becoming phenomenologically attuned to the currents, swells, and winds, the arc of the horizon and the motion of sea life teeming beneath. Such journeying is at the same time a medium of revitalization and an expression of cultural sovereignty: it fosters relationships between people and ocean, and between peoples separated by oceans, affirming the sustaining synchrony of past and present by retracing migratory paths and political missions (as in the 2007 journey of the wa'a to Japan and Micronesia). Such performances are not symbolic but performative in the most profound sense of the word, effecting a new (old) shape to things, through joint kinaesthetic action that is at once material, experiential, and ideational. To encounter this navigational practice (even superficially) is to reorder some of our most naturalized habits of spatial and political thought. It is to venture far from the familiar representational technologies of map and grid that lent fixity and purchase to the totalizing, objectivist imperatives of capital or empire. Here East and West are not geopolitical entities, but two trajectories among many, which both diffuse and isolate social collectivities; the ocean is not a blank space of passage, but a genealogical home and extension of self; the canoe is itself a maker of history, not an inert tool; and any understanding of political community must also include the ocean and its denizens, linked through the practical ethics of kuleana (responsibility, right) and pono.[1]

There are three things to notice here. First, these instances of Oceanic performance are contemporary formations—contemporary formations that are also evolving historical legacies, complexly interwoven with conceptual, institutional, and performance frameworks identified with "Western" modernity. Second, performance is how History/history *happens* in the Pacific; that is, it is both the medium in which the events of the past are brought to knowledge (History) and the engine of those events themselves (history).[2] Performance is a generative, motile process that propels, mutates, communicates, mediates association and differentiation between social collectives, humans and nonhumans, pasts and presents, through action (of, upon, between entities) that is affective, sensuous, imaginative, political, and material. What it is *not* is representational. It has no truck with the serial schema of representation—at once semiotic, aesthetic, and political—by which one entity (be it sign, person, object) stands (in) for another, which is taken to be both more real and less tangible. The Pacific world is material all the way down. Third, agency is attributed to a variety of actors, human and nonhuman. Actors exercise agency in the formation of associations over time and space, agency that could be understood as "political" in that it results in the fabrication of new polities, encompassing the dead as well as the living, objects and places as well as people.

What happens if we recognize the methodological rigor of this kind of thinking about performance? What happens if we engage it not as a whimsical holdover, strategic identity marking, or metaphorical habit, but as a theory (sometimes latent, sometimes emergent) of performance in everyday life, something not just to study but to *study with*? I venture that doing so is important to the practice of theater historiography not only because any basic ethical commitment to "engaging the Other" must necessarily engage the endogenous understandings of Other performers but also because it expands our disciplinary imagination to embrace a politics of performance (also an ecology and an ethics of performance) that diverges from the naturalized, but exhausted, paradigm of representation. It is not just that Oceanic thought makes nonsense of the oppositions around which the historiographic tradition (with its Enlightenment legacy) is organized— nature/society, idea/sign, body/mind, material/symbolic, subject/object, past/present, theory/practice, local/global, oral/textual, micro/macro, individual/society, spatial/virtual.[3] It is also that it makes palpable, in performance, a series of alternative ways in which they might be related. The encounter between Western and Oceanic thought may help "produce an art of the invention of political invention by putting hard questions to the given in experience."[4]

What I am advocating is two things. First, that we read and listen very carefully to historiographic theory from outside the precincts of our discipline and further, to theory that does not carry the imprimatur of academic respectability, recognizing that the segregation of literate epistemologies from (for example) spiritual discourse or the knowledge of craft is an artifact of a particular strain of Western modernity. Moreover, we need to recognize the theoretical productivity of practices themselves. Such an approach gives new life to the old saw that performance is a way of knowing (which scholars have tended to repeat at the same time as *they* have tried to do the knowing *for* the performance and performers, rather than—as actor-network theory [ANT] scholars suggest—following the actors, tracing the associations they make, scrutinizing the categories they employ).[5] If we define theory, with Sander Gilman, as a self-conscious, historicized awareness of the methodological approaches one uses to produce knowledge,[6] how can we understand reflexive performance itself as not only a way of knowing but also a way of knowing *how one might come to know*—the rhythms and health of an ocean, for example, or the power of things to create human collectivities? How does performance—quotidian performance, "traditional" performance, as well as avant-garde or theatrical performance—contribute to the theoretical project that has dominated the contemporary academic humanities, arts, and social sciences: "raising to the level of analytic attention the formative structures [and, one might add, political investments and possibilities] that lie beneath the surface of life and give it its shape"?[7]

Second, I am advocating for what might be called a coalitional theoretical practice that understands theory building as a dialogue between scholar and subject, and looks for points of resonance between their respective interests and investments. Theory, as Peter Galison has argued, does not stand outside of time and space (and too often in our discipline, we "apply" theoretical propositions as if they were some kind of universally applicable optical device—"theater," "theory," etymology: Gr. teatron, seeing place!—that will miraculously reveal the hidden truth of whatever we are examining), nor does it emerge solely from actors' categories.[8] Our impulses toward theorizing stem from historically specific conditions and political needs that may or may not be shared by those we study, whose own historiographic dispositions are, like ours, always inevitably hybrid. I find myself drawn to Oceanic performance in part because of a desire to bring to critical attention a region that is extraordinarily vulnerable to the whims of transnational capital, ecological catastrophe, and neocolonial exploitation, and that—due to the hegemony of the Euro-American spatial imagination—is often framed as vacant, inconsequential, or passive.[9] In equal part, I am compelled by the intersections between Pacific thought and exploratory theoretical projects underway in Euro-American humanities and social sciences that chafe against the Enlightenment inheritance of the disciplines and their dominant epistemologies. While trends in academic theory are slow to circulate in Oceanic discourse, Pacific thinkers have long recognized that to be legible in Euro-American academic circles, they must frame their insights as a critique of and alternative to this same epistemological inheritance, which has historically dismissed or objectified Oceanic thought. Oceanic insight, then, is not simply incommensurable with normative Western logic, but knowingly counter-to (and thus in part shaped by) that logic: this is the ground for careful, mutually transformative allegiance.

I want to make a brief sketch of one such countermodernist, radically antiobjectivist theoretical tradition, which has received little attention in either theater or performance studies, even while it makes performance a central term, method, and metaphor. I refer to a strain of philosophical romanticism or vitalism that might go under the (not uncontroversial) moniker of "postrepresentational theory" or "the new materialism." Scholars working in this vein are interested in the soft tissue rather than the skeletal structure of material life; in the forms and forces of circulation and connectedness that make themselves empirically felt even as they elude conventional ways of knowing through observation. They understand the world as in generative flux, aiming to capture the "onflow" of everyday life through methods that might be embodied, sensuous, imaginative, emotive, or creative. So while the materialism of this school of thought gives weight to things, it is to things as processes, relations of forces and affects; things as they coevolve with bodies in practice; things brought into relation with one another through continuous processes of encounter, become part of hybrid assemblages. The focus in this work, then, is necessarily on events, enaction, motion, practice, *performance*—not on what things are, but on how they happen, where they go. Its proponents are interested not so much in matter as in the dynamism of processes of mattering: the "polyrhythmic fluctuations of the everyday,"[10] the ways in which accumulations of practices (or "styles") over time lend stability and thus intelligibility to bodies, and also in how play works as a process of performative ex-

perimentation, producing variation. This is not a subject-based philosophy: it is fundamentally antihumanist as well as anticognitivist, abjuring
the individual agent in favor of the action of collectives, the force of affect
and sensation in thought, the intelligence of materials, and the skills that
produce selves, worlds, objects, facts. At the same time, it honors human
powers of fabulation, invention, imagination, and expression.

This new materialism refuses the division of things from ideas, sociality
from materiality, agency from structure, discourse from matter, and the
human from the nonhuman, moving to "reformulate the conflictual relations within the triad: nature/matter/human" laid down by older forms of
materialism[11]—an impulse that makes it the natural ally of both performance studies and Oceanic thought.[12] The implications of vitalism for
method are striking. Method must surrender the quest for certainty at the
root of modernist epistemology—the idea that by following certain steps
we can arrive at stable conclusions about how things really are (a precept
equally at the root of post-structuralism, as it is practiced in theater/per-
formance studies, and positivism). Instead it must become a slow, plural,
vulnerable, experimental, curious, concrete, messy, modest process of engaging with different realities. Grand, view-from-above theorizing about
the edifice of power (abstract generalizations that we give names like
"globalization," or "social forces," or the current bête noire "neo-liberal-
ism") is of less value to this project than intimate, pedestrian, haptic techniques.[13] This method would trace the scene of immanent forces—political forces, violent forces, as well as benign ones—as they make themselves
known locally in the experiences, textures, rhythms, and intensities that
"move through bodies, dreams, dramas, and social worldings of all
kinds."[14] It means slowing "the quick jump to representational thinking
and evaluative critique long enough to find ways of approaching the complex and uncertain objects that fascinate us."[15] As Kathleen Stewart has argued of the subject of her recent *Ordinary Affects*, "The question they beg
is not what they might mean in an order of representations, or whether
they are good or bad in an overarching scheme of things, but *where they
might go and what potential modes of knowing, relating, and attending to things
are already somehow present in them in a state of potentiality and resonance.*"[16] It
is a potent proposition that would make immediate sense to a Hawaiian
navigator or a Māori conservationist.

Further, if realities are made through enactment, if objects exist in a
complex present, their identities ephemeral, multiple, and shaped through
the associations they perform,[17] then our processes of knowing (themselves
a performance of associations) shape the things that are known. Scholars

have no privileged position here, and those studied (human and nonhuman, alive and dead) have equal rights to disclosure: the ocean makes its
paths and pasts known; the midden pit teaches conservationists how to
know/practice their ancestors' relation with shellfish. It follows that theory
and practice (including artistic practice) cannot be thought separately: the
objective of knowing not facts or truths, but practices and practical knowledges becomes a *practical task*, and creative research (which ought, as Paul
Carter argues, to be "an acknowledged tautology") a natural way to pursue
it.[18] This may seem like an unlikely basis for historiographic method, especially where history's textualist tradition equates evidence with the document; yet it is a particularly apposite basis for a historiography of an oral
culture, or for that matter, a nonfoundationalist historiography of literate
culture. It takes the sensual experience of a complex, material, unstable
present as the locus and genesis of historical understanding, the site at
which past objects (places, persons, things, ideas) are present-ed (brought
into association with present agents) as meaningful historical actors.

There has been little take-up of this strand of thought in theater/per-
formance studies, however, despite its interest in performance, artistic
praxis, and embodied knowing. I venture that this has much to do with the
entrenched dominance of representation as the organizing paradigm of
our (inter)discipline. Representation makes of theater both a metonym of
and a model for, on the one hand, Western political process and, on the
other, Western, post-Enlightenment historiography; an isomorphism that
flatters and legitimizes the work of our discipline. In this paradigm, theater
is an affair of the State founded in the regime of democracy: in the virtual
enclosure of the agora/theater, a public gathers for the event of an inquiry
into truth, morality, and ethics; actors are deployed as delegates that manifest polities, as incarnations of points of view (inevitably in discord);
textual referents are invoked, historical discourses elaborated, outcomes
made available for interpretation, evaluation, rationalization. As Badiou
has argued, theater's role (no matter what its subject) is to talk about the
state of the State through an "inventory of all the parts of a closed situation, a catastrophe." Theater, he goes on, both aims to elucidate our temporal site (tell us "where we are in history") and executes its thinking in the
past tense, saying "what the State *will have been* by lending it the fable of a
past."[19]

State politics, theater, and historiography, then, operate according to
mutually reinforcing representational logics that normalize very culturally
specific conceptions of historiography (deliberative, evaluative, moral,
aiming at the representation of the past and the disclosure of truth), poli-

tics (agonistic, discursive, statist, human, aiming at the truthful representation of subjects), and performance (a second-order, virtualizing process, more mimetic than inventive, in which subjects become objects in the representation of an external referent). It is also an entirely human affair: non-human collectives are consigned to the status of background, set. This has resulted, I think, in unfortunate disciplinary limitations. Non-Western modalities of performance, invited into the disciplinary fold by the vaunted inclusivity of the term, come under pressure to conform to the representational paradigm or forfeit their historiographic legibility and political significance. In turn, terms get stabilized (such as the actor-agent-individual human equation), scholarly goals are prescribed (reading signs, determining meaning, detecting hidden structures, evaluating moral valence), while the murkier performative terrain of everyday life—the residual in-between states, "'what is left over' after all distinct, superior, specialized, structured activities have been singled out by analysis"[20]—fades into the disciplinary background, and a definition of performance as framed, heightened, specialized, dominates the field, little challenged.[21] Thus, scholars have examined the musical and dance performances exchanged between Polynesian peoples and European explorers as reciprocal representations of political intent, a mimetic groping toward a semiosis-in-common, for which the ultimate referent was the drama of imperial power or of Polynesian kingship; but the divergent practices, technologies, and philosophies of navigation that brought both groups (at different times) to those beaches, and that were the (material, experiential, spatial, political, cosmological) engine of history for both—these only haunt the edges of the account.[22]

The persistence of the representational paradigm has shaped the field's interdisciplinary affiliations, making the intersection with popular culture and art criticism seem natural and welcoming linguistic models of performativity (which confirm-critique entrenched beliefs about the foundational nature of prior textual referents mobilized through repetition and rupture). Meanwhile our students find social sciences work on performance arid, irrelevant, and lacking in evidence of creative agency, in part because they implicitly recognize agency as a dramatic property of the individual subject-protagonist. Though performance studies built its early reputation on renouncing purely symbolic, representational approaches in favor of performance as the "most fecund metaphor for the social dimensions of cultural production," its entanglement with theater historiography makes the pull of theatrical-political-historiographic logic felt.[23] Joseph Roach's work from the 1990s on genealogies of performance (dense networks formed across time and space from a flux of mobile material—techniques, bodies, spatial formations, texts, commodities, but also crucially habits and attitudes), or Pollock's refleshing of performance history ("relieved of their respective isolation within discourses of history, performance proves powerful; history proves affective, sensual, and generative"), anticipates the thrust of vitalist thought.[24] But Taylor, continuing in this scholarly vein, analyzes the evidence of kinaesthetic practice (the repertoire) only as it is made visible *by containment* within the theatrical scene of colonial, textual historiography (the archive) or its revenance in contemporary theater, performance art, and protest. In this analytic context, pre-Columbian materials do not appear to be generative of associations, inventive, changing, vital practices of knowing, but are instead representations (mnemonic repetitions) of suppressed memories, absent or eliminated Others, superseded worlds.[25]

There is an urgency to admitting other cultural formations of performance, and the political rationalities they incarnate, into our disciplinary imagination. The decline of political participation—and (not coincidentally) theater attendance—in Western representational democracies indicates a broader loss of faith in representation and its concomitant idea of demos. At the same time, the networked, dispersed, heterogeneous, and ephemeral solidarities that characterize a global and information age defy representability. We have not only to think of other ways than representation in which humans and nonhumans might act, invent, or express politically, but we have also to develop analytic practices to grapple with "political imaginations shaping popular politics all over the world today that escape normative understandings of the political" (from Al Qaeda to America's own increasingly nonrational forms of political affiliation).[26] There are still other pressing problems that demand a reinvention of our historiographic apparatus. One might consider, for example, the new imperative to admit nonhuman agencies into the domain of both historiography and politics supplied by the challenges of a post-climate-change era. Dipesh Chakrabarty has argued that the fact of climate change challenges a historiography founded on the distinction between human and nonhuman ("natural") history, geological and historical time, the chronologies of species and capital.[27] The humanist, and theatrical, tenet that "man makes himself" is no longer tenable in the era when humans have proven a geological force and geology promises to have catastrophic bearing on human futures; the acquisition of human freedom can no longer be thought (pace Hegel) as the achievement of autonomy; nor can the State be the stage for our most urgent dramas or the ultimate, sufficient vessel for our political desires. Our planetary moment demands that we assay the limits of historical understanding. How might plumbing modalities of performance, such as the Oceanic, contribute to such a project? And how might the fruit of such a project benefit Oceanic interests?

NOTES

Epigraph: This is the epigraph to Edouard Glissant's *Poetics of Relation* (Ann Arbor: University of Michigan Press, 1997).

1. For the examples in these paragraph, I offer thanks to Garry Nicholas of Toi Māori Aotearoa, Paora Tapsell, whose doctoral thesis, "Taonga: A Tribal Response to Museums" (D.Phil., School of Museum Ethnology, Oxford University, 1999), and book *Māori Treasures from New Zealand Museums: Ko Tawa* (Auckland: Auckland War Memorial Museum, 2006) contain eloquent explanations of this logic; Huhana Smith, of the Te Papa Tongarewa National Museum of New Zealand; Karen Ingersoll and Noelani Wilson, for their respective work on Kanaka Maoli voyaging; Vincent Diaz, for comments at their panel at the recent Native American and Indigenous Studies Association conference; Waimaria Erueti; Kingi and Joe Biddle; and Ngamaru Raerino of Ngā Aho Whakaari.

2. I am employing the Historie/Geschichte, story/discourse distinction central to post-structuralist historiography, aware that the logic and politics subtending the relation-separation of narrative and event in Oceanic thought should not be assumed to be commensurate with that in the Western tradition.

3. Subramani, "The Oceanic Imaginary," *Contemporary Pacific* 13, no. 1 (2001): 149–62.

4. Nigel Thrift, *Non-Representational Theory: Space, Politics, Affect* (London: Routledge, 2007), 3. The proposition here is not that indigenous insight will save Western modernity from its own disenchantment (the classic primitivist gesture of colonial appropriation), nor is the point to idealize some pure strain of indigenous political wisdom and justice. (The Oceanic political has its own histories of violence and injustice, its own struggles to admit contestation and critique). I am also not suggesting that we, as a discipline, cultivate and claim expertise in indigenous epistemology. (Indigenous knowledge systems have their own regimes of training and credentialization that require a depth of commitment and length of apprenticeship that most scholars located in the United States cannot responsibly attempt, even were they granted access.) At the same time, studying Oceanic performance with only the tools of Western theater historiography, no matter how reflexively or deconstructively applied, is plainly inadequate, saying much about the West's past and present sins of omission, misrepresentation, and misinterpretation in its encounter with Oceanic performance and little about the political imagination of Oceanic peoples (or Oceanic objects, for that matter).

5. The ANT literature is extensive. For good recent surveys of the work, see Bruno Latour, *Reassembling the Social: An Introduction to Actor-Network-Theory* (Oxford: Oxford University Press, 2005); John Law and John Hasard, eds., *Actor-Network-Theory and After* (Oxford and Malden, MA: Blackwell, 1999).

6. Sander Gilman, quoted in Stanley Fish, "Theory's Hope," *Critical Inquiry* 30, no. 2 (2004): 377.

7. Fish, "Theory's Hope," 377.

8. Peter Galison, "Specific Theory," *Critical Inquiry* 30, no. 2 (2004): 381.

9. Epeli Hau'ofa, "Our Sea of Islands," in *Asia/Pacific as Space of Cultural Production*, ed. Rob Wilson and Arif Dirlik (Durham and London: Duke University Press, 1995), 86–98.

10. Gregory J. Seigworth and Michael E. Gardiner, "Rethinking Everyday Life: And Then Nothing Turns Itself Inside Out," *Cultural Studies* 18, nos. 2–3 (2004): 141

11. Henri Lefebvre, "Toward a Leftist Cultural Politics: Remarks Occasioned by the Centenary of Marx's Death," in *Marxism and the Interpretation of Culture*, ed. C. Nelson and L. Grossberg (Urbana and Chicago: University of Illinois Press, 1988), 87; quoted in Seigworth and Gardiner, "Rethinking Everyday Life," 151.

12. The tradition reaches from pre-modern precursors, such as Spinoza and Leibniz, to the twentieth-century thinkers Tarde, Bergson, Benjamin, Deleuze, Whitehead, and Lefebvre, to significant feminist theorists (Grosz, Probyn, Berlant, to name just a few), and to contemporary scholars in fields as diverse as philosophy, history, sociology, science studies, anthropology, and economics (e.g., Serres, Carter, Thrift, Latour, Ingold, and Callon). One can see the imprint of this tradition in the recent flourishing of interest in affect that addresses "the sociability of persons across things, spaces and practices" (Lauren Berlant, "Critical Inquiry, Affirmative Culture" [*Critical Inquiry* 30, no. 2 (2004)]: 2). This broadly post-humanist literature turns to the human without resurrecting a metaphysical subject, moving beyond the intersubjective drama of empathy/sympathy to focus on the preindividual character of affect as it circulates in the spaces between subjects or registers on/in the body. It has proved an equally sharp tool for examining the modern corporation's affective engineering of its workforce and the nonconscious, asignifying, extra-linguistic means by which art extends intensities over time and space (Nigel Thrift, "Performing Cultures in the New Economy," *Annals of the Association of American Geographers* 90, no. 4 [2000]: 674–92; Simon O'Sullivan, "The Aesthetics of Affect: Thinking Art beyond Representation," *Angelaki* 6, no. 3 [2001]: 125–35). The mark of vitalist thought is visible in the recent deluge of work on biopolitics that attends to the intimate practice of life through parsing the processes, techniques, technologies, and knowledges through which human existence is managed. Finally, vitalism has also influenced actor-network theories in sociology and science studies that eschew totalizing explanatory meta-objects (such as "the social"), focusing instead on the unstable effects produced by cumulative performances of linkages and famously insisting that both humans and nonhumans are actors within such assemblages. See, for an excellent précis, Latour, *Reassembling the Social*.

13. This discussion is informed by my reading in the ANT literature. John Law's elegant summary also helped formulate these thoughts (*After Method: Mess in the Social Science Research* [London and New York: Routledge, 2004]).

14. Kathleen Stewart, *Ordinary Affects* (Durham: Duke University Press, 2007), 5.

15. Stewart, *Ordinary Affects*, 5.

16. Stewart, *Ordinary Affects*, 5, emphasis added.

17. Annemarie Mol, *The Body Multiple: Ontology in Medical Practice* (Durham: Duke University Press, 2002), 43.

18. Paul Carter, *Material Thinking: The Theory and Practice of Creative Research* (Melbourne: University of Melbourne Press, 2005), 7.

19. Alain Badiou, "Rhapsody for The Theatre," trans. Bruno Bosteels, *Theatre Survey* 49, no. 2 (2008): 207.

20. Henri Lefebvre, *Critique of Everyday Life: Volume One*, trans. J. Moore (New York and London: Verso, [1947] 1991), 97; see also Seigworth and Gardiner, "Rethinking Everyday Life."

21. Even materialist methodologies in theater studies transect the field by dividing the thinginess of the production process from the idea-ishness of productions (their aesthetic, literary, semiotic dimensions) and assigning both different roles with respect to representational function. See, e.g., Ric Knowles, *Reading the Material Theatre* (Cambridge: Cambridge University Press, 2004). For a nonrepresentational argument about the performative work of framing, see Bruno Latour, "On Interobjectivity," *Mind, Culture, and Activity* 3, no. 4 (1996): 228–45.

22. I refer here to two inspiring studies, influential in the field of Pacific cultural and performance studies: Greg Dening, *Performances* (Chicago: University of Chicago Press, 1996); Christopher Balme, *Pacific Performances: Theatricality and Cross-Cultural Encounter in the South Seas* (Basingstoke: Palgrave Macmillan, 2007).

23. Joseph Roach, "Culture and Performance in the Circum-Atlantic World," in *Performativity and Performance*, ed. Andrew Parker and Eve Kosofsky Sedgwick (New York: Routledge, 1995), 46.

24. Della Pollock, "Introduction: Making History Go," in *Exceptional Spaces: Essays in Performance and History*, ed. Della Pollock (Chapel Hill: University of North Carolina Press, 1998), 2.

25. See Diana Taylor, *The Archive and the Repertoire: Performing Cultural Memory in the Americas* (Durham: Duke University Press, 2003). I am overstating my case here, and I think the book is rightly celebrated for the possibilities it opens up for historiography—but the choice to focus on theatrical/historiographic context, I believe, has a limiting effect on what can be made of practice.

26. Dipesh Chakrabarty, "Where Is the Now?" *Critical Inquiry* 30, no. 2 (2004): 460.

27. Dipesh Chakrabarty, "Climate of History: Four Theses," *Critical Inquiry* 35, no. 2 (2009): 198–222.

*Intra*disciplinarity in Theater History

Anne Oldfield's Mrs. Brittle via Brecht's Not/But

JAMES PECK ∽

Some twenty-five years ago, the discipline of theater history embraced interdisciplinarity. Reacting to a prevalent empiricism within the field as it was then constituted, many theater historians turned to adjacent forms of knowledge for interpretive paradigms to revitalize research and analysis of the theatrical past. I might cite many superb books and articles to support this assertion, though the trend is so common that in its broad contours the claim scarcely needs defending. Methods drawn from anthropology, sociology, semiotics, cultural studies, post-structuralist identity studies, and numerous other scholarly discourses now often shape arguments about theater history. This intellectual habit—enlisting the hermeneutic lenses of related discourses in the humanities and social sciences to establish the cultural work of the theater—is a widespread though not uncontested historiographic pattern. A recent spate of work inflected by cognitive neuroscience extends this tendency to the hard sciences. One indicator of the extent to which self-consciously interdisciplinary methods are staking a claim to the center of theater history might be the recent *Theatre Histories: An Introduction*, by Phillip B. Zarrilli, Bruce McConachie, Gary Jay Williams, and Carol Fischer Sorgenfrei.[1] This comprehensive theater history survey text introduces an array of interdisciplinary influences on the contemporary practice of theater history, framing each in a box designated "interpretive approach." Twenty-five years ago, interdisciplinary researchers were insurgent voices poised to transform the field; today, the field is so transformed that an array of interdisciplinary methods figures prominently in a widely used survey textbook.

The interdisciplinary turn has greatly enriched the practice of theater history. Interdisciplinary approaches reveal theater as an ideologically invested cultural process that mediates social relations in historically significant ways. Here, I'd like to argue for the value of what I'm going to call *intra*disciplinarity. In the present moment, theater history would also benefit from intellectual dialogue with epistemologies developed in the arena of performance practice. I refer here not to scholarly writing about contemporary theater and performance, though much of it is powerfully enabling. Rather, I am suggesting that theater historians rework theatrical techniques forged in the hurly-burly of the rehearsal hall.

In *The Archive and The Repertoire: Performing Cultural Memory in the Americas*, Diana Taylor creatively adapts theatrical technique for historiographic purposes. Taylor certainly works in an *inter*disciplinary mode: Latin American studies, critical race theory, and feminist theory figure prominently in her argument. But she also works in an *intra*disciplinary mode. She reworks the age-old performance method of the scenario—a rough narrative to guide improvisational performances such as those of the Commedia dell'Arte—into an analytic approach especially well-suited to performance history. "The *scenario*," defined as a common cultural story that traverses aesthetic and social realms through repeated reenactments, "includes features well theorized in literary analysis, such as narrative and plot, but demands that we also pay attention to milieux and corporeal behaviors such as gestures, attitudes, and tones not reducible to language."[2] Taylor's many trenchant analyses demonstrate the hermeneutic advantages of a critical praxis rooted in the epistemologies of performance. We would do well to remember that the history of theatrical technique contains many comparably rich ways of knowing with promising and largely untapped applications for theater history.

By way of example, I consider an episode in the career of the early eighteenth-century actress Anne Oldfield. In the season of 1708–9 Oldfield was excluded from the management of the Haymarket Theatre on the basis of her gender. On March 4, she and several other leading actors broke from the Drury Lane Theatre to protest the high-handed and erratic behavior of manager Christopher Rich.[3] Oldfield initiated the split when Rich, in apparent violation of their agreement, withheld one-third of the profits from her yearly benefit performance. The rebel actors immediately entered negotiations with entrepreneur Owen Swiney, who had acquired a license to perform plays at the rival Haymarket Theatre. Initially Oldfield, the established leading lady of the company, was proposed as one of its new managers. However, the potential actor-manager Thomas Doggett objected to a female presence on the management team. "Our Affairs," he argued to comedian and playwright Colley Cibber and leading man Robert Wilks, "could never be upon a secure Foundation if there was more than

Figure 19.1. Anne Oldfield, by Edward Fisher after Jonathan Richardson. Courtesy of the National Portrait Gallery.

one Sex admitted to the Menagement [*sic*] of them."[4] Six days later, on March 10, Doggett, Cibber, and Wilks signed an agreement with Swiney. Cibber reports the ensuing negotiations with Oldfield: Doggett "therefore hop'd that if we offer'd Mrs. Oldfield a *Carte Blanche* instead of a Share, she would not think herself slighted. This was instantly agreed to, and Mrs. Oldfield receiv'd it rather as a Favour than a Disobligation: Her Demands therefore were Two Hundred Pounds a Year Certain, and Benefit clear of all Charges."[5]

Figure 19.2. Thomas Doggett, by Johann Zoffany. Courtesy of the Hampden-Booth Theatre Library.

Theater historians have largely accepted Cibber's account of this incident, albeit with minor variations of emphasis.[6] However, I propose to demonstrate that Oldfield did not, as Cibber rosily implies, accept this deal with a gracious sense of relief from the burdens of management. Rather, she concretely sought entrees to management throughout the ensuing year through interpersonal, legal, and symbolic means.

To make this case and tease out its implications for the relationship between gender and theater management in the eighteenth century, I will examine these events through the lens of a rehearsal technique adapted from Bertolt Brecht, what he calls "fixing the not . . . but."[7] Brecht advocates that everything on stage occur in such a way that it includes the possibility it might have occurred differently. The characters do "not this, but rather that." Brecht explains the approach in "Short Description of a New Technique of Acting that Produces an Alienation Effect":

> When [the actor] appears on the stage, besides what he actually is doing he will at all points discover, specify, imply what he is not doing; that is to say he will act in such a way that the alternative emerges as clearly as possible, that his acting allows the other possibilities to be inferred and only represents one out of the possible variants. . . . Whatever he doesn't do must be contained and conserved in what he does. . . . The technical term for this procedure is "fixing the 'not . . . but.'"[8]

The not/but as here described is a modus operandi for performers. But it is not a value-free rehearsal practice; it is a technique to give body to a philosophical perspective on human action. "'Fixing the not-but,'" writes Meg Mumford, is an "interpretive strateg[y] rather than simply [a] formal device."[9] The not/but highlights contingency in human affairs. It instantiates in both the rehearsal process and the production Brecht's conviction that history is lived in the microconduct of daily life and that it is open-ended. The not/but directs attention to paths not taken, underscores the provisional quality of all historical arrangements, and dramatizes the view that for better and worse humans construct social reality in an ongoing process.

Critical methods focus the historian's attention: they privilege certain kinds of objects and evidence, suggest archives, and establish priorities. A historiographic practice adapted from Brecht's not/but would emphasize the conditional qualities of historical events. The historiographic not/but foregrounds decisive occurrences but gives copious attention to alternatives. It prioritizes interactions that crystallize the social relations of a given era but maintains conceptual space for atypical events or perspectives. It seeks to account for evidence that does not contribute to the dominant historical trajectory but rather marks visions of human society foreclosed by the eventual progress of affairs. It opposes the teleological. In these respects, one promising adaptation of the not/but shares the concerns of many critical historiographies. In Walter Benjamin's memorable phrase, a historical practice grounded in the not/but might "brush history against the grain" and unfold possibilities that did not come to pass.[10] It might draw attention to openings for a more equitable society eradicated by dominant or emergent power arrangements. It might reinsert those alternatives into the historical record and aim to implant them in public memory as options yet awaiting realization.

From the perspective of the not/but, Cibber's complaisant account of Oldfield's acquiescence must be approached with tremendous skepticism. Indeed, Oldfield had much to object to in the outcome of the negotiations; her contract was lucrative, but as a manager she would have made much more money and been in a better position to shape the direction of the company and the progress of her own career. Nor did she accept these terms "instantly," as Cibber states, but some six weeks later, on April 21. What's more, the documentary record attests that Oldfield actively sought managerial status long after committing herself to this arrangement. Though Swiney and the actor-managers moved forward with their plans for the Haymarket, the legality of their enterprise remained in dispute. Consequently, Swiney maintained an ongoing negotiation with the Lord Chamberlain for the rest of the year. During that time, Oldfield continued to wrangle for a place in the management. Her bid for a share surfaces in a letter from Swiney to the Lord Chamberlain written late that fall, proba- bly in November. Swiney proposes a profit-sharing agreement involving "four Actors" rather than three. Oldfield's lover, the Whig politician Arthur Maynwaring, the details of the letter indicate, had entered negotia- tions on Oldfield's behalf and persuaded Swiney to accept her as a fourth manager.[11] Unfortunately, on December 24 the Lord Chamberlain ratified the initial partnership among Swiney, Doggett, Cibber, and Wilks, legally validating Oldfield's exclusion from the managerial team.

To this point, Brecht's not/but is a pertinent but inessential touchstone. Intellectual habits common to critical historiographies shape this capsule analysis. I enlist the archival record to contest a prevalent view that Oldfield capitulated gracefully to a glass ceiling excluding her from the privileges, responsibilities, and rewards of managerial leadership. I show (with relative ease) that for the rest of the year she used her interpersonal influence to seek a place in management via legal negotiation. Clearly, I could have made these points without reference to Brecht. However, Brecht's not/but does clarify Oldfield's next effort to shape the progress of her career. "Barred, as a woman, from full participation in profits and managerial decisions," writes Joanne Lafler, "she would have to exercise her power in less formal ways."[12] Lafler does not specify what these means might be or recognize that in actuality Oldfield continued her quest to join the management. In February 1710, Oldfield turned to the symbolic public authority of the playhouse. A historiography adapted from the theatrical practice of Brecht's not/but keenly illuminates the stakes of this performance.

In the early eighteenth century, an actor's benefit was a valuable portion of her or his yearly income. Company members received rights to the theater for an evening, typically paid a small "house charge" to cover staff salaries and other building expenses, and pocketed the remainder of the proceeds. They chose the play and sold tickets themselves, hoping to pack the house with sympathetic fans. For her benefit performance two months after the Lord Chamberlain's ruling, Oldfield selected the character of Mrs. Brittle in Thomas Betterton's *The Amourous Widow; or, The Wanton Wife.*

Brecht's not/but reveals Oldfield's performance of Mrs. Brittle in this benefit as a canny, semiotically charged interruption of the smooth progress of playhouse affairs. This performance reopened the seemingly conclusive events of December, reminding all those with ears to hear that the future of the management at the Haymarket remained emphatically contingent. The recent history of *The Wanton Wife* was propitious for Oldfield's purposes. First off, three years earlier the role of Mrs. Brittle had established Oldfield as the unambiguous leading comedienne of the English theater. In 1707, Oldfield bested the senior actress Anne Bracegirdle in a widely publicized competition when they performed this role on successive nights to establish who was the superior actress. An anonymous biography of Oldfield published shortly after her death gushes that Oldfield "charm'd the whole Audience to that Degree, that they almost forgot they had ever seen Mrs. Bracegirdle, and universally adjudged her the Preheminence [*sic*]."[13] The author's rhetoric is effusive, but subsequent events attest that following this contest Oldfield supplanted Bracegirdle in the audience's favor. Bracegirdle retired within the year, and Oldfield assumed many of her roles. Oldfield's portrayal of Mrs. Brittle promised to remind spectators of her popular appeal, competitive spirit, and mental toughness. Moreover, *The Wanton Wife* was written by Thomas Betterton, the unrivaled leading man of the English Restoration theater and by this time its august statesman. In the early 1700s, Betterton had managed the theater at Lincoln's Inn Fields in tandem with two prominent actresses, Elizabeth Barry and Anne Bracegirdle; Barry in particular functioned as a de facto comanager with major responsibilities for the selection of repertoire. What's more, the three of them led the troupe of actors that founded the theater in 1695, in a highly publicized breakaway from the tyrannical management practices of the same Christopher Rich.[14] For theatergoers acquainted with the managerial strife at the Haymarket, the choice of a play by Betterton could have recalled a moment within the last decade when men and women indeed collaborated in running a theater.

These connections between the managerial drama and Oldfield's performance in *The Wanton Wife* are speculative. However, the content of the play—one scene in particular—establishes a vivid relationship between

Oldfield's bid for a share in the management and her performance as Mrs. Brittle. The comedy has two plots: the first concerns a love-starved widow searching for a virile male partner; the second, in which Oldfield appeared, focuses on the unhappy marriage of a young, stylish, aristocratic woman and a niggardly merchant-class husband. Oldfield's character Mrs. Brittle relishes tasteful aristocratic pleasures outside the home: fine clothes, cards, and most especially theater. Mr. Brittle fears that her expenses will bankrupt him and her circulation in polite society cuckold him. Mr. Brittle was normally played by the man who expunged Oldfield from the management, Thomas Doggett. The archive does not definitively establish that Doggett performed the role that night. However, ridiculous money-grubbing merchants filled his line, and he is the only actor known to have acted the part that season; it is very likely he appeared.[15] The role also echoed prominent features of his managerial persona: he was an irascible tightwad. Cibber, for example, reports frequent disputes between Wilks and Doggett over financial matters, Wilks advocating expenditure for the house's "Glory" and Doggett preferring "Lucre."[16]

At her benefit in February 1710, Anne Oldfield performed Mrs. Brittle as a witty, incisive, and resistant theatrical intervention in her professional relationship with Thomas Doggett. In *The Wanton Wife*, the most aggressive and recurrent disputes between the Brittles revolve around Mrs. Brittle's frequent trips to the theater. Mr. Brittle insists that his wife stop attending plays; Mrs. Brittle counters that she will go to the theater whether he likes it or not. I quote their argument at length, as it transmutes into dialogue bearing upon the professional relationship between Oldfield and Doggett:

BRITTLE: Whither away in such haste?

MRS. BRITTLE: I'm going abroad Husband. Good bye.

BRITTLE: Hold, hold by your Leave, I'll know for what, and whither your sweet Ladyship is going?

MRS. BRITTLE: Why to the Play, Sweet Husband.

BRITTLE: Hum! to the Play.

MRS. BRITTLE: Well, Good bye Husband—I shall be too late and then there'll be such crowding, I shan't get the first Row in the Box, for 'tis a new Play; and I had as life not go, as sit behind.

BRITTLE: Hold, hold, pray stay if you please.

MRS. BRITTLE: Indeed, but I can't.

BRITTLE: Indeed, but you must not go Wife.

MRS. BRITTLE: Indeed, Husband, but I shall.

BRITTLE: I say again, you must not.

MRS. BRITTLE: Must not! Who will hinder me?

BRITTLE: Why, that will I.

MRS. BRITTLE: I say, No.

BRITTLE: But I say, Yes.

MRS. BRITTLE: Don't you pretend to't.

BRITTLE: Don't you provoke me I say. Is this the Trade you intend to drive?

MRS. BRITTLE: Yes, indeed is it.

BRITTLE: I say, No.

MRS. BRITTLE: But I say, Yes.[17]

In the fictive world of *The Wanton Wife*, a paranoid husband seeks to control his independent wife. Mr. Brittle asks, "Whither away in such haste?" and after an initial attempt at evasion Mrs. Brittle replies, "Why to the Play, Sweet Husband." But recent events at the Haymarket expanded this interchange into a simultaneous public conversation between an actor-manager and the leading lady about her efforts to advance in her profession: Doggett asks, "Is this the Trade you intend to drive?" and Oldfield answers, "Yes, indeed is it." Doggett: "I say, No." Oldfield: "But I say, Yes." The circumstances of that evening's performance certainly invited all present to impute Mrs. Brittle's proclamation into Oldfield's bid for managerial status. It was her benefit. A house of patrons present in support and appreciation of the actress incontestably demonstrated her ability to attract money to the theater.

The not/but gives weight and historical resonance to this theatrical moment. Brecht states that as the role unfolds, an actor should "discover, specify, imply what he is not doing" so that the "alternative emerges as clearly as possible," other possibilities can "be inferred," and the plot "only represents one out of the possible variants."[18] A theater history informed by the not/but would especially value performances that halted the unfolding of events to frame the possibilities available in a given historical moment. It would attend to the options not taken and theorize the reasons for this. It would unpack theatrical moments that deferred a sense of closure in order to promulgate an open future. Choosing this play for her benefit, Oldfield recalled and reopened her bid for a spot in management. I imagine Thomas Doggett faced with a dilemma. Refuse to perform, and further alienate the popular leading lady? Agree to perform, and face this chiding exchange in front of her fans? I imagine Anne Oldfield relishing this scene. I see her turning to the audience, inviting them to join her in a face-off with Thomas Doggett or his erstwhile understudy. I hear her lending a wry, personal nuance to Mrs. Brittle's insistence that she will continue to pursue her theatrical trade: "But I say, Yes."

Clearly, I am enlisting my theatrical imagination to fill out these possibilities. I'm not saying that the not/but tells us *for sure* what Anne Oldfield and Thomas Doggett thought or felt in these moments. However, *something* lively and fraught happened around this performance, probably in that onstage moment, and whatever occurred had the potential to undo the sense of closure implied by the Lord Chamberlain's order six weeks earlier. This theatrical moment framed the managerial drama in the manner of the not/but. It highlighted choices made and options rejected and did so in a way that undermined the inevitability of the current situation. Indeed, in February 1710 it was by no means clear that the new Haymarket management structure would hold. And in point of fact the London theater scene was so unstable that by the end of the year Doggett, Cibber, and Wilks were compelled to secure a new license and move to Drury Lane.[19] In early 1710, Oldfield had good reason to hope that the decisions barring her from management were not finalized but might yet be overturned.

Brecht's not/but gives priority to contested social behavior—to actions and nonactions that assert or resist characteristic power arrangements. This imagined encounter between Oldfield and Doggett is an effulgent moment not only because of the seeming personal rivalry the scene evokes, as piquant as that is. It also encapsulates a then-unfolding shift in gender relations that took place across the eighteenth century. A large bibliography of work in eighteenth-century studies charts the creation of gendered spheres in this era, with men designated for the public arena and women relegated to domestic identities. Michael McKeon persuasively connects this trend to the simultaneous creation and ascendancy of bourgeois class positions like those occupied by Thomas Doggett and his business partners.[20] From this vantage point, Oldfield's clever artistic riposte was not narrowly personal. Rather, it publicly marked limitations placed on her economic power by a surging ideology that excluded women from positions of leadership within the rapidly evolving institutions of commercial society, even as those institutions opened new vistas for merchant-class men. Her "But I say, Yes" is one small piece of that large history. It is a reminder that powerful women recognized the injustice of these developments as they occurred and sought legal and, when that failed, symbolic means to oppose them.

For Doggett's part, the commercial leaders of early eighteenth-century England worried that trade was a feminized, irrational activity; the image of the market as a hysterical woman in need of discipline is a pervasive metaphor of the period.[21] Upper-class women often bore the brunt of projections arising from fears about the instability of the marketplace, fashionable women figuring as sites of displacement for the superficiality and cupidity of commercial society.[22] Doggett's insistence that "our Affairs could never be upon a secure Foundation if there was more than one Sex admitted to the Management of them" is perhaps a symptomatic manifestation of this anxiety about the compromised masculinity of business. Anne Oldfield was herself a stylish participant in polite society and played many fashion-conscious women of means.[23] Walking the boards, she often embodied the venal, capricious, and artificial aspects of commercial society that Thomas Doggett repressed to constitute himself as a stable, productive merchant-class man. The hysteria with which Barnaby Brittle insists that his wife stay away from the theater perhaps captures something of Doggett's hysteria at the thought of sitting down to business with Anne Oldfield, a symbolic condensation of the aspect of himself he most loathed.

Brecht's not/but illuminates the tensions packed into this reverberant moment in Anne Oldfield's benefit performance of February 1710. We know now that though Anne Oldfield went on to a long and storied acting career, she never became a theater manager. The not/but recovers the historical stakes of this performance early in her career. It gives these events vital historical attention—vital not because they determined the course of history but precisely because they did not. In 1709–10, Oldfield used her full resources—a legal action against Christopher Rich, personal connections with a Whig politico, and her access to the symbolic public arena of the playhouse—to move into management. This never happened for both interpersonal and broadly social reasons. Lamentably, Oldfield's exclusion from the management of the Haymarket established a precedent barring women from the managerial ranks of London theater that would last for well over a century.[24] Consequently, it is especially important that theater history not accept Cibber's blithe version of events but emphasize Oldfield's unsuccessful though multiform efforts to direct history along another path. Not/But.

Brecht's not/but gives historical resonance to this moment in theater history. It focuses attention on the stage as a site of symbolic contestation and endows the encounter between Oldfield and Doggett as Mrs. and Mr. Brittle with sly wit and resistant possibility. It helps the analysis resist a teleological tendency of much historical practice to privilege efficacious action and causal narrative and instead gives rhetorical emphasis to a path not taken, an opportunity squelched. Extrapolating from this example, I'm suggesting that performance techniques, reworked to address the tasks of history, can help historians find and analyze such historically charged moments. Theatrical techniques were created to give dimension, intelligence, and feeling to theatrical events. They are therefore readymade optics to research theatrical events and discover their dimension, intelligence and feeling. I am not suggesting—emphatically not suggesting—that theater history forsake interdisciplinarity. Without doubt, interdisciplinary methods help theater historians address consequential issues of identity, power, and historical change. The reader will no doubt have noticed that even in this short paper I invoke the idioms of several interdisciplines, including eighteenth-century studies, women's studies, cultural studies, and psychoanalysis. Though I have not emphasized my debt to the insights and methods of those fields, they thread through my argument. Observing that *inter*disciplinary operations have established themselves firmly in the contemporary practice of theater history, I have accented rather the potential of *intra*disciplinary methods. The history of the theater already encompasses a rich repository of interpretive approaches: artistic practices, at their best, *are* critical practices. Creatively adapted, these too could direct our inquiry, guide our analysis, and inform our efforts to locate in the theatrical encounter the frisson of social experience as it moved across the skin.

NOTES

1. Phillip Zarrilli, Bruce McConachie, Gary Jay Williams, and Carol Fischer Sorgenfrei, *Theatre Histories: An Introduction* (New York: Routledge, 2006).

2. Diana Taylor, *The Archive and the Repertoire: Performing Cultural Memory in the Americas* (Durham: Duke University Press, 2003), 28.

3. A detailed reconstruction of these events may be found in Judith Milhous and Robert D. Hume, "The Silencing of Drury Lane in 1709," *Theatre Journal* 32, no. 4 (1980): 427–47. See also the documents assembled and annotated by Milhous and Hume in *Vice Chamberlain Coke's Theatrical Papers, 1706–1715* (Carbondale and Edwardsville: Southern Illinois University Press, 1982), 116–46.

4. Colley Cibber, *An Apology for the Life of Mr. Colley Cibber: With An Historical View of the Stage during his own Time*, ed. Robert Lowe (London: 1889), 2: 70–71.

5. Cibber, *Apology*, 2: 71.

6. A comprehensive account of Oldfield's career is Joanne Lafler, *The Celebrated Mrs. Oldfield: The Life and Art of an Augustan Actress* (Carbondale and Edwardsville: Southern Illinois University Press, 1989). I am indebted to Lafler's thorough archival research. See also Oldfield's entry in Kalmin A. Burnim, Philip H. Highfill Jr., and Edward A. Langhans, *A Biographical Dictionary of Actors, Actresses, Musicians, Dancers, Managers, and Other Stage Personnel in London, 1660–1800* (Carbondale and Edwardsville: Southern Illinois University Press, 1987), 11: 101–11.

7. I am not the first to propose affinities between Brecht and the theater of the long eighteenth century. Brecht himself, collaborating with Benno Besson and Elisabeth Hauptmann, adapted George Farquhar's 1706 comedy *The Recruiting Officer* into *Trumpets and Drums* in 1955; it was his final completed play. An English translation is in *Collected Plays, Vol. 9*, ed. and trans. Ralph Manheim and John Willet (New York: Vintage Books, 1973). The British director Max Stafford-Clark drew upon Brecht for his production of *The Recruiting Officer*, chronicled in *Letters to George* (London: Nick Hern Books, 1989). From a critical perspective, Elin Diamond approaches the plays of Restoration playwright Aphra Behn through Brecht's acting technique of gestus. See her "Brechtian Theory/Feminist Theory: Toward a Gestic Feminist Criticism," *Drama Review* 32, no. 1 (1988); 82–94, and chaps. 2 and 3 of *Unmaking Mimesis* (New York: Routledge, 1987). Jocelyn Powell, *Restoration Theatre Production* (London: Routledge, 1984), employs Brecht's theory of the social gest to illuminate Restoration comedy's matrix of fashion, identity, and power.

8. Bertolt Brecht, "Short Description of a New Technique of Acting That Produces an Alienation Effect," in *Brecht on Theatre: The Development of an Aesthetic*, ed. and trans. John Willet (New York: Hill and Wang, 1957), 137.

9. Meg Mumford, *Bertolt Brecht* (New York: Routledge, 2009), 69.

10. Walter Benjamin, "On the Concept of History," in *Selected Writings, Volume 4, 1938–1949*, trans. Harry Zohn (Harvard University Press, 2003), 392.

11. Milhous and Hume, *Vice Chamberlain Coke's Theatrical Papers*, 130–31.

12. Lafler, *Celebrated Mrs. Oldfield*, 66.

13. *Authentick Memoirs of the Life of that Celebrated Actress Mrs. Anne Oldfield Containing a Genuine Account of her Transactions to the Time of her Death* (London: 1730), 22.

14. For a detailed account of the daily operations of the theater at Lincoln's Inn Fields, see Judith Milhous, *Thomas Betterton and the Management of Lincoln's Inn Fields, 1695–1708* (Carbondale and Edwardsville: Southern Illinois University Press, 1979). A summary of eighteenth-century managerial practices generally may be found in Judith Milhous, "Company Management," in *The London Theatre World, 1660–1800*, ed. Robert Hume (Carbondale and Edwardsville: Southern Illinois University Press, 1980), 1–34.

15. Emmett L. Avery, ed., *The London Stage 1660–1800, Part 2: 1700–1729* (Carbondale and Edwardsville: Southern Illinois University Press, 1960), 197–232.

16. Cibber, *Apology*, 1: 111.

17. Thomas Betterton, *The Wanton Wife* (London: 1706), 28–29.

18. Brecht, "Short Description," 137.

19. Milhous and Hume, "Silencing of Drury Lane," 446.

20. Michael McKeon, "Historicizing Patriarchy: The Emergence of Gender Difference in England, 1660–1760," *Eighteenth-Century Studies* 28, no. 3 (1995): 299.

21. An influential articulation of this thesis may be found in J. G. A. Pocock, *The Machiavellian Moment: Florentine Political Thought and the Atlantic Republican Tradition* (Princeton: Princeton University Press, 1981), 453.

22. See, e.g., Laura Brown, *Ends of Empire: Women and Ideology in Early Eighteenth-Century English Literature* (Ithaca: Cornell University Press, 1993), 112.

23. Elsewhere I have connected Oldfield's career to the pervasive links between

commercial society and female fashion. See my "Anne Oldfield's Lady Townly: Consumption, Credit, and the Whig Hegemony of the 1720s," *Theatre Journal* 49, no. 4 (1997): 397–416.

24. Helen E. M. Brooks, "Women and Theatre Management in the Eighteenth Century," in *The Public's Open to Us All: Essays on Women and Performance in Eighteenth-Century England*, ed. Laura Engel (Cambridge: Cambridge Scholars Publishing, 2009), 73. Brooks demonstrates that though no woman achieved the status of manager in the London theater, numerous eighteenth-century women successfully managed provincial touring companies. For a narrative of the actress-manager that extends from the Restoration into the nineteenth and early twentieth centuries, see Jo Robinson, "The Actress as Manager," in *The Cambridge Companion to the Actress*, ed. Maggie B. Gale and John Stokes (Cambridge: Cambridge University Press, 2007), 157–72.

History Takes Time

PATRICIA YBARRA ∾

> The general tenor of recent scholarship on American Theatre is as
> predictable today as it was ten years ago. Because in the minds of
> most theatre people, the theatre is always "now," scholars tend to
> write about current productions or trends of the recent past.
>
> —Walter Meserve,
> "The State of Research in American Theatre History"

Walter Meserve's essay reveals a profound disappointment with the state of
theater scholarship that does not end with his concerns about history.
Meserve ultimately makes a generational argument: he claims that only the
senior scholars in his field are writing full-length works he considers contributions to the field, while the few promising junior scholars are writing
only articles. Few young scholars, in his opinion, "aspire to the mastery of
the material which will produce major scholarship."[1] He is especially dis-
dainful of the essays he reads that seem to be "snatches of dissertations
forced upon editors by someone frantically seeking tenure or promotion."[2]
For him, such "publication becomes an exercise in practicality and expedient effort."[3] And, to his consternation, "very few historians are sufficiently
devoted scholars to apply for and receive Guggenheim Fellowships or
other awards from the National Endowment for the Humanities, the
Rockefeller Foundation, and the American Council for Learned Societies."[4] There is much to take issue with in Meserve's essay—primarily the
fact that Meserve sees historians as autonomous subjects whose own lack of
devotion, rather than the conditions of their workplace, inhibit their work.
There is also his claim that, while the recent "surveys, general observations, memoirs, descriptions, expository and critical essays on various topics, studies of theatres and playwrights, essays on popular entertainment
and ethnic or racial theatre . . . contribute meaningfully to an understanding of the American theatre," few, to his judgment, "suggest insight into
that theatre."[5] "Insight," here, is a curiously untheorized term that disar-

ticulates labor from knowledge production as it mourns a lack of comprehensiveness and totalizing explanation of "American" theater. At this moment, Meserve does not remind us that insight calls for spending extensive time with materials and that the heavy teaching loads and production requirements often required of theater scholars stop them from having that time. What Meserve does reveal, though his point may be lost under all of his harsh scolding, is that history takes time.

In this essay, I look back at theater research in order to intervene in what I see as Manichean and rhetorical agons in our field between research and theory or history and theory, history and historiography, past and present(ism), older generations and my own. Often, arguments that are waged as ideological or theoretical ignore or deemphasize material conditions. This is a mistake. Rather than framing our debates as purely methodological—that is, making claims for and against the necessity of empirical archival research as evidence of universal standards of rigor, or for theory rather than positivist narratives—we might be better served by understanding how different modes of research have been shaped by the emergence of neoliberal economics within our institutions.

Neoliberalism is a set of policies, an ideology, and mode of governmentality that first emerged in the United States in the 1970s. Neoliberal economic policy privileges the free reign of market forces (i.e., trade liberalization) and the privatization of all institutions as the most efficient and worthy modes of creating economic prosperity.[6] Within universities, this has led to corporate sponsorship privileging modes of research that generate profit; the increasing employment of "flexible" (i.e., cost-efficient) teachers who receive few regular benefits from the university; the undoing of "inefficient" faculty governance; and a growing tendency for education to be measured and rationalized by quantitative assessments that show "return" on university education as product.[7] These expectations generally stifle innovative pedagogy, disenfranchise the liberal arts because of the humanities' lack of profitability, and implicitly guide faculty and students toward research that will meet standards of prestige and profitability within these rubrics. Thus, the neoliberal university's modes of assessment and institutional rewards circumscribe the possibilities of historiographical research by underscoring productivity, marketability, and entrepreneurship as markers of success—which does not bode well for historiographical projects.

Like many others, I have felt profound discomfort that graduate students seem to be completing fewer and fewer projects that ask them to leave the twentieth and twenty-first centuries or to work in languages other than English. Young scholars' reluctance mirrors that of the field in general, where books about contemporary English-language theater often dominate the scene. Informally, I often find that graduate students and junior scholars are discouraged from doing projects that take them out of their own time and space, because they seem too unwieldy or challenging to complete during their tenure as a funded Ph.D. student or as a tenure-track professor who needs a book contract by the third or fourth year of teaching. At the same time, it is worthwhile to see what has remained consistent in our field in the last fifty years, so as to historicize many of the field's anxieties (including my own) about the marginalization of historical and historiographical projects.[8]

I begin by considering the 2004 issue of *Theatre Survey's* "Forum," "Theatre History in the New Millennium," a collection of short essays that engage the material conditions of today's academy. David Savran claims that as the corporate university engulfs us, it is more important than ever to "reconstruct the history of the historical labour of dehistoricization";[9] Marvin Carlson asks us to be less parochial—thanking rather than decrying performance studies for helping us to move beyond the European and U.S. canons when doing our work;[10] Thomas Postlewait looks back at history and historiography to assess just how Ph.D. programs in theater might train their students, arguing for historical research as part of a focused agenda in a difficult time for the humanities;[11] Joseph Roach's essay argues for making the labor of our "studio colleagues" visible in our own research.[12] All of these authors understand institutions and infrastructure. Roach and Postlewait both openly gesture toward the *longue durée* of the underscholared theater department, with or without the bloated theater apparatus.[13] Most of the authors seem to think there is a crisis afoot that we as performance scholars are going to have to weather to remain viable. They are probably right. More problematic to me is the trouble these essays and our field as a whole have talking about labor when we talk about our work.

Many of us, it seems, are embarrassed by or resentful of labor, especially when it does not produce results in an expedient way. Bad theater is disappointing because theater requires the labor of others—often of people with no artistic stake in the product—to make it. A failure on stage makes it seem as though that time was "wasted." Historical research, as those who do it know, can be equally frustrating. There is quite simply a lot of rote labor to do when you work on historical materials, and while history departments understand this, theater departments often don't. So, if one is trying to be efficient, so as to save, bolster, or begin one's career as a performance/theater historian/historiographer, the natural place to cut corners is

in those places where one is not thinking, but cataloging, digging, or orga-
nizing-but-not-yet-formulating, or "sharpening the cutting edge" of
theater/performance studies.[14] Nonetheless, most scholars know that rote
labor, as well as the less mundane but equally frustrating failures of
thought, takes time.

Postlewait's essay for the *Theatre Survey* forum lists recent award-
winning works of history and historiography.[15] Of the nineteen award-
winning books Postlewait categorizes as historical studies, only three are
first monographs. One of those first books is written by a scholar in a history department, and neither of the other two used their dissertation as
material for their first book, which may account for the twelve-year lag between Ph.D. completion and book publication by one author and the
change of topic to contemporary material from early modern material by
the other.[16] Securely tenured scholars wrote most of the award-winning
books, even if they returned to the research of their dissertation and
reimagined it. And while one might say simply that mature scholars write
better books, I think that having the job security to be able to take the time
to write these books and not publish them until they are ready might also
contribute to their quality. It takes a long time to "sharpen that edge," and
it is worth the wait. This is not to say that no first books have been great
historical studies. Two recent winners of the Errol Hill Award are first
books: Daphne Brooks's *Bodies in Dissent* (2006) and Jill Lane's *Blackface
Cuba, 1840–1895* (2005). Yet both of these models of historiographical
practice of the nineteenth- and early-century Americas had decently long
gestation periods as dissertation and postdoctoral projects.

Looking back at the list of doctoral projects in process from 1949 to the
present historicizes the seeming dearth of historical and historiographical
work in theater and performance studies, particularly among young scholars. Annual lists of doctoral projects and the databases of Dissertation
Abstracts International are an admittedly faulted metric within which to
understand a history of the field, but a survey of them suggests that my
concerns about the present presentism of the field are, in fact, presentist.[17]
To my surprise, the emphasis on contemporary projects was consistent
over time, as was a dearth of work on subjects more than eighty years removed from the time of writing, with the exception of dissertations on
early modern, Restoration, and eighteenth-century England, and a smaller
section of U.S. regional histories that included the last half of the nineteenth century. A survey of these lists admits preference for work on twentieth-century European and U.S. theater in both historical and literary
studies, with the key playwrights of modernism receiving a lot of attention.

The nineteenth-century United States fluctuates as a topic but finds a place in studies of professional regional theaters, genre studies, and later (greatly indebted to Brooks McNamara) studies of popular culture. Another peak of interest in historical U.S. materials comes after the work of Rosemarie K. Bank, Joseph Roach, and Bruce McConachie in the late 1990s.[18] There was also early interest in Asian theater, which I attribute to the geopolitical configuration of the Pacific Rim in the post–World War II years, some time before performance studies led scholars to work on "non-Western" topics later in the century. The majority of studies of historical practice focus on acting and scenography from the sixteenth to the nineteenth centuries in the United States and Europe.[19]

It is true that many dissertations before the early 1980s largely confine themselves to analyzing theater autonomous from social conditions, except as said conditions provide "context." Yet the line in the sand drawn between theater history and theater history as cultural history is perhaps overdrawn. While many regional U.S. histories are often simply narrations of historical material, some attempt to do cultural history within the context of close analysis of rich local archives.[20] A good number go no further than making claims about the theater being reflective of social attitudes, but others speculate about theater as constitutive of said attitudes in their conclusions.[21] It is true that the list exemplifies a curious split in many cases between positivist research on historical topics and literary or theoretical studies of more recent phenomena—at least until the 1980s, when the influence of post-structuralism and new historicism produce theses on early modern theater and dramatic literature in English departments. Where historiography comes into the picture is bit harder to determine. While a dissertation on American theater historiography dates from 1979 (followed by three more), one rarely sees historiography as an operative word in dissertation titles even after the mid-1980s.[22] In fact, almost 90 percent of dissertations that mention theater and historiography in their abstracts were written after 1990; interestingly, only a little over a third of these were written in theater departments. [23] In short, the lists suggest that in theater studies the lure of the present is consistent and that English-language histories of non-Anglophone theaters has always been scarce. Projects that require extensive translation, archival research, *and* historiographical theorizing have always been quite rare at the dissertation stage. Looking at these lists also makes one realize that theater history and historiography were never at the center of theater studies. There is only one year (1971) in which theater history is set apart as its own category in the list of topics for doctoral dissertations, in the list of "Doctoral Projects in

Process."[24] And in context, this categorization does not seem driven by a desire to solidify theater history as a discipline. It may merely be a fluke.

This evidence could be used to support a number of "old" theses about theatrical historical research: that its birth in English departments defined its subject and methodology, that theater history was always marginalized, that theater departments do not support research as well as other humanities departments because they are anti-intellectual; or simply that theory replaced history in theater history studies in the 1980s. These theses are not entirely false, but their partial truths obfuscate the complexity of how methodological changes in our field are impacted by labor and impact labor. Two excellent recent dissertations make this clear: Samuel Shanks's "Acting Technique, Social Performance and the Popularization of the Nineteenth Century Theatre" (2008) and Andrew J. Gibb's "Staging Continuity: Theatre, Performance and the Social Imaginary in Transitional California, 1836–1859" (2008). Both of these studies are theoretically complex and historiographically daring, but they are also local and containable as research sites: Gibb relies on readily available archives near his home site in Santa Barbara, Shanks on New York and Philadelphia archives and other anthologized and collected materials. Both of these scholars circumscribed their sites—and, one might even argue, wrote local studies—so as to labor harder at understanding the materials themselves. So it is not that theory has replaced history as some of our disgruntled colleagues may suggest, but that there has been a move away from doing histories of nonlocal *past* phenomena because more is expected of a history today, including a knowledge of cognate fields of cultural history; economic analysis; a clearly articulated nonpositivistic methodology; and enmeshment in gender, class, and critical race theory. While the evidence in the doctoral theses list shows a complicated picture, it is clear that students opt to think more deeply about what is near and now because they have time to do so. The turn to theory for historians and historiographers asks that scholars do more labor, not less, which quite simply translates into the necessity for graduate students to have more time, not less, to do dissertations not geographically or temporally close to them. This is necessary in a world in which theater historians are expected to become cultural historians of theater and performance in historiographically rigorous ways. These students are also now regularly competing for jobs and publication space with scholars of performance in American studies and other disciplines, whose students are trained to compete for grant money with much more regularity than those in our own discipline. How can we ensure that our students have the time to do the research and thinking they need to do?[25] How can we teach students to think about their work as labor, in a Marxian sense, rather than erase it as we mystify "innovation" as brilliance? Doing this is more productive than demonizing theory as a refuge for the trendy or the lazy, or dismissing historical research as inherently old-fashioned or boring, both of which make the mistake of casting the theater historian as a curiously autonomous subject (again).

To perhaps err toward the anecdotal, I would like to look at how our institutions might inhibit historical theater and performance research—especially those that require foreign languages. In my own university, the neoliberal move toward so-called objective standards and goals has necessitated that we list clear goal statements and timelines for our graduate students, which push them toward a five-year completion date for the Ph.D. This hard five-year rule often discourages students from riskier projects or ones that require language acquisition. Exemplifying the self-management particular to neoliberal life, students *perceive* the lack of time and themselves choose topics closer to their temporal and geographical homes. They may be right to be preemptive. Some state universities ask students to complete their degrees in four years. Who knows if this will become a reality in private institutions, too? I am unsure how a student can do historical research (primary and secondary) and complete a Ph.D. in five years; six to seven is more realistic, especially considering the theoretical sophistication expected of a dissertation and how quickly those students will have to turn a dissertation into a book—a new pressure scholars of other generations may not have felt.[26] Perhaps this is the reason why we see less and less work on theater and performance before 1900 from anywhere around the globe from younger scholars these days. Certainly, past pressures on graduate students in theater often forced them to wait until later in their career to pursue these projects.[27] But they got that time later. A surprising number of top scholars worked on the materials of their dissertations until they were associate professors. Some even became historiographers when they were professors—Thomas Postlewait's dissertation, for example, is a comparative literature thesis on memory as past in Ibsen, Beckett, and Pinter. [28] Some major scholars of Asian theater did a modern Western theater or drama thesis first, because projects on Asia either were not thought to be doable or were not yet thought of as possibilities by the authors.[29] And while I am glad that most students would not be dissuaded from writing about non-Western theater today—in fact, the number of jobs calling for scholars who can cover this material has skyrocketed—the need for efficiency is shutting down second chances. How does one expand one's field of interest or do a difficult historical project as a second project in today's climate? These anxieties have certainly informed my own choice of projects.

An analysis of the work of three distinguished theater and performance historians bears out the importance of the time we no longer have: Rosemarie K. Bank (Ph.D., 1972), Joseph Roach (Ph.D., 1973) and Bruce McConachie (Ph.D., 1977). These scholars (and they are not exceptions in their generation) published their respective first monographs twenty-four, twelve, and sixteen years after they submitted their dissertations. Bank's *Theatre Culture in the United States, 1825–1860* (1996) is on a topic related to her dissertation on frontier melodrama;[30] Roach's *Player's Passion* is on a topic different from his dissertation on Vanbrugh, but well within the long and wide eighteenth century;[31] and McConachie's *Melodramatic Formations* is closely allied with his dissertation, entitled "Economic Values in Popular Melodrama 1815–1860."[32] They all worked through the transition that occurs in the field methodologically, abandoning their base in textual analysis and the history of repertories, and moved toward theater historiography.

In his dissertation, McConachie uses literary analysis of the plays and cognitive theory of audience reception together to argue that melodramas were a site in which audience's ideas about money were reinforced. His readings of the plays are careful and lengthy, but his evidence about audiences and repertoires is taken from published sources. Only later does he do the archival research (funded by major grant organizations), which allows him to see certain cultural formations that he comes to theorize with Fredric Jameson and Raymond Williams as melodramatic formations.

Bank is already thinking about the concepts of race and genre in 1972 that will become key, in deeper form, to her arguments in 1991. In her work on spatial historiography, conceptualized with Michal Kobialka, she historicizes how categories structure knowledge of nineteenth-century theater (i.e., how the legal definition of sexual commerce in the early nineteenth century destabilizes the "prostitutes in the gallery" refrain of the period's moralizers).[33] Yes, it's Foucault that produced the possibility of this work—but it's Foucault and the archive—an archive well outside of theater collections and outside of "collections" at all.

Roach's research on the eighteenth century in the *Player's Passion* changed as he expanded his archive to include cultural history and the history of science. His deep knowledge of a period of history made him a more adventurous scholar. Is it not the time Roach takes to write a book (ten to eleven years, on average) that allows him to see what is there although not "there," as in the case of *Cities of the Dead* (1996)? Certainly, post-structuralist thought, new historicism, feminism, queer theory, and critical race studies indelibly changed all of these authors. But it was time that made their work insightful.

What this essay asks, then, is that we take labor into account when we make arguments about methodological shifts and developments in our field. Recent American Society for Theatre Research (ASTR) conferences show surprisingly little work pre-1900, to the point where it is classified as an underresearched area eligible for special research fellowships.[34] Some might argue that the new focus on geographical diversity in this organization has led scholars to abandon the European and U.S. past for a post-colonial present, but the reality is more complicated.[35] Most non-Western countries have performance traditions before 1900, but we see little of that work. And what is so "Western" about medieval Spain, after all? Not much if you look at its history—but figuring out exactly how to write that history of performance takes more time than most programs allow. Rather than blaming the vogue for geographical or ethnic diversity (which still some-how ends up showcasing research done in English and on the recent past, with few exceptions), let's first understand how labor works into the picture and conjoin that to the series of debates about history and historiography in our most popular journals, from the late 1960s to present.[36] What is curious to me about these essays, is, with few exceptions, how little is mentioned about labor.[37] Roach links institutional shifts to an imperative to do collaborative work that will bestow validity on practitioner's university work as labor; Postlewait mentions the possibilities that computer databases may allow for more large-scale quantitative theater research that was previously impossible; Kobialka tells us how destabilizing historiography should be to (neoliberal) academic institutions.[38] Yet little is said about how to advocate for ourselves as laborers within those institutions and to make a claim for that labor as a *political* act that eschews fast thinking and efficient production as the highest values of humanities scholarship.[39] Fast and efficient are not always better. After all, to write about representational practices, one must understand the modes of representation in which said performances are enmeshed, as well as understanding the actual practices of theater and other forms of expressive culture of the period, in addition to theorizing one's "archive."

In unofficial chats in conference hotel bars, there occurs a strangely fa-miliar quarrel of ancients (so-called positivists and archive hounds) and moderns (theory-obsessed youngsters who do no research). But the reality is that outside of our "rhetorical" roles we are really just subjects in a neo-liberal order, caught in a Manichean dyad that obfuscates the true condi-tions of production. The panic we all feel about production is part of a system in which inefficient and less profitable disciplines are downsized in the face of those with better applications in the "real world," prestige, or funding opportunities. Within our own universities we need to publish more, but not publish so much from our book that a publisher no longer sees it as a profitable enterprise for their press. We model applied theater instead of theater for social change, perhaps because it sounds more productive. We are compelled to internationalize, but not necessarily question the way the funds for international projects were created from capital that emerged from relationships of radical inequalities. And even if we do accept the money, it is unclear that such moves lead to more expansive research on the past "elsewhere," despite how good winning the grant looks to the administration. (And if we do not win those grants, how are we to account for the labor of grant writing?) And those concerns are only the luxury of those who happened to find tenure-track jobs, as we continue to move toward a model that exploits contract teachers to make the budget lines match up at private and public universities. Most of those instructors have no right to research funds or time to do scholarship at all.

The modes of late capital have in fact transformed the process of scholarly production into a business that quantifies our products but does not value intellectual process as labor. This quantification discourages certain types of historical research due to its labor time. Careful attention to the radical difference of the past—at the level of practices, representation, and representational practices—is often less expedient but more necessary than ever as we try to make the "history of the historical labour of de-historicization" visible. Neoliberalism threatens to flatten the past into the present by making it unprofitable to care about the past. To rewrite labor into our history of professing performance might be one way to mitigate against this rising tide, if only we take the time to listen to what we hear. I learned more than I imagined reading those lists of doctoral theses, but as I was reading I had to counter the voice in my head that said, Why am I doing something so time consuming to write a small portion of an invited publication pretenure? Shouldn't I be preparing an article for submission to a peer-reviewed journal instead? How can I make sure my labor is visible in a footnote? And there I am back in the efficiency model, right when I am writing about its problems. I am complicit in that system.

What would it mean to not be complicit? What would it mean to refuse our managerial role as enforcers of ridiculous timelines? What would it mean to quit "self-managing" our labor and realize we are not "managers" but laborers? We might have to slow ourselves down and start refusing to be sped up—adopting tactics from the assembly line and admitting that we might work in one.[40] We might have to take the first step in helping our advisees to do the same thing. And we might have to be the ones who find ways to make that possible for them—even if it has a cost to us—because we are better able to afford it.

NOTES

Epigraph: Walter J. Meserve, "The State of Research in American Theatre History," *Theatre Survey* 22, no. 2 (1981): 125.

1. Meserve, "State of Research," 125.
2. Meserve, "State of Research," 126.
3. Meserve, "State of Research," 126.
4. Meserve, "State of Research," 126.
5. Meserve, "State of Research," 125.
6. David Harvey, *A Brief History of Neoliberalism* (London: Oxford, 2005).
7. See Stanley Aronowitz, *The Knowledge Factory: Dismantling the Corporate University and Creating True Higher Learning* (New York: Beacon; 2000); Randy Martin, ed., *Chalk Lines: The Politics of Work in the Managed University* (Durham: Duke University Press, 1998); David Savran, "Neoliberalism and the Education Industries," *TDR* 53, no. 1 (2009): 26–29.
8. See Rosemarie K. Bank's comments in Rosemarie K. Bank, Harry Elam, John Frick, Lisa Merrill, and Don B. Wilmeth, "Looking Back to Look Forward: Assessing Future Directions in American Theatre Studies," *Journal of American Drama and Theatre* 19, no. 2 (2007): 9–35, for a complementary argument about theater scholarship in today's academy.
9. David Savran, "A Historiography of the Popular," *Theatre Survey* 45, no. 2 (2004): 211, quoting Pierre Bourdieu, *Masculine Domination*, trans. Richard Nice (Stanford: Stanford University Press, 2001), 82.
10. Marvin Carlson, "Be Less Parochial," *Theatre Survey* 45, no. 2 (2004): 177.
11. Thomas Postlewait, "Theatre History and Historiography: A Disciplinary Mandate," *Theatre Survey* 45, no. 2 (2004): 181–88.
12. Joseph Roach, "The History of the Future," *Theatre Survey* 45, no. 2 (2004): 275–78. The term "studio colleagues" comes from Oscar Brockett, "Research in Theatre History," *Educational Theatre Journal* 19, no. 2 (1967): 166–73.
13. See Joseph Roach, "Reconstructing Theatre/History," *Theatre Topics* 9, no. 1 (1999): 3–10.
14. I borrow William Worthen's phrase here from "Acting, Singing, Dancing and So Forth," *Theatre Survey* 45, no. 2 (2004): 267.
15. Postlewait, "Theatre History and Historiography," 182–83.
16. Jeffrey Ravel, author of *The Contested Parterre: Public Theater and French Political Culture, 1680–1791* (Ithaca: Cornell University Press, 1998), is in the French Department at Cornell. Catherine Schuler's 1984 dissertation was on Brecht and Shaw. David Román's *Acts of Intervention* (Indianapolis: Indiana University Press, 1998) was a shift from his work on Golden Age Spanish drama. He also does not teach in a theater department.

17. See "Graduate Theses in Theatre, 1949–1961," and "Doctoral Projects in Process in Theatre," published in *Educational Theatre Journal* (1949–78) and *Theatre Journal* (1979–2008).

18. Bruce McConachie, *Melodramatic Formations: American Theatre and Society, 1820–1870* (Iowa City: University of Iowa Press, 1992); Rosemarie K. Bank, *Theatre Culture in America 1825–1860* (London: Cambridge University Press, 1997); Joseph Roach, *Cities of the Dead* (New York: Columbia University Press, 1996).

19. Of 190 Ph.D. theses that had "theatre history" as a keyword (eliminating about 15 I consider under theater historiography), 97 were on the United States (all but 22 after 1900), and 56 were on England or Canada (13 were early modern or restoration, 9 were eighteenth century, 12 were nineteenth century, the rest contemporary).

20. See, e.g., Eugene Kerr Bristow, "Look Out for Saturday Night: A Social History of Professional Variety Theater in Memphis, TN, 1859–1860," Ph.D. diss. (University of Iowa, 1956).

21. See Pauline Wright Schaffer, "The Position of Women in Society as Reflected in the Serious American Drama from 1890 to 1928," Ph.D. diss. (Stanford, 1966); Joanne Marie Loudin, "The Changing Role of the Comic Heroine in American Drama from 1900–1940," Ph.D. diss. (University of Washington, 1974); Dorothy S. Pam, "Exploitation, Independence and Solidarity: The Changing Role of American Working Women as Reflected in the Working Girl Melodrama," Ph.D. diss. (New York University, 1980).

22. Maarten A. Realingh, "American Historiography of the Theatre," Ph.D. diss. (Bowling Green State University, 1979); Robert Staggenborg, "'New Literary History' and the Post-Modern Paradigm: Implications for Theatre History," Ph.D. diss. (Louisiana State University, 1983); Roberta Rankin, "A Historiographical Study of William Dunlap's *History of the American Theatre*," Ph.D. diss. (University of Missouri, Columbia, 1996); Andrew Ryder, "Between Relativism and Realism: Postpositivist Theatre History Writing in the United States since 1974," Ph.D. diss. (Bowling Green State University, 1997).

23. I read abstracts from projects that had "theater and historiography," "theater historiography," or "performance historiography" as a keyword. Of the 140 theses on theater or performance, 50 were written in theater departments; most others were written in English, history, German, and Spanish departments.

24. Between 1949 and 1972, after which the list adopted the system used by Frederic Litto's *American Dissertations on the Drama and the Theatre* (Kent, OH: Kent State University Press, 1969), the categorization of theater dissertations fluctuated.

25. See Lisa Merrill on grant funding in "Looking Back," 24–25.

26. The fact that the market demands first books earlier in one's career, and that this may place expectation on students to write more publishable and polished dissertations, is not mentioned in Joseph Berger, "Exploring Ways to Shorten the Ascent to a Ph.D.," *New York Times*, Oct. 3, 2007, http://www.nytimes.com/2007/10/03/education/03education.html (accessed Mar. 1, 2009).

27. Many scholars in earlier generations wrote theater dissertations in five years or less.

28. Thomas Postlewait, "The Design of the Past: Uses of Memory in Henrik Ibsen, Samuel Beckett, and Harold Pinter," Ph.D. diss. (University of Minnesota, 1976).

29. See, e.g., Haiping Yan, "Samuel Beckett and His Critics: A Cultural Redefinition," Ph.D. diss. (Cornell University, 1990); Rakesh Solomon, "Albee on Stage: Playwright as Director," Ph.D. diss. (University of California, Davis, 1986); James Moy, "John B Ricketts' Circus, 1793–1800," Ph.D. diss. (University of Illinois, 1977).

30. Rosemarie K. Bank, "Rhetorical, Dramatic, Theatrical and Social Contexts of Selected American Frontier Plays, 1870–1906," Ph.D. diss. (University of Iowa, 1972).

31. Joseph Roach, "Vanbrugh's English Baroque: Opera and the Opera House in the Haymarket," Ph.D. diss. (Cornell University, 1973).

32. Bruce McConachie, "Economic Values in Popular Melodrama, 1815–1860," Ph.D diss. (University of Wisconsin, Madison, 1977).

33. Rosemarie K. Bank, "Time, Space, Timespace, Spacetime: Theatre History in Simultaneous Universes," *Journal of Dramatic Theory and Criticism* 5, no. 2 (1991): 72–75.

34. A new scholarship for understudied topics, which includes Africa, Asia, Latin America, and pre-1900 research, was added at the 2007 executive committee meeting in Phoenix, Arizona.

35. E.g.: Unsettling Theatre: Memory, Map and Migration, 2008, and Desti-Nation, 2009.

36. I acknowledge Andrew Ryder's helpful introduction in "Between Relativism and Realism." See Ryder, Thomas Postlewait and Bruce McConachie, eds., *Interpreting the Theatrical Past* (Iowa City: University of Iowa Press, 1989) for extensive bibliographies of theater historiography.

37. *The Historiography of Theatre History*, ed. Alan Woods, *Theatre Studies* 21, supplement (1974–75), is an exception.

38. Tom Postlewait, "The Criteria for Periodization in Theatre History," *Theatre Journal* 40, no. 3 (1988): 299–318; Michal Kobialka, "Inbetweenness: Spatial Folds in Theatre Historiography," *Journal of Dramatic Theory and Criticism* 15, no. 2 (1991): 85–100; Roach, "Reconstructing Theatre/History."

39. Rosemarie K. Bank, "Physics and the New Theatre Historiography," *Journal of Dramatic Theory and Criticism* 15, no. 2 (1991): 63–64, and "Time, Space"; Kobialka, "Inbetweenness."

40. This formulation is Harney and Moten's in *Chalk Lines: The Politics of Work in the Managed University* (Durham, NC: Duke University Press, 1999), 164–66.

"I'll Cover You"

An Interdisciplinary Duet on Rent and Collaborative Musical Theater Historiography

JUDITH SEBESTA AND JESSICA STERNFELD ❧

In his essay "Toward a Historiography of the Popular," David Savran discusses various reasons for the dismissal of musical theater as a topic of serious scholarly consideration.[1] This dismissal has been theorized in numerous essays and books on the musical during the past decade, including Stacy Wolf's manifesto "In Defense of Pleasure"[2] and Bud Coleman and Judith Sebesta's introduction to their anthology *Women in American Musical Theatre*.[3] Aided by a recognition of popular entertainment in general as worthy of consideration, historians of musical theater during the past fifteen or so years have enjoyed a legitimization of their work heretofore unseen. But it is time to move beyond apologia to engage more actively in the work of musical theater historiography—primarily via collaboration and interdisciplinarity.[4]

Musical theater cannot be fully understood unless the sum of its various parts—including libretto, lyrics, music, and often dance—are examined. Because few individual historians are well versed in the analysis and interpretation of all these parts, it is necessary to engage in a historiography that mirrors the collaborative nature of musical theater creation. Furthermore, it is time to move past attempts to *define* the musical—a complex, multivalent form with many subgenres. Instead of asking, "What is the musical?" a more pertinent question today may be, "*Where* is the musical?" After a brief overview of trends in musical theater historiography, we will attempt to engage in such work by examining one musical through the eyes/ears of both a theater historian and a musicologist. This collaborative exploration of Jonathan Larson's *Rent* in the wake of its closing nearly thirteen years after it opened on Broadway will attempt to provide a model of interdisciplinary exploration of the many locations in which just one musical—albeit, we will argue, an important one—has been and continues to be situated in order to pave the way for further such collaborative historiographies. In our last section we will "perform" a more casual, dialogic duet on our mutual experiences viewing the recently released DVD of the final Broadway performance.

The only direct predecessor to this essay is Alicia Kae Koger's groundbreaking "Trends in Musical Theatre Scholarship: An Essay in Historiography," published in 1992 in the *New England Theatre Journal*. Koger's agenda in the essay is to "demonstrate how assumptions about the nature and content of the American musical have influenced most writing about the form and how some scholars have broken with the standard approach, suggesting alternative and enlightening directions for future inquiry into America's most popular theatrical form."[5] Koger points to the work of Julian Mates, Gerald Mast, Joseph Swain, Lehman Engel, and Allen Woll as models for such future inquiries. Interestingly, her savvy suggestions for future inquiry have played out as predicted in the eighteen years since she published the article, although she was a bit shortsighted in terms of how expansive the oeuvre on musicals would become. Some of the influential work done in the last few decades employs methodologies Koger suggested; others break new ground. For a partial survey of the approaches and insights put forth recently, one might explore Allen Woll, *Black Musical Theatre;* Bud Coleman and Judith Sebesta, *Women in American Musical Theatre;* John Clum, *Something for the Boys: Musical Theater and Gay Culture;* Andrea Most, *Making Americans: Jews and the Broadway Musical;* Joseph P. Swain, *The Broadway Musical: A Critical and Musical Survey;* Jessica Sternfeld, *The Megamusical;* Elizabeth Wollman, *The Theater Will Rock;* Banfield, *Sondheim's Broadway Musicals;* Mast, *Can't Help Singin';* John Bush Jones, *Our Musicals, Ourselves;* Raymond Knapp, *The American Musical and the Formation of National Identity* and *The American Musical and the Performance of Personal Identity;* Stacy Wolf, *A Problem Like Maria;* Bruce Kirle, *Unfinished Show Business;* David Román, *Performance in America;* and Ethan Mordden's series of books by decade.[6]

Drawing on both Koger and Savran, and exploring the works listed here, it is possible to identify some basic categories of work on musical theater and its history, with the caveat that many books, and articles, cross these categories to serve a number of functions, as this list likely indicates. Historical overviews have begun to proliferate, as have encyclopedias and bibliographies, biographies, studies of individual shows, theoretical analyses of trends, and works that place musicals in theatrical or cultural context. The growing wealth of books on musical theater history that fall into these categories and beyond raise a number of issues regarding the study of musical theater history in the twenty-first century. The continued bias against the study of popular forms has already been mentioned, as has been David Savran's 2004 confrontation of this bias that appeared in a special issue of *Theatre Survey* on historiography, in which he argues for the "overruling of long-standing, class-based prejudices about the superiority of art to entertainment."[7] Other pertinent issues include the increasing commodification of the musical, the availability of materials and the use of digital technologies, the value of evolutionary/progress narratives that privilege the book musical, questions of authorship and authenticity, and the need for collaborative and interdisciplinary study of the form. It is this last issue that we wish to confront with the collaborative, interdisciplinary, locational, and explorative duet on *Rent* that follows.

In the Past: Puccini

Anyone familiar with Puccini's *La Bohème* (1896) will spot its influence on Larson's *Rent* almost immediately. Although the musical's plot seems to have been derived from several sources, including Larson's own experiences among friends and acquaintances in the Village, the basic structure and all of the main characters have parallels in Puccini's opera. Several scenes are so close to the original that a few lines are nearly word-for-word translations: "Light My Candle," for example, chronicling the meeting of (and immediate chemistry between) Roger and Mimi, borrows heavily from Puccini's librettists Illica and Giacosa. When Musetta shows off at the café in an effort to make Marcello jealous, she sings the famous aria "Quando m'en vo": "When I walk alone along the street / all the people stop and stare, / and seek out all my beauty, / from top to toe."[8] This text gets loosely translated as "Every single day / I walk down the street / I hear people say, / 'Baby, so sweet,'" in Maureen's angry duet with Joanne, "Take Me or Leave Me." Although this is where the text of Musetta's number (known as "Musetta's Waltz") ends up, it is not where its music ends up. The catchy arpeggios of the accompaniment figure that support Musetta's melody become Roger's favorite guitar riff; he plays it several times when he doesn't know what else to play, and Mark even teases him in "La Vie Boheme" about needing to come up with something "that doesn't remind us of 'Musetta's Waltz.'"

This quotation is the only direct, recognizable borrowing from Puccini's music, and it appears one last time in the most crucial of positions: as the climactic moment of the climactic song, "Your Eyes." Roger serenades a dying Mimi with the song he struggled to write all year; as early as "One Song Glory," early in the first act, he admits his struggle to write something that will last, "before the virus takes hold." Larson, then, has saddled himself with a nearly impossible set of tasks for this eleven o'clock number: it not only must serve as the emotional peak of an already emotional show that has already carried its audience through one death; it must also justify the year it took Roger to compose it, and finally, it needs to raise Mimi from the dead. She hears his song as she is dying but takes Angel's advice given from beyond the grave ("Turn around girlfriend and listen to that boy's song") and returns to Roger.

This is an Orpheus situation, as played out in dozens of operas before. Mythic musician Orpheus, as told in Ovid, must convince the gods of the underworld through a song that his pain at losing his beloved Eurydice is unbearable; she must be returned to life and to him. His song is so beautiful that Pluto and the other gods of hell relent and return Eurydice to Orpheus (with conditions). In *In Search of Opera*, musicologist Carolyn Abbate notes that almost every composer of an Orpheus opera avoids writing this song, instead substituting a preview song involving less pressure.[9] Abbate argues that this is a wise suppression on the composers' and librettists' parts, since any song would fail under such pressure, and composers risk crossing the line into accidental comedy when they take the risk of writing the song itself: "Suppressing Orpheus's primal song seems to distinguish great Orpheus operas from silly ones. Lesser composers put Orpheus directly in front of Pluto and are diminished by their hubris."[10]

Perhaps some sort of substitution would help with Larson's Orpheus song. "Your Eyes" lacks an interesting melody and is saddled with square lines ending in predictable rhymes ("your eyes" / "goodbyes"). Most jarringly of all, the diegetic song blends into Roger's climactic cry of "Mimi!" (similar to Rodolfo's in the Puccini opera when he realizes Mimi has died), and to accompany this tragedy, Larson gives us the arpeggios of "Musetta's Waltz" on an electric guitar in the band. To anyone who knows the opera, this is a distracting and disappointing moment, confusing in that it's unclear where Roger's song actually ends and anticlimactic in that the music set up to be the most gut-wrenching of the show is not Larson's at all, but Puccini's fake-sweet ditty for Musetta. It may have been impossible to write a satisfying song for Roger given the nearly insurmountable Orpheus-like expectations, but "One Song Glory" is far more dramatically effective and less predictable, as are a host of other numbers in the score.

Off-Broadway

For years before it was a Broadway musical, *Rent* lived off-Broadway; its dramaturgical location in the East Village mirrored its developmental one, both certainly in keeping with the bohemian spirit of Puccini's opera. The

musical's genesis at the New York Theatre Workshop (NYTW) is no secret, in spite of initial claims in the press when it opened off-Broadway that
it "came out of nowhere."[11] This myth, cited alongside the oft-mentioned
tragic tale of Larson's untimely death of an aortic aneurysm the night of
final dress at NYTW, was quickly dispelled. In reality, while artistic director Jim Nicola's decision to work with the first drafts of the musical came
about through fortuitous circumstances, it saw several months of development and a successful workshop production before opening.[12]

Off-Broadway's importance in the twenty-first century as a site for musical theater development has been underhistoricized and undertheorized,
with the few articles on the subject appearing primarily in *American Theatre*. The significance of the area in nurturing the work of creators of musicals—and as a proving ground for their shows—is clear; what is not as
clear are the detrimental effects of this "system." Workshopping in general
has come under some scrutiny by director Susan Schulman and composer
Jeanine Tesori, who both claim that directorially staged workshops can
whitewash inherent flaws in a work and that readings of scripts may be
more useful.[13] Indeed, *American Theatre* published an article in 2006 titled
"How to Survive the Workshop Syndrome," which included advice by such
artists as Andrew Lippa and Tesori.[14] Although Larson's relationship with
NYTW was obviously eventually a productive one, sources indicate that it
was also stressful for him. Clearly, the system is not perfect and is in need
of more careful examination by historians and others.

Still, what is also clear is that in its off-Broadway setting, so similar to
the setting within the show, *Rent* very quickly *did* prove itself; it was only
there until April 1, when it transferred to the Nederlander, uptown. In
spite of a small house and thus relatively small audiences, reception soon
after opening at NYTW in January was wildly enthusiastic; actors reportedly found themselves answering phones to help meet demand for tickets.
Rent's themes of poverty and homelessness and transgressive equality for all
were well-suited to the downtown location, but would they play uptown
amid the increasingly Disneyfied theater district? Like *Hair* or *A Chorus
Line* before, it seemed a risk.

Broadway

In an article in the *Wall Street Journal*, Jeffrey Seller acknowledged the risk
inherent in moving *Rent* to Broadway: "One million people said don't go to
Broadway. They said the downtown people won't go up, and the uptown
people, because of the subject matter, won't come. . . . I was scared to

death."[15] When one considers the off-Broadway ticket sales, glowing reviews, and the awarding of a Pulitzer, however, *Rent*'s transfer seems less risky. And in order to avoid losing the connection with the downtown milieu, the creators and producers—minus Larson, of course—looked for ways to bring it uptown. This included selecting the rundown 1,185-seat, low-rent (relatively speaking) Nᵢderlander on 41st Street, which in 1996 had yet to be affected by the gentrification of Times Square and indeed was described by Jeffrey Trachtenberg in the *Wall Street Journal* as a "dark, seedy location."[16] Furthermore, designers hung photos of the Lower East Side in the theater and styled the lobby to suggest a funky Village club. The final—and perhaps most significant—effort by producers to connect with the downtown, off-Broadway location was to offer tickets that would mirror NYTW prices. They set aside the first two rows for same-day sales at twenty dollars, "creating big lines in front of the Nederlander Theater and all but guaranteeing that young, enthusiastic fans are in prominent seats."[17] Those who clamored for the seats—known as "Rentheads"—became key to the long-term success of the show, and the fandom created by the availability of the cheap seats is worth examining in order to better understand the significance of *Rent*.

Potential audience members waited in line for hours for the coveted tickets, which eventually were disbursed via a lottery, sometimes even camping out overnight ("urban camping").[18] Individual Rentheads saw the show dozens, hundreds, even reportedly over one thousand times in one case. A wall of graffiti appeared outside the theater, on which celebrities and other fans inscribed passionate messages about the show, many claiming that it had changed—or even saved—their life. The rapturous fans became a phenomenon rarely seen for a Broadway show, with perhaps only the tween fandom of *Wicked* coming close since. A number of aspects of *Rent* account for the musical's appeal to young audience members: the positive, hopeful, utopian messages; the notion that you can create your own family in the absence of the "original"; the urban orientation; the outsider status of characters. Original cast member Idina Menzel claimed, "They see people in the show that represent them."[19] The show seemed to capture the zeitgeist of the decade. Ben Brantley argued in his review, "Like [*Hair*], this production gives a pulsing, unexpectedly catchy voice to one generation's confusion, anger and anarchic, pleasure-seeking vitality."[20] *Rent*'s marketing as a "lifestyle philosophy," as David Savran put it, has attracted young audiences who could likely identify with the "no day but today" message more than more mature spectators. Savran called the show not lowbrow or highbrow but "hipbrow."[21]

But those once-hip spectators have matured, and the show has lost its edge and immediacy for some as *Rent*'s run has continued into the new century. In spite of the recent closing of the show due to decreased ticket sales, the Renthead phenomenon has continued, and young audiences via tours, the film, and other opportunities to see the show have continued to be enraptured by it. Nothing makes this clearer than the final performance on Broadway, captured on DVD along with several featurettes about related events, including one on the final lotteries for the twenty-dollar seats. In it, Rentheads sign the wall of graffiti one last time—"No day but today— RENT saved my life"; "Thank you RENT, I will never forget you"—and sing songs while waiting in line. Several provide emotional, tearful interviews, including a mother and daughter who saw the show every time they visited the city—apparently nearly a hundred times—and a man who was an original Renthead and was diagnosed with AIDS shortly after first seeing it. His partner claims that the lyric "No Day but Today" has become a mantra for their lives.

Anthony Tommasini of the *New York Times* was the last to interview Larson, speaking with him the evening he died, and in the same publication, he mused nearly thirteen years later: "With the closing of the Broadway production, the phenomenon that is 'Rent' will start to fade." But he admitted: "Passing through Portland, Me., to see some friends, I was delighted when their younger daughter, just 16 months old, came toddling into the living room when her daddy put 'Seasons of Love' on the CD player. 'She just adores it,' he said. Sure enough, Jonathan Larson's newest fan started dancing, all smiles, arms waving, hips swiveling."[22] While it may have seemed most suited to its off-Broadway beginnings, without the Broadway run, *Rent* most assuredly would have had less of an impact, and the Renthead phenomenon—in its broadest definition even including a sixteen-month-old—would never have occurred.

On DVD

As we discovered in the early phases of our collaboration, one of the most valuable things that working with others does is encourage new areas of exploration—areas that might not be our main ones, but also ideas and insights that might not have come to us working alone. Even very like-minded scholars, such as we are, have very different takes on certain aspects of the material, as would any scholars in different but related fields or any two people anywhere. Our collaboration began as a series of brainstorming emails, and in that spirit, we offer this section—musings on our mutual experiences recently viewing the DVD of the final performance of *Rent* on Broadway—as a model for one possible future for musical theater historiography.[23]

JESSICA: Although I am enormously grateful, as a scholar and teacher of musicals, to have a recorded version of the live stage show, I found the camera work distracting almost throughout and downright detrimental to the show at times. With far too many close-ups, quick jumps, unsteady cameras, and odd angles, it was often unclear what exactly was happening on stage. The same issue exists with other films of stage productions, *Cats* perhaps being the most grievous. I appreciate close-ups when seeing the whole stage would not add to my understanding of the moment—during ballads with little movement, for example. But "You Okay, Honey?" was filmed so awkwardly that it was hard to follow, as were most of the scenes involving the chorus.

It's inevitable that a filmed musical will tell the viewer where to look, unless one camera were simply placed in the audience and left alone. But this camera work makes some (overly) bold viewing choices. For example, Angel's exit as he dies, wrapped in the parachute-like sheet, received a close-up. I confess this moment never stood out to me before, being as it is upstage and the action downstage continues as Angel quietly slips away, with a beatific glance back at his friends. The camera's choice makes Angel even more of an angel, if that's possible!

JUDITH: I agree completely that the camera work is problematic; that was my first reaction upon viewing the DVD, and it was difficult to get past at first. For example, the close-ups and quick cuts in the "It's Beginning to Snow" montage—one of the chorus numbers you mention—are so frustrating and hard to follow. Perhaps this "cinematography," if you can call it that, is meant to appeal to the MTV generation; the techniques seemed similar to those used for music videos (not that you can even see those on MTV anymore!). Or maybe it was designed to mirror the techniques a young, somewhat amateur filmmaker like Mark himself might use? But I think I may be giving the creators of the DVD too much credit here. . . .

Recordings of theater productions do certainly seem anathema to their inherent liveness, but I agree that they are invaluable to those of us trying to reconstruct such an ephemeral thing. And they can be done well, I would argue, as with Stephen Sondheim's musicals available on VHS/DVD: *Sweeney Todd*, *Into the Woods*, and *Passion*. In the former, "Nothing's Gonna Harm You" is a good example of what you mention earlier: a ballad with little movement, and with great control the camera stays largely in close-up on Mrs. Lovitt and Toby seated on the stairs that lead to the source of potential harm about which Toby sings.

Once I had watched the entire DVD and managed to get past the camera work, I found that more problematic for me was how much the show seemed to have lost its "edge," its transgressive nature, about which I have written extensively elsewhere.[24] In spite of working in what is most often inevitably a commercialized medium (and Larson *was* eager to create a *Broadway* musical, according to those closest to him, regardless of other claims that he eschewed the commercialism inherent there), by all accounts Larson and his collaborators worked to support, in a variety of ways, the rebellious character of the bohemian life about which he wrote. Costumes that looked so appropriately grungy (or "out there," in the case of Angel's drag) to me when I first saw the show in 1996 now look like something you could purchase at the Bloomingdale's boutique where copies eventually were sold—vintage chic (distressed jeans, for example) is everywhere now. Perhaps most striking to me—and this is more your area—was how much the performers sounded like Broadway singers—not rock singers, as originally intended.

JESSICA: I agree that the entire tone of the show now feels much more like performance than it did originally. This is not to say that the original cast wasn't as calculated and rehearsed as any other cast for any show, but *Rent* in its early days came across as somehow much more raw and honest than most musicals. The idea that these people—not their characters, but the performers themselves—had something to say, and wanted to convey it with great earnestness and sincerity, has been replaced by a cast that seems to be trying to relive or re-create that natural earnestness. Other shows that feel in their original incarnations like natural outpourings of a group of disenfranchised youths with something to say—*Hair, Jesus Christ Superstar,* even more cynical shows like *Avenue Q, Urinetown,* or even *The Cradle Will Rock*—always face the struggle to either update the message for the present or make it feel immediate despite becoming dated.

It may also be a question of overexposure. The more times I saw "Seasons of Love" sung by the cast on various television shows, the less sincere it felt. If they weren't in the moment, telling the rest of the story, how could we believe their sudden "spontaneous" display of heartfelt group bonding?

You're absolutely right that some of the voices are far more Broadway than rock, compared to the original cast. Adam Pascal, the original Roger, has a very strong growl to his voice, which added a certain amount of street credibility—and also risk. One was never sure if he'd manage the high notes, with all that breath and gravel in the way of the pitch. Will Chase, the DVD's Roger, has a gorgeous tenor—thrilling in a new way, without the risk but with a commitment to the high notes that Pascal does not attempt. Similarly, Daphne Rubin-Vega (the original Broadway Mimi) has a voice full of air and crack, and the DVD's Renee Elise Goldsberry has a reliable, lyrical instrument that sounds more polished and less like it could fall apart at any moment.

JUDITH: I hate to sound like I am joining the ranks of those critics of the original production who dismissed the popularity of the show as mere maudlin emotionalism in the wake of Larson's untimely death, but I can't help but wonder if the earnestness and sincerity of the original cast wasn't an authentic desire to communicate Larson's themes of love, of hope, of living today as if it is your last. Perhaps the further casts got from those circumstances, the less raw and honest the performances seemed. But not having seen all the cast members perform, this could be a dangerous generalization to make.

JESSICA: I agree that the immediacy of the message was probably inevitably diluted by time and distance, and I also agree with your suggestion that over the years, some cast members may have been more invested in the message than others. As I discovered when researching the various touring companies, it became something of a rule—a casting qualification—for performers to express their belief in the show's messages and their respect and love for Larson's memory. I may be slightly more cynical than you, because although I agree that the show still packs a wallop of a message, I can't shake the sense that at least some of those involved with it are acting the roles of the actors who came before them.

The DVD offers an excellent glimpse of devoted Rentheads, not only in the audience for the performance but (as mentioned earlier) in the special features, such as the mini-documentary showing fans hoping to be chosen in the cheap ticket lottery. The cast, to their great credit, stay firmly committed to the performance and to their characters throughout, acknowledging the unusual nature of putting on the final performance only during the bows at the end. The audience, also to their credit, manages to restrain itself from excessive cheering during numbers, reserving it for the opening sequence (as the cast bounds on stage, invading Roger and Mark's apartment and simply standing around with pent-up energy, awaiting the choral refrains of the opening number) and appropriate applause points.

JUDITH: The DVD does include another bonus feature with footage of some original and other past cast members waiting in the wings during the finale, so that they can go on to join the current cast members in an encore of "Seasons of Love." It has a celebratory feel to it but also feels a bit like "milking" these final moments for all they are worth. The actor playing Angel in this version runs on stage, tears in his eyes, for the closing lyric, "No day but today." Then the audience members, standing, give an ecstatic reception to the past cast members who come on stage to sing Larson's anthem to love. The camera cuts to a spectator blinking back tears, others singing passionately, clapping and crying. The ages visibly range from seniors to teenagers, and the feeling of community is palpable. So I have to admit to getting chills (and even some tears when the camera cut to Larson's emotional sister) as I watched these final moments and recalled how I felt when I first saw the show. I had just started a full-time faculty position after graduate school, and *Rent* completely reaffirmed my desire to teach, study, and do theater. And I thought Larson's musical would change the face of Broadway! Of course, most critics/historians agree that it hasn't. But as I hope we have demonstrated in this essay, evidence suggests that it has changed the lives of many individuals, sometimes in radical ways.

We both hope that through this essay, we have demonstrated as well the potential that exists through such collaborative explorations of musicals. Together, our descriptions, analyses, and interpretations of *Rent* are grounded in and enriched by six viewings of live productions, as well as countless viewings of mediated productions and musical numbers/scenes. Together, we believe that we have offered a fuller consideration of "where" *Rent* is and a more complex, layered understanding of Larson's show. For example, a musicologist can explore the bohemian spirit in Puccini's opera, while a theater historian can then situate the musical within its bohemian off-Broadway roots. The latter, well versed in audience studies, can analyze reactions that spectators have voiced about the show, while the former, working in musical signs and layers of meaning, can analyze the enormous impact on the audience of nontexted musical moments. Just as *Rent* has no one location, nor does it have one analysis or interpretation; it has many "wheres" and, as we hope this article suggests, benefits from as many shared readings among colleagues.

NOTES

1. David Savran, "Toward a Historiography of the Popular," *Theatre Survey* 45, no. 2 (2004): 211–17.

2. Stacy Wolf, "In Defense of Pleasure: Musical Theatre History in the Liberal Arts [A Manifesto]," *Theatre Topics* 17, no. 1 (2007): 51–60.

3. Bud Coleman and Judith A. Sebesta, "Introduction," in *Women in American Musical Theatre* (Jefferson, NC: McFarland, 2008).

4. Both Savran and Wolf mention the importance of these techniques to the study of the musical; their increasing de facto importance to theater historiography is evident in Henry Bial's call for multiple and contradictory authorship (Henry Bial, "The Theatre Historian as Rock Star," *Theatre Topics* 17, no. 1 [2007]: 81–86). Indeed, *Theatre Histories: An Introduction*, with its four authors (Phillip Zarrilli, Bruce McConachie, Gary Jay Williams, and Carol Fisher Sorgenfrei [New York: Routledge, 2006]), threatens to supplant the long-established supremacy of Oscar G. Brockett's *History of the Theatre* as *the* text, the recent addition of a second authorial voice, Franklin J. Hildy, notwithstanding (Oscar G. Brockett and Franklin J. Hildy, *History of the Theatre*, 10th ed. [Boston: Allyn & Bacon, 2007]). In William Condee's essay "The Future Is Interdisciplinary," Condee points out that "interdisciplinary studies should encounter a beast that, if examined solely with the tools of the discipline, would leave out major body parts—parts that are inexplicable within the discipline" (William Condee, "The Future Is Interdisciplinary," *Theatre Survey* 45, no. 2 [2004]: 238).

5. Kae Koger, "Trends in Musical Theatre Scholarship: An Essay in Historiography," *New England Theatre Journal* 3, no. 1 (1992): 1–2.

6. Allen Woll, *Black Musical Theatre: From* Coontown *to* Dreamgirls (Baton Rouge: Louisiana State University Press, 1989); John Clum, *Something for the Boys: Musical Theater and Gay Culture* (New York: St. Martin's Press, 1999); Andrea Most, *Making Americans: Jews and the Broadway Musical* (Cambridge: Harvard University Press, 2004); Joseph P. Swain, *The Broadway Musical: A Critical and Musical Survey* (New York: Oxford University Press, 1990); Jessica Sternfeld, *The Megamusical* (Bloomington: Indiana University Press, 2006); Elizabeth Wollman, *The Theater Will Rock: A History of the Rock Musical, From* Hair *to* Hedwig (Ann Arbor: University of Michigan Press, 2006); Stephen Banfield, *Sondheim's Broadway Musicals* (Ann Arbor: University of Michigan Press, 1995); Gerald Mast, *Can't Help Singin': The American Musical on Stage and Screen* (Woodstock: Overlook Press, 1987); John Bush Jones, *Our Musicals, Ourselves: A Social History of the American Musical Theatre* (Lebanon, NH: Brandeis University Press, 2003); Raymond Knapp, *The American Musical and the Formation of National Identity* (Princeton: Princeton University Press, 2005); Raymond Knapp, *The American Musical and the Performance of Personal Identity* (Princeton: Princeton University Press, 2009); Stacy Wolf, *A Problem Like Maria: Gender and Sexuality in the American Musical* (Ann Arbor: University of Michigan Press, 2002); Bruce Kirle, *Unfinished Show Business: Broadway Musicals as Works-In-Process* (Carbondale: Southern Illinois University Press, 2005); David Román, *Performance in America: Contemporary U.S. Culture and the Performing Arts* (Durham: Duke University Press, 2005).

7. Savran, "Toward a Historiography," 211.

8. Giacomo Puccini (music), Giuseppe Giacosa and Luigi Illica (libretto), trans. Peggie Cochrane, booklet accompanying *La Bohème*, Decca recording 289466070-2, Teatro alla Scala, cond. Chailly (1999) 87.

9. In one of the earliest operas, e.g., Monteverdi's *Orfeo* of 1607, Orpheus sings to the boatman on the river Styx (who is actually so unimpressed that he falls asleep), then to Eurydice and the world at large as he sneaks across the river. The

action then jumps to an impressed set of gods who have already decided to release the girl; some unheard song, apparently having taken place during intermission (from the audience's perspective), has persuaded them. Gluck and Calzabigi's *Orfeo ed Eurydice* (1762) similarly shows Orpheus singing only to the gatekeepers, avoiding the moment when he sings for the gods.

10. Carolyn Abbate, *In Search of Opera* (Princeton and Oxford: Princeton University Press, 2001), 27.

11. Quoted in Stephanie Coen, "Not Out of Nowhere: A Breakthrough Musical's Developmental Odyssey," *American Theatre*, July–Aug. 1995, 15.

12. *Rent*'s years-long developmental odyssey has been well documented, but a brief overview is crucial here in order to explore the larger context of the musical's beginnings off-Broadway. Apparently accurate legend has it that in 1992 Larson biked by the 150-seat theater, still under construction, decided he liked its look, and returned the next day to drop off a tape with songs and a libretto. Nicola recognized the nascent show's potential and arranged for two readings in the summer of '92 and the spring of '93. Larson spent time at the theater's summer residency program, and a Richard Rodgers Foundation grant of $45,000 supported a workshop production in November of '94. The enormously successful workshop led eventually to *Rent*'s off-Broadway opening at the NYTW on Jan. 25, 1996.

13. Mark Dundas Wood, "The Workshop Cover-Up," *American Theatre*, Sept. 2002, 12.

14. No author listed, "How to Survive the Workshop Syndrome," *American Theatre*, Apr. 2006, 39+.

15. Quoted in Jeffrey A. Trachtenberg, "How to Turn $4,000 into Many Millions: The Story of 'Rent,'" *Wall Street Journal*, May 23, 1996.

16. Trachtenberg, "How to Turn $4,000."

17. Trachtenberg, "How to Turn $4,000."

18. Also known as "squatters," to mirror characters in the show, Rentheads have an entry in Wikipedia, which acknowledges that the term now has a more general use to include "someone who is obsessed with or at least a very big fan of the musical *RENT*," ("Renthead," *Wikipedia*, 2009, http://en.wikipedia.org/wiki/RENT-head [accessed Feb. 26, 2009]), as well as urban dictionary.com, which in defining the term uses it in a sentence that reflects the enthusiasm of the fans: "Those Rentheads in the front row can get pretty annoying with all their whooping and hollering between songs." The term also is defined there as "a disciple of the late, great, Jonathan Larson," adding an almost religious quality to the phenomenon "Renthead" (*Urban Dictionary*, 2009, http://www.urbandictionary.com/define.php?term=renthead [accessed Feb. 26, 2009]).

19. No author listed, *No Day But Today*, documentary, *Rent*, DVD, Columbia Pictures, 2006.

20. Ben Brantley, "Rock Opera a la 'Boheme' and 'Hair,'" *New York Times*, Feb. 14, 1996.

21. David Savran, "*Rent*'s Due: Multiculturalism and the Spectacle of Difference," *Journal of American Drama and Theatre* 14 (Winter 2002): 12.

22. Anthony Tommasini, "Like Opera Inspiring It, 'Rent' Is Set to Endure," *New York Times*, Sept. 6, 2008.

23. We recognize that the Internet and television, as well as the reception of

the 2005 Chris Columbus film on the big screen, are also crucial locations in which the identity and history of this show have been forged. *Rent*'s presence in Cyberspace is significant; a recent Google search of "Rent the musical" turned up 53,800 hits. Besides the official show Web site mentioned earlier, many are Renthead sites, from "Rentheads United," a charitable organization; to a Renthead group on flickr, where members can share photos of "anything *Rent* related"; to an entire site on "You might be a Renthead if . . ." (http://members.tripod.com/Melissa_Umlor/ renthead. html). There are even a few "I hate *Rent*" groups online, the existence of such countergroups evidence of the cultural significance of the groups who love it. A Mar. 30, 2009, YouTube search for "Rent the musical" resulted in 2,750 hits, ranging from a nine-minute promotional video from the original cast production to Rentheads filming themselves performing songs from the show at home (see also "'Rent' on the Net," *Billboard*, Nov. 23, 1996, 82). On TV, the cast made several appearances with tamed versions of their numbers—on Rosie O'Donnell's talk show, for instance, and the television broadcasts of the Democratic National Convention and the Tony Awards. Due to space restrictions, however, we are not able to devote attention to our research and discussion of these areas in this essay.

24. See Judith Sebesta, "Of Fire, Death, and Desire: Transgression and Carnival in Jonathan Larson's *Rent*," *Contemporary Theatre Review* 16, no. 4 (2006): 419–38.

PS: Can We Talk about Something Else?

HENRY BIAL ∾

> The Gileadites captured the fords of the Jordan leading to
> Ephraim, and whenever a survivor of Ephraim said, "Let me cross
> over," the men of Gilead asked him, "Are you an Ephraimite?" If
> he replied, "No," they said, "All right, say 'Shibboleth.'" He said,
> "Sibboleth," [and] because he could not pronounce the word
> correctly, they seized him and killed him at the fords of the Jordan.
> Forty-two thousand Ephraimites were killed at that time.
>
> —Judges 12:5–6 (New International Version)

Most English speakers understand the two-letter abbreviation PS (or
"P.S.") to announce writing that appears after the main text of a document.
In a letter, for example, the PS appears below the author's signature. In the
days of handwritten correspondence, such addenda typically represented
new information or thoughts that had struck the writer after completing
the letter, but prior to sealing it for delivery. In the age of electronic mail
and cut-and-paste editing, the postscript is no longer, strictly speaking,
necessary. Like many vestigial behaviors, then, the postscript persists as a
kind of ritual. The PS designation is a metacommunication; it signals that
the text to follow is in some way qualitatively different from the text that
has come before. The postscript is writing performed in a different mode.
It may be afterthought or a sudden inspiration.[1] It may be commentary,
ironic or earnest, on the main text. It may be a hint at what's to come in the
next dispatch. Whatever its function, the persistence of the PS reminds us
that we can rarely write all we wish to, and that what we write even more
rarely says all we would have it say. The *meta*-metacommunication is: beware
the supplement.

It is therefore not entirely coincidental that in certain circles—the corridors
and meeting rooms of the American Society for Theatre Research,
the Theatre and Performance Research Association, the Australasian

Drama Studies Association, the Association for Theatre in Higher Education, the International Federation for Theatre Research, and countless university and college theater departments—"PS" is a shibboleth, a word used as a test to determine whether someone is One of Us or One of Them. The test is in two phases: First, does the conversant recognize PS as an abbreviation for performance studies? Second, does he or she have sufficient familiarity and comfort with the performance studies discourse to deploy the abbreviation with confidence? It is not enough to recognize the letters; you must pronounce them correctly. Of course, every discipline has its specialized vocabulary, unpronounceable by outsiders. Within and without the academy, the charge of "jargon" is answered by the rallying cry of "necessary linguistic precision." This is as true in theater studies as in any other endeavor. As Joseph Roach writes, "The hard words must now and then do the work that easier words fail to do, and in the history of theatre it has been ever thus: think, for example, of classical cruxes such as 'catharsis' and 'irony' or neologisms such as 'subtext' and 'defamiliarization.'"[2]

Hang around enough theater scholars, however, and you'll realize that something more than understanding is at stake when it comes to PS. After all, not all jargon words function as shibboleths. I may not know the distinction between a teaser and a tormentor, but this bothers me little unless and until I attempt to join the stagehands' union. The Gileadites who bequeathed to us the term *shibboleth* required such a test because the field of battle on which they had engaged the Ephraimites was in disarray, any semblance of front lines having broken down, and the visible difference between the two opposing tribes was slight. Indeed, the cause of the conflict in the first place was the accusation that the Gileadites were in fact renegades who rightfully belonged with and owed allegiance to Ephraim.[3] These, then, are the conditions in which a shibboleth is necessary: conflict between two groups who are not readily distinguishable, even to each other.

For the better part of two decades, scholars who identify themselves with PS have been playing the Gileadites to theater historians' Ephraimites. As in most academic battles, it is ink rather than blood that has been spilled, but the sentiments are little less intense for the difference. Performance studies has been accused of being ungrounded, ahistorical, and willfully obscure. Performance studies scholars have been called dilettante, sloppy, unemployable, unpublishable. Richard Hornby, writing in 1994, declared, "There is a growing tendency toward 'performance studies' in American theater departments, which is not an extension of traditional literary and historical study, but a rejection of it."[4] A dozen years later, Laurence Senelick satirically bemoaned the decline of theater history under the influence of performance studies, devoting stanza after stanza to this plague of scholars:

> Weak on the past, of cultural context free,
> They sing their scores to scales of "Me, Me, Me."
> ....
> Fixed on a narrow range of texts; these horses
> Are most at home with secondary sources.
> They're blind to wider culture, art, and praxis,
> And deaf from grinding homiletic axes.
> English their only tongue, and not the Queen's,
> They've not been taught the rudimentary means
> Of practicing their craft.[5]

Conversely, "PS people" have charged theater historians with intransigence, Eurocentrism, and lack of imagination. Following Richard Schechner's rallying cry that performance "is a broad spectrum of activities including at the very least the performing arts, rituals, healing, sports, popular entertainments, and performance in everyday life," PSers did not so much critique theater history's methods as its scope, noting that theater occupies only a fraction of this "broad spectrum."[6] As Shannon Jackson has pointed out, the rise of performance studies was part of a broader wave of challenges to the Western humanities canon, often characterized in the United States as the "culture wars" of the 1980s and '90s. "Performance studies," writes Jackson, "aligned itself with the canon-busters, calling for the recognition of heretofore excluded people and cultural forms."[7] These forms included the theater of oppressed or marginalized populations; feminist and queer theater and performance art; popular and vernacular entertainments such as vaudeville and minstrelsy; and a great many rituals, games, and spectacles that theater history had declared "out of bounds," more properly the study of other fields such as anthropology, sociology, and religion. Thus, though PS did not demonize theater history per se, the reluctance of some theater scholars to join the "performance studies project" was (perhaps inevitably) construed by many as naive at best, sexist, racist, or jingoistic at worst. Add to this conflict an ever-diminishing pool of resources (government art and humanities funding, teaching lines, publication opportunities, etc.), and the stakes increase, to the point where a generation of would-be theater scholars has been challenged to declare an allegiance to one camp or the other.

Indeed, as all too often happens in the academy, it appears as though institutional constraints have trumped intellectual concerns. Like Gilead and Ephraim, performance studies and theater history share a common genealogy, one linked to an historically marginal position vis-à-vis other academic disciplines. Yet this seems only to increase the potential for territorialism and misrecognition. Stephen J. Bottoms, for example, writes: "The expansion of Performance Studies over the last couple of decades seems both to have exponentially expanded the potential field of study for theatre-trained scholars, and to have contracted the field of Theatre Studies itself, by imposing a curiously limited and limiting definition of that which constitutes 'theatre.' All too often, theatre is now characterized as the acting out of dramatic literature in a purpose-built building, whereas performance is taken to encompass pretty much anything and everything else."[8] This move, suggests Bottoms, allows performance studies to lay claim to avant-garde and grassroots traditions that theater studies has *not* neglected. Moreover, it ensures that the theater history against which performance studies has often defined itself remains an indefensible straw man. Bottoms goes on to suggest that the rhetoric of performance studies' earliest formations may even betray a *"repulsion from theatre"* that configures the latter as always already trivial, in contrast to the more dynamic and efficacious concept of performance.

Taking a broader perspective, Jackson highlights how the development of new historicism, cultural studies, and other self-consciously interdisciplinary modes of inquiry were imperfectly doubled in theater and performance studies. "Often," she writes, "the 'cultural turn' was used to rationalize an expansion of interest beyond theatre to a wider network of performance forms. While this is a heuristic move, it had the effect of ignoring the ways that theatre itself can be richly theorized as an exemplary site for cultural analysis."[9] Significantly, Jackson cites Thomas Postlewait and Bruce McConachie's *Interpreting the Theatrical Past: Essays in the Historiography of Performance* (1989) as an important demonstration of theater history's own ability to make the "cultural turn." Postlewait and McConachie's volume, which provided in many ways a model for the book you are now reading, says little—despite its subtitle—about PS as either topic or tool. *He said, "Sibboleth."* One unfortunate result of this is that the area of theater historiography has until recently been neglected by PSers, though many of the authors and ideas contained within the pages of *Interpreting the Theatrical Past* continue to circulate in both disciplines.

In fact, subsequent work by that volume's contributors—including Roach, Marvin Carlson, Tracy Davis, and Erika Fischer-Lichte, as well as

Postlewait and McConachie themselves—is the primary reason that reputable theater historians no longer question the legitimacy of the "performance studies project." Nor is the existence of the latter considered a threat to the former. Bottoms, for example, writes, "I see the two fields as dance partners, capable of learning from and supporting each other, provided of course that the dance is between mutually respectful equals."[10] Roach, more expansively, asserts:

> Reconfiguring the history of theatre as a history of performance . . .
> strengthens, not weakens, the teaching of canonical works, from *The
> Tempest*, as one of a variety of masterworks, including Trinidadian
> carnival, which physically stage intercultural contacts in the Atlantic
> world, to Meyerhold's biomechanical exercises, which engage the
> problem of alienation of labor in a way that illuminates the neo-
> Taylorist "performance paradigm" in contemporary manufacture.[11]

Many, however, still question the centrality of performance studies to the theory, practice, and pedagogy of theater history. Conversely, though performance studies as an emergent field no longer defines itself by its opposition to theater history, such history is often relegated to the margins of a "broad-spectrum" approach. Given the intensity of the internecine jockeying and scrambling, the careful self-positioning in prefaces and introductions, the surfeit of conferences and seminars devoted to questions such as "What is theater history?" and "What is performance studies?" what is the next generation of theater and performance scholars to do?

Can we talk about something else?

Can we talk, for example, about what to do with surplus evidence? Globalization—through physical travel as well as digital media—has given us access to more data than any group of researchers has enjoyed before, and yet some of the most basic premises of our field remain contested. Are theater's origins in ritual? Were female spectators welcome in the Theater of Dionysus? How, exactly, did Molière die? Is the problem that we have too little information, or too much? Our postmodern understanding of history pulls us in two directions. We are conditioned to be skeptical of the archival record, acutely aware of the lacunae that power imbalances, chance, and performance's ephemerality inevitably produce. Absence of evidence, we repeat faithfully, is not evidence of absence. At the same time, our emphasis on contextualization and recapturing the voices of the unhistoried forces us to range ever farther into territory once the province of (inter alia) anthropology, archaeology, biology, cognitive science, philosophy, religion. How many scholars—how many entire subfields—have made the "cultural turn" only to find themselves at an infinite crossroads, unsure how many of humankind's turning points they are obligated to explore before declaring their analysis complete?

And yet, down each path is the promise of revelation. A curse tablet buried by a Carthaginian slave prompts a reconsideration of Roman comedy. A found object draws our attention to a story that has gone missing. An apparently apocryphal anecdote is cited and recited until it becomes a ghostly revenant. That it cannot be empirically verified is beside the point. It represents, perhaps, a different kind of truth, one as essential to the theater historian's enterprise as the archive, the footnote, and the eyewitness account. A seventeenth-century English theater impresario spent his formative years as a pirate captain. His unconventional career choice sheds light on his theatrical career, the politics of Restoration theater, and the origin of the pirate as a literary trope. Military records of the American Revolution hint at heretofore unsuspected Jewish involvement in the early American theater. Newspaper accounts, advertisements, and social-club records can almost, but not quite, be triangulated to identify a family of performers that might or might not be important to this story. How many new data points must we unearth before we redraw the graph of history? How do we decide what to include and what to exclude? How much are historians allowed to speculate? How much are we *obligated* to do so?

Can we talk about politics in ways that move beyond the artificial binaries of majority and minority, dominant and oppressed, hegemonic and marginalized? The work of "canon-busting" is certainly not complete, but it's time we recognize that the very act of theater history necessitates choices about what to include and what to exclude. Every act of memory, as the old saw goes, is also an act of forgetting. We have known for a long time that such acts have real consequences, that revisioning our history constitutes a strategic intervention in our present and future. For theater historians, definitions of genre and period performatively reinscribe certain aesthetic, chronological, and cultural demarcations at the expense of others. The coining of a term to describe a "new" theatrical phenomenon retroactively characterizes that which came before as "old." Contemporary criticism can also project into the past, such as when we identify elements of Theatre of the Absurd in Shakespeare. When visiting ethnographers have the responsibility for classifying and archiving indigenous theater, what context is lost? Whose interest is served? How much embodied knowledge, though lost to the archive, is transmitted through the performance tradition? Can observing contemporary performances of the indigenous repertoire help historians recover the lost essence of a drama? When considering the work of prior historians, then, how can we adjust for the fact that their ideological priorities and agendas were not only different from ours, but often circumscribed by social contexts we can scarcely imagine?

Meanwhile, how can contemporary understandings of gender, race, and class politics inform our readings of past moments in theater history? A play that was never produced frightened the English government into passing legislation subjecting theater to government censorship, an act that would influence more than two centuries of Anglophone theater. A multiple-axes (i.e., nonbinary) analysis of the identity issues involved reveals much about the forces that shaped and continue to shape the public discourse around performance and its relationship to power. In India, a generation of theater historians sought to establish the validity of Sanskrit literature that had been dismissed by British colonial historians during the period of British imperial rule. Rebelling even against this postcolonial impulse, the theater of roots movement performs theatrical forms and practices that were left out of colonial and neocolonial histories of the Indian theater, using the stage itself as a site of historiographic intervention. If theater history is never ideologically neutral, how do we become reflexive about our own political concerns vis-à-vis the contemporary performances we study? Can we talk about how and when to let our own deeply held beliefs influence what and how we choose to include in our own records and interpretations? And how will a future generation of theater historians assess our choices?

Can we talk about technologies and interdisciplinary approaches that provoke new understandings of what theater history is and how to conduct it? Digital recording technology, because of a different kind of turf battle, is most often discussed by theater historians in terms of imperfection and loss. But the digital archive also brings gains, offering a level of access, and a democratization of access, that theater historians of the last century (by which I mean the twentieth) could not have imagined. Can we talk about what we're going to do with that? Similarly, the growth of visual analysis as a means of understanding performance may soon approach or even overtake textual analysis. Not only does such analysis suit our increasingly visual world; it provides a tool for recovering the stories of those people whom text-based histories tend to underrepresent or misrepresent. Evolutionary and cognitive approaches promise to enhance our understanding of key theatrical elements such as emotion, recognition, and identification, making our analyses of these phenomena both more specific (in terms of process) and more universal (in terms of applicability) than would have been possible a generation ago. By situating human performance within a larger ecological framework, such analyses also point to a significant ethical obligation that theater historians would do well to consider. Even death bears historicization, and theater historians would do well to draw on new thinking in this area. This is especially true to the degree that theater history may inform acting or staging choices.

Can we talk about theater itself as a site of historiography, and historiography as a site of performance? The death of Molière exerts such a powerful hold on the imagination that it is rehearsed over and over in three centuries of dramas, poems, films, and commemorations. Creating conditions in which something unexpected yet palpably present may emerge, such representations offer us a chance to catch history unawares, as if by happy accident. In Brussels, members of a Latvian theater company invite the audience to witness a collective reading of a Russian novel. The theater group's behavior and the relationships they establish—or refuse to establish—with the audience simultaneously reflect, play with, and comment upon the novel's narrative, a lurid tale of a mystical Aryan cult. At once seduced and repulsed by the "community" performing itself in their midst, spectators experience something of the conflicted history of Latvian involvement in the events of World War II and the subsequent Soviet occupation. The excesses of another totalitarian regime, that of contemporary North Korea, are chronicled more explicitly in a big-budget musical spectacular, and a historian is faced with the dilemma of how to get at the true story of the show's creation. Conducting an interview for archival purposes requires its own kind of performance, one that is often difficult to calibrate. Allowing the subject too much control of the interview may fail to yield the desired information, while pushing too hard for answers poses ethical pitfalls and may not yield more accurate data. As in theatrical performance, often the most salient details resist transcription. In museums and classrooms, participatory performance is deployed to encourage historiographic consciousness. Challenged to act out scenes from the past, museum visitors and students have the opportunity to develop their own embodied knowledge of history, one that may be more "true" if less factually accurate than more conventional courses of study. What might be gained if we import these theaters of history into the classrooms where we teach the history of theater?

Can we talk, finally, about disciplinary issues that do not require the shibboleths of the PS/theater history (non)conflict? One aim of this book is to challenge the misperception that theater history and performance studies are intellectually or professionally opposed to one another. The concept of theater historiography as illustrated throughout the preceding chapters offers a space of critical and generative interaction between the two fields. Indeed, if we understand the term *theater historiography* to encompass the diverse range of issues and methods deployed by historians of theater and performance, we can see that the critical intersection between these once separate discourses is not just desirable but inevitable. Consider Philip Auslander's useful distinction between theater as an *"object-driven discipline"* and performance studies as a *"paradigm-driven discipline."*[12] Theater studies is defined by the objects under consideration: if you are studying the history of a theater event, site, or text, then you are, by definition, doing theater history, regardless of methodology. Meanwhile, nearly any event, site, or text can be studied *as* performance, regardless of whether there is general agreement to classify it as such. Which is to say that a scholar can take a "performance studies approach" to theater history, just as another can choose to focus their performance studies scholarship on the realm of performances recognized as theater. No shibboleth required.

Far better to ask whether both fields' commitment to interdisciplinarity has gone far enough. Have we sufficiently expanded our ways of knowing to allow for approaches to historiography that are truly Other? Far better to ask whether the history of theater practice offers modes of inquiry that can illuminate our historical scholarship. The rehearsal tools developed by a director such as Bertolt Brecht offer a provocative way to interpret the career of an eighteenth-century actress, not through staging her experience as drama, but through asking ourselves many of the questions Brecht would ask if he *were* to do so. Far better to ask how the incentive structures and accompanying constraints of the modern university are changing the terrain for all scholars, regardless of disciplinary identification. The forces driving change in the professional practice of theater history do not come exclusively from within the scholarly ranks, and we ignore challenges from without at our own peril. What happens, for example, when we insist that histories of an inherently collaborative art take the form of single-authored narratives? And taking a page from Brecht, what might happen if we consider alternative, collaborative ways of writing our histories?

The performance-studies-versus-theater-history rhetoric continues to haunt scholarship in both disciplines. Yet the concept of theater historiography, as illustrated throughout the preceding chapters, offers an opportunity for more productive—and more interesting—conversations about theater history as both a subject and a profession. Thinking about theater history in terms of historiography helps resolve the distinction between object-driven and paradigm-driven discipline by focusing our attention on the diverse interrogative modes in which theater history is practiced. Indeed, we might regard the most recent "historiographic turn" in both theater history and performance studies as an attempt to reconcile the two camps. Or to put it another way, there is a reason this book is not called "Theater and Performance Historiography: Critical Interventions." We believe that (1) theater as a concept is sufficiently expansive to include the variety of events, behaviors, and phenomena encompassed within these pages; (2) theater history by definition includes consideration of performance; and (3) the two fields are not in competition with one another, because they are constructed differently. If we look back at the essays in this volume, we can see that some of the most dynamic and productive scholars in the field today are untroubled by an imagined opposition between performance studies and "theater history proper." They have no desire to say "Shibboleth" or to demand that others do so. They are too busy making history.

NOTES

1. Often, the postscript is something we planned from the beginning to write. The PS artfully conceals this motive. Hence the not infrequent use of the PS to deliver opinions or suggestions that the reader might take amiss.

2. Joseph Roach. "Reconstructing Theatre/History," *Theatre Topics* 9, no. 1 (1999): 6.

3. Judges 12:4 (New International Version): "Jephthah then called together the men of Gilead and fought against Ephraim. The Gileadites struck them down because the Ephraimites had said, 'You Gileadites are renegades from Ephraim and Manasseh.'"

4. Richard Hornby, "Against Performance Theory," *TheatreWeek* 8, no. 11 (1994): 34.

5. Laurence Senelick, "THE ASTRIAD; or, The Pedant's Progress," *Theatre Survey* 47, no. 2 (2006): 188.

6. Richard Schechner, "Performance Studies: The Broad Spectrum Approach," *TDR: A Journal of Performance Studies* 32, no. 3 (1988): 4.

7. Shannon Jackson, *Professing Performance* (Cambridge: Cambridge University Press, 2004), 23.

8. Stephen J. Bottoms, "The Efficacy/Effeminacy Braid: Unpacking the Performance Studies/Theatre Studies Dichotomy," *Theatre Topics* 13, no. 2 (2003): 173.

9. Jackson, *Professing Performance*, 155–56.

10. Bottoms, "Efficacy/Effeminacy Braid," 185.

11. Joseph Roach. "Reconstructing Theatre/History," *Theatre Topics* 9, no. 1 (1999): 8–9.

12. Philip Auslander, *Theory for Performance Studies: A Student's Guide* (London: Routledge, 2008), 2. NB: This citation may prove difficult to trace, as the book was withdrawn from the market by the publisher in early 2009 in response to revelations that portions of the text were reproduced without attribution from *Theory for Religious Studies* (London: Routledge, 2004), by Timothy K. Beal and William Deal. There is little doubt, however, about the authorship of the passage cited here. By citing this text, I intend neither to condone nor condemn the volume from which it is drawn.

Contributors

HENRY BIAL (coeditor) is an associate professor and the director of graduate studies in theater at the University of Kansas. He is the author of *Acting Jewish: Negotiating Ethnicity on the American Stage and Screen* (University of Michigan Press, 2005), the editor of *The Performance Studies Reader* (Routledge, 2004, 2nd ed., 2007), and the coeditor (with Carol Martin) of *Brecht Sourcebook* (Routledge, 2000). He serves on the editorial boards of *Theatre Topics* and the *Journal of Dramatic Theory and Criticism* and is a former vice-president of the Association for Theatre in Higher Education.

SCOTT MAGELSSEN (coeditor) is an associate professor of theater and film at Bowling Green State University and the incoming editor of *Journal of Dramatic Theory and Criticism*. He is the author of *Living History Museums: Undoing History through Performance* (Scarecrow, 2007), the coeditor (with Ann Haugo) of *Querying Difference in Theatre History* (Cambridge Scholars Press, 2007), and the coeditor (with Rhona Justice-Malloy) of *Enacting History* (University of Alabama Press, 2011). Magelssen won the 2005 Gerald Kahan Award for the Best Essay in Theatre Studies by a Younger Scholar for his article "Performance Practices of [Living] Open Air Museums," which appeared in *Theatre History Studies*.

WENDY ARONS is an associate professor in the School of Drama at Carnegie Mellon University. Her research interests include performance and ecology, eighteenth- and nineteenth-century theater history, feminist theater, and performance and ethnography. She is the author of *Performance and Femininity in Eighteenth-Century German Woman's Writing: The Impossible Act* (Palgrave MacMillan, 2006) and has published articles in *Theatre Topics*, the *German Quarterly*, *Communications from the International Brecht Society, 1650–1850*, *Text and Presentation*, and *Theatre Journal*, as well as chapters in a number of anthologies. She recently guest edited a special issue of *Theatre Topics*, "Performance and Ecology," and is coeditor, with Theresa May, of the forthcoming anthology *Essays in Performance and Ecology*.

SARAH BAY-CHENG is an associate professor of theater and film studies at the University at Buffalo—SUNY (UB), where she teaches avant-garde drama, modernist film and theater, and contemporary intermedia performance. She is the author of *Mama Dada: Gertrude Stein's Avant-Garde Theater* (Routledge, 2004) and the editor of *Poets at Play: An Anthology of Modernist Drama* (Susquehanna University Press, 2010). Bay-Cheng's essays have appeared in journals such as *Theatre Journal* and *Theatre Topics* and in anthologies such as *Avant-Garde Theatre, 1890–1950* (Yale University Press, 2001) and *Theatre and Film* (Yale University Press, 2005). She is also a member of the international research group Intermediality in Theatre and Performance and is a founding member of the Intermedia Performance Studio at UB, a performance and research group devoted to digital technology in performance.

JONATHAN CHAMBERS is an associate professor in the Department of Theatre and Film at Bowling Green State University. His essays have been published in *Theatre Annual, Theatre History Studies, New England Theatre Journal,* and *Journal of American Drama and Theatre*. His book, *Messiah of the New Technique: John Howard Lawson, Communism and American Theatre 1923–1937,* was published by Southern Illinois University Press. Chambers is the former editor of *Theatre Topics.*

JOHN FLETCHER is an assistant professor of theater history and women's and gender studies at Louisiana State University. His work appears in *Text and Performance Quarterly, Theatre Survey, Theatre Topics, Laberinto,* and the anthology *Querying Difference in Theatre History* (Cambridge Scholars Press, 2007). At present he is consolidating his research on the proselytizing strategies of U.S. evangelicalism into a monograph, tentatively entitled *Preaching to Convert: Evangelical Outreach and Activist Performance in the U.S.*

BRANISLAV JAKOVLJEVIC is an assistant professor in the Department of Drama at Stanford University. He specializes in modernist theater and the avant-garde, and in his current research he focuses on the relation of the event to performance. His articles have been published in the United States (the *Drama Review, PAJ, Theater, Art Journal*) and abroad (Serbia, Croatia, Spain, England, Sweden). His book *Daniil Kharms: Writing and the Event* was published by Northwestern University Press. Branislav was awarded the Hellman Faculty Scholar Fund at Stanford (2009) and is the recipient of the Association for Theatre in Higher Education's (ATHE) Award for Outstanding Essay for 2008–9.

ODAI JOHNSON, an associate professor of theater history and the head of the Ph.D. program at the University of Washington, took his MFA from the University of Utah and his Ph.D. from the University of Texas at Austin. His articles have appeared in *Theatre Journal, Theatre Survey, New England Theatre Journal, Theatre Symposium,* and the *Virginia Magazine of History*. His books include *Rehearsing the Revolution* (University of Delaware, 1999), *The Colonial American Stage: A Documentary Calendar* (Associated University Presses, 2001), and *Absence and Memory* (Palgrave-Macmillan, 2005). Johnson serves as resident researcher for the Colonial Williamsburg Foundation's reconstruction of the Douglass Theatre and is currently working on a project entitled "Ruins: An Excavation into Ancient Theatre." He has also worked as a playwright and dramaturge at Sundance and Wordbridge.

SUK-YOUNG KIM is an associate professor of theater and dance at the University of California at Santa Barbara. Her coauthored book (with Kim Yong), *Long Road Home* (Columbia University Press, 2009), documents the testimony of a North Korean camp survivor. She has authored another book, *Illusive Utopia* (University of Michigan Press, 2010), which explores how state-produced propaganda performances intersect with everyday life practice in North Korea.

MECHELE LEON is an associate professor of theater and the artistic director of the University Theatre at the University of Kansas. She is a recipient of a National Endowment for the Humanities faculty fellowship, a Bourse Chateaubriand from the French government, and numerous other grants. Her first book, *Molière, the French Revolution, and the Theatrical Afterlife*, is published by the University of Iowa Press.

ELLEN MACKAY is an assistant professor of English at Indiana University. She has written on a wide range of theatrical subjects, including the performance of citizenship required for "naturalization" (*Canadian Theatre Review*), the pernicious mythology of Schechner's Dionysus in '69 (*Theatre History Studies*, winner of the Robert A. Schanke Award), the tendency of theaters to self-combust (*Theatre Survey*), and the politics of stuttering in Susannah Centlivre's *The Busie Body* (MLA Approaches to World Literature series, forthcoming). Her first book is *Persecution, Plague and Fire: Fugitive Histories of the Stage in Early Modern England* (University of Chicago Press, 2011), and she is well embarked upon another, on sea spectacles from Nero to Wagner.

ERIN B. MEE is the author of *Theatre of Roots: Redirecting the Modern Indian Stage* (Seagull Books, 2008 part of the Enactments series, edited by Richard Schechner), the coeditor (with Helene Foley) of *Antigone on the Contemporary World Stage* (Oxford University Press, 2010), and the editor of *Drama Contemporary: India* (Johns Hopkins University Press and Oxford University Press, 2005). Her articles have appeared in *TDR*, *Theater Journal*, *Performing Arts Journal*, *Seagull Theatre Quarterly*, and *American Theatre Magazine;* two of her articles have been included in books on playwrights Girish Karnad and Mahesh Dattani. She is an assistant professor of theater at Swarthmore College.

HEATHER S. NATHANS is an associate professor in the Department of Theatre at the University of Maryland. She is the author of *Early American Theatre from the Revolution to Thomas Jefferson: Into the Hands of the People* (Cornell University Press, 2003) and *Slavery and Sentiment on the American Stage, 1781–1861: Lifting the Veil of Black* (Cornell University Press, 2008). Her work has appeared in *Theatre History Studies*, the *New England Theatre Journal*, the *Journal of American Drama and Theatre*, *Early American Studies*, and the *Pennsylvania History Journal*. She is the president of the American Theatre and Drama Society.

JAMES PECK is an associate professor and the chair of the Department of Theatre and Dance at Muhlenberg College. He researches in two principal areas: intersections between eighteenth-century English theater and financial history, and the theory and practice of directing. He has published articles in many leading academic journals, including *Theatre Journal*, *Theatre Topics*, and *Theatre Survey*. His coedited book, with Francesca Coppa and Lawrence Hass, *Performing Magic on the Western Stage: From the Eighteenth Century to the Present* was published by Palgrave. He is the coeditor of *Theatre Topics* and was the book review editor of *Theatre Journal*. He has directed over fifty productions of plays, musicals, and operas at professional and university theaters.

NICHOLAS RIDOUT is the author of *Stage Fright, Animals and Other Theatrical Problems* (Cambridge University Press, 2006) and *Theatre and Ethics* (Palgrave, 2009), the coeditor (with Joe Kelleher) of *Contemporary Theatres in Europe* (Routledge, 2006), and the coauthor (with Joe Kelleher and members of the company) of *The Theatre of Societas Raffaello Sanzio* (Routledge, 2007). He teaches in the Department of Drama at Queen Mary University of London.

JUDITH SEBESTA serves as the chair of the Department of Theatre and Dance at Lamar University; she has previously taught at the University of Missouri, the University of Arizona, and the University of Evansville. She serves as the performance review editor of *Theatre Journal* and is a past secretary of the Association for Theatre in Higher Education. Her articles on musical theater have appeared in such publications as the second edition of the *Cambridge Companion to the Musical*, *Studies in Musical Theatre*, *Contemporary Theatre Review*, the *Journal of Theatre and Performance*, the *New England Theatre Journal*, *Theatre Annual*, and the *Sondheim Review*, and her coedited anthology, *Women in American Musical Theatre*, was published in 2008.

ROBERT B. SHIMKO is an assistant professor of theater history and dramaturgy at the University of Houston, where he heads the M.A. program in theater studies. His work has been published in the anthology *Querying Difference in Theatre History*, as well as *Theatre History Studies*, the *Theatre Journal*, and *Theatre Topics*. He received the 2008 Robert A. Schanke Theatre Research Award from the Mid-America Theatre Conference, and is past Theatre History Symposium Co-chair for that organization. He is also a professional dramaturge whose credits include productions at the Alley Theatre and the Guthrie Theater, among others.

ALAN SIKES currently teaches in the School of Theatre at Illinois State University. His book, *Representation and Identity from Versailles to the Present*, was published in 2007 by Palgrave MacMillan. His articles have appeared in the *Baylor Journal of Theatre and Performance*, the *Journal of Dramatic Theory and Criticism, Studies in Eighteenth Century Culture, Text and Performance Quarterly*, and most recently *Theatre Topics*. His work also appears in the anthology *Querying Difference in Theatre History*, published by Cambridge Scholars in 2007.

JESSICA STERNFELD teaches music history and musicology at Chapman University in Orange, California. Her book, *The Megamusical* (Indiana University Press, 2006), looks at the phenomenon of the blockbuster musicals of the last thirty years. She also contributed a new chapter to the second edition of the *Cambridge Companion to the Musical* and is serving as the guest editor (with Elizabeth Wollman) of a forthcoming issue of *Studies in Musical Theatre*. She has numerous articles in print and forthcoming and is a member of the editorial board of the *American Music Research Center Journal*.

MARGARET WERRY is an associate professor at the University of Minnesota, Twin Cities, in the Department of Theatre Arts and Dance. Her forthcoming book, *The Tourist State: Performing Leisure, Liberalism, and the Racial Imagination* (University of Minnesota Press, 2010), examines the relationship among tourism, performance, ethnic politics, and liberal statehood, looking at cultural policy and tourism practice in the South Pacific at the turn of the twentieth century and at the turn of the twenty-first. Her work has been published in *Public Culture, Cultural Studies, Theatre Journal, Performance Research, TPQ, Review of Cultural Studies, Education and Pedagogy*, and *Essays in Theatre*, and her research has been supported by grants from the Wenner Gren Anthropological Foundation, the Woodrow Wilson National Fellowship Foundation, and the American Association of University Women, among others.

E. J. WESTLAKE is an associate professor of theater at the University of Michigan. She is the author of *Our Land Is Made of Courage and Glory: Nationalist Performance in Nicaragua and Guatemala* (Southern Illinois University Press, 2005) and the coeditor of *Political Performances: Theory and Practice* (Rodopi, 2009). Her articles have appeared in *TDR, Latin American Theatre Review, Youth Theatre Journal*, and elsewhere. Professor Westlake cofounded and managed Stark Raving Theatre in Portland, Oregon. She worked as a director and playwright and won the Oregon Book Award in 1992 for her play *A.E.: The Disappearance and Death of Amelia Earhart.*

PATRICIA YBARRA is an associate professor in the Department of Theatre, Speech and Dance at Brown University. Her book, *Performing Conquest: Five Centuries of Theatre, History and Identity in Tlaxcala, Mexico,* was published by the University of Michigan Press. She has published articles and reviews in *Aztlán: A Journal of Chicano Studies, Theatre Journal, Modern Language Quarterly, TDR,* the *Journal of Dramatic Theory and Criticism,* and *Gestos.*

HARVEY YOUNG is an associate professor of theater and the director of the interdisciplinary Ph.D. program in theater and drama at Northwestern University. He is the author of *Embodying Black Experience: Stillness, Critical Memory and the Black Body* (University of Michigan Press, 2010) and numerous articles on black theater/performance. He is a past president of the Black Theatre Association and a former vice-president of the Association for Theatre in Higher Education.

Index

Abbate, Carolyn, 265
Abel, Lionel, 64
acquired rationalizations, 2
acting, 6, 53, 104–6, 152, 157, 162–74,
    188–90, 239, 253, 283; profession of,
    14
actor-network theory, 226, 230–31
Adamov, Arthur, 63–64
adaptationist literary theory, 151–56
Aeschylus, 23–24, 26; *The Eumenides,*
    23
African American theater history, 146
Albee, Edward, 64
alienation effect. *See* V-effect
American Civil War, 142, 145
American Revolution, 48, 281
American Society for Theatre Re-
    search (ASTR), 120n4, 257, 276
American studies, 254
Anand, Mulk Raj, 107
Anne of Great Britain, 90
anthropology, 2–3, 75–76, 79, 81–82,
    84, 86n22, 86n35, 135n8, 215,
    233n12, 235, 278, 280. *See also*
    ethnography
archive, 2, 4–6, 8, 23, 25, 29, 32, 41,
    89, 97, 121n11, 126–30, 137,
    199–201, 204, 206, 208, 211, 231,
    239, 242, 253–54, 256–57, 281–82
Ariés, Philippe, 165–69, 173n34
Aristotle, 32, 106
Arons, Wendy, 5
Association for Theatre in Higher Ed-
    ucation (ATHE), 277
Astor Place riots, 182
Aubrey, John, 33–34
audience, 4, 6, 8, 24–26, 45, 52–54, 63,

66–68, 70, 72n23, 100, 104–6,
    112–13, 127, 152, 177–79, 181–82,
    186–90, 193–94, 198, 205, 213, 215,
    241, 243, 256, 265–68, 271–72, 283
Aughtry, Charles, 64
Auslander, Philip, 127, 132, 284
Australasian Drama Studies Associa-
    tion (ADSA), 276–77
authenticity, 17, 76, 83–84, 126, 203,
    210–11, 215–16, 223, 264
Autos Sacramentales, 76
Avenue Q, 270

Badiou, Alain, 229
Bain, Ken, 208, 210
Baker, Lee D., 82
Balme, Christopher, 234n22
Banfield, Stephen, 263
Bank, Rosemarie K., 253, 256
Barba, Eugenio, 127
Baron, Michael, 178
Barry, Elizabeth, 241
Barthes, Roland, 65
Barton, Carlin, 13
Barton, I. M., 27
Bay-Cheng, Sarah, 5
Bayle, Pieree, 178
Beacham, Richard, 4, 26, 29
Bearden, Romare, 146
Beckett, Samuel, 62–66, 69–70, 255;
    Waiting for Godot, 62–63, 65, 67–71,
    73n32
Behn, Afra, 41
Béjart, Armande, 177–78
Belmont, Nicholas Longworth,
    142–44, 146, 147n15
Beloff, Zoe, 132, 136n25